FOOD

EDITED BY PAUL FREEDMAN

FOOD

The History of Taste

UNIVERSITY OF CALIFORNIA PRESS

BERKELEY LOS ANGELES

CALIFORNIA STUDIES IN FOOD AND CULTURE, 21
Darra Goldstein, Editor

Frontispiece: Jan Brueghel the Elder, *Allegory of Taste* (detail), 1618

Picture research: Georgina Bruckner and Josine Meijer

Essays by Hans J. Teuteberg and Alain Drouard translated by David H. Wilson

The quotation on p.284 is from Marcel Proust, *Within a Budding Grove*, trans. C. K. Scott Moncrieff and Terence Kilmartin (Chatto & Windus, 1982)

Designed by Mala Hassett

University of California Press, one of the most distinguished university presses in the United States, enriches lives around the world by advancing scholarship in the humanities, social sciences, and natural sciences. Its activities are supported by the UC Press Foundation and by philanthrophic contributions from individuals and institutions. For more information, visit www.ucpress.edu.

University of California Press
Berkeley and Los Angeles, California

Published by arrangement with Thames & Hudson Ltd, London

Cataloguing-in-Publication data for this title is on file with the Library of Congress.

ISBN: 978-0-520-25476-3 (cloth: alk. paper)

Manufactured in Singapore

17 16 15 14 13 12 11 10 09 08
10 9 8 7 6 5 4 3 2 1

CONTENTS

INTRODUCTION

A New History of Cuisine

Paul Freedman

Taste is not simply the preserve of a tiny aristocracy, of the court culture of the European, Abbasid or Chinese past or the 'foodie' cutting-edge of the present. In the social history of ordinary people, caloric intake, the threat of famine and the supply of urban centres are among the topics that have given us an idea of the fragility and difficulty of pre-industrial life. The relevance of the history of food in its most basic sense needs no justification. The exchange of products resulting from the discovery of the New World, the dependence of societies on one overwhelmingly important food source (as with nineteenth-century Ireland and the potato), or the impact of modern warfare on civilian diet are all clearly major topics. In the mid-twentieth century historians' interest in the conditions of society, and particularly the history of ordinary people, inevitably involved questions of how peasants or workers lived in the past; how well or ill-nourished they were; how they coped with the unpredictability of harvests, food supply and prices.

In contrast, accounts of the culinary tastes of the comfortable classes of society were until recently regarded as relevant only to a kind of anthropology of ceremony, such as the elaborate excess of the Burgundian court of the fifteenth century where musicians were placed in baked pies and edible tableaux depicted battles, sieges and allegories. Otherwise the history of cuisine has tended to be viewed as merely part of the history of fashion, hence of frivolity.

Yet the idea that a society's soul is revealed by its cooking has, in fact, been with us since earliest times. According to Greek classical and also Chinese tradition, barbarians eat raw or crudely cooked meat rather than observing the civilized practices of cooking, and this is an essential aspect of their barbarism. The Huns, and eight hundred years later the Mongols, were reputed to 'cook' slabs of meat by placing them between the thigh of the horse-rider and his mount. In this and many other cases, the identification of a populace by its cuisine is the preoccupation of outside observers and their stereotypic ideas more than an activity of self-reflection. Such comforting contempt can be applied either to crude lack of taste (as in widespread opinions about the blandness and inadequacy of British or American food),

Previous page: *The Sense of Taste*, one of the 'Lady and the Unicorn Tapestries' woven in the late 15th century, probably at Tournai and now in the Cluny Museum in Paris. The tapestries exemplify the five senses and the pleasures they offer. Here the lady is looking at her pet bird while reaching into a footed bowl offered by a servant. The bowl contains some sort of sweet. The monkey in the foreground is sampling the confectionary.

or excessive sophistication (popular British mistrust of 'mucky French sauces' that goes back to the early eighteenth century). It can encompass dislike of people who seem obsessed with food preparation (a common complaint in the United States against immigrants), or who have a more generous definition of what is edible than does the observer. This last distinction between a narrow and broad view of the food spectrum has at times had dramatic historical consequences. According to an authoritative account of postwar Soviet foreign policy by Vladislav Zubok and Constantine Pleshakov, Khrushchev's first doubts about China, which later contributed to the Sino-Soviet rift, arose during a trip in 1954 when he and his entourage were served the famous Cantonese specialty 'A Battle of the Dragon and the Tiger' (*long hu dou*), which features snake and cat, provoking a horrified reaction from Khrushchev and tears from two members of his delegation.

Gastronomy expresses an outlook, an aesthetic. Some perceptions of quality seem to continue for centuries, thus already in the Middle Ages the wines of the Bordeaux and Rhine regions were acknowledged as superior. Other perceptions change dramatically: wines sweetened with sugar and spices were greatly esteemed in ancient Greece and medieval Europe, but now, with few exceptions, are regarded as dubious Christmas novelties at best. The Roman Empire's attachment to fish sauce is often thought of as alien and unimaginable, and it certainly differs from European preferences of recent centuries. As will be seen, cuisine changes faster than most people think. Even if, as in China, basic principles were elaborated long ago, ingredients, preparation and fashions have shifted dramatically. The Prophet Muhammad's favourite meat stew, *tharīd,* is still a Bedouin staple, but many tastes of the Caliphate have been superseded. There was a time when Italian cuisine flourished without tomatoes or eggplant, when pasta was an edible container for cooking rather than a food in itself. Yet there are certain durable and distinguishing aesthetic principles: the relation between rice (or other starches) and their accompaniment in Chinese cooking, the importance of wine in the Christian Mediterranean, the preference for numerous small spiced dishes in much of India.

Food reflects the environment of a society, but is not completely determined by it. People who live near the seashore will tend to consume more fish than those who inhabit the mountains, but there are islands such as Sicily that relegate seafood to a surprisingly minor place, or England that has sometimes consumed immense quantities of fish, but tended in the past century to avoid all but a few species and methods of preparation. Contrast this with the craze for seafood that has long characterized Madrid, a place that has to overcome logistical obstacles to satisfy a craving inexplicable by reference to proximity or convenience. Sometimes environmental conditions are a challenge leading to the invention of foods, such as sherbets and other snow-desserts in the Middle East, a relief from the very conditions that would seem to discourage their elaboration.

A 16th-century kitchen displayed in the Heimatsmuseum at Schloss Adelsheim, Berchtesgaden. Tour guides tend to invite unflattering comparisons between cooking then and now. Traditional methods produced excellent results, but certainly required effort and a large labour force. European kitchen design was influenced by the availability of an ample fuel supply and the aristocratic taste for roasted and boiled meat.

This book offers comparisons among a wide range of places and across extensive time periods, culminating with the modern phenomena of global choices, the rise of the restaurant and the double-edged sword of food technology. Inevitably, this means the cuisine of some cultures receives more attention than others, such as those of India, Mexico and Japan. What gives a certain unity to the very different culinary worlds described is a preoccupation with taste understood not only as flavour but the production of an impressive and artistic effect. We see this in the attention to colour and display in medieval Europe described in Chapter 5 and in the heroic efforts necessary to produce the classic French cuisine of the eighteenth and nineteenth centuries discussed in Chapter 8, or in the account given in Chapter 6 of France's imitators throughout Europe. The preparation of food has involved a craft that, unlike metalwork or glass-making, is by definition ephemeral and so hard to reconstruct. It is also a daily production undertaken by ordinary people as well as by masterful and acclaimed exponents.

Visitors to historic houses of the pre-modern world are always taken to the kitchens where the guides often invite them to pity people in the past with such questions as: 'How would *you* like to have to prepare meals without modern conveniences, using these tools?' With the advent of modernity and the desire for convenience and time-saving, much in the way of difficulty, of art, experience, calculation and sheer effort has been replaced by the attractions of speed, convenience and easy variety. Food has tended to become more of a hobby than

Monks belonging to the Benedictine Rule, such as those depicted in this fresco of 1505–8 by Sodoma, dined in silence. They might listen to readings from edifying texts of Scripture, saints lives or secular knowledge while they ate. Meat was usually not permitted except for monks recuperating in the infirmary, but grand monasteries such as Cluny in Burgundy elaborated recipes for fish. Many monasteries and convents were famed for medicinal preparations including cordials and pharmaceutical sweets known as electuaries.

a craft. Exponential growth in the volume of writing about food and the production of cookery books has coincided with a decline in how much cooking is actually being undertaken in the home. The modern affluent consumer's taste for changing cuisines, evoked by the imagined Europeans' excursion to an Ethiopian restaurant at the opening of Chapter 10, implies a desire for new sensations and a strategy to avoid boredom more than a search for perfection within a single cuisine tradition. Such attention to novelty does not necessarily mean an interest in intrinsic quality – the vogue for tinned pineapple and cheese crackers in postwar Germany was an expression of middle-class affluence and mild global sophistication rather than a culinary choice based on freshness or *terroir*.

There is now, however, a tremendous anxiety about food simultaneous with an enthusiasm for innovation; a sense of limitless possibilities as more cuisines enter the sophisticated urban first-world marketplace together with belated anxiety over such developments as genetic manipulation, artificial enhancements and the exhaustion of a once bountiful nature (so that luxuries from ortolans to Caspian Sea caviar are either unavailable or about to be unavailable). Seafood has enjoyed a tremendous popularity even as the global fisheries have reached the point of no return. Wild shrimp or wild salmon are now luxuries. From a gastronomic point of view, we live in both the best and the worst of times.

***

Throughout history recurrent patterns emerge in how people thought about food and its place in daily life and the expression of taste. There are many points of similarity and difference across time and continents, as well as how cultures dealt with outside influences: the introduction of New World products such as potatoes and peanuts to Europe, but also to China; or the much-debated question about the extent to which Islamic cuisine was the model for medieval Europe. Although the culinary worlds discussed in the following chapters had their own identity, they were not completely isolated and it is worth examining some patterns and questions that inform the argument of the book as a whole.

The first concerns diet and health. We can define health broadly enough to include spiritual health and so also the prohibitions of different religions. Of the cuisines considered here, Islamic food has the most obvious and extensive rules about what is not fit to eat. Some of these regulations are enduring and firm, notably the ban on pork. Others, such as the attitude towards wine, have been at various times more malleable. Jewish limitations on what is acceptable have been traditionally even more restrictive. In neither case, it goes without saying, has this meant a depreciation of the enjoyment of food.

Christianity has been more inclined to impose restrictions based on liturgical time (fasting days, Lent) or degree of dedication (monastic diets) rather than forbidding completely the consumption of particular foods, but Christianity has had a stronger anxiety about gluttony than Islam or Judaism. While all religious and philosophical traditions regard habitual over-eating with distaste, Christianity lists gluttony among the deadly sins and defines it to include connoisseurship rather than simply gross indulgence. In the sixth century, Pope Gregory the Great identified several kinds of gluttony, such as eating too much (*nimis*), eating with unbecoming eagerness (*ardenter*), or not waiting until normal decent mealtimes (*praepropere*). Enjoying food that was too expensive (*laute*) or too dainty (*studiose*) was also sinfully gluttonous. Excessive daintiness encompassed both fussiness over the preparation of food and medical (or hypochondriacal) concerns with it. The careful consideration of food so beloved in the Chinese and Islamic traditions, to say nothing of modern culinary writers, was dismissed entirely by the medieval Christian tradition.

That over-eating or indulgence in certain foods is dangerous is a constant theme and yet ever-changing in its specific focus. Melons and other raw fruit or large eels such as lampreys were regarded as dangerous in the Middle Ages and Renaissance, even if (or perhaps because) delectable. A concern with balance expressed by the theory of bodily humours (fluids defined as cold, moist, hot or dry) was essential to European classical, medieval and early modern thought and was incorporated into Chinese notions of equilibrium and propriety, where they remain strong to this day. China, which had relatively relaxed and omnivorous standards of what foods are permitted, has nevertheless many complex secular, more-or-less medical ideas of what is appropriate physically and spiritually. Western theories of humours were expressions of scientific speculation but often corresponding to religious or philosophical ideas of nature and cosmology. The balance of flavours (sour, sweet, sharp, salty, and so forth) produced culinary rules and conformed to notions of health. The use of spices in China, the Islamic world and in Europe until the eighteenth century reflected both a taste for certain sensations and theories of humorally hot and dry ingredients balancing essentially cold and moist meats and fish.

Vegetarianism and its intermittent popularity provides a case-study for the interrelationships among diet, religion and health. In the Islamic world, the primacy of meat is unquestioned and has the sanction of traditions dating back to the founding of the religion. In the Christian West, meat was mistrusted as an encouragement to sensuality and so prohibited or severely limited (usually to invalids) in monastic rules. Little in the way of a complementary praise of vegetables developed, however, as they were regarded with a degree of contempt as more appropriate for consumption by peasants than by the well born. A vegetarian diet was a penance. There was official opposition to the practice of voluntary vegetarianism among laymen since this was identified with the Manichaean heresy and its teachings about the evil of created matter and flesh in particular. The Cathars or Albigensians in the thirteenth century revived this aspect of Manichaean dualism. Their violent suppression in the Albigensian Crusade and its aftermath gave such teachings an especially bad name. Buddhism and other religious traditions of India and China extolled vegetables as did certain Greek philosophical schools, but this did not always encourage the development of what can properly be called a cuisine rather than simply preaching abstemious indifference to food.

In the modern world, concerns about the interrelation of health and food have produced any number of odd combinations: fads for diets coinciding with a growth of obesity; fears about ties between various foods and disease (eggs, saturated fats, trans-fats) coinciding with increased consumption of artificially processed ingredients; exaggerations of the benefits of one or another kind of food (vegetarianism, oat-bran, high-protein regimes). At the most basic statistical level, life expectancy in developed countries has increased significantly in recent decades and rates for fatalities from heart disease and other conditions related to diet have fallen, so that it can be argued that such anxieties are unjustified. They may be symptoms of a sense of displacement because of the separation from the sources of food and even from its day-to-day preparation – of being at the mercy of a food industry whose organization of farms, fisheries and livestock into immense and ecologically damaging factories has created justified but not squarely recognized anxieties. A basic reluctance actually to face the stove may also contribute to a sense of deracination. Over twenty-five years ago in the United States, Pierre Franey's *60-Minute Gourmet* and a sequel, books that offered (more-or-less) French recipes that could be accomplished within an hour, raised eyebrows for what seemed like scandalous brevity. Now the American magazine *Gourmet* has recipes that can be accomplished in 10 minutes. Ruth Reichl, the editor of *Gourmet*, author of several intriguing and important volumes of culinary life history, points out that the United States currently has more prisoners in its gaols than it has farmers, and has taken it as her mission to increase awareness of where food comes from, the environmental context and consequences of agriculture, and to encourage people to use their kitchens for their intended purpose.

Fortunately, health concerns do not necessarily discourage, at least for very long, the pleasurable consumption and contemplation of food. Such delight may be thought of as closely linked to sexual pleasure, an association expressed by films such as the Japanese *Tampopo* (1985), the Mexican *Like Water for Chocolate* (1992), or the Spanish *Jamón, Jamón* (1992). The restaurant was a place of assignation in nineteenth-century Paris and eighteenth-century Yangzhou. Part of the Christian mistrust

A scene from *Like Water for Chocolate*, a film set in early 20th-century Mexico in which injustice, selfishness, violence and cruelty are resisted, if not always overcome, by the power of food cooked with emotional intensity. Both the dishes themselves (quails in rose-petal sauce) and their manner of preparation (wedding cake with the tears of the slighted lover) have magical effects.

The two Catholic deadly sins, gluttony and lust, were thought to complement and encourage each other. They are quintessentially physical sins as opposed to the mental transgressions of pride or envy. This meal in a bath-house/brothel from a German manuscript of about 1470 is allegorical rather than an accurate portrayal of ordinary medieval dining habits.

of gourmandise is its supposed kinship with lust, yet, as with the more dangerous attractions of drink, beyond a certain point indulgence becomes a disincentive to sexual desire and attraction.

Societies and historical periods differ greatly on the intellectual or philosophical worth of opinions and guides concerning the pleasures of the table. It is striking that in China, discriminating knowledge of food was a requirement for the sophisticated and scholarly elite, equal in importance to poetry or art. Thus cookery books and discussions of food were not only written for great patrons but often by them. In the Caliphate of Baghdad, poems in praise of meals were recited and collected while in Umayyad Córdoba, the musician Ziryab retooled his career to become a food stylist for Caliph 'Abd al-Rahman II and permanently affected Spanish gastronomy. In contrast, the medieval West produced over one hundred cookery books, but almost nothing by way of comment on food by sophisticated lay patrons. Banqueting and appreciation of food reached great heights in late medieval Europe, but there were no noble amateurs that we know of, no Christian parallel for the invention of the sour meat stew *ibrahīmīya* by the half-brother of the caliph who gave his name (Ibrahim al-Mahdi) to it.

The Renaissance writer Platina's *De honesta voluptate et valetudine* (On Correct Pleasure and Good Health) constitutes a discriminating guide to gastronomy, one that eschews gluttony, ostentation, or over-reliance on expensive ingredients. It is comprehensive and descriptive rather than just a collection of recipes, but it is only minimally discursive and does not share the sensuous lyricism of the Arab or Chinese writers. Platina praises moderation and frugality (or at least claims to do so), and rejects the notion that the celebration of food encourages gluttony and lust. His work is more in the nature of a compendium than a sustained meditation on cuisine.

The definitive European treatise on gourmandise comes much later with Brillat-Savarin's *La Physiologie du goût* (*The Physiology of Taste*) of 1825 whose scientific and medical pretensions are indicated by the title, but whose further purposes are communicated by subtitles that combine magisterial authority with innovative panache: 'Méditations de gastronmie transcendante: ouvrage théorique, historique...' (meditations on transcendent gastronomy: a theoretical, historical work...). As with Platina, taste, health and pleasure are compatible, a view that always has to be defended in Western culture. More than anyone previously, however, Brillat-Savarin made discrimination and the maintenance of standards an ally of pleasure and, in some sense, one of its constituents. Part of the pleasure of knowing about food comes from the possession of knowledge and taste that can devise rankings (of wines or restaurants, for example), establish hierarchies, and in so doing, confer a sense of self-satisfaction and social distinction.

The connection between social status and food runs through the essays in this book. In 1404, a Florentine notary named Lapo Mazzei wrote a letter to the important merchant of Prato, Francesco de Marco Datini, to thank him for a gift of partridges. Lapo protests that these birds are really too good for him, and this is not just a slightly servile expression of gratitude but quite carefully calibrated. At one time, Lapo explains, when he was a member of the Florentine government, it was not only his privilege but his obligation to eat partridges, but now that he has returned to ordinary social status, it is inappropriate for him to do so.

The European Middle Ages had an elaborate code of what foods were appropriate for what sorts of people. White wheaten bread, game, delicate or unusual birds, large fish and exotic spices were meant for nobles. Peasants should stick to their supposedly natural diet of dairy products, strongly flavoured root vegetables, garlic, and porridge or dark bread. Some of this gastronomic stratification masked anxiety over the rise of newly rich people and erosion of social boundaries, and the proliferation of sumptuary laws that defined who could wear what sort of clothing responded to the same unease. Yet the sense that class determined food preference was given a medical or what might be called cultural overlay. It was not as if peasants necessarily wanted or could appreciate the delicate food of the wealthy, any more than the modern imagination expects caviar or Italian white truffles to constitute an important unsatisfied gratification of the poor. In fact, food choices symbolically reinforced comfortable assumptions about class and status. A number of medieval stories recount the unexpected gastronomic consequences of social mobility. In one a well-off peasant marries into a better class and his new wife prepares all manner of elegant up-to-date dishes for him that give him terrible indigestion. He is restored to contentment when she serves him what he is used to: beans and peas with soaked bread. According to a Renaissance medical work, partridges were not good for rustics and correspondingly a French social observer credited the greater intellectual acuity of the upper classes to their diet of delicate foods such as partridges rather than beef and pork.

These distinctions have certainly not gone away even if partridges are no longer such a key social marker. There are certain persistent stereotypes of lower-class foods, such as less desirable kinds of organ meats, as well as new ones that stem from technology – canned vegetables or artificially enhanced convenience products such as Spam. Yet the preferences of ordinary people, or their perceived preferences, have an occasionally powerful political as well as social meaning. It is not quite true that on the campaign trail in the 1990s Labour politician and spin-doctor Peter Mandelson mistook mushy peas, the northern English working-class favourite, for guacamole, but the story has an emblematic durability epitomizing New Labour and its isolation from the proletarian world. On the other hand, much was made in June 1939 of a picnic at which the United States president served hot dogs to King George VI and Queen Elizabeth, publicity that promoted a democratized image of both Roosevelt and the monarchs.

The meals that symbolize and confer the highest degree of social prestige tend to be characterized by quantity, variety and the rarity of what is served. Service for the Qianlong Emperor of China seems grotesque in the immensity and variety of dishes presented, such as the breakfast menu of 1779 described in Chapter 3, but so were routine meals of medieval European and Islamic notables, or for that matter those of the bourgeoisie of the nineteenth-century Russian and British empires, as advised by Elena Molokhovets and Mrs Beeton respectively. The latter, in her celebrated book of household management, suggests for a mere party of eight dining in the spring a first course of Mock Turtle Soup, Brill and Shrimp Sauce and Broiled Mackerel à la Maître d'Hôtel, followed by an entrée of Lobster Cutlets and Calf's Liver and Bacon aux Fines Herbes. A second course consists of Roast Loin of Veal, Two Boiled Fowls à la Béchamel, Boiled Knuckle of Ham with Spinach or Broccoli. The third course is Wild Ducks accompanied by Apple Custards, Blancmange, Lemon Jelly, Jam Sandwiches, Ice Pudding and Potatoes à la Maître d'Hôtel. Dessert and Ices conclude this elaborate (if not at the moment particularly attractive) meal.

Certain foods were associated with luxury to the extent that their presence at a sophisticated meal was almost a necessity: lobster, caviar, truffles, foie gras fit this description in the late nineteenth and early twentieth century. These things change, so that before the nineteenth century, lobster and caviar had occupied a more modest place in the hierarchy of prestige, while in the eighteenth century the long culinary, symbolic and social power of spices that dated back to the Roman Empire collapsed. As Timothy Morton put it, 'yesterday's banquet ingredient becomes today's Dunkin' Donuts apple-cinnamon item.' What then are today's partridges, things that a person of high estate *must* consume? Lobster has become too affordable in many countries while on the other hand truffles and caviar are so prohibitively expensive as to have become bizarre exotica. There is really nothing in the way of particular dishes that fulfil a more than local or temporary role in gastronomic fashion. This is not only because of eclecticism or decreasing novelty (now anyone can have asparagus out of season if they wish), but because in our time food is defined more as personal style than a rigid attribute of class, except perhaps for *lower*-class foods. And even here, there are traditional, seemingly authentic lower-class foods that can be elevated to esteem with some tweaking: polenta, gazpacho, various international forms of so-called 'street-food', 'gourmet' hamburgers…. Most strongly in our time is a longing for what is regarded as peasant food, a rusticity that reflects not so much admiration for a class that is now in the process of extinction in Europe, but rather a response to the transformation of *terroir* into factory and the desire to connect with a tradition of hearty authenticity.

The real Mrs Beeton has only recently been distinguished from the legendary figure whose much reprinted cookery book is often taken as defining the taste of Victorian England. The plates show savouries and fruit desserts from the second edition of *Mrs Beeton's Book of Household Management*, published in 1869. Presentation for the desserts, then and now, tends to be more frivolous. The savouries include preparations of now-neglected animal parts accompanied with extraordinarily rich ingredients: pig's feet with truffles or calf's ears prepared with the complex Sauce Financière based on Sauce Veloutée but with mushrooms, brains, Madeira, olives and sometimes truffles as well.

Taste has tended to become adventurous rather than codified; a statement of individual choice instead of mere etiquette. This allows for greater exuberance and less fatiguing repetition, but eclecticism has not completely eliminated the relation between food and social standing. High status is now identified by access to certain levels of what once would have been routine quality (free-range poultry, wild seafood).

The same societies that defined luxurious foods and developed an extensive discourse surrounding them, also reacted against what was perceived as excessive elaboration to rediscover simplicity and purity. This could, as just stated, take the form of paying attention to peasant or popular dishes, mostly those requiring considerable cooking time (slow food) enhancing simple but artisanal ingredients. Simplicity is a reaction against what might be called, paradoxically, the limitations of excess, its narrowness amid infinite choice (not foie gras, again!), and its tendency to interfere with the intrinsic quality of primary products by excessive manipulation and gratuitous flavouring. In some cases this might be a redefinition of luxury. In the fourth century BC, the Greek Sicilian chef Archestratos of Gela wrote a poem in praise of the life of luxury (*Hedypatheia*) but his instructions are to search out quality, freshness and elegant simplicity in preparation. Establishing French grand cuisine in the seventeenth and eighteenth century meant rejecting the distortions and ostentations of medieval food in favour of purity and intrinsic quality. Pleasure, delight and true flavours were extolled over what was regarded as an unpleasant legacy of excessive use of spices, childish artifice and lack of respect for primary ingredients. Yet of course this movement towards simplicity would itself become complex, rule-bound and ponderous.

The oscillation between magnificence and simplicity, between artifice and authenticity, is particularly typical of the current culinary scene, where the two contradictory trends flourish simultaneously rather than one era succeeding another. How many articles has one read about famous chefs cooking the simple dishes of their family traditions on their days off? This is not just a question of style or fashion, the culinary equivalent of rising and falling hemlines, but an expression of a modern sense of loss that exists alongside variety and experimentation.

The cuisines discussed here all had an international sway. French cuisine in the nineteenth and twentieth century might express the wealth and variety of a particular *pays* with many inimitable elements dependent on special places and conditions (truffles in Perigord, Calvados in Normandy) but that could be successfully marketed for export. In *The Brothers Karamazov*, Ivan recklessly buys luxuries such as Cognac and French paté to waste on his peasant drinking companions. It is notable that these were readily available in the nineteenth-century Russian provinces, just as at the other end of the world, Gold Rush San Francisco could produce a fine French restaurant called 'Au

Poulet d'Or', known to the locals as the 'Old Poodle Dog'. How French all of this was in the sense of intimate knowledge of that country may be questioned, but there was a very varied and large-scale export of taste and it was not simply for display. That symbol of the American gilded age, the railroad tycoon Diamond Jim Brady, loved Sauce Marguery (the recipe filched from Paris) so much, he declared, he would eat it even if it were served on a Turkish towel.

Certain fashions travelled the world long before the modern era. Marco Polo in about 1300 wrote that the amount of pepper imported into the Chinese port of Zaitoun (modern Quanzhou) was a hundred times what was received in Alexandria for the European market. Even if this is an exaggeration, the medieval desire for pepper grown in India extended from China, throughout the Muslim world and to the farthest western reaches of Europe.

French cuisine in the last centuries is not really national but rather a collection of regional items turned into a grand cuisine and pruned then for export. In this sense, national cuisines are sometimes considered to be fictions or modern conveniences with the only really enduring culinary traditions being based on regions. Certainly cassoulet or choucroute would become staples of Parisian restaurants, but they remain essentially identified with Languedoc and Alsace. The latter is a region that has not always consistently been part of France and neither province has been consistently French-speaking. Italian food is also more a form of packaging for export than a national reality. The country's political unity dates only from the late nineteenth century, and the styles of cooking between Sicily and Milan are as different as any national distinctions. While looking at broad culinary worlds that encompass many regional specialties, we should not overlook the differentiation among regions and the process by which certain items are either limited to one place by availability or taste (*pa amb tomàquet*, grilled bread rubbed with garlic, olive oil and tomato, extends out of Catalonia to Aragon but not beyond), incorporated into metropolitan definitions of national cuisine (tripes à la mode de Caen) or even fictitious inventions (chicken chow mein) or re-imports (pizza).

***

In *The Politics* (Book 1, 7), Aristotle cites cooking as a typically 'servile' branch of knowledge, a skill appropriate to slaves. The observation occurs in the context of demonstrating that masters are distinguished from slaves not by knowing how to do things, but by their character. It is fitting that a domestic servant have the ability to prepare food, but this is not a craft that confers honour in the way that knowledge of hunting and war do. The master of a household is concerned not with the acquisition of lower arts such as cookery, but merely with their use.

We seem to have progressed along a road of increasing prestige in our age of celebrity chefs, yet, as discussed in Chapter 2, the classical world was not completely in accord with Aristotle's formulation and could lavish fulsome attention to culinary matters, elevating the best practitioners to the status of stars. Only part of Athenaeus' *Deipnosophistae* survives, but even so, this rambling collection of arguments and observations from the early third century AD comprises fifteen books that reveal a passionate culture of cookery and in which there are elaborate descriptions of feasts and discriminating information on gastronomic lore.

Similarly, in our era, the history and culture of food have been objects of great attention. Certain specific subjects have proven especially popular, such as collections of local recipes, reminiscences of the food of childhood, or evocations of vanished graciousness. In the category of local culinary knowledge there are entire books devoted to a single typical dish, for example, the aforementioned Catalan *pa amb tomàquet* that allegedly cannot be duplicated elsewhere, despite the seeming ordinariness of its ingredients. Another example of local pride comes in an introduction by Eudora Welty, one of the greatest American writers of the later twentieth century, to a recipe collection assembled by the ladies affiliated with the Jackson (Mississippi) Symphony League. Welty uses this opportunity to describe how mayonnaise was first brought to Jackson not long after 1900. A recent recipe collection from the same part of the world, *Being Dead is No Excuse*, gives an account of dishes traditionally served after southern funerals, their recipes and social meaning.

Among reflections on childhood, Proust presents far more complicated meals recalled in pleasurable detail than the mere madeleine. In a memoir of growing up in postwar Livorno, Patrizia Chen recalls the contrast between the bland timbales, plain pasta and steamed fish served to her grandparents and their cook's more creative and variegated creations on her own, accompanied by the rapt young author. A poignantly comical example of cultural loss in reference to a superior cuisine of the past is evoked in a review of an English translation of the classic nineteenth-century Russian cookery book *Podarok molodym khozyajkam* (A Gift to Young Housewives) by Elena Molokhovets. In her review essay, Tatyana Tolstaya describes the amazement of Russians of the Soviet era marvelling (in fact laughing uproariously) at this book with its lost world of extraordinary appetites and the means to satisfy them with the most astonishing ingredients. The book's subtitle promises economy and reduction of expenses to the merely middle-class household, yet, according to Tolstaya it seems to describe a race of magnificent gluttons:

> Where is the creature who, rising at dawn, spends two and a half hours roasting chamois in time for breakfast? Or who tosses back a jigger of vodka in the morning and sits down to consume beer soup with sour cream (Rhine wines are served in the middle of breakfast, punch at the end; or the

The Merchant Wife's Tea by Boris Kustodiev captures a
prosperous, quiet occasion and expresses an everyday kind
of joy. Painted in 1915, a time of war and pre-revolutionary
social upheaval in Russia, by an artist who was suffering from
a paralysing tubercular illness, this picture is a reminder of
the fragility of enjoyment and the radiance of memory.

other way around), and with barely time to recover, again drinks vodka or wine for midday dinner (with hors d'œuvres: marinated fish, smoked hare, stuffed goose or pears in honey, ninety versions to choose from) and applies himself to soup with champagne and savory pies (the champagne is *poured in* the soup!), upon which there follows yet another bountiful meat dish, and then a heavy dessert drenched in sugar and fat. After that, it's not long until evening tea with five types of bread, veal, ham, beef, hazel grouse, turkey, tongue, hare, four sorts of cheese.

China in particular, as revealed in Chapter 3, seems to have excelled in recollections of the food of better times, such as Zhang Dai's lovingly detailed memories of the crabs, clams and junket enjoyed before the fall of the Ming Dynasty, or the evocation of the restaurants of Kaifeng in the early thirteenth century by Meng Liang Lu, including Mother Song's fish soup, or the pig cooked in ashes at a place in front of the Longevity-and-Compassion Palace.

And yet, if the cuisine of the past evokes such powerful associations, its academic study has only recently been able to justify itself as something other than the history of elite fripperies or of antiquarian fussiness. In his edited collection *Food Nations*, Warren Belasco laments the combination of dismissiveness and bemused wonder that writings on the history of food receive even now from academic historians. Introducing a series of his essays on the culinary history of the Middle Ages, Bruno Laurioux dates the first (Western) interest in the gastronomic past to eighteenth-century France, where it formed part of the polemic between the moderns and the ancients, but after that, the history of food meant the quantitative study of 'rations and provisioning' (*rations et de ravitaillement*) until only just in the last few decades has the qualitative study of the consumption and preparation of food for reasons other than survival been taken to have a scholarly value.

This book concerns the culinary accomplishments of several civilizations of the past and present, especially their basic principles and aesthetic preferences. Although primarily concerned with the pleasures of dining experienced by those fortunate enough to have some choices, basic questions about survival and nutrition are also considered. Chapter 1 on prehistoric humans, and chapters 7 and 10 about the impact of technology and globalization, focus on ordinary people and their struggle for an adequate diet. Throughout, however, there is a concern with the history of *taste*: how people thought about food – its ingredients, preparation and presentation. The book examines how food preferences and culinary principles varied in different societies and is informed by the belief that taste says something important about specific places and times. Food is considered as a form of social history, revealing the impact on dining of, for example, postwar prosperity, or the technological revolutions and the desire for convenience. In addition to these objective considerations, the authors also explore the subjectivity of food: the experience and satisfactions of its preparation and consumption and the pleasures of discussing meals, dining and recipes.

Chapter 1 on Prehistory uses the archaeological evidence to investigate the conditions under which early humans consumed food. Before agriculture and the domestication of animals, taste was determined by the difficulty of obtaining sufficient fat and carbohydrates so that taste, if certainly determined by biological imperatives, was nevertheless paramount. Fondness for the limited repertoire of sweet tastes available (honey) and a sense of discrimination between different kinds of fats (from different parts of animals) are indications of preferences within the constraints of the culinary environment. Once animal-herding starts, there are contrasting preferences for cereals, for the domination of one dietary element, and different attitudes towards dairy products.

In the classical world, examined in Chapter 2, taste changed from the ceremonial but simple roasted meat of the Homeric era to the complex aesthetic of Greek Sicily and Imperial Rome. Characteristics shaped by particular needs and desires of Ancient Greece and Rome would be repeated in subsequent food cultures: the importance of trade, imported luxuries and oscillation between a tradition of simplicity and what was perceived by some as innovation and others as degenerate excess.

The Chinese culinary principles discussed in Chapter 3 go back in some cases more than 2,000 years, but changes were introduced by new religious and philosophical doctrines, expansion of the Chinese empires and, eventually, the availability of New World products. The immense range of foods on offer imparted a permanent richness to the cuisine, encouraged also by an unusually prolific commentary and appreciation for dining, regional specialties, recipes and connoisseurship.

Islamic cuisine in the Middle Ages, as revealed in Chapter 4, would combine elements of the Arabian desert tradition with Persian, Indian and Byzantine cuisine to form a sophisticated, subtle and varied group of food customs. The incorporation of culinary ideas from the Mediterranean to Central Asia and the Indian Subcontinent would create a zone of mutual exchange and would influence regions beyond the borders of Islamic religious culture, including China and Europe.

Medieval Christian Europe, discussed in Chapter 5, developed a magnificent, highly decorative cuisine, based in certain respects on Roman precedents mingled with adaptations from Islamic Spain, Africa and the Middle East but with its own aesthetic of flavours, ceremony and presentation. The famous medieval passion for spices is set in a context of shared enthusiasm over several cultures and eras, with a consistent, long-term taste for sharp, complex and fragrant sensations.

Overleaf: The venerable practice and tradition of drinking tea continues in contemporary China in many different ways and settings, including this institutionalized form at a session of political advisers in the Great Hall of the People in Beijing, 2005.

Chapter 6 covers the period between roughly 1500 and 1800 when Europe first continued and eventually broke with ancient and medieval traditions of humoral theories of balance and highly spiced food in favour of greater emphasis on primary ingredients and the adaptation of the divers products resulting from the exploitation of New World resources. The introduction of tea, coffee, maize, tomatoes and chocolate, and the huge expansion in the consumption of sugar, would revolutionize diet, taste preferences and in turn social and economic organization on a global scale.

By the nineteenth century France had come to dominate the culinary style of the European (and soon American) world. Chapter 8 discusses the principles of French cuisine and the differences between its regional and bourgeois origins and the grand cuisine that emerged as a world trend in the nineteenth century. It was, however, already in the process of change and diminution by 1920.

Other chapters describe attributes of modern dining, those resulting from changes in how and where food is provided (restaurants, for example), and the impact of modernization in the technology of food cultivation, preservation, transport, packaging and marketing. The restaurant, a feature of China from early times but developed in Europe only in the late eighteenth century, would come into its own beginning in the nineteenth century. The conditions that encouraged the rise of the restaurant are outlined in Chapter 9, as well as the changes in what was served (types of cuisine), forms of service (emphasizing elegance, intimacy, or convenience), and the place of the restaurant in European and American society. Chapter 7 on the birth of the consumer age uses the case of nineteenth- and twentieth-century Germany to show the transformations brought about by new methods of transporting and preserving food, the choices introduced by better crop yields, industrialization and rising living standards, and the upheaval created by the growth of cities and the reduction in the number of people involved in agriculture. The contemporary situation, the ambiguous benefits of choice, are considered in the final chapter. After an initial phase of reconstructing and surpassing the patterns of pre-war consumption, a change in the direction of fewer rules, greater eclecticism and globalization has accelerated the pace of innovation. How food is acquired, distributed and prepared is now at the centre of discussion of sustainability, globalization and the world of the future.

If all history is, in a sense, a dialogue between tradition and innovation, how today do we weigh up in culinary terms the ever beguiling tension between them? What seems to exemplify the higher end of dining now is a double or even contradictory view of what taste should strive for. On the one hand, the uneasiness over where food comes from, coupled with a periodic shift towards simplicity, has led to a cuisine of *authenticity* in which quality, naturalness, seasonality and local ingredients are paramount and the style of preparation is designed to highlight the primary products. To some extent this involves the reinvention of the wheel – at one time all chickens were free range because there was no mass production of poultry; before recent advances in fish-farming, all salmon was wild salmon. Within the context of advancing technology, homogenization and separation from agrarian life, the ability to preserve and evoke 'heirloom' produce or naturally raised meat has a certain luxurious ostentatious simplicity.

Among the best-known pioneers in this rediscovery is Alice Waters's restaurant Chez Panisse, located in Berkeley, an apparent paradox in the country that has gone the furthest towards artificiality and mass production. California is both the centre of American agribusiness and now a region with some of the most carefully nurtured and delightful food products. The publicity for Chez Panisse (for example on its website) states a desire to base the menu on sustainability, local small-scale production, and of course on the intrinsic quality of ingredients. The restaurant's menu describes the specific, small-scale provenance of much of what is offered – Laughing Stock Farm pork, Quinault River steelhead, Wolfe Ranch quail – a menu innovation now widely imitated in the United States and Britain. As Patric Kuh has pointed out, local specificity as well as detailed cooking methods characterized the menu of Chez Panisse from its beginnings in the 1970s ('Monterey Bay prawns sautéed with garlic, parsley and butter'), in contrast to the standardized (if to many Americans impenetrable) French vocabulary of the previous era. Of course, preparation accounts and their evocations of boutique-farm origins would become exaggerated, ritualized and comical in the hands of lesser imitators. Compare such elaborate descriptions with the concise listings in a Tour d'Argent menu from about 1960 that includes fifteen varieties of its famous *Caneton*, a few with bare descriptions (*Caneton au quartiers de Pêches*, *Caneton de la Cerisaie*) but mostly mysterious to the mere neophyte: *Caneton Raphaël Weill*, *Caneton des Vendanges*. There is, of course, a decipherable vocabulary of French geographical descriptions in classic cuisine, so that a Grenoblaise sauce is butter and capers, or a Rouennaise sauce involves duck or chicken livers, Crécy indicates carrots, and so forth, expressing a sense of regions or towns and their specialties, but developed before the industrialization of food production made specific artisanal origins a matter of special privilege. The Grenoblaise capers are seldom specified as to origins (Tunisian versus Italian, for example), and certainly not by whichever caper farm raised them.

Not quite the same, but in the similar category as a dissent from modernization and homogeneity is the Slow Food movement, an explicit response to the imperial conquests of fast food and the consequent standardization and degradation of taste. The Slow Food movement, started in Italy in 1986, attempts to restore not only the sense of place and seasonality to what is eaten, but a traditional or at least not mass- and convenience-oriented method of cooking.

A particular emphasis is on biodiversity, the preservation and reintroduction of breeds and varieties that have been cast aside as inconvenient to standardized production and packaging.

Along with the emphasis on local and seasonal ingredients is another, seemingly contradictory, tendency towards artifice and innovation, manifested, for example, by various fusion cuisines combining ingredients from different cultures, especially European dishes made with the addition of Asian or African spices and flavours (cream sauce with vanilla; lemon-grass infusions, hoisin sauce). Artifice includes reversals of expectations: clashing ingredients, mixtures of plebian and elegant, alchemical transformations of ingredients. Some of this goes back to the effects produced by the *nouvelle cuisine* of the 1970s, whose penchant for the unexpected (maple syrup with seafood) became notorious and was often mocked. In fact, however, as discussed in Chapter 8, *nouvelle cuisine* began as a rediscovery of quality of ingredients and extolled simplicity against a tired traditionalism of over-rich sauces and rule-bound complexity. *Nouvelle cuisine* in a sense extends on either side of the borders of simplicity and artifice, for if on the one hand its advocates praised freshness and integrity, they also wanted to expand the imagination of the chef, embracing such French 1968 slogans as 'everything is permitted' and 'it is prohibited to prohibit'. They were advocates of that elusive attribute we are exploring here, taste, understood in this instance as originality rather than tradition. In keeping with the exaltation of the new, the *nouvelle cuisine* movement truly begins the cult of celebrity chefs who emerge as inventors of new sensations, not, as with Carême, Escoffier or Point, guardians and definers of a grand heritage.

The innovative restaurants of Catalonia, capital of contemporary trends, evoke some of the precedents of the *nouvelle cuisine*, promoting intensity of flavour and unusual combinations, but their stylishness is considerably more playful, global and eclectic. Thus the Barcelona restaurant Comerç 24 has offered items such as 'cotton candy' flavoured with anchovy, basil and tomato among its starters, along with an ultra-sophisticated version of the Spanish fast-food grilled sandwich classic the 'bikini', here made with Jabugo ham and zucchini. The intrinsic quality of the ingredients is less important than their manipulation.

The best-known restaurant in this category is Ferran Adrià's El Bulli on the Costa Brava. Rather ordinary ingredients (such as canned mandarin oranges) are transformed by a kind of alchemy into foams, powders, frozen creams. Rather than the earnestness of California naturalism there is a surreal emphasis on metamorphosis and unexpected juxtaposition. Adrià describes his food as 'creative', a 'vanguard cuisine' and 'conceptual'. The heartland or *terroir* is here the imagination. There is a special place for *trompe-l'œil*: 'risotto Milanese' has the right look, taste and texture, but is made with bean sprouts rather than rice; duck foie gras is frozen into a consistency and colour resembling

the South American grain quinoa and served with consommé which you are instructed to eat alternating with the powder ('quinoa helada de foie-gras de pato consommé'); cauliflower is fragmented so as to resemble cous-cous ('cous-cous de coliflor con salsa sólida de aromáticos'), and the humble peasant dish of cooked breadcrumbs is flavoured with artificially created truffles ('migas al falso tartufo'). How much this sparkling inventiveness can be effectively imitated remains in question. Adrià has a lot to answer for in the proliferation of restaurants offering dubious food transformations. In Anthony Bourdain's bestselling *Kitchen Confidential* (2000), the chef of El Bulli is dismissed simply as 'that foam guy', but clearly his influence has only grown in the years since that was written.

The simultaneous success of authenticity and creativity is not completely new. A similar polarity, at least in aspiration, between seasonal simplicity and baroque effect could be seen in the 1950s and 1960s, as a look at menus from two restaurants owned by the same company in New York reveals. Joseph Baum, founder of Restaurant Associates, ran a fleet of restaurants that included the Four Seasons (still one of the grand restaurants of New York City), which as its name implies emphasized seasonal ingredients, and the long-extinct Forum of the Twelve Caesars whose bombastic menu offered exotic, magnificent and often somewhat ludicrous suggestions. The Four Seasons was unusual for the 1950s in paying attention to seasonal ingredients beyond the well-known appropriateness of game in autumn or lamb in spring. Its menus now seem more exotic and extensive than the careful temporal appropriateness of a Chez Panisse and they seldom communicate any sense of where the ingredients come from. Among the 'seasonals' in a winter menu from *c.* 1959 are Wild Mallard Duck, Pressed; Suckling Pig with Stewed Apples; Woodcock Flamed in Cognac; Lake Sturgeon in Cream 'Muscovite'; and Terrapin Maryland. An exception to the lack of interest in origin is the Whole Perigord truffle and Prosciutto in Parsley, at $8.75 a reminder of a world we have lost. What the Tureen of January Fruit starter was, is difficult to determine. A 'variety of seasonals' for the spring of the same period includes Bouché of Sweetbreads Fine Champagne, Veal Cutlet with Primeurs, Suckling Kid in Lemon and Parmesan Crumbs along with a Tureen of March Fruit.

The Forum of the Twelve Caesars made no claim to follow the rhythms of nature. In a 1957 menu, capital letters and arch formulations abound, announcing such categories as EPICUREAN TROPHIES OF THE HUNT which includes 'Epigrams of Venison, Sautéed with Truffle and SAUCE VITAE'. A note laments the unavailability (because of local 'sumptuary laws') of pink flamingos, larks and thrushes, but offers as a consolation 'the noble Peacock' cooked by 'our ARMIGERIUS and his kitchens' according to 'one of the most delightful recipes of their ARS COQUINARIA'. The Wild Fowl of SAMOS are cooked (rather oddly considering the historical

The first page of this menu from the short-lived but spectacular New York restaurant Forum of the Twelve Caesars shows a typically great variety of offerings, an arch tone and comical, sketchy but ostentatious learning. Even though $7.50 for the truffles roasted in ashes was real money in 1957, the availability of this dish evokes a lost world.

DINNER

CENABIS BENE . . . APUD ME — CATULLUS

'YOU WILL DINE WELL AT MY TABLE' — THUS MIGHT A CAESAR INVITE HIS
GUESTS TO SHARE THE EPICUREAN TREASURES GATHERED FOR HIM FROM ALL THE
ROMAN WORLD — TONIGHT WE INVITE YOU TO SUP WITH THE CAESARS: YOU WILL
DINE WELL!

PROLOGUE

SHELL-BORNE OUT OF THE SEA

The Oysters of Hercules 1.65   Oysters and Pink Caviar 2.25
'WHICH YOU WITH SWORD WILL CARVE'   A LUCULLAN FANTASY
Cherrystone Clams 1.10   Nearby Oysters 1.10   Little Neck Clams .95
Alban Crabmeat set in Avocado Coronet 2.65   Shrimp from the Golden Gulf 1.75
A Cocktail of Fresh Lobster 2.50   A Salad of Bay Mussels and Roe 1.50
TRIBUTE TO TRITON—an Offering of Various Shellfish 2.85

GUSTATORIES — VARIED AND COLD

Artichoke with Strasbourg Livers 2.25   A Cocktail of Fresh Fruits .95
Adriatic Anchovies, Whole and Marinated 1.10   The Leeks of Rome, APICIAN STYLE .85
Lentils and Sausages, Sweet and Sour 1.35   Smoked Game Fish, SAUCE VITELLIUS 1.65
Half Grapefruit with Avocado Slice, Honey Dressing .95   Iced Seasonal Melon 1.25
The Great Heather-Smoked Scotch Salmon 2.75   Herring of the Far-Off North Sea 1.10
FROM THE HERDS OF EPICURUS—Various Hams Served with Delightful Fruits 2.45
Belgic Pate with Wild Boar, Sauce of Damascus Plums 3.00
CAVIAR IMPERATOR on an Ice Throne with Vodka and Other Accompaniments

MORE PROVOCATIVES — HOT

Snails on the Silver Gridiron 1.85   Snails in Dumplings, Green Butter Sauce 1.75
A Dish of Scallops with SAUCE VOLUPTAS 1.50   Beef Marrow on Toast, A LUCULLUS ORIGINAL 1.45
Leek Pie with Hot Sausages .95   The Golden Eggs of CRASSUS 1.10
THE GREAT FORUM ARTICHOKE, Filled with a Puree of Oysters 1.65
Grilled Fresh Sardines, IBERIAN MUSTARD SAUCE 1.35   Crayfish Filets in a Light Dill Sauce 1.65
Oysters in SENATE DRESS 1.65   Oysters ANOTHER WAY 1.75
Wild Boar Marinated and Served on the Flaming Short Sword 2.35

ROMAN RAMEKINS CALLED MINUTALS

FAVORITES OF THE AUGUSTAN COURT

LUCANIAN—Lamb, Sausage, Dill 1.10   SYLVAN—Venison, Red Wine, Chestnuts 1.10
APICIAN—Egg, Red Wine, Marrow and Leek 1.25   PISCATORIAN—Mousse of Pike, Lobster Sauce 1.10
TARENTINE—Chicken, Mushroom, Truffled Cream 1.25
LUCRINE—Oysters and Artichoke Hearts 1.35

MUSHROOM AND TRUFFLES

'THE RELISH OF THE GODS'

Great Mushrooms Stuffed with Snails, Gallic Cheese and Walnuts, Glazed 1.85
Wild Mushrooms Served Cold in a Marinade with Basil, Peppercorns and Anchovies 1.95
Black Truffles and Artichoke Bottoms Flamed in Mustard Cream 2.75
Fresh Truffles HERCULANEUM—Prepared 'Under the Ashes' 7.50
Mushrooms of the 'SINCERE' CLAUDIUS—An Emperor's Design 1.75
Egg Mushrooms with Roman Beans seasoned with Chervil and Shallots, SERVED COLD 1.50

gestures) with New World vegetables: Sherried Tomatoes and Crusty Corn (maize). The desserts include 'The Crepes of the Mad Nero' (flambé) and 'Frozen Omelette THULE'.

There are consistent oscillations between natural simplicity (or its affectation) and the spectacular effects of artifice (with the corresponding inclination to a certain vulgarity). The vogue for the ostentatiously 'simple' *nouvelle cuisine* coincided with one of the last manifestations (at least in the United States) of the spectacular traditions of *haute cuisine*: the much-publicized meal of the New York restaurant critic Craig Claiborne at Chez Denis in Paris (November, 1975), which cost the then unheard-of sum of $4,000 for two and consisted of thirty-one courses and eleven wines.

Ingenuity, artifice, sustainability and authenticity have certain points of common contact. Our gastronomic era is faced with the necessity of giving up certain kinds of food because of scarcity and corresponding attempts, with varying degrees of success, to duplicate the original product. With Caspian Sea caviar now illegal in many countries, attempts to make domestic farmed sturgeon produce something comparable have gained urgency.

The good news is that awareness has grown about issues relating to food, how it is produced and consumed. Taste, in its most literal sense, has resisted modernity and efficiency. Fifty years ago, nutritionists and food scientists were entranced by sterile dreams of hygiene, convenience and artificial flavours and seemed ready and able to destroy all interest in the actual savour and complexity of food. The future was to be one of de-natured ease, square tomatoes for better packaging, Tang instead of troublesome orange juice; of margarine, frozen food and sugared breakfast cereals. This did not happen, at least to the degree planned, nor in the 1970s did the microwave oven drive out other, more nurturing methods of preparation. The heavy, pretentious and poor quality 'continental' food served in American and English restaurants of the 1970s – what Calvin Trillin called the 'La Maison de la Casa House' sort of places – is no longer dominant. The chicken Kiev of that era has been relegated to the culinary back of the freezer. In a rearguard and not wholly successful combat, taste has withstood the impact of technology, packaging and the producer's and retailer's convenience.

As discussed in Chapter 10, the 1970s can now be seen as a turning point. In 1977, the denunciation of American standards by John and Karen Hess was published after the former had been fired from the *New York Times* for his scathing restaurant reviews. In 1979, there appeared Calvin Trillin's more good-humoured collection on the surviving glories of American vernacular regional food in contrast to the dubious pretension of the 'Continental' regime (its essays had been published separately throughout the 1970s). Chez Panisse opened. In Europe the era of post-war reconstruction ended and with it the continuation of trends towards re-establishing or expanding the pre-war patterns of dining. The sometimes competing desires for variety, global cuisine, authenticity, *terroir* and experimentation were all established.

What is declining is a sense of a core or series of core cuisines, and especially the international sway of French cuisine. In New York, a city with thousands of restaurants at all price levels representing hundreds of nations and regions, the most endangered species are the elegant French restaurants of which only a few remain. This is not so much a reflection of the economics of owning a restaurant that produces a costly, labour-intensive cuisine, since there seems to be no limit to what high-end restaurants can charge (the most expensive restaurant in New York in 2006 was Japanese), but rather a shift in taste. In a 2003 *New York Times* article extolling the creativity of the 'Spanish' cooks of Catalonia and the Basque region, Arthur Lubow wrote with a certain patronizing pity about the failure of the French to keep up, but the French could just as plausibly be credited with refusing to follow fashion by their stubborn maintenance of certain established standards of authentic culinary practice and aesthetics.

An optimistic take on the future is that the movement towards authenticity will affect more than the wealthy amateurs of the great world capitals and influence countries that have rich culinary traditions but are not themselves in privileged places in the world economy. When the food in Ethiopia develops an authentic élan, benefiting its population in ways beyond what is popularly presented in Europe and America, that will be an accomplishment. There are some hopeful signs of the spread of movements that combine ecological stewardship, biodiversity, and revitalization of culinary traditions and practices in Asia and Latin America. Food and the future of food are matters of taste, but also of human freedom (as Sidney Mintz has shown in a study of slave diets in the New World). The way we collect, process, sell, buy and prepare food is both a necessary industry and a daily art that expresses what it is to be alive.

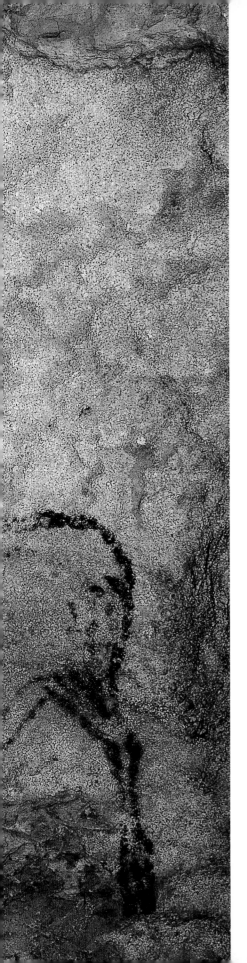

1 HUNTER-GATHERERS AND THE FIRST FARMERS

The Evolution of Taste in Prehistory

Alan K. Outram

Discussing prehistoric peoples' taste in food is something of a challenge. By definition, prehistoric peoples left us with no written record of their likes and dislikes. Prehistorians must use the archaeological record as their primary source of evidence. They must sift through physical remains left by people thousands of years ago. In fact, archaeologists spend much of their time rooting around in ancient garbage for the remains of peoples' food and items of material culture. Through finding food remains, it is possible to demonstrate *what* people ate and, through the discovery of such items as hearths, ovens, cooking pots and serving vessels, it may be possible to shed light upon *how* food was prepared and consumed. However, trying to understand *why* people chose to eat what they did, and whether they enjoyed it, is a far from simple matter. Archaeologists must use many lines of evidence in order to address an issue as complicated as taste. These include the study of material culture, food residues, structural evidence, environmental context, ethnographic analogies, art, medical knowledge and the remains of humans themselves. They are helped in their work by the very recent development of a raft of new biomolecular techniques for analysing past diet.

This chapter cannot possibly outline all the details of past diets, let alone tastes, for all cultures around the world within the several million years of our prehistory. What it does aim to do is to illustrate how archaeologists can get at issues of dietary taste and flag up a number of significant and interesting issues relating to food and taste within a very broad chronological framework. First of all, it is necessary to discuss our lines of evidence in a little more depth.

The types of food remains that archaeologists find are usually limited to those that are resistant to biological decay. Unfortunately, many food remains, being made up of organic matter, rot away quite easily. Perhaps the most obvious class of remains to survive well are animal bones. Bones are largely inorganic in makeup and, providing the soil is not too acidic, they tend to survive well for many thousands of years. Discarded animal bones can tell us significantly more than

Above: A reconstruction of a prehistoric hearth from Sweden shows a pot being used for cooking. Soot on the outside of vessels is evidence of such use, but not all cooking in pots was carried out like this in prehistory. Sometimes heated rocks, called 'pot-boilers', were added to the contents, because the pottery could not survive being on a fire.

simply what species of animal people were choosing to eat. Zooarchaeologists can establish whether animals were wild or domestic, hunted or farmed. They can tell the age and sex of animals and reconstruct the demography of herds. With regard to hunted animals, this might tell us something about the hunters' preferences, whether these relate to good management of the wild herd, the season of the hunt or, indeed, to their particular taste. For farmed animals herd structure is more significant, since farmers will keep different ratios of male and female animals and cull at different ages depending upon what they primarily wish to exploit from that herd. Dairy herds look very different to meat herds or wool herds, for instance. Such husbandry choices will be influenced by economy and environment, but also by taste and cultural preferences. Bones often also bear the scars of butchery. Marks of cutting, chopping and sawing frequently form clear patterns that indicate how a given culture went about dividing up a carcass for distribution and consumption. Butchery is a very culturally engrained practice which, even today, shows very clear regional differences and can relate to current fashion and taste in meat consumption.

Mammals, reptiles, birds and fish will all leave bones for us to find, but what of invertebrates? Molluscs and some crustaceans will leave their shells. Shells do not provide us with quite the same range of evidence as bones, but, for some molluscs that lay down annual growth rings, it is possible to tell something about age selections and even the season of collection. Insects do not have an inorganic exoskeleton, but one made from protein. This protein, called chitin, is quite tough, however, and tends to survive quite well in soils where bacterial action in limited, perhaps by low temperature, acidity or a lack of oxygen. After careful recovery, insect remains can often be identified to species level. In many cases, these insects were not themselves eaten, but they provide indirect evidence of what was eaten and how it was stored. Insect species are often very specific in their activities and diet. Different species can be very accurately associated with the presence of particular foodstuffs or animals or storage conditions.

Under normal burial conditions, plant food remains do not survive well. Archaeologists see the best plant remains where biological decay has been inhibited by extreme conditions such as permanent water-logging, desiccation or permafrost. Such archaeological sites are relatively rare, but they open up an invaluable window into the range of organic foodstuffs otherwise missing from most archaeological excavations. Plant foods do survive in normal soils in several forms, however. As a result of cooking accidents, or more major disasters, some plant foods or debris, such as seeds, chaff, nuts and nutshells, will become burnt and carbonized. The carbonized remains retain their shape and can be extracted from the soil and studied. Seeds and nuts can tell us what was being eaten, but waste products such as chaff and weed seeds can tell the archaeobotanist even more. They can indicate how the plant was processed and stored and the presence of different weeds can imply different seasons of ploughing and harvesting. Evidence for plant foods and the general environment also comes from the survival of pollen. Pollen is best preserved in acidic, anaerobic conditions, but its proteinaceous shell is so hardy that it survives to a certain extent on many archaeological sites. It provides evidence of what was growing in the area of a settlement. Another way in which plant foods leave evidence is through impressions. It is not uncommon to find the impressions of plants in the clay of pottery vessels.

Recently developed biomolecular analytical techniques have opened up new avenues for exploring human diet. Some of these

techniques can also be applied to more cultural questions relating to how food was consumed, which, in turn, might tell us something about taste. Fundamental to several of the new methods is a better understanding of stable isotopes. The number of protons in the nucleus of an atom determines which element it is, but some have extra neutrons in the nucleus that make them heavier. For instance, carbon has three isotopes. Carbon-12 has equal numbers of protons and neutrons, Carbon-13 has one extra neutron and Carbon-14 has two. Carbon-14 is not stable and radioactively decays at a known rate. This fact has been the basis of radio-carbon dating which has been used since the late 1940s. Here we are interested in the stable isotopes. For many years it was thought that stable isotopes behaved in exactly the same way in chemical reactions, but it has transpired that, while their chemical properties are the same, many reactions are prejudiced when it comes to atomic mass. Biological tissues end up with different stable isotope ratios as a result of the origin of their constituent parts and the processes they have been through.

This has been revolutionary in facilitating the determination of human diet from the study of human remains. The human skeleton can reveal something about diet without chemical analysis. We can examine the dentition for different wear patterns and signs of decay associated with particular diets. Certain conditions, such as rickets, reveal particular dietary deficiencies and the general health and stature of a population are often related to the quality and abundance of food supplies. The stable isotopes ratios within bones, however, can give a clearer indication of what was being eaten. The isotopes of carbon and nitrogen are particularly useful in this respect. Carbon isotope ratios can tell us the extent to which people were exploiting marine food, because the carbon cycle in the sea is very different to that on land. Furthermore, this method can tell the difference between two major classes of plants which handle their carbon differently. This has been helpful in identifying the development of maize as a foodstuff in North America, for instance. Nitrogen tells us about trophic level, which relates to how far up the food chain one is. Herbivores and vegetarians are at the bottom, then omnivores of various levels followed by carnivores. If a carnivore eats another carnivore then that is even higher. This happens quite commonly with fish. Pike are carnivorous fish and humans eat them regularly. This would give a very high trophic level.

The other main area of development has been in the study of food residues found in vessels, particularly pottery ones. Fats and waxes, derived from the original contents of vessels, soak into the fabric of pottery where they can survive for thousands of years. For some time, analysts have been able to give a vague indication of vessel contents from the particular fats and waxes present. For instance, they could identify specific waxes from brassicas, the cabbage family of plants, or be able to say the pot contained animal fat. Stable isotope ratios have refined the technique greatly, allowing species of animal to be determined in some cases, or even whether the fat came from meat or dairy products. Alongside this there has also been progress in identifying protein residues. This has been successful in some later prehistoric examples, but the preservation of protein residues tends not to be as good as that of fats. The importance of these methods of residue analysis is that they tie together the consumption of food with material culture in a way that studying bones and seeds does not. We can begin to say much more about cultures, fashions and tastes if we can demonstrate the context of their consumption. What was consumed from fine, decorated wares? What was consigned to coarse pottery? Which foodstuffs were traded long distance in containers, such as amphorae, and were a valued commodity? Were particular foods associated with ritual or funerary vessels?

How might we be able to see which foods were selected by taste and which by necessity? The two things can be strongly connected. We have a tendency to crave what we particularly need. For example, we get a sweet tooth when quick energy is needed, and so on. However, particular tastes, taboos and fashions might actually become apparent because the nature of particular peoples' food choices seems illogical. Archaeologists who spend a lot of time modelling past environments in great detail and discussing the calorific requirements of past human groups are often labelled as 'environmentally deterministic'. This is meant as a great insult in archaeological circles, since such an approach appears to deny the rich tapestry of human cultural choices. Such studies may seem dull but they are useful, however. Only by knowing all the details of what was available in a given environment and which food resources were the most obvious for exploitation can we begin to identify the fascinating choices that humans make. For instance, if an island society was struggling to live off the resources of the land, then why did they choose to ignore abundant marine resources? It could have been for practical reasons, or due to a cultural taboo or simply a matter of taste. Such a holistic approach allows us to identify interesting questions which can then be investigated in more detail.

Archaeologists often appeal to the ethnographic record for ideas about the ways in which past societies may have behaved. Modern

These storage jars, or 'pithoi', were found in a shop in the Minoan city of Akrotiri dating to 16th century BC. Akrotiri is exceptionally well preserved because it was buried under ash from the eruption of the Santorini volcano on Thera. This has provided an excellent insight into how the inhabitants stored their food.

Western culture is very divorced from the kinds of society that existed in prehistory. By studying recent and modern communities that more closely resemble prehistoric ones, in terms of technology and social and economic organization, they hope to be made aware of possibilities beyond their immediate experience. They may even be able to draw analogies. Ethnographic analogy has gone in and out of favour within archaeological circles. It still forms a major part of many archaeological interpretations and is invaluable in throwing up possible explanations for things modern Western cultures would have little understanding of. However, ethnographic analogy comes with a health warning. Recent and modern 'primitive' peoples are not prehistoric peoples and they are not preserved in aspic. Their cultures are dynamic and are affected by their changing surroundings. Furthermore, the environments in which surviving primitive cultures live are not always a good analogy for the past. For instance, there are no hunter-gatherer groups on record that live in an environment equivalent to temperate Europe. Ethnographic analogies are useful, but should be drawn with caution.

Our earliest ancestors may have had a very different sense of taste to us. What some of us might just force ourselves to eat in life or death desperation may well have been bread and butter to our hominid forebears. Establishing the diet of our very early ancestors is an incredibly difficult task. The earliest hominids date back to around 5 million years ago, in Central East Africa, but there is virtually no evidence relating to their food. Before about 2 million years ago, we can only make crude inferences about diet based upon skeletal morphology and dentition. Although the evidence is not always consistent, early hominids appear to have retained some ape-like tree climbing abilities and studies of tooth wear suggest that plant matter was still a major part of the diet. Perhaps they ate very similar things to modern great apes. One branch of the *Australopithicus* family (*boisei*) gained the nickname 'nutcracker man' on account of its heavy-duty, plant-processing dentition. From about 2 million years onwards, we begin to see more structured archaeological sites, where hominid remains are associated with animal-bone refuse and stone-tool production. Famous sites associated with *Homo habilis* include Olduvai Gorge in Tanzania and Koobi Fora in Kenya. Initially, it was simply assumed that these hominids were hunters and these sites contained the remains of their meals and tools. In some cases this interpretation has been completely reversed. At the cave site of Swartkrans in South Africa, a site dating to about 1.5 million years ago, large numbers of animal bones were discovered in association with the remains of the hominid species *Paranthropus robustus*. In a landmark volume entitled *The Hunters or the Hunted*, C. K. Brain put forward a very detailed and convincing argument that the cave had originally been just a shaft into the ground that was unsuitable for occupation at the time. Its contents were not the food of hominids, but the food of wild animals including leopards. Indeed, Brain identified

This horse bone was found at Boxgrove, West Sussex, England, in levels pre-dating the arrival of anatomically modern humans. It bears cut marks from stone tools indicating butchery of horses by the site's inhabitants. Such marks need to be carefully identified with the aid of a microscope, to avoid confusion with scratches or tooth marks.

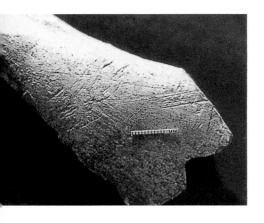

Ethnographic studies help archaeologists think about different ways of doing things, that otherwise might not have occurred to them. This fisherman in Guilin, China is using a cormorant to fish. The cormorant catches the fish, but cannot swallow it because of a ring around its neck.

leopard tooth marks on a hominid skull. At this site the hominids were the prey. However, this is certainly not the case at many of the *Homo habilis* and later sites, but it is still not entirely clear that hominids were gaining their food from hunting.

Detailed studies of butchery and the carnivore tooth marks on bones from several sites, including Olduvai, show some very interesting patterns. Archaeologists have argued that the cut marks made by stone tools do not match expectations for the butchery of fresh carcasses of hunted animals, as established through ethnographic and experimental studies. In some cases, the butchery is concentrated in areas where meat was limited and carried out in a way that might indicate that the tissues were no longer entirely fresh. More importantly, some hominid cut marks overlie, and were therefore later than, carnivore tooth marks. This all implies that hominids at this date were not great hunters but, in fact, scavengers. They were probably high-ranked scavengers, but were, nonetheless, picking over the largely devoured carcasses of big cat kills that were in less than fresh condition. The debate over the extent to which hominids hunted or scavenged extends at least as far as the Neanderthals, some 150,000 to 28,000 years ago. It is clear that Neanderthals hunted large game, but some suggest that they scavenged too.

The implications for taste are blatant and simple. Prehistoric people had a stomach for things we would not dream of eating today. They would regularly eat things that we would think had gone off. We can

In Kazakhstan a woman milks a mare to make a traditional drink called koumiss. The milk is fermented, but can also be smoked as well. It is certainly an acquired taste. Perhaps Kazakhs developed this taste because in the past they were unable to keep the milk fresh.

demonstrate that they ate semi-rotten food, but did they enjoy it? It is highly likely that they did. While researching early horse domestication in Kazakhstan, this author was offered a bowl of koumiss by a local horse herder. This is a drink made from fermented mare's milk. To the modern Western palate it is utterly vile. It provokes all the body's natural reactions to rotten food. Traditional Kazakhs love it. The herder was asked why he did not drink the mare's milk fresh. The answer is actually obvious; they cannot keep the milk fresh without a refrigerator. However, he had obviously never thought about it and paused before replying that the fresh milk tasted of nothing. The above discussion was about early hominids scavenging from potentially semi-putrid carcasses, but the point about acquiring the taste for 'off' food is relevant for the whole of prehistory and beyond. It is clear that some prehistoric peoples stored food very little, but there is also evidence of various storage methods such as smoking and drying. Also, they simply tolerated food that we might define as being 'off'. Some of the entomological evidence can attest to that. Taste depends upon what one is used to.

Whether from hunting or scavenging, it seems that the quantity of meat in the diet may well have significantly increased from the time of the tool-using *Homo habilis* onwards, when hominid brains start to get much larger. One theory, called the 'expensive tissue' hypothesis, suggests that eating more meat allowed hominids to evolve a smaller digestive tract. The gut uses up a lot of metabolic energy and the hypothesis suggests that wasting less metabolic resources on digestive tract has allowed for development in another type of expensive tissue, the brain. It is possible to extend this theory further and suggest that the first cooking of food would have made food even easier to digest. The first use of fire for warmth and cooking is attributed to *Homo ergaster/erectus*. The most famous early site with evidence for fire use is that of the Zhoukoudian cave in China, dating to between 500,000–240,000 years ago. Leaving evolutionary biology aside, the introduction of cooking clearly takes discussion of taste to a new level. People from that time onwards did not just choose what to eat, but how they liked it cooked. While with *Homo erectus* this decision may have merely been between rare and well done, the technology and variety of cooking method would soon have as significant an influence on decisions of taste as the ingredients used.

With the arrival of *Homo sapiens*, between around 100,000 and 12,000 years ago, depending on where one is in the world, the debate about scavenging subsides somewhat. Our own species may well have opportunistically scavenged on occasion. This cannot be ruled out, but it is clear that we were highly effective hunters and gatherers from the start. The diet of hunter-gatherers varies tremendously depending upon the environment in which a particular group lives. In general, however, diets tended to be much more protein rich than we are used to. Hunting largely supplies protein, with accompanying animal fat. Important plant foods like nuts contain a balance of protein, fat and carbohydrates. Good sources of carbohydrate tend to be more limited. Wild seeds, fruits, roots and tubers will be the principal source, and many of these are only seasonally available. Modern Western diet, of course, is based upon farmed staples that are very high in carbohydrates. Carbohydrates are the easiest source of energy to our bodies and, in the form of sugar, they are even more easily metabolized. Modern Western society has an (over) ample supply of refined sugars. There is strong evidence that many hunter-gatherer groups in the past would, at certain times of the year, not only *need* sources of fat and sugar, but would have *craved* them. Necessity may well have driven taste.

Today, in the modern Western world, fat tends to be seen as a dietary villain. Fat is bad for our health and bad for the body beautiful. It is very high in calories and blocks our arteries. This paradigm is shifting, however. *Dr Atkins' New Diet Revolution* (1992) was not the first diet book to suggest that eating plenty of protein and fat, along with a low carbohydrate intake, was a healthy thing to do, but it was the first to catch on in a big way. Science is taking its time to catch up, but, at the time of writing, a number of properly controlled, independent, long-term studies have been published that back up Atkins's claims. This author was not at all surprised. Viewed over the *longue durée*, it is the modern combination of vast quantities of refined carbohydrate with high-fat foods that is anomalous, not the diet Atkins proposed.

A cave painting from De Val del Charco de Agua Amarga in Spain most likely dates to the early Holocene period, *c.* 8000–6000 BC. It depicts a hunter in pursuit of a wild boar. Other paintings of this period, from the Spanish Levant, show people hunting in large groups using bows and arrows.

While no hunter-gatherers would have quite the access to carbohydrates that we do today, some had better sources than others. Those who lived principally from hunting animals, particularly high-latitude or Ice Age hunters, would have had very limited access to carbohydrates indeed. Small amounts would have been seasonally available from nuts, berries and a few other plant sources. A further, and critical, problem is that the animals they were hunting would be, for much of the year, rather lean. Eating just lean meat (protein) is very problematic. Digesting protein alone for energy is actually very inefficient and, if sustained, can cause damage to the liver and kidneys, dehydration, loss of appetite (even though one is starving) and the digestion of one's own muscle mass. Adding some carbohydrate to this diet is the best way to prevent these problems, but that was not an option for many hunting communities. Fat also has a 'protein sparing' action and a certain amount of fat is necessary in the diet. The body requires some 'essential' fatty acids and fats are also a good source of vitamins such as A, D, K and E. Seeking good sources of fat is the only solution in this situation.

Ethnographic accounts of hunters the world over suggest that it is often the fattiness of the animal that is most important, not how much meat it yields. Hunters tend to target animals they perceive to be fatty and will often test their kill, by cutting to the fat layer

Above: American bison (or buffalo as they are popularly known) once roamed the plains of North America in huge numbers, but they became threatened by over-hunting. Large herds, such as this one in Custer State Park, South Dakota, USA, are now protected. Bison can provide huge quantities of meat and fat as well as excellent large hides for clothing and covering structures.

Opposite: The most common subjects of Ice Age artists in Western Europe were the animals they hunted. The antler carving of a bison from La Madeleine rockshelter, in France, dates to around 15,000 BC. The most commonly hunted animal at this site was reindeer; bison would have been a particularly prized quarry.

under the skin, to see if they were correct. If the animal turns out to be lean they may even abandon it entirely. Having warned against the inappropriate use of ethnographic analogies, it seems safe to use one here because this pattern is so universally present and the accounts so broad-ranging, from Alaska to Africa and Siberia to Australia. We have little experience of the problem, but pioneers in North America knew it all too well. During Lewis and Clark's famous coast-to-coast exploration of the continent between 1803 and 1806, Lewis writes in his journal on 17 April 1805: 'we met with a herd of buffalo of which I killed the fattest I conceived among them; however, on examining it I found it so poor that I considered it unfit for use and only took the tongue.' On 25 April 1805 he wrote: 'we met with two large herds of buffalo, of which we killed three cows and a calf. Two of the former were but lean; we therefore took their tongues and part of their marrow bones only.' The tongue and marrow bones (see below) were the best sources of fat. The rest was left to rot. Captain Randolph B. Marcy also discusses the issue with some clarity in his 1859 work *The Prairie Traveler.* 'We tried the meat of horse, colt, and mules, all of which were in starved condition, and of course not very tender, juicy, or nutritious. We consumed the enormous amount of between five and six pounds of this meat per man daily, but continued to grow weak and thin, until, at the expiration of twelve days, we were able to perform but little labor, and were continually craving for fat meat.'

In this modern reconstruction of the rendering of bison bones for grease, hot rocks were used to boil the water; the fat then settled on the surface. This is a laborious process requiring a lot of effort and fuel, yet there is much archaeological evidence for it, indicating the value placed upon fat by prehistoric hunters.

He not only needed fat, but *craved* it. The ethnographic record shows that fat is fairly uniformly liked by hunter-gatherer peoples. Indeed, despite decades of medical advice, most people in the modern Western world secretly, or not so secretly, enjoy fatty foods. It is very safe to conclude that fat sources were both important and very much to the taste of most prehistoric groups.

In fact, there is plenty of evidence that prehistoric peoples went to great lengths to exploit fat sources. One of the most reliable sources of fat in an animal is the skeleton. Long bones contain marrow cavities and marrow is primarily fat. Inside the ends of long bones and in the vertebrae and ribs there is spongy bone, which is also largely filled with fat. When an animal is starving it uses up the fat beneath its skin and surrounding its muscle first, before mobilizing the fat in its bones. Even an animal that dies of starvation will still have much of its bone fat remaining. That is why Lewis, and most hunter-gatherer groups, targeted the marrow bones. To obtain the marrow is simple: you break the shaft of a long bone and poke the fat out. However, fat is so important that many hunters wanted to exploit the fat trapped within the spongy bone as well, and this is very difficult. To do this you have to break up the bones into little pieces, which is a very labour-intensive job. The fragments then have to be boiled in water to render out the fat, which floats to the surface and can be skimmed off after cooling. This may not be difficult in a modern context, but in an early prehistoric context, without metal cauldrons, this had to be carried out in pits, buckets or pots by heating up rocks and adding them to the water to bring it to the boil. This involves an incredible amount of effort and fuel for a relatively limited amount of fat. This practice, well known from many ethnographic and archaeological examples, leaves a very clear pattern in the archaeological record. There are large amounts of fire-cracked rocks, which were used to boil the water, mixed with lots of bones that are broken up in a very particular way.

Prehistoric hunter-gatherers not only had a particular taste for fat, but they would also have had taste preferences for particular kinds of fat. Several ethnographic accounts relating to Inuit and other Native American groups make it clear that the grease extracted from limb bones was preferred to that produced from vertebrae and ribs. The quality is related to levels of blood production that occur within those bones and the actual types of fat present in marrow or grease. The make-up and texture of the fat changes as you move down the leg of an animal. Just as we might discuss the best cut of meat, prehistoric people might well have been as interested in the choicest marrow and grease. These preferences are not just hypothetical, and can occasionally be seen in the archaeological record. This author has studied a bone assemblage from Greenland, where grease rendering was occurring on a large scale. However, it seems that the ribs were avoided almost entirely. A lot of blood is produced in ribs, and the grease rendered from them has a reputation for being rather poor. This selection was probably largely driven by taste.

We can also be fairly sure that prehistoric hunter-gatherers had something of a sweet tooth. It is no accident that the taste buds that sense sweetness are on the tip of our tongues. Their presence there is an adaptive trait in our evolution. As outlined above, carbohydrates were in limited supply to hunter-gatherer populations in most environments and, in particular, sugar-rich foodstuffs were rare. Carbohydrates are very easily metabolized for energy and sugars are particularly easily absorbed. Carbohydrates are not only good because of their 'protein sparing' action, but they are also good to help people fatten up. People put on fat when their blood-sugar levels are high. Most modern people are not aiming to put on weight, but your average hunter-gatherer wants to provide an energy buffer for hard times. A taste for sweet things would have advantaged early humans in terms of natural selection. Sugars are relatively rare in the natural environment, but a sweet tooth would predispose an individual to seek them out, hence advantaging that individual over others. The ethnographic record shows that hunter-gatherers, such as the San and Hadza in Africa, will target sweet foods when they are available with a great enthusiasm and put on weight as a result. This genetic trait serves many modern societies less well. We have a vast supply of refined sugars and we lap them up in huge quantities, getting ever more obese. People very often ask why all the tasty food is bad for us. Well, it is because sweet and fatty food was hard to come by back in our evolutionary past and our prehistoric forebears really needed it. Unfortunately we have a glut, but still cannot help ourselves.

In prehistory, sources of sugar would have included fruits and berries, honey, maple syrup and a few other plant extracts. Collecting berries is simple enough and they are even storable by drying them. Berries can also be incorporated into pemmican. Pemmican is a well-known prairie food made from pounded dried meat, rendered animal fat and berries. Maple syrup is also known to have been added by some Native American groups. Pemmican is a high-calorie and very nutritious blend of protein, fat and carbohydrate, with a good range of vitamins, and stores really well. Direct evidence for prehistoric pemmican does not exist, but we know all the ingredients did. It seems very likely that it has been an important recipe for thousands of years. The evidence for the use of fruit and berries comes from the remains, usually carbonized, of seeds and pips.

Collecting honey is a risky business, as bees are genuinely dangerous, and particularly so in the absence of protective clothing. It is likely that the use of smoke to calm bees is a very old tradition. The Hadza of East Africa certainly employ this technique, with various degrees of success. The danger underlines the importance, or perhaps desire, people bestowed on this food. We have archaeological evidence for the gathering of honey. At Cueva de la Arana in Spain there is a very late

Rock art depicting the gathering rather than hunting of food is rare. The image from Cueva de la Arama in the Spanish Levant is mesolithic in date and shows the collection of honey; a somewhat risky activity. The figure appears to be reaching into a nest in a tree or rock fissure, with angry bees buzzing around. There is also a bag to keep the honeycomb in.

hunter-gatherer (*c.* 7,000 years old) cave painting of an individual collecting honey from a tree, with bees buzzing around. The painting is a little stylized, but what is depicted seems clear enough. In later periods in prehistory there is some evidence for bee keeping. Bronze Age, wickerwork beehives have been recovered from wetlands in Germany. Residue analysis of pottery might yield yet more evidence, as beeswax is decay resistant and chemically recognizable. There is also a very characteristic suite of pollen associated with honey, since bees visit a very particular set of flowers to collect their nectar and inadvertently collect pollen too. A number of Bronze Age vessels have been recovered from Scotland which contained pollen that could be associated with honey.

The land was not the only source of nutrition in prehistory. The sea is an exceptionally rich provider of food, including sea mammals, fish, molluscs, crustacea and even seaweed. Sea mammals and fish, in particular, have a distinct advantage over terrestrial quarry due to their constant fattiness. Sea mammals are covered in blubber and many fish are very oily. The extreme difficulties of trying to find sufficient fat to supplement an overabundance of lean meat simply do not apply in this context. Certain species of fish, including the cod family (gaddids), can be easily preserved by simple air drying, in appropriate climates, to produce what are called 'stock fish'. Blubber and fish can be rendered for oil, which can be stored as a foodstuff or fuel. To acquire some marine foods necessitates one to be sea-going, including harpooning or net fishing from boats, but other food can be obtained from the shore. Seals come ashore during their birthing season or can be hunted through sea ice. Whales sometimes beach themselves. Fish can be caught by hook or collected *en masse* in estuarine fish traps. Shell fish and some crustaceans can simply be collected at low tide. A great advantage of living by the coast is that you have access to all of these marine foods, but also access to terrestrial ones as well.

Many hunter-gatherers that live in a purely terrestrial environment find that they have to move around constantly to find sufficient food. However, there are plenty of archaeological examples of hunter-gatherer communities that had a very settled existence on coastlines, estuaries or, indeed, major rivers. An example of a sedentary hunter-gatherer site on a river is Lepenski Vir on the Danube and there are many examples of sedentary coastal settlements. One of the most famous hunter-gatherer cultures to have lived a settled existence by the sea is the Ertebølle Culture in Denmark. The Ertebølle belongs to the very late Mesolithic period (*c.* 4500 BC), when Neolithic farmers had already moved into areas of inland central Europe to the south.

A fish-trap basket from the Ertebølle Culture site of Lille Knabstrup, Denmark, *c.* 4500 BC. It provides us with an insight into the technology of a successful hunting and gathering society that resisted the adoption of farming for over a thousand years after their neighbours had taken it up.

We know that the Ertebølle people traded with the farmers for things such as polished stone axes. The Ertebølle people had permanent base camps, usually strategically placed to take advantage of both marine and terrestrial environments, and a series of smaller, temporary camps they used to exploit particular seasonal resources. Because of water-logging, there is very good preservation at some Ertebølle sites. We know that they had sophisticated estuarine fish traps that employed wooden hurdles to channel fish into baskets, because some of these arrangements have survived for 6,000 years in relatively good condition. Common features of these late Mesolithic coastal cultures are shell mounds. So many shellfish were collected that they formed huge mounds of waste shells. Many of these mounds are still obvious today in many parts of the world.

Some shell mounds are very old indeed. Some, in South Africa date back to around 100,000 years ago, while there are examples in Australia and Papua New Guinea that date to around 35,000 years ago. However, sedentary settlement of coastlines by hunter-gatherers and the mass exploitation of marine resources are generally seen as post-glacial, late Mesolithic phenomena. Why is this? Did people not have the taste for marine food before then? Some archaeologists have suggested that, as populations increased after the end of the Ice Age, hunter-gatherer societies became more complex, stratified and sedentary. This social change led to settlement, where the resources were good, on the coast. Many see this stage as part of a linear progression of increasing complexity that leads on to the adoption of farming. The truth of that matter may well have nothing to do with either changes in food preferences or society.

At the end of the Ice Age, as the glaciers melted, sea level rose considerably. It is still rising. The simple fact of the matter is that the vast majority of Palaeolithic and early Mesolithic coastlines are now underwater. So, when we compare Ertebølle with earlier neighbouring sites, it is not surprising that they do not look the same. The earlier

The shell midden in the foreground of this picture was created by Australian aboriginals on Fraser Island, Queensland. Shell middens are often very easy to spot by archaeologists, even when completely covered by vegetation. The shells create a very basic soil and, as a result, completely different plants tend to grow on them.

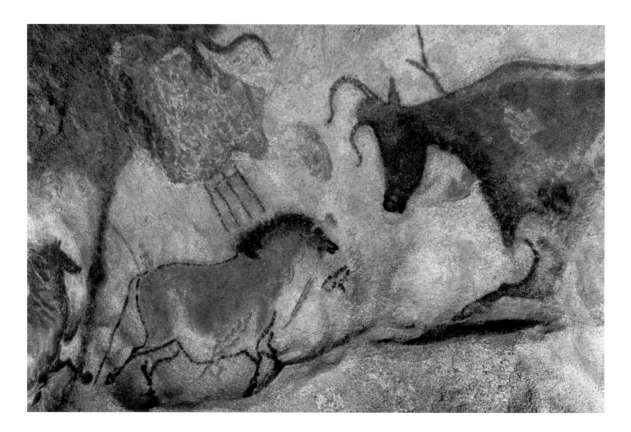

Above: An Upper Paleolithic painting from Lascaux Cave in France depicts two horses and an aurochs (wild cattle).

Opposite: A bison from Altamira Cave in Spain. Interestingly, reindeer, the most commonly hunted species, are portrayed less often. Perhaps they were so commonplace that they were of less interest to the artists.

sites were miles from the sea. It is very possible that much earlier, marine-based sites are sitting there on the sea bed waiting for us to develop techniques that allow us to investigate them. Indeed, this is beginning to happen. Late Palaeolithic cave art from sites such as Lascaux (France) and Altamira (Spain) famously portray animals such as bison, horses, aurochs and deer. These are all terrestrial animals that we know that people hunted and ate. In 1991, however, a diver called Henri Cosquer found an underwater cave off the French coast near Marseilles. Cosquer Cave, as it is now known, contains spectacular Palaeolithic pictures of marine life including seals, fish, auks and jelly-fish. Recent inter-tidal and underwater excavations off the coasts of Denmark and southern Sweden are also showing that significant coastal settlements existed before cultures such as Ertebølle.

In the Americas, there are now alternative hypotheses for the peopling of that continent. Orthodoxy, based upon assumption and very little evidence, has always suggested that land-based hunters arrived in America by passing across a land bridge from Asia. It is now clear that there are many very early coastal sites along the west coast of North America providing an alternative route that exploited marine foods. Even more controversially, but surprisingly plausible, once the evidence and ethnographic parallels are taken into account, it has been suggested that European Solutrean hunters could have made their way along the Atlantic sea ice to North America by exploiting marine resources in a way much like modern Inuit. Many other examples

Below: The semi-submerged Cosquer Cave in France provides rare evidence of the exploitation of sea foods by Upper Palaeolithic hunters. As well as the seal depicted here, there are images of fish, jellyfish and great auks. There appear to be lines entering the seal's body; are these spears?

could be given. In particular, much could be said about marine resources and the peopling of Australasia. What is clear is that seafood has been enjoyed and valued by people for a very long time. The exploitation of marine and coastal resources probably played a major part in early human colonizations around the world.

It should be stressed that hunter-gatherer diets vary greatly, but we have identified a number of themes in taste that can probably be applied across a wide range of past cultures in different regions of the world. As discussed, hunter-gatherers would have particularly needed, and probably craved, both fats and carbohydrates, particularly at certain times of the year. But what would happen if the balance of diet suddenly shifted as it did with the advent of agriculture? As agriculture spread, so did the mass availability of carbohydrates, and, furthermore, carbohydrates that could be stored for use year round.

There are a number of places in the world where people independently discovered how to farm plants for food. The big three are the Near East, Central America and China. In the Near East, about 10,000 years ago, cereals such as wheat and barley were first domesticated. Between around 9,000 to 8,000 years ago important staples such as maize and beans were first farmed in Central America and rice was first cultivated in China. However, there are other later centres of plant domestication, such as potatoes in the Andes, sorghum in Sub-Saharan Africa and a few other significant examples. The idea of farming, and the raw materials needed, spread from these various foci. In the actual

Above: The maize and beans shown here are traditional varieties, but ancient corncobs were much, much smaller. Archaeobotanists have tracked the crop's development by counting the number of corn cupules on specimens preserved either through desiccation or charring. Very early varieties are hardly recognizable.

Opposite: A Hopi woman, photographed in about 1902, is grinding corn to flour. The flat quern stone is called a 'metate' and the stone she holds is a 'mano'. These artefacts are identical to those found on ancient sites in North America. Very similar tools were used by early farmers across the world. In a British Neolithic context, the 'metate' would be called a 'saddle quern'.

centres of domestication, the wild versions of the crops would have already played a major role in peoples' diets before farming. However, in areas where farming was introduced, those foodstuffs would be very novel indeed. Imagine life without bread, potatoes, corn or rice and then imagine what it was like suddenly to have such commodities introduced in quantity, along with a completely new way of life. There is, of course, a vast amount of academic debate over the nature of the transition to agriculture in different regions of the world. There is argument over the speed of change, how complete the transition in economy initially was, and whether farmers moved and colonized land originally inhabited by hunter-gatherers. It is beyond doubt, however, that some areas adopted farming rather quickly and fairly completely. It could be argued that this is the case in southeast and central Europe, for instance, while the situation is rather more complex in Britain and even more confused in Scandinavia. Some of these dietary changes can be investigated with the use of stable isotope studies of human remains. A clear shift from marine to terrestrial diets is seen at the start of the Neolithic in Britain (c. 4000–2500 BC), for instance, and the arrival of maize is equally clear from carbon isotope ratios in American studies.

From the point of view of taste, it is interesting to know the extent to which we are dealing with farmers moving and colonizing or with indigenous peoples adopting a whole new range of foods and tastes. It is clear from the archaeological record that both things happened, depending where and when we are talking about. What is clear is that some groups adopted the new staple foods to the exclusion of many other possible resources. In the early Neolithic of Europe and the Near East, the result of the new diet appears to be a general decline in health. The new, carbohydrate-rich diet certainly resulted in many more dental caries (almost absent in the Mesolithic) and other health problems that could be associated with nutrient deficiencies. A more extreme case relates to early farmers in the South West of the USA. During the 'Pueblo II' phase, dating to around the eleventh century AD, the conditions for maize cultivation were good and the inhabitants of the area ate little else. They had beans as well, but did not do much with them. All the evidence points to an absolutely monotonous diet of corn and yet more corn. Archaeologists have also noted that they had little variety in the way they cooked it. There are no structures that indicate the production of bread. They just ate ground, boiled corn. The result was very bad health indeed. They were getting plenty of calories but were deficient in many other nutrients and had lots of dental problems. After a period of drought, and temporary abandonment of the area, the 'Peublo III' people who returned to the area had a much broader diet and were clearly in better health.

We can ask ourselves a number of questions about this. There are three possibilities from the perspective of taste. Firstly, they may have really liked their carbohydrate-rich diet and been perfectly happy

Remains of a joint of meat on a fragment of a wooden dish from a tomb in Jericho. It is unsual to find food presented this way on a plate. In this case, it was preserved because the tomb was undisturbed and the contents had been desiccated.

with it, even if it was monotonous. Secondly, taste actually may have been much less of an issue then than it is now. Perhaps some people in the past cared little about taste at all. Lastly, they may not have liked the monotonous diet but were forced through economic circumstances to put up with it. This final suggestion does not really fit the evidence. The Pueblo II people had lots of resources. It has already been suggested that early humans might have evolved to like carbohydrate and fat. Perhaps this abundant source of carbohydrate did satisfy their taste and satiate them to the exclusion of other possibilities. However, such a concentration was certainly bad for health. A worse situation has befallen modern Western cultures, however.

If we are hard-wired to like carbohydrates, we are even more fond of sweet things (as argued above). From the late nineteenth century onwards, refined sugars became very widely available in large quantities. Our sweet tooth has led us into consuming vast amounts of sugar, alongside an otherwise rich diet. The result of this is obesity and diabetes. Prehistoric tastes for carbohydrate rich diets may have led to health problems in the past, but we are facing a similar issue today.

The farming of animals came very slightly later than plant agriculture. Goats, sheep, cattle and pigs were all domesticated in the Near East between about 9,000 and 8,000 years ago. Horses and Bactrian camels were domesticated in Central Asia between about 6,000 and 5,000 years ago. Horses, it seems, were initially domesticated for food. The chicken was probably domesticated in Southeast Asia around 8,000 years ago, followed by the duck about 3,000 years later. Some other foci of domestication include turkeys in Mexico, llamas and guinea pigs in the Andes, rabbits in Europe and the reindeer in Scandinavia and Russia. Once again, generalization about the spread of livestock farming is not easy. In the Near East there was a period of time where only plant agriculture took place, but by the time farming arrived in Europe it was spreading as a package of mixed farming, and the degree of emphasis on plants or animals varied from region to region. On the other hand, in North America, the farming of plants continued without domestic animals. Plains Indian villages of about AD 1000, for instance, were large settled communities with maize and bean crops but animal products still came from hunted bison and deer. Conversely, in Central Asia, the economy was based on the husbandry of horses, cattle, sheep and goats, and agriculture was only introduced to areas of the steppe by Stalin, by force, in the mid-twentieth century.

Based upon the modelling of Neolithic herd structures in the Near East and southeast Europe, it appears that animals were initially simply kept for their meat. They were effectively 'walking larders'. Animals could be fed with crop waste or surplus grain and the animal would turn it into meat and keep that meat fresh (by living) until it was needed. Some archaeologists have proposed that there was a major change in animal husbandry at the start of the Bronze Age in these regions. This has become known as the 'secondary products revolution'. The secondary products in question are milk, wool and animal labour but we shall focus upon dairying here. In the Bronze Age in southeast Europe (*c.* 3300–1000 BC), it appears that herd structures changed to reflect animal husbandry that most appropriately fits a model of mixed meat and milk exploitation. It is clear, however, that by the time the farming package reached other regions of Europe, milking was already established. Analysis of animal bones from British Neolithic sites always hinted at possible dairy herds, but a recent programme of pottery residue analysis indicates that milking was widespread from the very outset of the Neolithic in that region.

The adoption of dairying is very closely tied to an issue of taste. If we look at peoples of the world today, we find groups, including many in the Far East and others in parts of Africa for example, who absolutely abhor milk. Underlying their disgust is a digestive problem. They are intolerant of lactose, the sugar in milk, because they lack the ability to manufacture lactase, the enzyme that digests it. Milk makes them feel nauseous. On the other hand, north-west Europeans and many other groups have high levels of lactose tolerance. This is clearly a local evolutionary adaptation. The interesting thing is that all our early ancestors were lactose intolerant as adults. Humans, like many other mammals, lose the ability to digest milk soon after weaning. The big question is how humans overcame this problem in various regions to become reliant upon dairying economies? If humans were all naturally disgusted by milk, who first tried it and why? How did those groups develop the taste for a diet of dairy products?

It is important to stress that lactose intolerance is not the same thing as milk allergy. Somebody who is allergic to milk can suffer very serious reactions, but lactose intolerance only results in discomfort. In fact, lactose intolerance does not stop milk being digested as a food. Studies have shown that lactose tolerance does increase in intolerant people when they are regularly exposed to milk products. An individual can adapt to milk drinking, to a certain extent. In the long run, those genetically predisposed to lactose tolerance might also be evolutionarily favoured within pastoral societies. It is clear, therefore, that past groups could become adapted to milk consumption. This still

The time between the Neolithic and Bronze Age is called the 'beaker period'. These vessels, such as the one from Wessex, England, shown here, have been associated with the consumption of beverages, possibly as part of a ritual.

does not address the question of overcoming an initial lack of tolerance or taste for milk. Of course, milk does not have to be consumed in its raw state. Indeed, cultured and fermented dairy products, such as yogurt, buttermilk, sour cream, kefir and the aforementioned koumiss, involve the breaking down of lactose by bacteria or yeast in advance of consumption. This clearly would have reduced problems associated with lactose intolerance, but this raises further questions about who would have first tried such products? This again suggests that our pre-historic forebears may have had a different perception of the strong tastes associated with 'off' food. We have lots of ethnographic information about dairying and its role in many world societies, but it is difficult to identify the manufacture of cheese, yoghurt and other products in prehistory. Fat and protein residue analyses can only tell us whether a milk product was present in a vessel, not what type it was. Zooarchaeology can only hint at milk production, not what was done with it. There are some European Bronze Age pottery 'strainers' that have been identified as possibly being associated with dairy processing, but there are alternatives to this interpretation. There is much we can speculate on, but it is clear that milking was widespread in some early farming communities.

Returning to fermentation, sugars can be turned into alcohol. No chapter on prehistoric taste would be complete without a discussion of the origins of brewing. In the Old World, brewing is certainly well in place by the time of the first great proto-historic civilizations. In the third-millennium BC, Sumerian and Akkadian texts make reference to beer that was probably made from barley. There are Mesopotamian illustrations of beer-drinking straws and Predynastic Egyptian models showing brewing vats. By classical times, large quantities of wine were being traded great distances in specially produced amphorae.

The evidence for prehistoric periods is rather less clear. In Europe, the arrival of alcoholic drinks is often associated with the spread of a particular type of pottery in the late Neolithic and early Bronze Age (2500–2000 BC). 'Beaker' vessels spread across most of central and western Europe at this time and, due to their design, these have long been thought of as drinking vessels. The deposition of beakers in funerary and ritual contexts implies that their function had some social importance. As well as pottery beakers, with or without handles, there are a number of very fine gold beakers from this period. Several beakers from British sites have produced residues containing high concentrations of immature pollen, which might be indicative of the presence of honey and meadowsweet that is known to be used as a flavouring for mead. This evidence has been used to strengthen the argument that beakers were associated with the early consumption of alcoholic beverages. In Egtved, Denmark, a Bronze Age grave of a girl has been excavated revealing excellent levels of preservation. A bucket made from bark was recovered that contained the remnants of cranberries, wheat and honey. This too could be the residue of a brewed drink.

An Egyptian statue of the 5th Dynasty, 2450–2325 BC, depicts a servant woman kneading barley as part of the process of brewing beer.

The antiquity of fermented-milk drinks such as koumiss (from mare's milk), shubat (from camel's milk) and kefir (from cattle milk) is hard to prove, but it seems likely that such drinks date back as far as the origins of milking itself, since it may actually have been quite difficult to prevent the milk from fermenting. All the archaeological, historical and ethnographic information we have suggests that alcoholic drinks have always had great social significance. Intoxicating substances are clearly going to be viewed differently to other foodstuffs, particularly in times before their powers were understood. If the association of 'beakers' with alcoholic beverages is correct, then it is not surprising to find drinking vessels associated with high-status and ritual sites. Where does this leave taste? It is impossible to know what prehistoric people thought about the taste of alcoholic drinks. Today it is often said that such drinks are an 'acquired' taste, and one tends to acquire the taste for social reasons. The same may be true in prehistory.

As well as looking at the varieties of food available to prehistoric peoples and the evidence we have for their likes and dislikes, it is worth examining the evidence for the addition of herbs, spices and flavour enhancers. Salt, the most obvious flavour enhancer, is very difficult to study archaeologically. Being so soluble, it tends not to leave residues and there is no way to identify its consumption from the human skeleton. We are reliant upon identifying salt-production sites. Salt can be mined as rock salt, but is more commonly produced by evaporating salt water from the sea, salt lakes or brine springs. In suitable climates, solar evaporation is possible. Natural evaporation of the salt lake at Zuñi, New Mexico, has probably provided salt at that sacred Native American site for thousands of years, while, in Early Formative, prehispanic sites in Veracruz, Mexico, pottery trays were manufactured for the purpose of solar evaporation. In prehistoric Europe there is evidence of salt production dating back to the Neolithic, but there is much clearer evidence from the Bronze and Iron Ages. The evidence takes the form of 'briquetage', which is coarse pottery formed into crucibles, pans and pillars. Briquetage is known from historic periods too. The pillars are intended to support the vessels above a heat source to encourage evaporation. Important European salt-production sites are often recognizable from the use of the Latin, *sal,* or Greek, *hals,* for salt. The Austrian site of Hallstatt lends its name to a whole period in the late Bronze Age and early Iron Age. The site and region is heavily associated with salt production, which may have led to the wealth that is displayed in the prehistoric cemeteries there. Salt was clearly valued, but it is a little less clear what it was valued for. As well as being a flavour enhancer, it is also a preservative. It is, however, clear that salty food was probably a feature of prehistoric diet.

Hunter-Gatherers and the First Farmers

The use of herbs and spices is even more difficult to assess archaeologically. There are many plants that can be used as flavourings and we use many still today. Pollen analysis will indicate that such plants were available in the past, and the survival of seeds might show that they were actually present on an archaeological site, but we have very little direct evidence for their use in cooking in prehistory. Linear B tablets from Mycenae provide us with some of the earliest evidence for their use. They refer to the use of coriander, cumin, fennel, sesame, celery seeds, mint and other herbs and spices. It is clear that some were used in cooking, but the records show that they were also employed in the production of scented oils. In the Americas, the chilli pepper is an example of a flavoursome plant that was farmed in prehistory. It was domesticated along with maize and squashes in Central America, where it was clearly used in cooking. Interestingly, however, it was not adopted as a crop further north until the Spanish introduced it. Was this a matter of taste? The use of herbs and spices in the past is further complicated by their use as medicines. In most cases, we are left unsure whether a given plant was used for flavouring, medicine, preservative, perfume or any combination thereof.

A problem that archaeologists face is that we know very little about prehistoric recipes. We know about the ingredients, but rarely get evidence for how the ingredients were combined to make the actual dishes people ate. On the whole, archaeologists are reliant upon ethnographic analogies when reconstructing possible recipes. Pemmican, described above, is a good example of a recipe we see ethnographically that most likely existed in the past, but proving it is difficult. Very occasionally we do find the burnt remains of a finished food product, rather than just ingredients. Burnt bread is not uncommon, for instance. It is, however, possible to tell a certain amount about cooking methods from studying cooking utensils and structures.

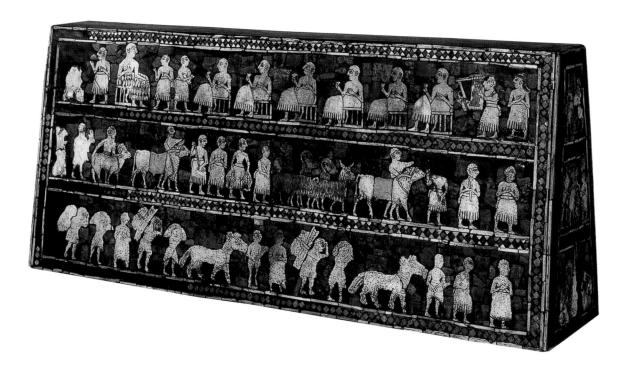

Cooking pots can tell us about boiling and chemical residues in the pots might tell us what was boiled. A wide variety of different oven and baking structures have been identified. These range from simple pits heated by hot rocks to complex, clay ovens. Bones sometimes provide us with evidence of the way meat was cooked. For instance, at the British Neolithic ritual site of Durrington Walls in Wiltshire it seems the people had a passion for roast pork. Pig bones dominate and they appear to have been butchered into joints. Only the bone ends are charred, suggesting that joints were roasted over the fire but the bone was only subjected to heat at the ends of the joint where it protruded out from the roasting meat. Feasting seems to have been one of the ritual activities that took place at this site.

Feasting and fine dining can be very important aspects of social activity in any society. Feasts can be used to display wealth and status through the conspicuous consumption of food and drink. Such display might involve eating rare, exotic or expensive foodstuffs. Alternatively, social status might be displayed through the finery of eating accoutrements. In this context, taste might not simply be an issue of what is favourable to one's palate, but a matter of fashion. Fashionable taste, and the wealth to support it, is often a mark of distinction in a class-based hierarchical society. Feasting certainly occurs in hunter-gatherer societies. For instance, Native Americans of the northwest coast, such as the Tlingit or Chinook, celebrate a feast called 'potlatch'. At these feasts gifts are given and much food is consumed. The events are usually designed to re-enforce social positions, but are also a forum for rivalry between powerful men, based upon levels of conspicuous consumption. We cannot prove it, but when we see evidence of mass consumption archaeologically, that apparently happened as a single event, we might well wonder whether such politics were being played out over meals in prehistory too.

The politics of feasting and fine taste certainly played their part in the formation of complex societies and the rise of civilization. In the Greek Bronze Age, for example, we see the rise of hierarchical societies based around palaces and these grow into the great Minoan and Mycenaean civilizations. The arrival of the first palaces is accompanied by a very obvious change in drinking and dining wares. Earlier in the Bronze Age, pottery was nice enough and was well made, but it was all very much on the same level. As palaces arrived, so did a clear pyramidal hierarchy of eating and drinking vessels. There are just a very few exquisitely fine pots, turned to be very thin-walled indeed, then a larger number of moderately fine wares, more coarse pots, and so on. As these pots tend to be found mixed together, it is possible that people are still feasting in large groups, but it is clear that the status of some is being displayed by what they are consuming their food from. Perhaps in the future, residue studies will reveal if they were eating and drinking different things too. Zooarchaeology has provided us with some evidence in this direction. In the Neolithic in Greece animal exploitation was concentrated upon domestic species, but the proportion of wild species significantly increases in the Bronze Age. This was certainly not economically necessary and this trend has been interpreted as representing the establishment of hunting as an elite sport. These new elites were affirming their position through exclusive tastes.

Such behaviour had effects well beyond Greece. Similar fine tastes appear to have been adopted in Bronze Age chiefdoms in central Europe. Elites started to import fine drinking wares from the palatial societies to the south. Extra value could be placed on such imports because of their exotic nature. Similar elite tastes are apparent in the 'barbarian' world that lay outside the Roman Empire. For instance, in the late Iron Age in Britain, prior to the Roman invasion, tribal chiefs clearly imported Roman goods including fine tablewares such as Samian pottery and amphorae. The amphorae, of course, were imported for their contents and may represent new elite tastes in foreign foods and wines, not simply dining habits.

In periods before people recorded their thoughts, we will only ever be able to speculate on matters of taste. However, archaeologists have come a long way in being able to reconstruct past diets and much more will be possible in the future with advances in biomolecular analyses that will allow us to gain a much more holistic view of food production and consumption. Most studies of prehistoric food have concentrated upon economic aspects. Such studies were all about how people survived but, while this aspect is still very important, it is clear that mere survival is not what life is all about. Recent trends in archaeological research have stressed the important differences between 'food' and 'diet' and have drawn attention to the social context within which food is consumed.

It seems that some matters of taste may well have been heavily influenced by hard-wiring relating to our evolutionary past or our dietary needs, while others were dictated by environment and availability. However, it is equally clear that there was a rich tapestry of choice in tastes operating in prehistoric societies. Such choices were driven by many social forces. Foods and drinks used in feasting might be chosen for their quality, exotic nature or even intoxicating qualities. Prestige in dining could have derived from quantity, rarity, novelty or fashionability of either the foodstuffs or the eating accoutrements. Religion and taboos would have played their part. Hardest to study of all, there must simply have been individual likes and dislikes, just like any of us have today.

2 THE GOOD THINGS THAT LAY AT HAND

Tastes of Ancient Greece and Rome

Veronika Grimm

'Mix stronger wine. A cup for the hands of each guest –
here beneath my roof are the men I love most.'
He paused. Patroclus obeyed his great friend,
who put down a heavy chopping block in the firelight
and across it laid a sheep's chine, a fat goat's
and the long back cut of a full-grown pig,
marbled with lard. Automedon held the meats
while lordly Achilles carved them into quarters,
cut them well into pieces, pierced them with spits,
and Patroclus raked the hearth, a man like a god
making the fire blaze. Once it had burned down
and the flames died away, he scattered the coals
and stretching the spitted meats across the embers,
raised them unto supports and sprinkled clean pure salt.
As soon as the roasts were done and spread on platters,
Patroclus brought the bread, set it out on the board
in ample wicker baskets. Achilles served the meat.
Then face to face with his noble guest Odysseus,
he took his seat along the farther wall,
he told his friend to sacrifice to the gods
and Patroclus threw the first cuts into the fire.
They reached out for the good things that lay at hand.

(*Iliad*, 9. 244–265)

This was the way for civilized people to receive guests, friends or strangers, in the ancient heroic world brought to life by the great epic poems of Homer. The first of these, the *Iliad*, recounts episodes from the long war of the Achaeans against Troy, full of raging emotions, bloody violence and devastating suffering; the other, the *Odyssey*, tells the story of the return to home of the most resourceful of the heroes from that war, a journey of ten years' duration, with dangerous adventures and narrow escapes across a more or less peaceful world that had almost lost by then even the memory of that great war. The Greeks of later ages cherished the epics of the Trojan War and its aftermath, and regarded the events sung by the bard as the beginning of their history. Homer's world was carved into the bedrock of their shared consciousness. Any discussion of the ancient Greeks, including the topic here considered, that of cuisine and taste, should start with Homer.

The events described in the epics are the creation of poetic imagination, but to make the story come alive for the reader the poet, like other storytellers, seems to have used the everyday realities of contemporary experience; thus the world that emerges as the background in many of the vivid narratives may indeed reflect social realities of Homer's own age, some enduring aspects of living which, by their conservative nature, would be slow to change. First and foremost among the routines of everyday life of great importance for the social historian is food and diet. Homer not only describes a surprising number of feasts but, compared to later Greek writers, his attitude to food and drink is wonderfully wholesome and uncomplicated, without pretentious disdain for those bodily needs that we share with the animals. No matter how brave his heroes are, how eager for victory and how merciless in slaughter, they cannot fight on empty stomachs. Food and wine 'is a soldier's strength and nerve', counsels wise Odysseus, long before it became widely accepted wisdom that an army marches on its stomach. Even the greatest grief and mourning has to pause for the demands of the body for sustenance, so Achilles urges food on the distraught Priam, who has come to beg for the return of his slain son's body from his killer. Achilles, putting aside his rage, prepares a feast for the old King, the father of his slain enemy, with his own hands.

But food and drink in Homer are not only a necessity, the sustenance of life and strength; they are also the source of joy and pleasure, the foundations for communal life. There are similarities and repetitions in the description of the many feasts, inducing some scholars to regard these passages as empty formulas. Indeed, the preparation of the many feasts follows a similar order, with enough variation left, however, to distinguish the occasions. The repeated sequence of the preparation of the feast has intrinsic interest, for this may have been the part of the epics most familiar to the poet's contemporary audience. The well-known course of the feast, similar to those during which the bards sang their stories, may have given the audience a short respite in the midst of the fast-changing events. The many feasts of the heroes commence, just as communal feasting will commence in ancient communities for centuries to come, with a sacrifice, a gift offered to the gods. The extent of the gift depended on the felt need or the felt indebtedness for divine favour. The gods on their part liked to receive as gifts what human beings liked to eat, the roasted flesh of domestic quadrupeds. While mortals ate just as gladly flesh obtained in the hunt, the gods accepted only the sacrifice of domestic animals. This is somewhat curious in light of the fact that, as Homer informs us, the

food of the gods is different from the food of mortals. The immortals sustain themselves on ambrosia and nectar. Why then should mortals sacrifice valuable meat? The gods, it was believed, enjoyed the smell of the burned sacrifice. Understanding this fact made the whole process more economical. The animal destined for the human banquet was slaughtered with solemn rite accompanied by prayer, the long bone was cut out from its haunch, a layer of fat was wrapped around it and this package was burned for the gods, who enjoyed the aroma of roasting fat. In the meantime,

> They skinned the animal quickly, butchered the carcass,
> expertly cut the meat in pieces, pierced them with spits,
> roasted them to a turn and pulled them off the fire.
> The work done, the feast laid out, they ate well
> and no man's hunger lacked a share of the banquet.
>
> (*Iliad*, 7. 362–366)

Unlike the obvious difference in the divine and human portions of the sacrificed animals, a custom that will provide later comic writers with a convenient target for their barbs, Homer's heroes always enjoyed an 'equal feast'. Whether the meat is of oxen, sheep, goat or pigs, the food is carefully shared out. Sometimes exceptional bravery or spectacular fighting is rewarded with an especially desirable piece of meat, giving posterity some idea of what pleased the ancient palate. No preference is shown among the heroes for any one of the four types of domestic quadrupeds. Not surprisingly, there is a strong preference for fat, marbled cuts of meat and for the 'long savory cuts that line the backbone'. Bread is the accompaniment of the meat, in ample quantities served up in wicker baskets. Large cups of mixed wine wash down the food, but only after libations are poured out for the gods.

In later ages the Greeks diluted their wine with water. Homer does not say what the heroes added, but the wine is often described as honeyed or sweet. On two occasions, once in the *Iliad* and once in the *Odyssey*, the mixing of wine is elaborated; the resulting mixture (the *kykeon*), however, is no longer, strictly speaking, a drink but more like a restorative porridge or posset. In both instances it is prepared by a woman, which is unusual, especially for the *Iliad*, where all the feasting is organized by men. This mixture contains Pramnian wine, a dark and strong drink, to which barley meal and honey are added and goat cheese is grated on top. It may have been heated to help the honey dissolve, but this is not explicitly stated in the text. What is clear, however, is that the preparation of this potion required considerable skill. In the *Iliad* it is given to exhausted and wounded fighters as a restorative, while in the *Odyssey* Circe, the sorceress, offers it to Odysseus' men who, as is well known, turn into pigs after drinking it. To keep the record straight, it is not the potion that does the trick but Circe's magic. Whatever its powers were, restorative or magical, this seems to be the mother recipe for a very long line of comfort foods, consisting of grains cooked in wine, milk or water and flavoured with honey or other sweet or savory substances, from the barley porridge of the ancients to the rice or semolina pudding of my own Hungarian childhood.

The diet of the Homeric heroes has stimulated some curiosity among both ancient and modern scholars. The problem they have all had to face is that, despite the great number and lengthy description of ancient meals, many of the ingredients and cooking techniques, familiar aspects of later Greek cuisine, are missing from Homer's accounts. There are no fish, so dear to later gluttons' hearts, on the heroes' board, no fattened fowl, no spices, no sauces, not even vegetables, except for an occasional onion, and no honey-cakes. Ancient scholars, always eager to see moral lessons in Homer, came to the ingenious conclusion that the poet, wishing to implant the virtue of moderation in the young, made his heroes' way of living frugal and contented. They argued further that Homer pointedly excludes the tricks of the culinary art for fear of its aphrodisiac and luxury-inducing effects.

The ancient commentators did not express any surprise concerning the large amount of red meat the heroes habitually devoured; some modern scholars, however, are sceptical about this, especially those who like to imagine the ancient

An *oinochoe* (wine jug), embellished with the head of Silenus, from the Tomb of Philip II, 4th century BC. Silenus, half-man half-beast, wild, mischievous but wise, together with satyrs, nymphs and maenads, formed the riotous companions of Dionysus, the god of Wine.

A gold-plated strainer and silver *kylix* (wine cup) from the Tomb of Philip II, 4th century BC. Ancient wine was often flavoured with aromatic flowers, herbs and spices. Sometimes the flavouring was placed into the strainer before the wine was poured through it into the drinking cup, other times it was steeped in the wine and the strainer used to prevent it from being poured into the cup.

Mediterranean world as almost completely vegetarian, where most people tasted meat only on the rare occasion of religious sacrifice, where oxen were used for ploughing, sheep for wool and only the rich could afford to eat meat or fish. The Homeric diet is indeed problematic for those who like to compare the ancient Mediterranean world to a contemporary Third World country, with little historical evidence or justification for the comparison.

As we have seen, the main ingredients of the Homeric feasts included only meat, bread and wine; but in fact the Homeric world seems to have contained a rich variety of other delicacies. The poet's descriptive language, the metaphors and similes he uses, reveal that both the author and his intended audience were at home in the settled agricultural milieu of the Mediterranean. Homer's view of a civilized community is a place where people produce grain to make their bread, where they have vineyards to make wine, orchards with apple and pear trees, pomegranates, figs and olives, and where well-planted gardens provide all sorts of fresh green vegetables throughout the year. Communities like this have meeting halls where the people come together for discussion and counsel. This is the picture of the Greek *polis* or city state. In contrast, he sees the sheep-herder as a man-eating savage who lives alone, not in a well-built house but in a cave, who does not till the land but subsists on milk and does not even know how to drink wine. This wild creature, the Cyclops, does not recognize even the most basic law of civilized life, the law of hospitality, which was protected by the father of the gods, Zeus.

The great value placed by the Greeks on hospitality was shared by peoples around the ancient Mediterranean basin who also ate many similar foods. The major components of the Mediterranean diet,

A 6th-century BC terracotta, from Tanagra in Boeotia, depicts a woman stirring with a long pestle. Is she churning milk or mixing the strength-giving potion of the Homeric heroes, the *kykeon*, made of Pramnian wine, honey, barley and cheese, or is she Circe, mixing the magical drink with which to turn Odysseus' companions into pigs?

discernable already in the Homeric epics, as we have seen, were grain, oil and an alcohol-containing liquid, a product of the fermentation of fruit or grain. The cuisine, which builds upon and enriches the staples, depends on the variety, nature and quality of added ingredients, on meat, fish, vegetables and seasonings, which in turn depend upon the nature of the land, climate, economics and social customs, and, of course, on the skill and inventiveness of the cooks. All of these may have contributed to regional variations in foodways and traditions.

Even the Greeks differed among themselves in their cuisine and food preferences. The Greeks of the ancient world were never organized as a unified nation; being Greek meant speaking Greek and sharing some aspects of culture; those whose language they could not understand they regarded as aliens, 'barbarians'. Through migration, colonization and trade, Greek-speaking settlements dotted the Mediterranean basin from Asia Minor to France, south Italy, Sicily and North Africa. Greeks measured themselves against other Greeks and competed with each other not only in athletics but in almost everything. Their history, which they believed to have begun with a great war, did indeed continue with almost never-ending wars, most of the time Greek cities fighting each other until the Roman Empire conquered them all and put a stop to their belligerence.

Not surprisingly, their competitive spirit could be discerned even in the disparagement of each other's cuisine. The Boeotians, for example, whose land was rich and whose Lake Copais produced the much sought-after big fat eel, were characterized as mean-spirited gluttons who ate the strangest things, such as weasels, foxes, moles

Ancient food was cooked over a wood fire or charcoal using braziers and gridirons, as this 5th-century BC terracotta figurine from Boeotia illustrates, or in more affluent circles, using earthenware or brick ovens. None of these gave the cook much direct control over the heat.

and fat geese, as well, of course, as gorging themselves on giant eels. Similarly, the Thessalians, rich in wheat, cattle and horses, were maligned as insatiable eaters, seekers of voluptuous food, heavy beef-eaters and useless inventors of many rich delicacies. The Spartans' reputation for great courage in battle was ridiculed famously by a Greek from the high-living south of Italy, who, after being a guest at a Spartan communal meal, remarked: 'It is no wonder that Spartans are the bravest men in the world; for anyone in his right mind would prefer to die ten thousand times rather than share in such poor living.' None came in for more righteous censure for high living and for luxury of cuisine than the Sicilian Greeks. The Athenians, on the other hand, who invented or at least spread most of these disparaging comments, painted their own portrait as frugal, upright, moral people, with 'simple taste', who were taught by their philosophers always to stop eating while still hungry and to starve themselves in the midst of plenty.

Before we discuss further the food customs and cuisine of the ancient classical world, a few words need to be said about the sources. For the classical period, as with the Homeric banquets, the main sources are literary. Accumulating archaeological evidence, where it exists, provides useful controls to the literature. Knowing the layout of ancient kitchens, the tools of the cooks, may give some insight into the sort of use they may have been put to. Analysis of bone and other organic remains, when these are found around ancient settlements, does add important information, which still has to be interpreted in light of the literary evidence. For the classical period, the literary evidence is not as straightforward and unproblematic, when it comes to food and its enjoyment, as were the Homeric epics. There is a great wealth of references to food in the extant literary works. In this literature, written by men for the amusement or edification of other men, food increasingly came to be a concern central for both one's moral and physical wellbeing. Eating and drinking were used by the writers for a great variety of purposes; unfortunately the straightforward description and analysis of the cuisine was not one of these. Instead, discussion of food often played an important role in the ethical teaching of the philosophers, who tended to agree that food was meant only for life support; anything beyond subsistence was luxury, luxury excited the passions and, once aroused, the passions would lead the way to certain moral degradation.

What many later philosophers considered as the best cuisine is well illustrated in Plato's *Republic*. Socrates, in a discussion of the nature of a just society, describes to his listeners the diet such a society would follow: 'For food they will have wheat-meal and barley-meal for baking or kneading. They will serve splendid cakes and loaves on fresh leaves…they will drink wine and pray to the gods with garlands on their heads.' When one of his listeners objects that this would indeed be very plain fare for a feast, Socrates consents to allow them some luxuries, 'salt…and olive oil and cheese and different kinds of vegetables from which to make various kinds of country dishes.' And for dessert he would give them 'figs and peas and beans, and myrtle-berries and acorns to roast at the fire as they sip their wine.' To which his companion exclaims: 'Really, Socrates, you might be catering for a community of pigs!' and asks Socrates to give to this ideal society the same type of foods that they themselves eat, a regular diet with meat. In response, the philosopher proceeds to show how the everyday comforts of their own civilized society with its meat-eating diet will generate more and more demands for luxury, 'for delicacies, scents, cosmetics and mistresses…for fine arts of painting and embroidery…gold and ivory.' He envisions a rapid expansion of the state with a multitude of useless occupations made necessary by the greed for endless luxuries, which will inevitably lead to wars and unjust societies.

Socrates seems to have objected to meat-eating for its possible social consequences; philosophers of various schools often advocated a meatless diet for fear of the effect of meat-eating on a person's body or soul. Some argued that the 'vapours' from the meat rise to clog the mind and thus make thinking sluggish. Others were influenced by current medical notions that regarded health as a balance between the four 'humours', blood, black bile, yellow bile and phlegm, and their 'qualities', the hot, the cold, the dry and the moist that, according to ancient medical ideas, constituted the body. Philosophy and medicine often influenced each other, sharing views about the human body, although neither discipline had much real understanding about how it functioned. These medical notions gave rise to philosophic anxieties that a diet rich in meat will unduly heat the human body, which in turn may lead to increased and dangerous sexual appetites. They tried to convince their listeners that variety in food is unnatural for human beings, whose digestive system, they argued, is not equipped to deal with it; they urged the adoption of a simple, one-staple diet, which, if followed, would give rise to serious dietary deficiency diseases.

Ancient moralizers understood that food and sex were necessary for the survival of the individual and the community, but appetite either for food or for sex was regarded with alarm, for it meant for them individual cravings that demanded more than one's just allotment. Moreover, a craving for strong, heating foods was feared for its power to stimulate a desire for sex.

Influenced by these philosophical and medical notions, anyone wanting to be seen as a balanced, self-controlled, upright and serious person would be expected to spend his or her energies on the improvement of the mind and to exert as little effort as possible on matters pertaining to the body, except for what was needed to maintain health. Comic writers, satirists and political rivals clearly realized that this kind of rigid and unnatural posturing could serve as an easy target for their irreverent, debunking wit. Consequently, the literature on food, in addition to medical theories and philosophical strictures, is full of brilliant confabulations of fantastic feasts, gluttony and the attendant lechery. Eating, drinking and the sexual habits of well-known persons, true or invented, became easy and convenient methods of character description or, more often, character assassination, employed even by serious historians.

Under the stern gaze of philosophers, who agreed that catering to bodily appetites was below the dignity of a man of character, ancient writers repeated *ad nauseam* the dangers of rich food, the immorality of lavish dinner parties, and so forth. The surviving ancient literature was transmitted through the ages by those who selected only what they liked or what they found useful. These later generations found the ancients' high-and-mighty attitude appealing, and were more interested in fasting than feasting, so, today, we have only a few pieces of evidence from which we can obtain some inkling of the flavours, aromas and methods of the ancient cuisine.

'When men of gentle breeding and culture are gathered at a symposium you will see neither flute-girls nor dancing girls...they are quite capable of entertaining themselves without such nonsense, but with their own voices, talking and listening in turn, and always decently, even when they have drunk much wine' or so stern Plato teaches (Protagoras 347). A wall painting from a tomb in the Greek colony of Paestum, Italy, c. 480 BC.

The most valuable source of evidence concerning Greek cuisine comes from the pen of an obscure Greek writer of the second century AD, Athenaeus, a native of Naucratis in Egypt. This author composed, in all likelihood while sitting in a library rich in Greek literature, a long literary dinner party with a large number of intellectuals as participants; it is called *Deipnosophistae*, or the 'Learned Diners', expressly in imitation of Plato. The innovation of Athenaeus is in the topic chosen for discussion; while Plato's dialogues focus on lofty topics such as the nature of justice or love, the interest of Athenaeus is in dinner parties. His fifteen surviving books contain quotations from an enormous range of Greek literature that without him would be completely lost to us. In the course of their discussions, the participants of his dinner party cite verbatim, with reference to author and title, from a very large number of lost comedies, historical works, literary commentaries, medical texts, cookery books, agricultural handbooks, and more, concerning eating and drinking and customs pertaining to these.

Reading the interminable banquet of Athenaeus' learned professors, one cannot help but be impressed by the wealth of writing that

Persephone, daughter of Demeter, the goddess who gave the gift of grain to humans, was abducted by Hades, the Lord of the Underworld, to be his wife. With Persephone in the Underworld and Demeter grieving, spring would not come, no grain would sprout and the world starved until Hades let her rejoin her mother for half of the year. The c. 470 BC terracotta relief shows the royal couple of the Underworld with Persephone's attributes, the stalks of grain and fruit.

must have dealt with food and drink in Greek literature. It seems that despite philosophic disdain for the appetites of the flesh, the flesh and its demands asserted themselves vigorously in all sorts of Greek writing. Food and the cooks that produce it appear as important participants of many a comedy on the stage. Hellenistic historians, recording the fortunes of ruling dynasties, whose fame and prestige were enhanced by their lavish hospitality, seem to have paid close attention to all details of the feasting and drinking, and of course to the sex life, of the rulers. Without perusing Athenaeus, few of today's students of Classical Greece would suspect that there were many famous Greek cookery-book writers in the ancient world. We can, for instance, thank Athenaeus for transmitting to later ages a substantial portion, about 350 lines, of a remarkable travel and cookery book, written in the fourth century BC, in epic hexameter poetry, by the Sicilian Archestratus of Gela or the neighbouring Syracuse. From Athenaeus we learn also about the popularity of a peculiar literary genre, the detailed description of a feast in the form of a letter written by a participant to an absent friend. The friend who received the report was expected to reciprocate with a letter describing another extravagant feast. Collections of these letters were, apparently, published and were read by many with great enjoyment. In fact, Athenaeus' own composition is put in a similar framework; he writes the *Deipnosophistae* as a first-hand report of a banquet to a friend, Timocrates, who could not be there.

The 'Learned Diners' of Athenaeus show no concerns with crop failures, farmers' worries, the poverty of the soil or the never-ceasing wars that must often have devastated the countryside. Their interest is firmly centred on the good life and its constituents, fancy food, wine and women, flower garlands and perfumes worn by the diners, party games, dances and the paraphernalia pertaining to all these. Athenaeus is indeed an expert on the literature of cuisine and taste; one needs to have patience, however, to extract the information, for his discussions are long-winded and the dialogues of the literati that connect the multitude of quotations from ancient writers reveal a worse than second-rate writer. Despite it all, Athenaeus is a goldmine for anyone interested in Greek cuisine and taste of the Classical and Hellenistic age.

This cuisine was based on the three gifts from the gods – grain, wine and oil – without which civilized people cannot live. Grain was the gift of the goddess Demeter, wine of the god Dionysus, while Athena was believed to have taught the people olive culture. Of Demeter's gifts the preferred grain was the naked variety of wheat, even though larger areas of mainland Greece were better suited to growing barley. Husked varieties of wheat and barley needed to be parched to get rid of the husks before they could be ground for meal. The parching destroys the gluten in the grain, making it unsuitable for bread baking. Barley and other husked grains were soaked in various liquids, made into soups, porridges or kneaded into flat cakes. Porridge and barley cakes

Wine was the gift of Dionysus, the most versatile and elusive of the Greek gods with myths and cults that often challenged established social norms. He travelled far and wide on the sea, on land on the backs of wild animals, and through the air with wings. On this black-figure wine cup by Exekias (c. 540 BC) from Vulci he is sailing on a ship.

remained a characteristic feature of the cuisine; most Greeks, however, even in regions where the growing of wheat was unprofitable, from early times on developed a preference for wheat bread. Both bread, produced from naked wheat, and porridge would serve as the basis of the meal, enriched with oil, cooked meat and vegetables, flavoured with herbs, spices or honey. The bread of Athens was famous for its excellent quality and a great cause of pride for the Athenians, who had to import their wheat, for the soil of Attica was not suitable for growing it. Thearion, a fifth-century BC Athenian, was credited with the invention of bread ovens and maybe even with the establishment of commercial bakeries. Plato mentions Thearion the baker as one of the three men who were 'the best at caring for men's bodies'; the other two being Mithaecus, a Sicilian cookery-book writer, and Sarambus, a producer or provider of wine. Plato, being a philosopher, meant the praise facetiously.

It appears that following Thearion the Greeks exercised great inventiveness and skill in bread making. Athenaeus mentions a number of learned treatises written on bread making and lists over seventy different sorts of bread. Breads may be distinguished by the kind of grain used: wheat, rye, spelt and millet, the last three used only by necessity, for wheat, as we have seen, was the preferred grain for bread. There were breads made of flour of different quality, white bread made of finely bolted flour, whole-wheat bread made with unbolted meal. Whole-wheat bread was thought to be 'laxative' and often recognized as more health-promoting; despite this, white bread was generally preferred as the finest and best tasting. Bread could be leavened or unleavened. Breads could be differentiated on the basis of the baking method: oven-baked bread; bread baked in the ashes; or baked on a brazier in a pan, which may have resulted in something like a pancake, eaten folded over some filling and dipped in wine – delicious, to judge by the poets' praises: 'smeared brazier bread, it is a soft and delectable compound.' Some even baked bread dough on a spit.

The variety of liquids, fats and seasonings added to the flour could change the consistency and vary the flavour of bread. Wine, milk, cheese and honey are mentioned, alone or in some combination, as liquids, while oil, suet or lard as added fats and poppy, sesame and flax seeds are the most often mentioned seasonings for bread. Finally, breads may have also been stuffed with cheeses of various consistency, raisins and other dried fruits or other sweet or savory substances. Bread served often as an edible plate upon which the meat or fish was served. The most highly praised bread was produced by Phoenician, Lydian or Cappadocian bakers.

The god Dionysus, according to legend, came to the Greeks from the East, from where he brought his miraculous but ambivalent gift, wine. Indeed, viticulture came to the Greeks from the East, from Anatolia in Asia Minor through Phoenicia, Palestine and Egypt, a long time before written history. By the period of the Homeric epics the Greeks were expert vine growers, wine producers and wine drinkers. During the Classical age, a fashion developed for drinking parties, *symposia,* at least among upper-class men. These drinking parties may have taken place as the continuation of a dinner, or the men may have gathered for the purpose of celebrating the gods Dionysos and Eros. Whichever way the symposium was organized, it was a men's affair; no wives attended, according to the literary evidence. The women who participated were there as musicians, entertainers and providers of satisfaction for the drinkers' appetites for physical or intellectual companionship. Light food was provided with the purpose of increasing the desire for drink. While the Wine-god and his power were celebrated at the symposium, the Greeks were well aware of the dangers involved in his gift. The god Dionysus himself taught the people – according to the poets – to drink only three cups, 'one to health, which they empty first, the second to love and pleasure, the third to sleep. When this is drunk up wise guests go home.'

Servants preparing food for a dinner party. The food was cut into bite-sized pieces by the servants before it was placed in front of the guests, who ate with their hands. Detail from a 6th-century BC Corinthian black-figure column-krater, Cerveteri.

Above: Attic red-figure *kylix*, 490–480 BC, showing a scene from a symposium: two guests, a flautist and a boy with a wine jug and ladle ready to refill the cups. The guests are playing kottabos, a game of competition to see who could dislodge a precariously balanced target by flicking at it the last drops of wine in his cup.

Opposite: Bronze krater depicting scenes from the divine wedding of Dionysus and Ariadne, 4th century BC, Derveni. The krater, a large jug, was used to mix wine with water; the ratio of the ingredients was decided by the symposiarch, the ruler of the party elected by the guests. It was believed that all would get inebriated equally.

Drinking more will lead to violence, uproar, drunken revel, black eyes, biliousness and one may end up in the hands of the policeman. The dire warning was repeated often and to some extent it was heeded, for the Greeks drank their wine mixed with water, which, depending on the ratio of water to wine, must have reduced the alcohol content. It is estimated that the wine they drank ranged from about three to seven percent alcohol, the range of strength of modern beers.

Wine was part of the diet of all Greeks. It may have even been healthier than drinking from the cities' water supplies. As Greek colonies were established around the Mediterranean basin, the love of wine and expertise in wine production went with the colonists. Western Greeks from Massilia (present-day Marseilles) introduced wine to the beer-drinking tribes of Gaul; Greek settlers on Sicily made the island known as Oenotria, the land of wine. What was Greek wine like? The literature mentions a variety of colours: white, golden and dark or black wine. Wines are praised as fragrant, smelling of flowers, violets, roses and hyacinths. If the wine did not have a fragrance in itself, as many of the sweet wines did not, then they could be perfumed with various additives, including spices or extracts of flowers. It appears that there was a strong preference for sweet wines, wines tasting like honey. Honey alone, or spelt kneaded with honey, was among the often-mentioned additives used in wine production, sea water was another. The former may have raised somewhat the alcohol content by adding more food for the fermenting yeast, while the latter was said to increase the sweet taste of the wine. Not all wines were sweet, the Pramnian, known already in Homeric times, was an austere, dark and strong wine, which kept for a long time. The poets praise 'old wine' (and blame women for liking old wine while they prefer young men). It is unlikely, however, that many of the wines could be kept more than a few years. Owing to problems of storage in large and porous earthenware containers, amphorae, wines would oxidize into vinegar, which itself was used as a drink and also as a popular flavouring of food. The most highly praised wines were those produced on the islands of the eastern Aegean – Lesbos, Chios, Cos – and in Thrace on the northern mainland.

The third gift to contribute to the sustenance of humankind, according to the Greeks, came from the goddess Athena, who planted the first olive tree in Athens and taught the people how to cultivate it. The olive tree came under cultivation in the area of Syria and modern Israel about six thousand years ago and from there spread westward around the Mediterranean basin. Anyone who has ever bitten into an olive fresh off the tree would agree that divine instruction was indeed needed to reveal the possibilities inherent in the foul-tasting fruit. The olive contains a glucoside that makes it too bitter to eat without elaborate curing. When the olive is pressed for its oil, the glucoside remains in the residue and does not flavour the oil. Both the cured fruit and the oil were of great importance in the diet of ancient Mediterranean peoples. The oil was used also as fuel in lamps, in place of soap for the body and as a base for the concoction of perfumes and medicines. There were variations in the quality, taste and of course in price of oils depending on the quality of the fruit, methods of extraction and storage.

Many and varied ingredients were added to the basic staples in the cuisine of the Greeks, as the work of Athenaeus testifies. In fact, the number of fish species enumerated in the literature quoted by him has convinced some modern scholars that fish was the preferred food, the prestige food, the luxury food of the Greeks. In support of this view they call attention also to the number of fish decorations used on painted pottery. Fish, indeed, must have been an important component of the diet, especially in the coastal regions. The social importance of it, however, may be exaggerated especially in relation to meat, if we take these literary sources as objective, straightforward evidence and disregard the internal demands and dynamics of the artistic genre. Most of Athenaeus' descriptions of dinner courses and their ingredients come from comic poetry. The more and more colourful marine creatures a cook on the stage could rattle off would make him, or the poet who created him, appear a more skilful virtuoso of word-play than the listing of meat from the usual domestic quadrupeds or barnyard fowl; although lists of these are also found in some comedy fragments. The same applies to the painted pottery; depictions of fish and other denizens of the sea appear to be more esthetic and decorative than a picture of a beef steak or pig's trotters.

During the banquets recounted in Athenaeus typically a number of courses were served to the diners; the first of these offered a selection of small plates with, for example, sea-urchins, cubes of smoked fish with capers, small slices of meat, a bulb (hyacinth, iris and asphodel bulbs were regarded as foods that promote sexual prowess), and some salad greens. Vinegary sour dressing was recommended often with 'biting mustard seed' for bulb vegetables or the salads included in the first course, for such condiments were thought to 'rouse the sensory organs' even of old men, 'dispel the sloth and bluntness of their desire, and make them glad to eat'. After the first course came wine. To drink much at this point was regarded as boorish bad form and also self-defeating, for it prevented you from enjoying the food that followed. The main course could present more fish, boiled or baked with wine, olive oil and seasonings. As well as fish there was meat. This could be kid, fat pork, lamb, boar, goose, duck, partridge or chicken, all prepared with a great deal of seasoning, which testified to a preference for strong pungent vinegary tastes. The vegetables that accompanied the fish or the meat would include peas-porridge, lentils, asparagus, white beet, cabbage and turnips. The turnips, for example, would be sliced and boiled in water or soaked in strong brine then dried and finally served in a sauce made of equal amounts of must and vinegar, mixed with raisins that were pounded together in a mortar with mustard seed. To finish the meal, there may have been a third course of sweet cakes, nuts and fruit, or the company may have settled in for the symposium, with the interest shifting from eating to some serious drinking.

Refinement in Greek cuisine appears to have been stimulated by both eastern and western influences. The ancient kingdoms of Lydia and Persia in the east represented for the Greeks fabulous wealth and the height of luxury, a luxury that they often deplored as 'effeminate' and decadent but envied secretly. The western influence came from their own colonies established early in the eighth and seventh centuries BC on the fertile lands of Sicily and southern Italy and which soon became very wealthy. The east contributed some rich and complex dishes, perfumes and the best bread and cake makers. Sicily provided the rest of Greece, and later the Romans too, with highly sophisticated professional cooks and cookery-book writers.

European cuisine as an art was born with the ingenuity of these Sicilian cooks. Their rich cuisine of many ingredients, elaborate sauces and seductive honey-cakes was enjoyed and admired but it also invited criticism, and not only from those self-appointed moral guardians who decried it for centuries to come as the beginning of every kind of decadence. In the fourth century BC Archestratos of

Gela, a Sicilian himself, a forerunner of future apostles of *nouvelle cuisine*, criticized his fellow-Sicilians not on moral but on culinary grounds. He is the author of the epic poem, the *Hedypatheia* (Life of Luxury), a culinary tour around the Mediterranean, that aims to teach the reader what to buy, where and when; what localities produce the best fish, meat, bread or wine. The guiding principle of the cuisine of Archestratos seems to have been: obtain the very best quality, as fresh as you can, everything in its proper season, and then cook it simply. As an example, to prepare grey mullet, a much sought-after fish, his advice is to buy the best quality, which comes from Miletus, then roast it whole in the embers wrapped only in fig leaves – the fish is tender, it must not be overcooked – and to serve it sprinkled with salt only. 'But let no Syracusan or Italian Greek come near you as you are making the dish,' he warns, 'for they do not know how to prepare top-quality fish but utterly ruin them by covering everything they cook with cheese and vinegar and silphium flavoured broth.' Hard-fleshed fish, he advises, may be good with a sauce of cheese and vinegar but soft-fleshed ones need only salt and oil, maybe a sprinkling of cumin. Simplicity seems to be his guiding principle also in the cooking of meat, for instance, his choice among the many methods he knows for the preparation of a hare is the simplest, that is to spit-roast the meat to medium rare, sprinkled with salt alone, without superfluous 'sticky sauces with too much cheese and oil'.

Interest in refined cuisine, simple or elaborate, seems to have spread not only among the Greeks but also up the Italian peninsula to the Romans too. The poet Quintus Ennius in the late third century BC wrote an adaptation of Archestratos' gastronomical poem for Latin-speaking readers, at about the same time that professional cooks and bakers started to arrive in Rome. The Romans developed an enthusiastic interest in good food and good wine, and as the empire expanded they put much thought and effort into the technology required to produce these.

The Romans succeeded in building their great empire and in maintaining it for centuries because they were pragmatic and willing to learn from anyone able to provide them with useful knowledge. They may have learned viticulture and wine production from their Etruscan or Greek neighbours but they contributed more to the development and spread of wine culture than any other people. They made a science of viticulture, developing several new grape varieties, some that were more adapted to northerly regions of the empire, even as far as

The fresco of a bread shop from Pompeii may depict a similar scene to the one conjured up by the Roman poet's epigram: 'Rise. Already the baker is selling boys their breakfast, and the crested birds of daybreak sound from every side' (Martial XIV 223). Some claim that the picture shows a distribution of bread by some official. In either case, the picture emphasizes the centrality of bread in the Roman diet.

Britain; they matched vines to the various soil types and made improvements in pruning and training the vines, in grape presses and storage methods. Consequently, a large variety of wines was available for the inhabitants of the empire. A similar course seems to have been followed in oil production and the development of Roman cuisine.

The Romans liked to look back on their early history with nostalgia for the 'simple life' without cooks and bakers, when their women ground the grain for the porridge that sustained them. When this ideal simple life ended and what caused its demise nobody knew for sure, but various culprits were suggested. Contact with 'luxurious' foreigners, the influx of Greeks and other 'aliens', were all popular targets. It is certain, however, that by the time their history began to be written the Romans were beyond the 'simple life' and well on the way towards the development of a great empire and a world-class cuisine. This cuisine was eagerly adopted by the peoples of the empire and it still stands at the foundations of Mediterranean and European food cultures. Sicilian Greek cooks coming to Rome undoubtedly had a strong influence and so did Roman contact with the East. But again it was the Roman determination to learn what is good and improve it that was responsible for the success. As in wine production, so in agriculture and food technology they experimented, improved and spread their knowledge. The Roman system of farming, with its pattern of fields laid out like brickwork, bordered by ditches and wattle fences, walled enclosures for orchards, vineyards, gardens for potherbs and vegetables, with an extensive network of roads that ensured communication and trade, is still discernable in areas of Europe that were part of the empire. The Romans should be thanked also for bringing many food plants, herbs and fruit trees such as the almond, cherry, peach, quince and medlar to northerly areas of Europe.

The surviving Roman handbooks on agriculture, horticulture and animal husbandry testify to the interest and the attention they paid to quality and variety of food for the table, and the energy they invested in producing it. References to food are ubiquitous also in the works of Roman poets, orators, historians, biographers and medical writers. Following the Greeks, advice about food and eating forms a significant part of the teaching of the various philosophical schools. The interpretation of the great number of references to food and feasting in this literature remains hotly contested, for, as in Greek literature, the purpose of Roman authors was rarely the objective description of taste or cuisine; most writers used eating and drinking as tools to express attitudes, strongly held and emotionally laden opinions. The poets and satirists found the depiction of ludicrous eating habits a convenient tool in the characterization of their targets. Against the philosophical background that emphasized frugality and the control of the appetites as the basis of morality, a good person could be described as a frugal eater while those that the poet disliked would be ridiculed as wallowing in horrendous amounts of the most outlandish food. Recognizing that food images have a wealth of sensuous associations, enticing or disgusting, Roman poets became masters of their use as vivid metaphors for the excesses, real or imagined, of their own society.

The Roman people, according to Cicero, hated private luxury but delighted in public munificence. It appears that he was right. Accusations of ostentatious luxury echo through the literature, heavily underlined by envy and often supported by the need to blacken the character of political opponents. This satirical literature was later put to use in political propaganda by early Christian writers who aimed to paint the pagan Roman Empire as the deepest pit of iniquity. They preached fasting and celibacy, accusing the pagans of insane gluttony and lechery, using Roman satire as evidence against them. From here it was a short step to the Roman orgies depicted by Hollywood.

Two examples from Roman literature, misused even today by some scholars, should be mentioned here, one as evidence for how the upper classes dined and the other for the poor peasants' fare. Neither

Above: Mosaic floor decoration from a triclinium, the dining-room of an elegant Pompeian house. The whimsical mosaic 'carpet' shows how the floor would appear after the diners finished the meal and left the room, with wish-bones, fish-bones and other inedibles dropped under the tables. This motif for floor-covering seems to have been popular for it appears in many areas of the empire.

Overleaf: In his 1969 film *Satyricon*, Federico Fellini proved that with the accumulated experience of 2000 years and in a new, and to the Romans unknown, medium, he could far outdo the ancient Petronius in conjuring up scenes of insane depravity and decadence that few Romans could even dream of.

can be taken as a realistic document of social history. The first of these, Trimalchio's dinner, is the longest surviving episode of the *Satyricon*, a fragmentary picaresque novel of low life around the Bay of Naples and south Italy, attributed to the aristocratic aesthete and courtier of Nero, Petronius, who lived in the first century AD.

Trimalchio's feast is a cruel satirical attack on an ex-slave who has managed to accumulate enormous wealth, surpassing by far even that of his master, and now in his pride he wants everyone to see his fortune. He throws his money around ostentatiously and puts on what he believes to be aristocratic and cultivated manners for friends and strangers to admire. There is historical evidence for an increasingly well-to-do class of tradesmen, artisans, merchants, many of them from among freedmen, who in the decoration of their houses, and probably in other aspects of their life also, attempted to imitate the aristocracy. Trimalchio is depicted by the author as a vulgar and ignorant

A tomb relief from Rome shows a butcher's shop with various cuts of meat and innards hanging from hooks and the butcher cutting up a pig's head. All parts of the animal, from head to trotters, were used as food.

nouveau-riche character, whose every effort to ape his betters turns out a disgusting failure. The meal, on which the episode centres, follows in vague outlines a Roman banquet in that it too goes 'from eggs to apples' that is to say from appetizers through main courses to desserts. In Trimalchio's banquet, however, just as in all other aspects of his house and household, everything is fabulously exaggerated and overblown in order to amaze his guests with his great wealth. All his efforts only succeed to expose his equally enormous boorishness.

It is well recognized that Trimalchio's feast is a satire, showing aristocratic disdain for the middle classes, a forerunner of a long-lived literary-intellectual conceit, the 'put-down' of the bourgeoisie, yet it is brought out as an example every time the banquets of the wealthy Roman elite are discussed.

The other often cited literary 'evidence', this time for the poor peasant's life, is the *Moretum*, a first century AD poem by an unknown author. The poem recounts in heroic epic metre and in minute detail how Simulus, a poor peasant, bakes his bread and prepares a herb and garlic cheese condiment, the Moretum, to go with it, for his daily sustenance. The upright hero, the poem asserts, has no meat in his larder; bread satisfies his hunger with onions and watercress as relish. Is Simulus so poor that he cannot afford meat? He owns a farm consisting of fields that he ploughs with a pair of oxen, and a fertile vegetable garden, the produce from which he sells at the town market for good money. He even owns a slave, a not very appealing African woman, whom we see tending the fire on the hearth.

Rather than presenting a faithful picture of peasant life in the Roman countryside, the unknown poet seems to be poking fun at the bucolic genre, with its nostalgia for the simple rural life, which was ever popular among the urban rich. Some farmers may have been very poor but this poem cannot be used, as it often is, to support the claim that most people in the Roman Empire lived on an almost vegetarian diet, that only the wealthy could afford meat.

There are, unfortunately, no surveys of food consumption in the empire; many sources of evidence suggest, however, that this dire view of its diet is far from realistic. Legal and historical evidence testifies to the concerns of the imperial administration with adequate food supplies, with the supervision of food markets and with the control of prices. Archaeological evidence, where it is available, also supports the view that the diet that was supposed to have been restricted to the privileged few was actually widespread. Evidence from the finds of butchered bones of domestic quadrupeds, for example, shows that pork, sheep, goat and beef were eaten all around the Mediterranean, with areas varying in their preference among these. The Romans' favourite meat came from the pig. Pliny the Elder in the first century AD wrote that 'there is no animal that provides more variety to the tongue: its meat provides nearly fifty flavours, while other animals only one.' Next to pork came beef and mutton in the preference of the

Pompeiian wall painting of a dining scene. For the Romans dinner was the main meal of the day. Dinner was a convivium, the place and time to enjoy companionship with food and wine. In contrast to the custom of Classical Greece, both husband and wife took part in Roman dinner parties.

urban population. The evidence from the bone data indicates that the cattle butchered for meat, instead of being old and retired from work as often claimed, were actually young animals, around three years of age, produced for the meat market. All parts of the animals, even the poorest, were used, suggesting that meat was central to the diet of most people, the same impression one gets from the literary evidence also if one is willing to discard the compulsively repeated ancient moral diatribe against luxury, upper-class excess and decadence.

Feasting, as everyone who is fond of Hollywood spectaculars knows, was central to Roman life. Indeed, the Romans, like most Mediterranean peoples, were deeply aware of the importance of hospitality and commensality in the cementing of communities, as the Pompeiian so aptly expressed it when he scratched the graffito on a wall: 'the one I do not dine with, he is a barbarian for me!' Dining together signified friendship, acceptance, connectedness. For this reason dinner parties were useful not only as a gathering of family and friends but also for furthering business and political interests. If read carefully the ancient literature distinguishes between dinner parties for intimate friends and great banquets given for state occasions or as a part of an important person's obligation to his position and to his clients. The distinction between dinner parties with the character of a public feast and those that represent a gathering of intimate friends is clear today. Looking at the Roman world this distinction is often

Bakers in the Roman Empire produced breads of great variety. Wheat ranked highest in preference. White bread made with finely bolted flour was most desirable. Breads were also made in a variety of shapes, judging from bread-molds found in the shape of pigs, hares and many others, such as the elaborate pie shape discovered at Pompeii.

ignored and the different occasions are often conflated resulting in the picture of the extravagant luxury of the Romans, a picture as justified as a depiction of a typical American dinner party on the basis of a banquet in the White House given by the President for a visiting foreign dignitary.

For the Romans, dinner was the main meal of the day. Neither breakfast nor lunch was of much significance, both light and fast meals, usually without company. Dinner was the main occasion for the leisurely enjoyment of both food and companionship; they called it *convivium*. Convivium signified 'living together'. They consciously distinguished themselves from the Greeks whose main communal enjoyment was the symposium, which meant 'drinking together'. The difference indeed was substantial: Roman wives attended dinner parties with their husbands, while Greek wives, as we have seen, were not welcome at their husbands' carousing. The Romans liked wine just as much as the Greeks but they drank it with the food. They frowned upon religious excuses for drunkenness, regarding both Dionysos and Eros, the gods who presided over the Greek drinking parties, as respected but dangerous forces.

Whether it was for family and friends, or a larger affair with many guests, the participants assembled for dinner after having visited the baths and dressed for the occasion. They had learned long ago from the Etruscans and Greeks the elegant (and quite uncomfortable) fashion of reclining on couches positioned around the serving tables. The custom demanded that one propped oneself up on the left arm, the right hand being left free for the food and the wine. They ate with their hands, the food having been cut into small manageable pieces before being served. Forks had to wait almost a thousand years yet before they were admitted to the dinner table. Spoons of various sizes were the only cutlery used by the diners.

The dinner, whether simple or elaborate, consisted of at least three courses: the *gustatio* or appetizers, the *primae mensae* or main course, and finally the *secundae mensae,* the dessert. Within each course a greater or lesser variety of dishes would be served, from which the diners chose according to their desire, 'buffet style'. Bread was the omnipresent accompaniment of the first two courses; often it served as a plate upon which to pile the meat or fish, or used instead of a spoon to soak up soup or sauce.

The *gustatio* often commenced with a sweet honeyed wine, the *mulsum.* There are various recipes in the ancient literature for its preparation, each proposing various but substantial quantities of honey to be dissolved in wine. A version produced by following a late Roman agricultural

A 2nd-century AD mosaic from a villa at Tor Marancia, Rome, shows fish, fowl and vegetables common in the Roman kitchen. Fruits, vegetables, eggs and fish, birds, animals and other commonly eaten foodstuffs were popular topics for domestic wall paintings and mosaics.

handbook, the *Geoponica,* by adding one part honey to four parts of dry white wine produces a very pleasant-tasting mead.

The first course, the appetizers, included various small bite-sized items such as eggs, snails, oysters and pieces of pickled fish, lettuce, sausage and the like. The main course again consisted of a variety of dishes, meat, fish and other seafood, porridge, pulses and vegetables. The dessert course, usually simple, included nuts, apples, pears or other types of fruit. More elaborate dinners offered honey-cakes and other sweetmeats.

For an understanding and appreciation of Roman cuisine, its tastes and aromas, its ingredients and preparation, we should turn to cookery books rather than rely on poetry and satire written by elite men, usually for the purpose of expressing distaste for the foibles of other elite men. There must have been all sorts of Roman cookery books; unfortunately, those who transmitted Latin literature to later ages did not deem them worthy of copying, with one exception, a collection of recipes under the name of Apicius, entitled *De re coquinaria* (On Things Pertaining to Cookery). Apicius was a famous gourmet who lived in the time of the Emperor Tiberius and about whom many fabulous anecdotes circulated. The cookery book attributed to him is actually a collection of over four hundred recipes from a wide variety of sources, combining recipes for the average households with some more luxurious ones. The language of the collection is late Vulgar Latin of the fourth or fifth century, when, in all likelihood, it was put together. The cookery book survives in two copies, both dating to the ninth century.

Scholarly opinions as to the cuisine that this collection reflects have ranged widely. On reading it, some claimed that the Romans had a 'destructive' cuisine, monstrous, extravagant and alien to modern sensibilities; a more charitable view regards it as a reflection of aristocratic luxury, on account of the many expensive ingredients the recipes call for, which, in their view, were unaffordable by most people, a problem to which I shall return below. Those, on the other hand, who having had some experience in the kitchen, and have attempted to reproduce the ancient recipes, often found them 'practical, good and even delightful'. There are many reasons for the lack of consensus; the most vexing problem is the fact that Apicius, or whoever wrote most of the recipes, did not bother to specify measurements or proportions for the ingredients, nor the order of their combination. There are few instructions for cooking methods or cooking times. Variations in any one of these would be expected to change the resulting product drastically. While many of the seasonings in the recipes are ancient versions of what we are familiar with today, a few of them have disappeared from the cuisine we are used to, and that adds to the problem.

The two most beloved seasonings, silphium and the infamous garum, the Romans inherited from the Greeks. Silphium was a fennel-like plant that grew wild in North Africa. Almost every part of the plant – the resin from the stalk, the dried and ground root and the

Arcesilas II, King of Cyrene, watching his workmen weighing bales of silphium, depicted on a Laconian cup from c. 565 BC. Silphium, a highly desired flavouring in Greek and Roman cuisine, was over-harvested and became extinct by the middle of the 1st century AD.

leaves – was used for seasoning. Whatever its taste was, it was highly desirable, for the Greek city Cyrenaica in North Africa, which collected it, became rich from trading it, a fact that was proudly advertised by the city's coins, which carried the picture of this plant. North African silphium apparently could not be domesticated despite the great demand for it. Its highly desired taste and possibly also the rumours about its powers as a contraceptive, caused it to be over-harvested and by the end of the first century AD it was extinct. The emperor Nero was said to have received the last Cyrenaican specimen. Thenceforth Roman cooks had to be satisfied with a somewhat inferior eastern substitute, the Parthian laser. It is believed that this substitute was asafoetida, derived from an Asian variety of the fennel family, which is still used today in Indian cuisine. Used in small amounts, asafoetida and, presumably, the ancient silphium, contributed a flavour similar to garlic, without garlic's lingering odour on the breath. Apicius uses silphium or laser in many savory dishes; garlic appears only once.

The other most common flavouring used by Roman chefs was fermented fish sauce, garum or liquamen. Anyone who has ever heard of Roman food must have shuddered with disgust upon learning that the Romans seasoned their food with rotten fish sauce. Despite the fact that it has been known for a long time that garum was made by salting fish and having it ferment with enzymatic and not bacterial action, and that this process and the resulting sauce is similar to the production of South Asian fish sauces used today, it is almost impossible to dismiss the claim that the Romans had a preference for the taste of rotting food.

Garum was produced in factories all over the Roman Empire. Methods for its production were described by agricultural writers. Like the South Asian fish sauces, garum varied in quality, taste, colour and, of course, in price. Fine-quality garum was like the modern Asian Nuoc Mam, a translucent golden-coloured liquid with a salty, nutty taste, subtle and aromatic with a hint of the sea; it has nothing to do with rotten fish.

The Roman cook worked with wood-burning hearths, charcoal-burning braziers, gridirons, earthenware or brick ovens, usually with very little control over the heat. The simplest oven, a portable device, the clibanos, turns up often in excavations. This is an overturned earthenware bowl under which fire is placed. When the floor under the fire and the bowl itself is hot enough then the bowl is lifted, the fire is raked out and the food to be baked is put in its place, the hot bowl is then replaced over the food and hot embers are piled around it. (I have seen the same device, a bowl, now made out of metal, used very effectively in a Bedouin tent in Israel. The camp fire was covered with an old tin washbowl and tasty flatbread was baked on the top of it.)

The cooking utensils found in the ancient kitchens are surprisingly similar to those we use today: long-handled frying pans, saucepans, cooking pots, small cauldrons, and the like, made from bronze and baked earthenware. Kitchenware collections in the archaeological evidence include bronze ladles, spoons and iron knives of varying sizes, cheese graters, strainers and the all-important ancient 'food-processor', the mortarium. Indeed, no Apician recipe can be reproduced without the mortar and the pestle. The ancient mortar was a heavy bowl with a rough interior to facilitate the grinding and mixing of ingredients by a wooden pestle, which was often topped by an iron head.

The collection named after Apicius suggests a sophisticated cuisine of many ingredients but not necessarily one that was beyond the means of average inhabitants of the empire. Some of the recipes may be fancy and expensive but many contain simple ingredients. What were the main ingredients of this ancient 'Mediterranean diet'? It may come as a surprise to some that all the foods that today are considered as characteristic of the area were unavailable to the Romans; there were no tomatoes, no potatoes, no green peppers, no aubergines, no oranges and, most surprising, no spaghetti or macaroni.

Even if pasta, in the shapes we know it today, entered the cuisine much later, the Roman diet was based on grain, as mentioned earlier. The cookery book confirms the central position of meat and fish in the diet. In addition to the four domestic quadrupeds, there are recipes for venison, boar, hare and dormice. Dormice, a small member of the squirrel family, were raised on farms in large quantities like farmyard fowl. They were fattened in earthenware containers that approximated their hibernating conditions. Not only muscle meat but almost all parts of the animals were cooked for food: head and trotters, heart, liver, testicles, tripe, udder, womb and even bone marrow. Blood,

Signboard for a well-stocked poulterer's shop from Ostia, AD 160–170. The shop is rich with merchandise, with cages under the counter, a wicker hamper and loaded baskets on top of it. Customers could bargain for live or slaughtered birds or other small animals for the table.

fat and scraps of meat were made up as sausages, stuffed into pigs' stomachs and intestines, and these were much enjoyed smoked and fried. Nothing was wasted. Roman cooking made use of a great variety of birds; in addition to the usual barnyard fowl, chicken, geese and ducks, often artificially fattened, there were also partridges and pheasants, turtledoves, pigeons, thrushes and fig-peckers, and some truly exotic winged creatures such as cranes, ostriches and flamingoes. Peacocks were much admired for their beauty as they ornamented private and public gardens, the less-attractive female of the species, if not kept for breeding, was fattened for the table of the rich. Fish seem to have been highly desired food and some fish may have been more expensive than meat. Oysters and mussels were farmed; sea urchins, octopus, squid, crayfish and prawns were available commonly, at least to coastal communities. Snails also were farmed and fattened on milk and bread-crumbs for the table.

Meat and seafood would be boiled and/or roasted, fried or baked. There was a variety of liquids available for marinades and as cooking media: oil, milk, wine, vinegar, garum and various combinations of these. Cane sugar was not known to the Romans, honey was their most important sweetener, together with various syrups obtained by boiling wine, must and various fruit juices in order to concentrate their sugar content. These decoctions added a pleasant complexity, more than just a sugary taste to food. In some cases they may have added dangerous poison also. The best way to prepare boiled-down must, according to the advice of experts, was to cook it in lead-lined vessels. The acid in the must would form lead acetate with the lead in the cooking pot. This is a white sugar-like crystal, which indeed tastes very sweet, but it is a dangerous poison.

Roman cooks, judging from the many remarks in the literature, seem to have concentrated their efforts on the seasoning of the food, in order to create a variety of tastes. Many different flavours could be achieved for a piece of roast meat with the addition of new sauces. The cookery book of Apicius lists a great number of sauces, causing, in large measure, the disapproval that the book receives. These sauces are claimed to be made up of exotic and expensive ingredients; with the aim of hiding the true nature of the food, and so on. A closer reading and attempts to reproduce the sauces could well prove the unfairness of the critics who read more carefully the satirical or moralizing literature of the Romans than their cookery book.

The ingredients that made up these 'wicked' sauces can be sorted roughly into four categories: spices, herbs, liquefiers and thickeners. The list of spices includes pepper, cumin, asafoetida root, seeds of celery, fennel, dill and rocket, dried berries of myrtle and laurel. Most of the fresh or dried herbs used for the sauces are commonly used flavourings even today: onions, shallots, leeks, coriander, cress, marjoram, oregano, savory, ginger and thyme. Some went out of culinary fashion, such as lovage, which was replaced by the similar but

The still life was highly appreciated as house decoration throughout the Roman Empire. This wall painting from Pompeii, of thrushes, a bowl of hen's eggs, and a wine jug with an elegant drinking cup, depicts the happy abundance of good things.

One of the many wall paintings found in the numerous taverns of Pompeii, depicting life in the establishment, a plebeian convivium in the Caupona on the Via di Mercurio. The streets of Pompeii were richly served with eating and drinking places, sixty of the ninety-six excavated street corners appear to have been occupied by bars and taverns.

milder tasting parsley or celery leaf. The bitter rue and catmint, pennyroyal and other more exotic members of the mint family, which were much appreciated by the Apician cook, do not seem to appeal to the modern palate.

The liquids that would be used in the sauces included garum, oil, vinegar or wine, honey or boiled-down must or fruit juice, mustard, stock, milk or water. To thicken sauces, the cook again had various choices: egg-whites or egg-yolks, wheat starch, ground pine kernels or crumbled pastry. Most of the sauces in the cookery book consist of ingredients from each of the four categories blended or cooked together; some have as few as three or four ingredients, while others may have eight or twelve. How much of each to use is not given. Some of the spices, such as pepper, may have been expensive because they

Relief depicting a greengrocer in his shop from Ostia, the old port of Rome. He seems to be selling cabbage, garlic, kale, leeks and onions. The wicker hamper under the trestle table may hold small birds, chickens or rabbits.

were imported, but a little of them usually went a long way. The other flavourings – herbs, seeds and berries – were abundant, many of them growing wild around the Mediterranean.

Were these sauces so exotic? Did they taste so strange? What did the most often used ingredients add to the overall flavour? The Romans loved pepper; it appears in most of the sauces. Next comes the fish sauce which contributed a salty taste with some depth of a nutty richness; add asafoetida with a flavour of mild garlic and lovage leaves with their taste reminiscent of celery and parsley. Salt, pepper, garlic and celery or parsley is not a very exotic combination for us; on the contrary, it is still the common basis of many savoury dishes today. The Romans seem to have preferred depth and complexity, flavours with many layers, combinations of peppery and pungent, sweet and peppery, and sweet and sour.

In addition to this varied and fine cuisine for the professional or home cooks there was a large variety of tavern fare, food and drink sold on the streets and even in and around the baths. Some upper-class writers sneered at the people who enjoyed tavern life and street food but, judging from the number of these establishments in the excavated parts of Pompeii, the people were not deterred by aristocratic disdain, they liked the food and the company, the plebeian convivium.

The Romans succeeded in building an empire that survived and resisted internal and external crises for over a thousand years. In the fifth century AD under increasing pressure of barbarian migrations the western part of it collapsed, while the eastern Roman Empire, much transformed, survived for another thousand years. The fall of Rome was accompanied by drastic changes in all aspects of life. The archaeological record for the early post-Roman centuries testifies to general impoverishment, significant reduction in population, production and trade, and in serious breakdown of communication. This, together with the rise of a new Christian ideology that aimed to focus attention on the soul and the afterlife while looking with disapproval on any concern with bodily enjoyment, caused significant changes in food customs and habits of daily life. While the Church claimed that the love of good food came dangerously close to the sin of gluttony, it was not, however, wholly successful in eradicating the enthusiasm for feasting. Through the early Christian centuries more and more feast days were introduced to relieve those of fasting; most of these were instituted to replace the enduringly popular pagan celebrations of the calendar. The ancient Romans bequeathed to posterity the appreciation of fine cuisine as the basis of civilized community life. This conviction, with the general outline of what a good meal should consist of, survived the collapse of the empire and often subverted the ascetical fasting culture that replaced it.

3 THE QUEST FOR PERFECT BALANCE

Taste and Gastronomy in Imperial China

Joanna Waley-Cohen

'Have you eaten?' This most common of daily greetings attests to the central position occupied in Chinese lives, now as in the past, by food and the whole range of activities surrounding it. These activities included the acquisition, preparation, presentation and consumption of food, often accompanied by intense discussion of every detail along the way. Indeed, few would argue with the proposition that Chinese culture ranks among the most keenly food-oriented in the world. This focus has sometimes been attributed to the prevalence in China until quite recently of terrible famine. Yet most observers now agree that generally Chinese people in the premodern period were fed reasonably well, perhaps even better than some of their counterparts elsewhere. The favourable impression made by the ordinary Chinese diet on foreign visitors, recorded centuries apart by such observers as the thirteenth-century Venetian merchant Marco Polo, and the nineteenth-century British plant-hunter Robert Fortune, lends support to this view. Thus hunger is not, or not the only, explanation for the strength of Chinese food culture.

The canonical classical texts that guided rulers since antiquity made popular welfare, which included ensuring that people had enough to eat, the principal goal of good government. Failure to attend to such fundamentals could provoke unrest, which in theory indicated an impending loss of the mandate of heaven and in practice often threatened a looming loss of power. At the same time, an interest in food that surpassed mere concern for sustenance was an integral feature of even ordinary people's lives, as we can tell from early folksongs wistfully contrasting daily fare with festival foods. For persons of refinement, an interest in and knowledge about food was from antiquity one of the essential attributes of the cultivated life, binding together gustatory and aesthetic taste. Thus, beyond food's immediate practical purposes, in different ways it has always played a significant part in Chinese political, social and cultural life.

Food also played a vital and varied role in the symbolic realm. Early texts governing the ritual behaviour around which Chinese society was organized paid enormous attention to the selection and preparation of

Previous page: Along with painting and poetry, an interest in and knowledge about gastronomy was one of the essential attributes of the cultivated life. Dinners and banquets were a routine part of social life, while every scenic outing, drinking party and poetry-society meeting tended to culminate in an elaborate repast served in beautiful surroundings. This painting is attributed to the 12th-century emperor Huizong of the Song dynasty.

Above: The figures from about AD 907–1125 are in a tomb at Xuanhua, Zhangjiakou, Hebei province. They were probably attendants intended to accompany the person buried in the tomb into the after-life, where the needs of the departed for nourishment were just as great as those of the living. Tomb decoration and burial objects of this kind often provide vital information about the practices of everyday life.

food, and to table manners, as well as to the appropriate alimentary offerings to be made to the ancestors, whose need for nourishment in the after-life was as great as that of the living. Those who adhered to the rituals counted as civilized, while those who did not ranked among the uncivilized or barbarian.

Further, early ritual texts associated cooking with civilization and established a cooking vessel, the *ding* or three-legged cauldron, as a symbol of the state. Thus civilized people were seen as 'cooked' while the uncivilized were defined as 'raw', characterizations that at the same time distinguished crucially between those who ate grains and refined their food by cooking it with fire, and those who neither ate grains nor used fire to cook their meat. This distinction between culture and nature, so clearly linking food practices to issues of identity, constituted a cultural version of 'you are what you eat' that retained its force at least into the late imperial period, when the degree of civilization of minority peoples within the empire still tended to be measured largely in terms of what they ate.

The early Chinese sense of cultural superiority rested on, among other justifications, the relative sophistication of its system of government in comparison with that of the neighbouring peoples. By association, cooking itself served as a useful metaphor for government – useful not only because it referred to an everyday activity and hence

The set of nesting wine or food cups with their own container, inscribed with characters indicating their intended usage, capacity or ownership, were buried so that their wealthy owners would find sustenance in the afterlife. Archaeologists found the remains of food – fish and pheasant bones and wheat – when they excavated this 2000-year-old tomb in 1972.

Early ritual texts associated cooking with civilization and established a cooking vessel, the three-legged *ding*, as the symbol of the state. Moreover, cooking often served as a metaphor for government, so that culinary talents, broadly conceived, were regarded as an apt qualification for ministerial office. This vessel dates from the 3rd or 4th century BC.

was readily comprehensible, but also because it seemed peculiarly apt. Thus in the fourth century BC the early Daoist text *Dao De Jing,* attributed to Laozi, claimed that 'Governing the country is in principle like cooking a small fish', meaning that great care and attention were in both cases essential. Indeed, culinary skills were thought to constitute a fine qualification for ministerial appointment. Perhaps the earliest of those who thus gained office was Yi Yin, who in the second millennium BC became prime minister of King Tang of the Shang dynasty. According to legend, Yi Yin was a foundling whose foster parents taught him to cook. His culinary skills brought him to the king's attention, and in his first audience he transformed the greatest philosophical issues of governance into a menu of foods to be coveted. Among other things, Yi Yin likened the whole world to a kitchen in which one prepares food, and proper government to good cooking. Just as in cooking it was necessary to understand flavours to blend them successfully; so in governing it was necessary to grasp people's sufferings and aspirations in order to satisfy their needs.

Yi Yin also laid out what became a classically influential culinary theory. He classified animal foods, for example, as falling into one of three categories: fishy, rank or 'muttony', depending on whether the creature involved had lived in water or had been carnivorous or herbivorous. All needed transformation by cooking in order to become pleasant to eat. Having once identified the correct category, the cook could select the most appropriate cooking methods for dispelling odour and producing delicious dishes, adding seasoning to achieve a balanced taste that was 'not excessively sweet or sour, lightly flavoured but not tasteless, tasting of fat but not greasy in the mouth', and so on. Many of Yi Yin's categories remain current today.

In general terms, the main characteristics of Chinese food culture were as follows. First, Chinese cuisine had at least the potential to be extremely varied. In the case of ordinary people this was mainly due to the fact that in a cuisine that rested on the infinite permutations of ingredients and seasonings, a huge variety of combinations was possible, although of course in practice poverty often sharply restricted choices. Moreover, for the most part potential ingredients were not limited by religious taboos, although one cannot discount the influence of Buddhist-inspired vegetarianism. For the elite, the range of combinations was even greater than those available to ordinary people because of the much broader pool of potential resources. And as Chinese-controlled territory expanded over the centuries, more and different foods became available, although access at first remained quite local. Besides, by no later than the Song dynasty (960–1279), increased agricultural output

combined with greater commercialization, expanding inter-regional trade and increasingly effective ways of preventing spoilage to make an enormous difference. Along with urban growth, these factors both made it possible to move beyond shaping one's diet to accommodate only immediately accessible ingredients and created the conditions for the development of a market in luxury foods.

In addition, China's age-old connections to other parts of the world, particularly in Central and Southeast Asia, led to a steady influx of imported foodstuffs, which sooner or later became incorporated into the repertory of possible ingredients. In some cases this involved such luxury items as birds' nests and sea cucumbers but imports also included such New World imports as peanuts and the sweet potato, subsistence crops that would grow where nothing else could be cultivated and hence could enlarge the food supply. Also derived from abroad was the taste for certain types of foods that could, however, be produced at home, such as yogurt and other milk products popular among Central Asians. Such foods sometimes fell out of favour for political reasons (e.g., because of association with the Mongols), but not because of any absolute Chinese distaste for dairy products. Thus a second major characteristic of Chinese food culture was that imports affected cuisine at every level and, as a corollary, what constituted 'Chinese cuisine' changed constantly.

Finally, but no less significant, diet was closely linked to health. This meant that eating properly – choosing the right ingredients and combining them in appropriate ways – was seen as the most reliable path to good health and longevity. This view gave rise to an extensive literature of nutrition and dietetics, which itself formed part of a much wider textual corpus covering everything to do with the production and consumption of food. It was also closely connected to classical ideals of frugality, moderation and balance.

To understand the context in which these characteristics took shape, we turn to a consideration of the position of gastronomy in the larger scope of Chinese philosophical thinking about the nurturing of the physical and mental aspects of human life. As we will see, these ideas remained important in Chinese food culture even as the pursuit of pleasure in eating became more prominent.

The period from approximately the fifth to the third centuries BC saw a revolution of ideas in China according to which, despite a lack of consensus as to whether human nature was originally good or bad, thinkers generally agreed that humans were capable of perfecting themselves. From this emerged a devotion to self-cultivation, whose ultimate purpose was, precisely, the attainment of perfection, or sage-hood. In conformity with a broad understanding that everything within the cosmos was interconnected, no sharp separation was seen between the mind and the body. Thus nurturing the body was just as important as the quest for intellectual and spiritual perfection. They were all part of an organic whole in which nothing functioned in

isolation. The close relationship between food and health also derived from this understanding, as did a more general view of the interconnectedness of the material and moral worlds.

From these notions it is easy to understand how gastronomy, in the sense of an intimate understanding of the properties of food and a quest to achieve perfect balance in one's physical intake, as well as the pursuit of gourmet pleasures, became an important branch of self-cultivation. In short, it was thought that eating right, understood as essential to physical wellbeing, formed one part of the way to moral propriety, and that neither could exist without the other. Regulating one's food intake to prevent or cure corruption of the body was a moral duty, therefore, not just something to be done for the sake of pleasure. Such considerations were, of course, infinitely more relevant to members of the educated upper classes than to the vast majority of people living at or near subsistence level, but it is likely that on some level these ideas impinged on most people's consciousness.

In this context, the Chinese by no means frowned on deriving pleasure from eating – to the contrary, the ideal attitude was an appreciation of food's qualities, broadly conceived, combined with a grateful awareness of the labour that had gone into its production. Gluttony, on the other hand, tended to meet with strong disapproval. While Chinese beliefs lacked an equivalent of the Christian-inspired seven deadly sins, which included gluttony, excessive eating clearly ran counter to Chinese ideals of frugality. Of course, frugality was a virtue often born of necessity, but it also constituted an important manifestation of the overall preference for balance and against excess in all matters. A number of seminal thinkers, including Confucius and his follower Mencius, enunciated these principles in their teachings and practice, asserting the authority of the ancient sage-kings for the rule that one should eat only when hungry and then only to satisfy one's needs, as those paragons had done. Confucius, for instance, was said to have eaten only sparingly – pleasure in eating does not feature much in his writings – while, in what became a cliché notable for its linking, once again, of food and government, Mencius and others criticized the ruler who enjoyed a banquet in his palace while outside in the streets people were starving to death.

It was often said that bad people counted gluttony among their failings or that they were brought to badness by gluttony. Some such tales involved luxury-loving rulers and their ministers, such as the stereotypically bad last minister of the Song dynasty, said to have hoarded vast quantities of sugar and pepper, and one Wang Fu, who was accused of possessing three larders full of pickled orioles. Other stories of gluttony surfaced in the folklore surrounding the stove god, the symbolic core of the family whose image adorned virtually every kitchen. The stove god was more often male than female, although tales of women gone to the bad through gluttony, or of gluttony as an indication of poor character, do exist.

Many accounts of the stove god's origin involve gluttony in one form or another, often with the theme of compelling a glutton forever to watch others enjoying food to which he no longer had access. In one such tale, a woman created the stove god by vanquishing a gluttonous king. In another, the stove god was originally an official who compelled every household in his jurisdiction to prepare a banquet for the enjoyment of his entourage, on pain of death. Eventually – not before the official's waistline had noticeably expanded, suggesting an association of plumpness with moral turpitude – a strongman rebelled and locked the official into a wall behind the stove. Nonetheless, in the end, in recognition of the official's talents as an imperial cook, the emperor decreed that he should be deified as the stove god.

Condemnations of gluttony competed with a strong inclination among the elite towards enjoyment of the good things to which their elevated social position seemed to entitle them, including good food. This attitude originated in the ritually reinforced distinctions between social classes. It contributed to the ranking of gastronomy among the arts of the cultivated gentleman, along with knowledge of painting and

Stories about the origins of the kitchen god often suggested that he had once been a glutton and was now condemned forever to watch others eat without being able to do so himself. As his image adorned virtually every kitchen, there was always a risk that he would report unfavourably on a family's behaviour to the celestial authorities.

poetry. From there it is easy to grasp how it was that poetic celebrations of epicurean pleasures and artistic depictions of favourite foods formed a coherent whole with scholar-gourmets' poetry and paintings. The Song poet and statesman Su Dongpo (Su Shi, 1036–1101) is a venerable example. His writings are full of references to the pleasures of food (or sometimes its absence), and he is credited with at least one dish named after him – 'Dongpo Pork'. In other words, the appreciation of food was understood as quite distinct from mere greediness.

This distinction remained in place at least through the late imperial period, when a number of sources celebrate enthusiasm for food and the eating binges that sometimes accompanied it, displaying a marked disinclination to denounce such pleasures. The early seventeenth-century writer Zhang Dai (1597–?1684), for instance, writing nostalgically of pleasures in better times, describes his father and uncles greedily vying to devour all the food at a family banquet. We will hear more of Zhang Dai's gourmet pursuits below. In similar vein, more than one later author included in his jottings accounts of men known for their unusual capacity for food. Thus, for example, the early nineteenth-century connoisseur Liang Zhangju recorded that,

> In the Qianlong era [1736–99] the top eater was Cao Wen'ge
> of Xinjian…people said that the skin of Wen'ge's stomach

was loose, and that he had to fold it over once or twice, and when he was full he would let out another fold. Whenever the emperor had meat to bestow, he would permit each of the princes, lords and great officials, to bring out a leg of mutton and give it all to Wen'ge, so that it filled up his sedan chair. Wen'ge would slice it up with a knife and eat it, and by the time he got home all the meat would be gone.

Cao Wen'ge's gorging of meat also smacked of reckless inattention to a diet that properly balanced meat and vegetables with such staples as rice and other grains. This departure from first culinary principles suggests that in later periods pleasure in food may sometimes have prevailed over concerns about self-cultivation.

***

Different varieties of rice, both dry- and paddy-grown, glutinous and non-glutinous, formed part of the Chinese diet from earliest times. As transportation networks improved after the 11th century, rice became widely available even in the north, where it competed with wheat and millet. Many wines were made from rice and other grains, partly using imported techniques learned from grape-wine manufacture.

The most fundamental principle underlying Chinese cuisine, and its most distinctive characteristic, is the *fan-cai* principle, which divides all foods into two categories. *Fan* literally denotes rice, but in this context encompasses all grains and such other carbohydrate foods as bread and noodles. Its purpose is to fill up the eater. *Cai* denotes the dishes made to flavour the *fan*, and is of secondary importance. All Chinese meals consist of different combinations of *fan* and *cai*. Of Confucius it was respectfully said that: 'Though there might be a large quantity of meat, he would not allow what he took to exceed the due proportion for the grain.'

Cutting skills are absolutely essential to the culinary process, so that dexterity with the knife carries considerable prestige. There are well over one hundred different ways to cut up food in Chinese cuisine, although generally all the ingredients in a single dish are cut up in the same way. The pottery tomb relief from which this rubbing of kitchen preparations was taken is from the period AD 25–220.

A serving of food without *fan*, such as a snack of fruit or dried fish, is not considered a proper meal. For the poor, not surprisingly, meals generally consisted primarily of *fan* with minimal *cai* as seasoning or garnish, while further up the economic scale the proportion of *cai* increased until, among the wealthy, dishes of different vegetables and meat constituted the main part of the meal, culminating with a bowl of rice served either to clean the palate or to 'fill up the cracks'. In such circumstances, to eat *fan* at the end of the meal could amount to a rude suggestion that the *cai* offered had been inadequate. These general principles have retained some of their force down to the present.

The essence of Chinese cuisine has long been the creative combination of different forms of *fan* and *cai*. This was not so much a case of 'you are what you eat' as 'you are how you prepare and serve what you eat.' When Chinese cooks combined *fan* with different vegetables and meats prepared and cooked in different ways – sliced, chopped or minced and then boiled, braised, or stewed, stir-fried or dry-fried, and so on, with more than one method sometimes applied to a single dish – they were able to create a diet that was almost infinite in its variety. In this way, the universal application of the *fan-cai* principle conformed to the modular approach to aesthetic production found in, for instance, the mass production in terracotta of slightly varied human figures for the tombs of the first emperor of Qin in Xi'an. This similarity underscores the ranking of gastronomy among the fine arts.

Beyond the *fan-cai* principle, much of the thinking underlying Chinese cuisine related directly to medical knowledge and concepts of health and the human body, which themselves derived from traditional notions of the cosmos. An important aspect of the view that everything was connected to everything else was the idea that the human body itself was a microcosm of the cosmos, and that both were animated by energy, or *qi*. In the case of the human body, that energy, which took different forms, resided in varying amounts in food. The goal in eating – the foundation of proper nutrition – is to achieve and maintain a perfect equilibrium between strengthening and weakening foods. This is achieved by balancing *yin* and *yang* forces within the body, *yin* and *yang* being the basic elements into which the cosmos is divided. These terms originally denoted the shady and sunny side of a hill, respectively. By extension, *yin* stands for what is cool (or cooling), dark and moist, and generally associated with female qualities, while *yang* represents what is hot (or heating), bright and dry, qualities generally regarded as male. These were not regarded as diametrical opposites but as complementary poles on either end of a spectrum on which any given item of food (or anything else) would be rather more *yin* or rather more *yang*, rather than categorically one or the other. Foods were divided into cooling and heating types according to their effect on the body – not the temperature at which they were served – with, for instance, green vegetables and such water-dwelling creatures as crabs ranking among cooling foods, and fatty foods, hot peppers and

The foundation of proper nutrition is to balance *yin* and *yang* forces within the body, *yin* and *yang* being the basic elements into which the cosmos is divided. This is done by classifying foods as more cooling (*yin*) or heating (*yang*). These ideas resonated with humoral theories similar to or derived from those known in the West. In the painting on silk from the Qing dynasty, two sages study the *yin-yang* symbol.

chicken soup ranking among heating foods, although the properties of individual foods were not fixed.

These early ideas about cooling and heating foods received further reinforcement and elaboration with the introduction in the early sixth century of the humoral system. According to this theory, the human body was affected by heat and cold, and to a lesser extent by wetness and dryness, and balance was essential to wellbeing. The humoral system may have reached China from the Western world as a consequence of the spread of Buddhism, or may have arisen independently; at any rate, its resonance with the *yin-yang* idea undoubtedly helped it take root in China. It was widely adopted and had an enormous effect on ideas about nutrition; in addition, those responsible for diet and health now sought ways to combine it with another important Chinese classification system – the linkage of items in a particular category into groups of five.

The primary such group divided the cosmos into five successive phases generated by *yin* and *yang*, namely, wood, fire, earth, metal and water. Those phases formed part of a comprehensive system of correspondences in groups of five; each group had its counterpart in every other group. The one most directly connected to food was the five flavours, that is, acidic or sour, as in vinegar; bitter, as in bitter melon and apricot kernels; sweet, as in honey and, later, sugar; pungent, as in ginger and garlic; and salty, as in salt and, later, soy sauce. Closely related were the five viscera, namely spleen, lungs, heart, liver and kidney, whose wellbeing depended on proper nutrition; their relationship to the five flavours affected the understanding of a particular medicine's properties.

Other groupings of five included cereals, namely rice, wheat, soy, glutinous and non-glutinous millet; domestic animals, namely cows, sheep, pigs, chickens and dogs; and any number of others such as seasons, cardinal directions (including centre), colours, social relations and so on. The acknowledged interrelationship between all these groups of five and their individual elements meant, among other things, that reference to one group or one individual element in a group had broader implications. As Su Dongpo observed:

> Salty and sour, both are part of what we enjoy;
> But the centre harbours the supreme flavour,
> one that never fades away.

Finally, on the subject of health and hygiene, it is noteworthy that freshness and cleanliness has always played a central role in Chinese cuisine. Confucius, who notwithstanding his canonical status preferred to call himself a transmitter of existing ideas rather than an original thinker, was famously fastidious about what he would and would not eat, and in terms of modern hygiene his principles seem eminently sensible:

Food and food culture became a defining characteristic of city life in Song China. Both memoirs and artistic depictions, such as this scroll, probably partly factual and partly idealized, devote much attention to the pleasures of different kinds of public eating establishments, ranging from simple stalls in the street selling single types of food to large-scale restaurants of various kinds.

He did not eat rice which had been damaged by heat
or damp and turned sour, nor fish or flesh which was gone.
He did not eat what was discoloured, or what was of a
bad flavour, nor anything which was ill-cooked or was
not in season.

**

The remainder of this chapter focuses on questions of gastronomy and taste from the thirteenth to the nineteenth century, a span of time in which China is variously considered to have shown both late imperial and early modern characteristics, depending on the criteria used. Scholarly opinion varies on the question of when China's early modern age may be said to have begun. Most historians, however, would agree that in the last millennium China saw three major periods of what we would recognize as large-scale consumerism, a trait associated with modernity in the West. These periods were the southern Song (1127–1279); the late Ming (*c.* 1550–1644); and the latter part of the eighteenth century, which marked the turning point in the fortunes of the Manchu Qing dynasty (1636–1912). In each period the consumerist phenomenon involved food as well as a broad spectrum of other goods and manufactures.

In 1127, northern invaders forced the Song court to move its capital from Kaifeng in Henan province to the port of Hangzhou, south of the Yangzi river. During the Song, two linked transformations took place, in agriculture and in commerce. Cultivators increasingly moved beyond self-sufficiency, growing cash crops as well as diversifying into producing handicrafts and weaving textiles. They sold these at market and bought food with the proceeds, often using money instead of a system of direct exchange. In consequence, a market for certain goods developed on a national scale. The effects of these transformations were far-reaching. For our purposes, the important point is that much more food, especially rice, became available, and that the variety of foods was enormously increased. This was partly because of the commercialization of agriculture, partly because of imports, and partly because such hitherto limited crops as tea and sugar entered into general use, making everyday commodities out of what once had been luxuries. More people than ever before moved into employment other than food production, giving rise to a new merchant class. Foodstuffs moved with other goods along inter-regional trade routes and were sold at periodic markets in centres both large and small.

These developments contributed to the growth of large cities whose inhabitants – from workers and artisans to merchants, scholars and officials – bought their food at market stalls, in teahouses, wineshops and large-scale restaurants, some of which were capable of serving hundreds of people at a single sitting. Thus public eating establishments arose in China at a relatively early stage in comparison with, say, France, helping to normalize the idea of eating outside the home. None of the descriptions and memoirs of life in Hangzhou (the southern capital) that have come down to us fails to mention the huge variety and deliciousness of the food available, sometimes in great detail, while much of the poetry of the era dwells on the same topics, signifying unmistakably the pivotal role of food and food culture in the self-identification of the era.

The inland early-Song capital of Kaifeng was already known for its southern-style restaurants that kept gourmets supplied with fresh-water fish and seafood in pristine condition and with rice brought up from the south, in addition to those that provided such more usual northern foods as red meats, poultry and wheat noodles. The trend towards restaurant specialization and the importation of delicacies from afar increased once the capital moved south to Hangzhou, because it became a city not only of sophisticated residents and sojourning traders but also of refugees from all over, unable to return home. Restaurants appealing to regional tastes, and to such special dietary groups as Muslims, proliferated at both the luxury and more popular levels, while still others specialized in particular kinds of dishes, as we know from a reminiscence of the first half of the thirteenth century written in 1275, just before the Mongol invasion:

> Formerly...the best-known specialties were the sweet soy soup at the Mixed-Wares Market, pig cooked in ashes in front of the Longevity-and-Compassion Palace, Mother Song's fish soup and rice served with mutton. Later...there were the boiled pork from Wei-the-Big-Knife at the Cat Bridge and the honey fritters from Zhou-Number Five in front of the Five-span Pavilion.

Of 'Mother Song' it was said that she had once worked for a rich house-hold in Kaifeng and had moved south with other refugees. Finding others who shared her nostalgia for home cooking, she figured out how to reproduce her specialty fish soup in Hangzhou, using local carp, and sold it at a stall in the marketplace with such success – apparently it smelled irresistible – that the emperor heard about it and became one of her patrons. Although a majority of chefs and restaurateurs were male, she was only one of a number of Song-period women of whose food expertise we know. Another authored a collection of recipes from the Shanghai area and Zhejiang province (in which Hangzhou is located), entitled *Zhongkui Lu* (Records of Home Cooking), one of the earliest collections of recipes to be published independent of agricultural or dietary guidelines. New printing technology meant that at least in theory anyone could buy and read this work; although we do not know the extent to which it did in fact circulate, a number of later collections drew heavily on some of its otherwise lost recipes.

祭神

一年農事週民庶皆安逸歌謠
遍社村共享昇平世五風君德
生十雨蒼天濟當年后稷神留
與後人祭

欽天監五官臣焦秉貞畫
鴻臚寺序班臣朱圭鐫

The state promoted agriculture by encouraging the composition and dissemination of treatises such as the *Gengzhi tu* (Agriculture and Sericulture Illustrated), a series of twenty pictures each on the cultivation of rice and silk, accompanied by an appropriate poem. Qing emperors, including Qianlong, appended their own poems and had the work reprinted several times.

In the late thirteenth century the Song were destroyed by the Mongols, who made China under the Yuan dynasty the easternmost part of a vast transcontinental empire within which ideas and goods, including foodstuffs, travelled freely. Under the Yuan there was, broadly, a distinction between the cuisines of the north-west, which were strongly affected by the Muslim-influenced food cultures of Central Asia, and the south and east, which remained relatively free of these influences.

We turn now to the late sixteenth century, the next major period of consumerism, when the Ming who had succeeded the Mongols in 1368 were already entering the declining years of their dynasty. Late-Ming China's unprecedented agricultural prosperity and thriving regional and national markets gave at least the lower Yangzi region a superficial resemblance to Hangzhou under the southern Song, with widespread commercialization and urbanization. But Ming China was not under siege as the Song had been three hundred years earlier, and moreover it was tightly integrated into the developing global economy, not least because silver from the New World and Japan had become a leading commodity just at the moment when the Chinese economy was becoming increasingly dependent upon it. As important in terms of the Chinese diet were such New World imports as maize, sweet potatoes, peanuts, potatoes, chilli peppers and tomatoes, all of which reached China around this time.

Late-Ming China also boasted a burgeoning consumer culture that bestowed enormous prestige upon the possession and enjoyment of material goods, encouraging a new market in luxuries. In this hedonistic atmosphere, not only was collecting all the rage, but the scope of what one might collect continually expanded, until both expert knowledge and eventually taste itself became marketable commodities. At much the same time, the exponential growth of printing and publishing provided further momentum for these developments by making it possible to inform a much wider public about the aesthetic and other possibilities open to them.

A Ming dynasty wine jar from the Jiajing period (1522–66). Both wine made from grapes and the technology for making it were imported into China but more commonly Chinese wines were made of grains such as millet and rice. Drinking games were popular forms of entertainment among the elite, with the loser of each round draining his glass; descriptions abound of drunken parties.

The late-Ming commodification of taste, together with the commercialization that made more luxury goods available, prompted a resurgence of interest in gastronomy, in which gustatory and aesthetic taste came together in ways that, because of the still strong connections of nutrition to both health and self-cultivation, could still be framed as morally acceptable despite a primary focus on pleasure. That possibility was particularly inviting to those members of the elite disquieted by the realization that the cultivation and taste upon which their class reputation and identity largely rested was available potentially to anyone with money to pay for it. But for many, the interest in good food and drink simply harmonized with the pleasurable fashions of the age and had very little to do with anything but pure self-indulgence.

In Chinese cuisine the flavour and consistency of freshwater fish is considered superior to that of seafood. According to legend, the Kangxi emperor (1662–1722) once stopped for dinner at a simple inn when he was travelling to the south. Entranced by the subtlety of a fish dish he was served, he renamed it 'Palace Gate Fragrant Fish'. This Ming dynasty bowl dates from about 1600.

The writings of three late-Ming authors serve to give some sense of the epicurean life of the period, both in terms of food itself and in terms of the ways in which such men both shared and perpetuated their pleasures and their knowledge by writing about or, in some instances, painting them. Certainly, partaking of food and drink was customary at every social gathering, at some of which, not surprisingly, gastronomy itself was the *raison d'être*. These three authors are Gao Lian, whose prescription for elegant living included lengthy discourses on food and drink; Xu Wei (1521–93), a well-known oil painter and poet whose work is full of references to food, and Zhang Dai, a survivor of the Ming-Qing dynastic transition whose nostalgic reminiscence of the pleasures of life under the Ming abound with descriptions of gastronomic delights. I have selected these particular writers among many possibilities because each represents a different variation on the themes outlined above, in order to give an overview of the gastronomic culture of the time.

All three authors lived in and around the prosperous lower Yangzi region of Jiangnan, which included rich farmland and the great cities of Nanjing, Suzhou, Yangzhou and Hangzhou, centres among other things of a thriving textile industry. In many ways this region's wealth and power rivalled those of the political capital, Beijing, and its material prosperity and cultural efflorescence made it the epicentre of elite social and cultural life. While Jiangnan cannot be taken as typical of the whole of China, there is no doubt that both in contemporary perceptions and in retrospect it served as the repository for the very essence of Chinese elite culture. From a gastronomic point of view, the cuisine of Jiangnan and especially Suzhou, best known for its aquatic fare, became particularly fashionable after prime minister Zhang Juzheng (1525–82), in transit, lavished his praises upon it. A number of contemporary accounts testify that Suzhou chefs and Suzhou dishes became extremely popular at this time, both in elite kitchens of the region and in Beijing.

The first of the three, Gao Lian, a sixteenth-century figure whose precise dates are uncertain, was in many ways the most influential. Gao's social status was ambiguous in that he was both a scholar whose accomplishments made him acceptable to the cultural elite and a successful merchant whose family was known for its patronage and philanthropy. He may have been employed at one time at the imperial banqueting hall. At a time of increasing eclecticism in intellectual and ideological life, Gao was a Daoist who lived in retirement in the city of Hangzhou and devoted his energies to questions of health and longevity. In harmony with a general trend towards articulating standards of good taste, Gao's *Ya Shang Zhai Zun Sheng Ba Jian* (Eight Discourses on the Art of Living from the Studio Where Elegance is Valued) was a work of connoisseurship suggesting ways in which one might perfect both one's material surroundings and one's metaphysical existence. Of its eight main sections, one was devoted to ways of prolonging life and avoiding illness, one to medicine, and one to food and drink. The latter occupied three of the nineteen chapters of the complete work and drew on the recipes of the Song *Zhongkui Lu,* referred to above, among other more recent culinary texts. It was reprinted several times in the thirty years following its initial publication in 1591, indicating that the information it offered was greatly in demand.

Gao discussed, among other things, tea and the best spring-waters with which to make it; soups and broths; grains; noodles; wild and domestic vegetables; preserved meats; sweets; fruits; brewing; medicinal recipes; and the relationship of spiritual matters to food. Noting that he has avoided discussion of fancy foods, which he regarded as unsuited for those such as himself who seek to lead a frugal and quiet life, Gao launched his discourse on food and drink with the following salvo in favour of moderation and healthy eating, identifying the connections between proper eating on the one hand and physical and moral strength on the other:

> Nutrition is the essential factor sustaining human life. It is through this means that, within a single person, *yin* and *yang* come into play and the five phases succeed one another (in proper order). Since everything depends on nutrition, once that is delivered [in the appropriate combination] then the stomach's vital force is complete, then the body's energies can flourish and so the bones and sinews are at [full] strength.

Yet Gao also reproduced mouth-watering descriptions of certain delicacies, showing he had not relinquished a fondness for good food. Thus he echoed, among others, Song poet-gourmet Su Dongpo's poem 'Old Gourmet':

> …taste the finest meat from a pig's neck, a crab [in autumn] just before frost, cherries simmered in honey… lamb steamed in almond milk. Clams half done then steeped in wine, under-cooked crabs soaked in wine…

The dual concern with the palate and with nutrition and longevity made Gao's work very compelling. But its appeal had a further dimension. By embedding a discussion of food within a work avowedly devoted to connoisseurship and good taste, Gao achieved another, more subtle goal. He expressly placed food and drink among those objects whose connoisseurship was essential for the person of refinement, underscoring his point by claiming the authority of Su Dongpo and Huang Tingjian (1045–1105) – one a poet-gourmet, the other a famous calligrapher who had written a short work on nutrition. In addition, by thus setting out rules of good taste, not least by the elision of gustatory and aesthetic taste, he pointed the way forward, for anyone capable of reading his book and following his prescriptions, to attain the level of cultural sophistication to which his work as a whole staked a claim. It was at once a claim for exclusivity and a blurring of the boundaries through commodification, and it bore little relation to eating to satisfy hunger.

As we will see, at least some of the delicacies Gao mentioned, such as autumn freshwater crabs, make such regular appearances in later culinary and gourmet texts as to suggest that he was quite successful in establishing certain benchmarks of good taste – it may, of course, merely demonstrate that he actually did have good taste and that the crabs were, simply, delicious. And he may have been following the prescriptions of others: compilations of lore about crabs, among other delicacies, were a longstanding literary genre. At any rate, as the authors of the great eighteenth-century imperial bibliography, among others, would note, Gao's work both launched and set the tone for what has been called a gastronomic movement among Chinese men of leisure.

For many, the question was not only what represented the acme of good taste, but what they could afford. Every scenic outing, drinking party and poetry-society meeting seemed to culminate in an extravagant picnic, sometimes cooked on the spot by the host's own cook. Contemporaries observed that, along with the fashion for leisure touring, lavish banquets, expensive restaurants and indulgence in pricey delicacies increasingly were becoming a hallmark of elite life in the late Ming. Not surprisingly, this dilemma troubled many less affluent aspirants to the good life, among whom was the well-known artist-poet Xu Wei.

Both Xu Wei's paintings and his poetry reveal a strong interest in food. Xu often exchanged his work for rare and expensive foods that he could not otherwise afford, in a system of exchange that was not

Food in Chinese culture can suggest more than just gastronomy. A plate of porcelain delicacies from the Qianlong period cleverly suggests, through a series of puns, a wish for many successful sons. The character for 'seed' is the same as that for sons, so the pomegranate implies fruitfulness; that for the crab's hard shell is the same as that denoting the ranks in the highest level of civil-service examinations, and so on.

uncommon but seems to have been particularly pronounced in Xu's case. Thus, for example, in return for a gift of bamboo shoots from a military official on the northern frontier he produced a painting of bamboo:

> I made a meal of soup with carp and grain
> I rack my brains wanting to respond but with difficulty
> All I can do is cut up a visiting card
> Sketch bamboo to match [your] spring dish.

Later he did another, similar, bamboo painting for the same official, noting that he hoped 'in jest' it would serve as a reminder of the earlier gift, perhaps prompting more bounty. Thus some of Xu's food paintings – which also included crabs, fish, grapes, pears and other fruit – were not reciprocations for gifts already received but were done either in hopes of provoking such a gift, or simply to find a way to obtain seasonal delicacies beyond his means:

> At night by my window, guests and hosts talk
> It's autumn on the river and the crabs and the fish are fat
> I don't have the money to buy crabs to go with the wine
> I think I'll paint something to pay for it.

Xu also composed poems celebrating many different foods, including some of the recent imports from the New World, then still something of a novelty.

In the first decades of the seventeenth century the veneer of Ming prosperity began to wear thin. The dynasty fell prey to political factionalism, whose destructive effects were compounded by a series of natural catastrophes. In 1644, peasant rebels brought down the dynasty and occupied Beijing. Shortly afterwards, Manchu invaders from the north-east overcame the rebels, going on over the next few years to conquer the rest of China. The Jiangnan region, once the intellectual, cultural and economic hub of the empire as well as its gastronomic heart, was particularly hard hit because the new rulers, the Qing, understood full well the need to crush Chinese elite opposition at its very core. A ten-days' massacre in the city of Yangzhou was only the worst of many such episodes in the wars of dynastic transition, in which many people lost everything, if not their lives.

A well-known *bon vivant* of the late Ming who survived into the Qing was the essayist Zhang Dai, once conspicuous for his ubiquitous presence at social occasions and for his extravagant way of life. After the transition, Zhang was reduced to poverty and often went hungry. His poignant and detailed memoir of his earlier life was almost all that remained to sustain him. It consisted of a series of anecdotes and vignettes, many of which describe Zhang's former life in which, as he put it, he 'painstakingly researched the daily pleasures of the mouth and stomach'.

In one of his most evocative descriptions, Zhang recorded in loving detail the pleasures of a crab club that he and his friends had formed each year expressly for the purpose of gathering to enjoy river crabs during their short autumn season. There is no reason to suppose that the crab club existed only in his imagination, and we may speculate that it was not unique. After asserting that crabs, along with another local delicacy, blood clams, naturally combine the five flavours without needing seasoning, Zhang continued:

> Their shells, as big as a serving-dish, curve up, while their purple claws are as big as a fist. The flesh that comes out of their little claws is glossy like an earthworm. The open shell is full of unctuous 'meat', holding together in jade-like fingers and amber morsels. It is a sweet and velvet-smooth dish to which even the 'eight most delicious foods' cannot compare. As soon as October comes around, I get together of an afternoon with my friends in the Crab Club to cook the crabs for ourselves. We plan on eating six apiece, but for fear that if they get cold they will lose their flavour, we cook them as we go along. For side dishes we have plump salted and dried duck, junket, blood clams steeped in wine like amber pearls, and cabbage cooked in duck juices like slabs of jade. For fruit we had mandarins, and dried chestnuts and caltrops; for drink, Yuhubing wine; for vegetables, Bingkang bamboo shoots; for rice, new harvest white rice from Yuhang. Finally, to rinse the mouth, Snow-Orchid tea When I think of it today, it is really as though we had tasted the offerings of the immortals come from the

A silk handscroll of the 16th or 17th centuries depicts a scene entitled *Whiling the Summer Away*. Leisure touring became increasingly popular in the late imperial period, and might well involve female companionship. Most entertainers were trained in music and dance but some young women also included culinary skills among the range of services they offered potential clients.

celestial kitchens, reaching the point of total satiation and intoxication.

Zhang reverts several times to the topic of 'Snow-Orchid tea', a tea he named himself in tribute to its piquant taste, greenish colour and delicate aroma. He recalls a particular teahouse in his hometown, Shaoxing, where he thought the best Snow-Orchid tea was served. He attributed this to the teahouse's exacting standards: they would infuse the tea only in water drawn from a particular spring and only when the water had just come to the boil, serving it only in a pot that was always kept scrupulously clean by being washed after every use, a comment that suggests that such was not always the case. Other vignettes relating to tea show connoisseurs competing not only to guess what kind of tea they were drinking but to demonstrate the sensitivity of their palate and sophistication of their knowledge by identifying the spring from which the water had been drawn. One is vividly reminded of upper-class Englishmen, centuries later, competing to identify the vintage of a bottle of port and even its shippers.

As to the accompanying junket – after lamenting the way it had generally ceased to be made properly, Zhang describes in another passage how he once had devoted considerable time and care to making it himself:

> I myself milked the cow and at night I put the milk into a basin. Next morning a layer of curds ('milk-flowers') had formed, about a foot thick. I boiled it for some time in a copper pot. I infused orchid blossoms in snow-runoff water. I added four cups of this infusion to one catty of milk and boiled it and boiled it until the liquid became like jade and the solids like pearls. Unctuous as snow, silken like hoar-frost, this dish gives off a fragrance that surpasses

the orchid's and permeates the viscera. It is like a true gift of the gods.

According to Zhang, the junket thus made was both delicious and versatile. It was just as good served hot or cold, preserved in wine or vinegar, or simmered in sugar. In this depiction of a milk-based luxury dish, Zhang also confirms for us the continuing, if occasional, presence of dairy products in the Chinese diet.

The unsettled years of the Ming-Qing dynastic transition were certainly no time to worry about gastronomy, except as an object of nostalgic reminiscence. Many, seeking to understand how the Ming could have fallen, reacted against the devotion to pleasure and the intellectual open-mindedness that they feared might have fatally undermined the dynasty. But life slowly resumed a degree of normality. By the late seventeenth century, Jiangnan was gradually regaining its role as economic and cultural centre of the empire, and rebuilding its great cities. The Ming loyalism of the early post-transition years gradually subsided with subsequent generations, and as it became clear that the Manchus were there to stay. And Manchu suspicions of Jiangnan's political loyalties vied with individual emperors' predilection for luxury goods, many of which, including fine textiles and cuisine, originated precisely in that region.

During the long eighteenth century, approximately from the 1680s to the 1810s, overall peace and prosperity gave rise among other things to renewed commercialization, accompanied by the resumption of an increasingly rampant consumerism. One important consequence was that Jiangnan became ever wealthier and the daily life of the scholars, merchants and other residents who thronged there ever more given over to life's pleasures.

Qing rulers' mistrust of the Jiangnan scholarly and intellectual elite led them to seek ways to draw its members into the imperial orbit. One potential means to achieve that goal was by sharply limiting their subjects' ability to function independently of the throne in any sphere, a tactic that it was hoped would pre-empt any formation of cliques or the factionalism that had laid low the Ming. Especially under the Qianlong emperor (r. 1736–95), these goals led to imperial involvement in – which *ipso facto* meant assumption of control over – intellectual and cultural trends that had once enjoyed a relatively autonomous existence. The bid to co-opt elite practices was discernible in a number of areas, such as ritual studies and the intellectual movement favouring evidence-based research over abstract philosophizing. This strategy became habitual, so that its extension to the field of gastronomy seemed only natural, whether or not in that particular instance the underlying motivation was really political. In any event, the lavishness and eclecticism of the imperial table could not but make court cuisine a model to emulate. Thus any account of taste and gastronomy in the late eighteenth century needs to take account of what was happening

A portable tea-ceremony chest dating from the period of the Qianlong emperor. Qing palaces did not have rooms set aside for dining or for taking tea; instead, meals were brought to the emperor wherever he happened to be at the appropriate time. Also, when the emperor travelled away from the palace, as he frequently did, he sometimes took his favourite cooks with him so as not to be deprived of his preferred cuisine on the road.

both at court and among the Jiangnan elite who, according to one contemporary account, 'ate like kings'. Here a caveat is again necessary: it is important to bear in mind that while Jiangnan may have represented a pinnacle of 'good living' outside court circles, as in the Ming it was not necessarily representative of the empire as a whole, particularly when one takes into consideration the strikingly multiethnic and multicultural character of the Qing empire.

Records of earlier imperial kitchens are for the most part limited to statistics about the often astonishing number of people employed to take care of food and nutrition at court and the ways in which they were organized. For the Qing, however, especially under the Qianlong emperor, detailed information is preserved in the court archives about the actual meals served, including daily menus, tableware, and the names of cooks responsible for particular dishes. We know, for instance, that Suzhou cuisine became the Qianlong emperor's favourite – he sometimes recruited good Suzhou chefs away from his officials – but that he also enjoyed such Manchu snacks as sweet- or savoury-stuffed 'bobo' buns, shaped to convey a message such as longevity or happiness. He loved to eat duck, and he often drank tea with milk, a Manchu custom about whose influence on English practice we can only speculate. The emperor's devotion to Buddhism evidently did not prevent his enjoyment of animal foods, but on religious festival days and some other special occasions he ate only vegetarian dishes. Buddhist influence, in combination with the exigencies of sheer poverty, had created a strong vegetarian tradition in Chinese cuisine. At the imperial level, it is likely that many of the dishes served to the emperor were vegetarian imitations of meat and other non-vegetarian fare. Sometimes these meals were prepared for

Qianlong in a monastery to add an aura of sanctification. On such days the entire court also had to follow a vegetarian diet. Finally, in a strikingly humanizing anecdote, we learn that on at least one occasion the emperor declined to eat some food his mother sent over, and asked his chef to make him something else instead.

Generally, he took two meals a day, one at about 6 a.m., by which time he had already been dealing with affairs of state for some time, and one between noon and 2 p.m.; in the evening he had some light snacks. He always ate alone at a small table, as was customary for everyone dining at court; his food was served wherever he wished to take his meal, and no single room was set aside for the purpose.

The imperial kitchens went to great lengths to procure the best ingredients from imperial farms and orchards, from tribute submitted by senior officials and princes, and from all over the empire, including Jiangnan, as well as employing chefs with particular specialties. Freshness was ensured by the use of ice stored in specially constructed caves, which also served to cool the ambient temperature in summertime, a practice not limited to the imperial court.

The quantity of food required to supply the palace was astonishing, not only because there were thousands of people to be fed but because typically far more food was served to the emperor than he could possibly consume, as we can see from the record of an autumn breakfast in 1779:

> hot pot with bird's nest and duck; sautéed chicken with soft bean curd; lamb; a stew of duck, dogmeat and pork; bamboo shoots…bird's nest with chicken; various thinly-sliced meats; deep-fried duck with meat; quickfried pork; quick-sauteed chicken eggs; sautéed chicken feet; cured pork; doughnuts; chicken soup with dumplings…lamb with steamed gruel and a fruit congee (the latter two untouched). On another table were fourteen dishes of eight-treasure bobo buns, four dishes of yellow greens; three dishes of milk. On a third table some baked goods, and on a fourth, eight plates of meats.

The emperor ate lightly, sampling only a few of these dishes; his leftovers were distributed in a prescribed order among concubines, imperial family members, high officials, and occasionally foreign visitors whom the emperor wished to honour. This menu suggests rather minimal attention to issues of nutrition. But nutrition was not the main point; the array of dishes served to the emperor constituted one among many ways of exposing to public view his boundless riches; it formed part of the mythology surrounding the emperor or, in modern terms, was part of imperial public relations. In any event, Qianlong lived to the ripe old age of eighty-eight and, according to

The Qianlong emperor was fond of drinking tea with milk, a custom more familiar to his Mongolian, Tibetan and Manchu subjects than to Chinese, who preferred their tea plain. The Qing court possessed a number of ewers of this kind, which may have been modelled after vessels used for buttered tea in Tibetan Buddhist ceremonies.

In the 18th century, imagined Chinese decorative styles or chinoiserie became the height of fashion in Europe. This was mirrored by a taste for things European at the Qianlong court, to which the French presented a set of tapestries intended to adorn the emperor's European-style palaces. François Boucher's study for a tapestry cartoon, entitled *Feast of the Chinese Emperor*, was executed in c. 1742.

British ambassador George Macartney, was still physically spry and mentally acute a few years before his death.

Both at court banquets and for daily meals, each person's food allocation was carefully worked out according to a strict system of gradation. Banquets, in particular, often consisted of both Manchu and Chinese dishes: Manchu cuisine to represent the empire and Chinese dishes to respect the presumed taste of Chinese guests. Still, the prestige of imperial cuisine meant that a number of Manchu culinary preferences, such as roast meat, found their way into elite Chinese kitchens, and Beijing food, with its Manchu inflections, became popular in Jiangnan just as the cuisine of Suzhou and Yangzhou found favour in the capital. It was not long before it would become fashionable, when Manchus and Chinese dined together, for a Manchu host to serve Chinese dishes and vice versa. From this it is evident that considerations of social class and mutual interest, rather than any issue of ethnic distinction, governed elite social relationships.

In the late eighteenth century the city of Yangzhou claimed a particular imperial connection, both because its cultural world was dominated by salt merchants grown wealthy from imperial monopolies and because it was a regular stop on the frequent imperial southern tours intended precisely to reinforce such bonds. Yangzhou was a cultural and gastronomic mecca even among the cities of Jiangnan. Among other things, the leisure activities of its elite often involved picnic outings to view a scenic spot, perhaps accompanied by the exchange of poetry or political views (the two were not necessarily distinct), or visits to one of the restaurants for which the city was famous. In addition to many individual memoirs of city life, we are fortunate to have a detailed account of Yangzhou which pays considerable attention, among many other topics, to its gastronomic delights. Li Dou's *Yangzhou Huafang Lu* (Record of the Painted Pleasure Boats of Yangzhou), published in 1795, offers tantalizing glimpses of a culinary culture at its height, giving us some sense of the epicurean possibilities open to elite Chinese men in the late eighteenth century.

Li's description of Yangzhou's main fish market depicts a scene in which all kinds of different fish were rushed three times daily from fisherman's boat to city restaurants 'as though on wings', to ensure peak freshness. The choice was enormous, for 'Huainan marine resources are the best in the world'; best of all were the bream, whitefish and perch, with abalone ranking not far behind. Crabs came from three nearby lakes and from the Huai river; the latter were larger but the lake crabs were more highly prized by crab connoisseurs for their intense flavour. Near the market one could smell two stores selling dried, salted and pickled goods, for which Yangzhou, then as now, was famous: fish and shellfish; jellyfish; squid; the fins of various ocean fish passed off as sharks' fin, an expensive luxury, and vegetables.

Many teahouses also served snacks, and some had a particular speciality. The finest served sesame buns, stuffed with sweetmeats or meat, or with fresh or dry vegetables, which were so delicious they became all the rage. Other sought-after treats included different kinds of steamed buns and dumplings; soup buns and fried breads, for all of which there was almost continuous demand. Other popular dishes included such regional specialities as pressed salted duck, a Nanjing dish, and five-fragrance wild duck, more often associated with distant Sichuan province than with Jiangnan. Perhaps the popularity of duck-based dishes in Yangzhou partly reflected imperial tastes.

Outings on one of Yangzhou's many waterways always involved eating and drinking as well as musical and sexual entertainment. Most of the famous pleasure-boats of Yangzhou – in effect floating brothels catering to different social classes – were individually huge and often moved in convoy, but lacked their own kitchen. So the one that did offer cooking facilities was in great demand. It was not unusual for a gentleman to bring along his own cook on pleasure outings of this kind, along with all the equipment needed and kitchen hands to help prepare a feast. Some private cooks had a reputation for particular dishes, such as Wu Yishan's roasted beancurd; Tian Yanmen's deep-fried duck, Wang Yinshan's boneless fish, and Wang Wen-mi's honey-boiled cakes. An alternative arrangement was to have food delivered to a pleasure-boat from one of Yangzhou's many catering establishments. Wine vendors drifted nearby ready to supply whatever was needed.

The momentary delights of Yangzhou gastronomy were replicated in different forms in other great cities of Jiangnan and elsewhere. More far-reaching and more durable may have been another important strand of late eighteenth-century food culture, namely a growing literary genre centred upon gastronomy. As we have seen, neither recipe collections nor interest in gastronomy was in any way new, but from the seventeenth century they formed part of a trend that steadily gathered momentum and, at the same time, gained in respectability.

Scholars created their cookery books for different reasons. For some, writing about food may initially have seemed a safe haven at a time of dangerous politics, although that aspect of its appeal probably diminished in proportion to increasing imperial interest. Others may have been deliberately following such eminent predecessors as the renowned Yuan dynasty painter Ni Zan (1301–74), whose recipe collection was notable among other things for an absence of outside influence despite Mongol rule, perhaps as a form of oblique resistance. Some were primarily concerned to transmit knowledge about health and nutrition as these related to particular types and combinations of food. Still others may have chosen to tread the path taken by the late-Ming writer Chen Jiru (1558–1639), who consciously turned his back on public life to teach and to write for payment, whether in the form of popular books on life's pleasures or more formal eulogies such as tomb inscriptions. Chen was notably successful in this somewhat unconventional career, becoming almost a brand name whose involvement in particular projects sometimes was invoked by publishers as a marketing device. Whether or not Chen was familiar with Gao Lian's *Eight Discourses*, he formed a link between that group of late-Ming writers who supported themselves in part by the marketing of their good taste and connoisseurship and those who, like Zhang Dai, lived to see the interruption of that way of life as the result of the dynastic transition. It was recorded that Zhang once met the well-known older man when, as a small boy, he was out riding with his grandfather.

Those who, consciously or not, emulated Chen Jiru included the late seventeenth-century writer Li Yu (1611–?1680), whose *Xianqing Ouji* (Casual Expressions of Idle Feelings) was a collection of essays on such topics as recreation, travel, women, diet, hygiene, drama and architecture. It formed part of a much wider œuvre that also included erotic fiction, popular drama and the well-known *Jiezi Yuan Huazhuan* (Mustard-Seed Garden Manual of Painting). Other collections of recipes published in the early to middle eighteenth

Festivals, such as the one depicted here, provided the occasion not only for celebration but for great conviviality, together with abundant feasting and drinking. Zhang Dai recalled attending such an occasion near Hangzhou in 1633 with all his friends. 'Each one brought a bushel of wine, five baskets of grain and ten varieties of vegetables and fruits, and a red carpet on which to sit and eat.'

Overleaf: The Jiangnan region, with its fertile land, its network of lakes and rivers, and its relatively mild climate, is famed for the wide range of its local products, including vegetables and aquatic fare. Markets selling fresh and dried goods are a common sight throughout its cities, great and small. Today, pollution is endangering the continuation of some of the characteristic dishes of Jiangnan cuisine.

century included one by the official dynastic historian Zhu Yicun (1629–1709), which focused on health and diet but also included a number of unusual and luxurious foods such as bear's paw and deer tendon as well as vegetarian imitations of elaborate meat dishes. Still others had a regional focus, such as *Tiao Ding Ji* (Records of the Harmonious Cauldron), a huge compendium of recipes mostly from the Jiangnan area.

The best-known work in this genre came at the very end of the eighteenth century. Yuan Mei (1716–98) abandoned a promising official career to make his living as a writer in Nanjing. His *Suiyuan Shidan* (Recipes from Sui Garden), published in 1796 probably after having circulated in manuscript for some time, appeared at almost exactly the same moment as Li Dou's work on Yangzhou, and no doubt Yuan, who lived not far away in Nanjing, was familiar with much of what Li was describing. But Yuan's interests were somewhat different.

Suiyuan Shidan is a collection of recipes that Yuan, who had retired from the imperial bureaucracy after a short but evidently lucrative career, had collected over a period of several decades. Some of these recipes he obtained by consulting the cooks of friends at whose house he had enjoyed a particular dish – a practice in which he was not unique among scholarly collectors of recipes at this time, who often prefaced their collections with an explanatory comment to that effect. Certainly Yuan also had some knowledge of cooking rather than relying completely on professionals; it is clear that he tested recipes before including them, although it seems likely that Yuan's cook actually carried out the test, perhaps under his employer's watchful eye. Other recipes Yuan found in earlier collections. Not all met with his satisfaction – he criticized Li Yu – but some he thought worthy of reproduction, such as 'Yunlin Steamed Goose', which he named for Ni Zan (Ni Yunlin) on whose recipe he based his own.

How did late eighteenth-century writings on gastronomy differ from those of the late Ming? Each group of works reflected the intellectual interests of its time. The earlier books were, in effect, manuals of taste – works that established an aesthetic standard for food, taking account of issues of health and nutrition. The later works, including that of Yuan Mei, shared those goals, but added another that was derived from a movement known as 'evidential research' whose operating method was to seek truth from facts. Yuan and others collected recipes either from books or from chefs whose work they had sampled, and then tested them. Empirical observation and practical experimentation was a driving force of the whole project, built upon concern for eating for pleasure, good health and the reinforcement of criteria of taste.

Yuan Mei has sometimes been compared to the almost contemporary French gastronomic writer Jean-Anthelme Brillat-Savarin (1755–1826), whose famous *Physiology of Taste* appeared in 1825. The comparison presumably derives both from Yuan's strong opinions about cooking and because of his insistence on the importance of gourmet knowledge. Among his many prescriptions, Yuan was adamant that cooks should always use the best-quality ingredients – he endorses some and demolishes others – rejecting anything not absolutely fresh; they should strive to achieve balance in seasoning and to respect the natural flavour of an ingredient; they should pay close attention to hygiene; use separate pans for different flavours; and pour water onto tea-leaves only when it reaches boiling point.

Yuan's opinions extended to social behaviour and rules of etiquette. He often criticized others for departing from his standards, for instance those who judged quantity more important than quality. He once derided an eminent official at whose house he had been served expensive but, in Yuan's opinion, completely tasteless food – in fact none other than the birds' nests often enjoyed, presumably in more palatable form, by the Qianlong emperor. And he claims once to have begged a friend to save their relationship by never inviting him back for a meal. These criticisms demarcated his work from simple recipe collections, yet all shared an interest in researching and recording recipes based on actual practice.

Thus gastronomy in imperial China consisted of two main branches, procuring and savouring the best and rarest foods, and writing about them. One was transient, if time-consuming, while the other was more permanent; a concern for health and nutrition permeated both. Both were a normal part of a gentleman's activities; while most food writers were also gourmets, many gourmets also wrote about food. The surviving corpus of texts on Chinese gastronomy show an uncanny resemblance to the *fan-cai* principle that ordered gastronomy itself, in that they changed along with broader intellectual trends yet retained the same core concern for flavour, health and good taste. It was a case of infinite variation within a single modular form.

4 THE PLEASURES OF CONSUMPTION

The Birth of Medieval Islamic Cuisine

H. D. Miller

More than once in the Qur'an, first in Surah 2: 172–173, Muslims are enjoined by Allah to 'eat of the good things wherewith We have provided you', and forbidden to consume that which is unlawful, specifically, carrion, blood, pork, improperly slaughtered animals, intoxicating drinks, and anything consecrated to anyone other than Allah. Thus, from the beginning foodstuffs are divided for Muslims into two categories, halal and haram, or that which is permitted and that which is prohibited.

Over time, as Islamic legal practice became more sophisticated, and as the Arabs conquered more culinarily adventuresome cultures, certain schools of Islamic jurisprudence would further forbid to Muslims the consumption of other items, especially carnivores, raptors, some shellfish, most insects and reptiles, and 'animals with fangs'. But even with these injunctions, there was still a wealth of ingredients from which early medieval Muslim cooks could begin to construct an identifiable Islamic cuisine. Grains, milk, honey, vegetables, fruits, nuts, properly slaughtered quadrupeds, fish, fowl and freshly killed game were all deemed halal, suitable for the Muslim diner, and all were used extensively by Muslim cooks.

In the beginning, however, in the desert cities of Mecca and Medina, the dining habits of the earliest Muslims were humble indeed, and it is unlikely that the Prophet and his followers had the opportunity to consider whether or not more exotic fare, such as crabs and oysters, were to be permitted to the faithful. Instead, one gets the impression while reading through the Hadith (the collected sayings and traditions of the Prophet Muhammad and his early followers) that Muhammad was a man who enjoyed what might be considered good, honest, country cooking, or at least the Arabian Desert version. Grains, meat, milk, dates, and other typical fruits of the desert, all simply prepared, figure prominently among foods mentioned in conjunction with Muhammad's dining habits, habits that other pious Muslims at least initially sought to emulate.

Preparations for feasts could be quite elaborate, as this scene from a 15th-century Mughal Muslim manuscript attests. Here, cooks chop food and tend to their pots, while a butcher slaughters a goat as his assistant holds a bowl to catch the blood for disposal.

Of the things Muhammad consumed, meat was the most highly praised, 'the lordliest food of the people of this world and of Paradise is meat,' he is reported to have said. In fact, the eating of meat would almost become a religious obligation for Muslims, who are commanded by Allah to sacrifice a lamb during the Eid al-Adha, the festival celebrating the end of the pilgrimage to Mecca, and to distribute part of that sacrificial meat to the poor. For Muhammad, who thought eating with a knife a fussy foreign affectation, preferring instead to use his teeth to gnaw roasted meat from bones, no meat dish, no dish of any kind, could compare to *tharīd*, a humble meat stew thickened with crumbled bread. Later Muslim cooks would prepare this dish in dozens of complicated varieties, but the only variation specifically mentioned in the Hadith is one made with dried meat and gourd, a vegetable the Prophet is said to have thoroughly enjoyed, so much so that others took pride in mentioning that they too liked eating it.

Also to be found on the leather dining cloth of the Prophet (leather because the Prophet never ate from gold or silver dishes, nor sat at a table, nor ate fine, thin bread) were *khazira*, thin broths with bran, *hais*, a mixture of dates, curds and ghee, *sawiq*, a thick wheat or barley porridge, *silq*, Swiss chard usually mixed with grain and long simmered, and occasionally the roasted haunch and legs of desert hare. Likewise, fresh cucumbers, melons, fresh and dried dates, and hearts of palm were also present, and 'Aisha, his favourite wife, whom he said 'surpassed all other women as *tharīd* surpasses other dishes,' related that he had a sweet tooth, which he satisfied with honey and dates. All of these were typical dishes of an impoverished desert people making do with what they could find. Even today, most are still eaten by the Bedouins of the Arabian Desert.

Over and over in the Hadith the Prophet Muhammad is seen dining heartily on the humblest of foods, and when food was scarce, as it was when the Prophet and his earliest followers were forced to flee Mecca, he makes do with a mouthful of bitter leaves, or the worst quality of dried dates, or a few cups of barley in water, never complaining, never failing to give thanks to the One who provided it. 'Eat from what is placed in front of you,' was his motto, and others noted that 'he never criticized food. If he liked it he ate it, and if he disliked it he left it.' And of that, only a single dish falls into the latter category, that which was disliked by Muhammad, and that was lizard. The traditions tell us that one day when a roasted lizard was placed in front of Muhammad he would not touch it. His fellow diners quickly asked if it was haram, 'no,' said the Prophet, 'I just don't like it.' Of course, such dislike was enough for later Muslim legal minds to deem lizard unsuitable for consumption by the faithful.

While dining, Muhammad was also insistent that proper etiquette be observed and that hospitality be extended even when there

Desert hare, taken with snares, falcons or dogs, was a favourite of the earliest Muslims and continued to appear on the plates of urban sophisticates long after the desert had been left behind for the city. Decorated serving dishes, like this one from Eygpt or Syria featuring the image of three hares, would have been common in the upper middle-class homes of the medieval Muslim world.

A young man holding a glass is depicted on the wall of a bathhouse in Cairo, from about the 12th century. Although alcohol was forbidden for Muslims, there existed throughout the Classical period a strong tradition of poetry, both low and high, in praise of wine. In pious upper-class homes *sharbat*, a soft drink made from fruit juices and sugar, would have been drunk.

was little available: 'Food enough for two is food enough for four, and food enough for four is food enough for eight,' an injunction that is perfectly consonant with the legendary hospitality of the Bedouin.

Despite the austerity of this early Muslim diet, or perhaps because of it, the Qur'an and the Hadith abound with references to the food and drink that await the faithful in Heaven. There were rivers in Heaven, a river of wine that does not intoxicate, of milk that does not spoil, and of pure honey, that flow through gardens filled with fruit trees of every sort, where one sits upon a golden throne, and the 'flesh of fowls' is served up by buxom, brown-eyed houris, while slim youths keep one's gold and crystal goblet forever filled. Undoubtedly these were powerful incentives for those who were usually grateful for even the meanest meal.

As Islam grew in the years following the death of Muhammad in 632, first during the reign of his immediate successors, the four so-called Rightly Guided Caliphs, and then during the boom years of their successors, the Umayyads, the demographics of the religion's

فصادف من رؤوسا بنجار أن أقلم بها الجار الجار فدعا
إلى ماذينة الجفلا من أهل الحضارة والفلاح حتى بثرت
دعوته إلى القافلة وجمع في مايز الفريضة والنا فلة
فلما الجنا منادية ورجلانا دية أحضر من أطعمة البلد
والبك من ما حلا بالفم وحلى بالعين صورة البساط

adherents changed. Expansion out of the Arabian Desert around Mecca and Medina brought the early Muslims into immediate contact with Greeks, Egyptians and Persians, and eventually, by the end of the first Muslim century, Berbers, Franks, Indians and others, many of whom readily converted to the new religion. Each group encountered, each region conquered added its own particular flavours and dishes to the cuisine that was developing out of the alimentary restrictions laid down in the Qur'an. Muhammad's beloved *tharīd*, the meat stew with bread, was soon improved with spices such as cinnamon and cardamom and exotic vegetables such as cardoons and carrots.

By the middle of the seventh century, the Umayyad caliph Mu'awiyah had relocated the Muslim capital out of the desert into newly conquered Damascus, a Byzantine colonial capital that was undoubtedly the most cosmopolitan city the nomadic Muslim raiders had ever seen. Unlike the inhospitable Hijaz, where many of the first Muslims would have been happy to have been able to put an honest roast lizard on their leather dining cloths, late seventh-century Syria was an agricultural and culinary Eden. Proximity to Mesopotamia, the mountains of Lebanon and the Mediterranean Sea, along with a well-established system of oases irrigated by the Barada river, and called the Ghuta, around Damascus itself, meant that the variety of food encountered in the city far surpassed the simple desert staples of grain, dates and meat. Mecca may have been a major trading stop on the route from the Yemen to the Levant, but it was, and is, a desert city with few agricultural resources.

The move from Mecca to Damascus also brought the early Muslims into direct contact with Byzantine and Persian cuisines, and with the opulent customs and habits of a Greco-Roman colonial court.

Opposite: Here a convivial meal of roast chicken is eaten with the forefingers of the right hand, as the Prophet Muhammad had dictated was proper.

Right: No medieval Muslim feast would have been possible without meat, which the Prophet Muhammad referred to as the 'lordliest food of the people of this world and of Paradise.' Here all of the steps of the process are shown, from proper slaughter, to cooking, to serving.

'Shake the trunk of the palm tree towards thee: it will drop fresh, ripe dates upon thee. Eat, then, and drink, and let thine eye be gladdened!' Qur'an 19:25–26. Mentioned in the Qur'an more frequently than any other plant, the date palm was thought to be one of Allah's special gifts, and thus worthy of being the subject of a mosaic on the Treasury of the Umayyad Mosque in Damascus.

The Umayyads, the powerful descendants of the third caliph 'Uthman, and those of his nephew the fifth caliph, Mu'awiyah, wasted little time in relocating into the now vacant Byzantine palaces, nor in adopting the regal style of the Byzantine court. In short order they began to erect new public buildings, such as the Grand Mosque, in a style that synthesized Byzantine and Persian elements into something distinctly Muslim. Meanwhile, a similar metamorphosis was taking place in Islamic kitchens, as Persians, Byzantines, and others from throughout the far-flung empire, contributed their own foodstuffs, techniques and spices to the mix. The result was the birth of an identifiably Muslim high style of dining. So that while the poor were still mostly eating what the Prophet ate, those at court, and those who imitated the court, were dining on far grander fare in which expensive spices, exotic ingredients and elaborate preparations were served up, not on humble leather, but on gold and silver.

Together, the imperial style and the imperious and impious manner in which the Umayyads ruled combined to stir up unrest among those who felt excluded, especially among the Shia and the non-Arab Muslims of Iraq and Khurasan. By 750, led by the descendants of Muhammad's kinsman Ibn 'Abbas, and riding under the black banner of revolution, these dissident factions had defeated the Umayyads in battle. Fittingly, dinner was the final downfall for the remnants of the Umayyad family, as in that same year, the newly installed Abbasid caliph, Abu al-'Abbas, slaughtered the last of them during the final course of what was billed as a reconciliation feast. Only a single Umayyad escaped, 'Abd al-Rahman, who made his way across North Africa to newly conquered Iberia, where he would install himself as ruler.

The Abbasids, who were beholden to Persians and Iraqis, promptly moved the Muslim capital eastwards, first to Kufa, and then finally, in 762, to Baghdad, a planned city on the banks of the Tigris river. Built in three concentric rings, with the caliphal palace and grand mosque at the centre, and largely constructed from and on the ruins of older Babylonian and Sassanid cities, Baghdad quickly became the centre of the Muslim universe. And it was in Baghdad that Muslim cuisine reached a zenith of lavishness and sophistication.

By the beginning of the ninth century, during the reign of the legendary caliph Haroun al-Rashid, the fashionable of Baghdad were already completely obsessed with food, not just with fancy eating, but also with reading and writing about the culinary arts, and even with the act of cooking itself. In such a climate of epicureanism, good cooking was not just something to be performed by menial servants in the hidden confines of the imperial kitchen, it was an activity fit for the caliph himself. Indeed, in the stories of the *Arabian Nights*, one of the most charming of Shahrazad's tales has Haroun al-Rashid, in disguise, cook for a pair of lovers a meal of fish he has freshly caught himself from the Tigris river.

After dinner was cleared away, drinks were served and the evening's entertainment began. A 16th-century miniature depicts the Persian poet Nizami reading from his 'Treasury of Secrets' while musicians provide accompaniment.

If cooking fish was an activity not beyond the dignity of the Abbasid caliphs, who soon after the remove to Baghdad had adopted the remote, semi-divine style of the Persian kings, along with their extravagant dining habits, then writing about cooking was surely of equal worth. One of the indispensable literary works of medieval Islam is *The Fihrist*, a late tenth-century annotated bibliographic index compiled by the Baghdadi bookseller Ibn al-Nadim. *The Fihrist* lists dozens of cookery books and specialized culinary tomes, the earliest dating to the second half of the eighth century, and almost none of which, unfortunately, survive.

In the ninth and tenth centuries, cookery books and books on dining etiquette were so popular because standards of connoisseurship in Baghdad were so high, and thus a well-bred gentleman was expected to know a bewildering variety of topics related to dining, from which wines went with which dishes, to how to stack desserts in an eye-pleasing manner, to the latest culinary innovations in spices, to famous poems suitable for recital during dinner. Even more impressive were the names of the individuals who composed such volumes. Among those mentioned in *The Fihrist* as having authored culinary tracts are the high-ranking men of the empire, senior civil servants, courtiers, generals, poets and others, including the great historian and geographer al-Masudi, and the prince Ibrahim al-Mahdi, the half-brother of the caliph Haroun al-Rashid, who is famous for having invented the eponymous *ibrahimīya*, a sour meat stew made with verjuice or vinegar.

For medieval Muslims, however, the most important of the genres of Arabic culinary literature would have been the 'poems of the table', elaborate poetic paeans to food and dining that were recited at dinner parties. Some of the greatest of these are contained in a lengthy passage in the historian al-Masudi's *Meadows of Gold*, in which he describes an unusual feast held by the Caliph al-Mustakfi (r. 944–946). At al-Mustakfi's literary dinner each attendee was instructed to come prepared to recite a famous poem in praise of a particular dish, which would then be promptly prepared and served in exactly the manner described. The participants dined that day on an incredible variety of foods, from appetizers, to chicken, to roast kid, to fish, on through to a number of desserts, all the result of their literary efforts and a well-stocked kitchen. They were only thwarted in the matter of fresh asparagus, which was out of season, and thus had to be sent away to Damascus for.

Although unusual in the manner in which the menu was set, such elaborate feasts as the one described by al-Masudi were entirely normal in the context of caliphal dining. The humble desert hospitality advocated by Muhammad had, after three centuries, given way to a lavishness unheard of since the fall of Rome. On holidays and special occasions, thousands of people would be served a dinner of multiple courses at the caliph's expense. And when the caliphs dined with friends at home they could boast of the fact that no less than 300 different dishes might be presented in a single sitting. As with the number of women in the caliph's harem, the number of dishes served at dinner was about more than just the pleasure of consumption, it was also a way for the caliph to express his wealth and power, and for the citizens of Baghdad both to take pride in the majesty of their government and to live vicariously through the exploits of the great man.

Of course, from the very beginning of the Abbasid period there were dissidents to the cult of the stomach, including many physicians who objected on grounds of good health. Their dietary treatises, most of which are based on earlier Greek medical theories, abound. A few of these, such as *Kitāb al-aghdhīya* (The Book of Foods) by the tenth-century Cairene doctor Ishaq b. Sulayman al-Isra'ili, were even translated into Latin, where they enjoyed long, influential lives as books worthy of consultation by European physicians. Back in Baghdad, the Jewish, Muslim and Christian doctors who wrote these Arabic dietary tracts were often prominent figures at the caliph's court, men who were frequently consulted during the preparation and consumption of food, going so far in some cases as to be given the frustrating power to forbid the caliph a dish judged unhealthy.

A few of those who objected to the conspicuous consumption of the fashionable, however, did so on moral grounds, that excessive devotion to the stomach prevented true enlightenment. Such was the case with Salih b. 'Abd al-Quddūs, who wrote in the late eighth century that 'we live among beasts always looking for new grazing but who do not seek to understand. If you write about fish and vegetables, you garner much merit in their eyes, but if you expound truly scientific subjects they find it boring and irksome.' Indeed, so boring, irksome and heretical did the Caliph al-Mahdi find the works of 'Abd al-Quddūs that he had him executed in 793.

Medieval Baghdad sat at the busy centre of a vibrant Islamic world, a world that stretched from the Indus river to the Atlantic Ocean. Exotic foods and culinary traditions poured into that centre, influencing what was eaten and how it was eaten. But, equally important was the influence that the fashionable gourmands of Baghdad had on the wider Islamic world. One famous example of how the culinary culture of Baghdad influenced the world is found in the story of Ziryab, a freed slave and musician from Baghdad who found a position in Córdoba, in the Andalusi court of 'Abd al-Rahman II, the great-grandson the last Umayyad. Ziryab, hired to be a musician, became instead one of the greatest arbiters of taste the world has ever seen.

Córdoba in the early ninth century was not Baghdad. At the far western end of the world, and only recently wrested away from the semi-barbarian Visigoths, it was a city in which unrefined, gluttonous excess was one of the few ways the upper classes thought of expressing their wealth. Although there was a great variety of food, and it was plentiful, it was often unimaginatively prepared, served in heaps, and consumed in a near frenzy by diners armed with knives, teeth and

The fashion for refined dining, like the clothes, hairstyles and musical tastes of the upper classes of Baghdad, was often spread to the more remote areas of the Muslim world by professional entertainers who had been trained in the capital. The image is from an early 13th-century Spanish or Moroccan manuscript.

wooden spoons. The appearance of Ziryab in Córdoba around 822 put an end to this. Although hired as a musician – and he was a musical genius – he quickly set the standard for how elegant Andalusi ladies and gentlemen behaved in matters of etiquette, fashion and dining. He changed local hairstyles, modes of dress, grooming habits and musical tastes, and he influenced Spanish and European dining habits down to the present day. In the kitchen he taught Andalusi chefs new dishes from the east, and convinced diners that asparagus, that old Damascene delicacy, was worth a try. Some of the dishes he introduced are still served in Spain, including one, *ziriabí*, a dish of roasted and salted broad beans from Córdoba, that bears his name. One of his most famous innovations was the introduction to al-Andalus of the practice of dining in courses. Although dining in such a manner was not unheard of in Baghdad, it was not common. However, it became the elegant standard in the western half of the Muslim world, and under Ziryab's direction meals would begin with soup, followed by fish, and then fowl or meat, then desserts, ending with a small bowl of pistachios or almonds, in other words, from soup to nuts, a style of dining that has persisted.

Ziryab is the most spectacular example of a process that spread the dining habits and dishes of Baghdad outward to the rest of Islam, and then on to Europe, where with regional variations some of these same dishes are still served today. But many more of these dishes have disappeared or mutated over the intervening centuries, leaving behind little beyond their names. Most scholars of the history of Islamic cookery

Below: A glass goblet from 14th-century Upper Egypt is etched with a fish motif, indicative of the importance of the Nile river in the diet of medieval Egyptians. Among Muslims of that period only the Andalusis and Maghrabis loved fish more.

have noted that what now passes for Muslim cuisine is a greatly simplified and changed version of what was available in Baghdad during the time of the caliphs. What then were the characteristic flavours of this medieval Islamic high cuisine? Luckily, a handful of cookery books has survived to tell us. Among the most important of these are two that share the simple name *Kitāb al-tabīkh* (The Book of Cookery). The earlier of this pair, a Baghdadi cookery book that dates from the tenth century and was written by the almost otherwise unknown Ibn Sayyar al-Warraq, is probably the earliest cookery book to survive from the medieval period in any language. It is, however, a work more encyclopaedic than practical, listing hundreds of foodstuffs, dishes, drinks, cooking implements, ingredients and recipes, but in never enough specific detail to satisfy fully the erstwhile modern cook. By comparison, the second *Kitāb al-tabīkh*, written in 1226 by Muhammad al-Khatib al-Baghdadi, is much shorter, but also much more explicit than its predecessor in regard to ingredients and specific instructions for preparation, so that the careful modern chef can make an honest attempt to recreate the flavours of medieval Baghdad.

Al-Baghdadi's *Kitāb al-tabīkh* is a highly personalized work, in which the author describes in detail the preparation of 164 dishes he himself enjoys, explicitly leaving out those more mundane recipes that are 'well known and in common use'. Thus some of the very common but humble staples of the medieval Iraqi table, such as okra and beans, are missing from his recipes. Yet at the same time, because of the detail al-Baghdadi provides for the recipes he does include, we are still given an excellent glimpse into the high cuisine of the caliphal city. Additionally, *Kitāb al-tabīkh* was a book that enjoyed long life, both in its original form and as the base of a second book, *Kitāb wasf al-at'ima al-mu'tāda* (The Description of the Familiar Foods), a book that adds dozens of recipes to al-Baghdadi's original. Copies of this latter version, probably dating from the eighteenth century, can even be found in the Ottoman libraries of the Topkapi Palace.

One other thirteenth-century Arabic cookery book survives to give us a look into the cuisine of the western Muslim world. That work, edited and translated into Spanish by the Arabist Ambrosia Huici Miranda and published under the title *La cocina hispano-magrebí en la época almohade según un manuscrito anónimo*, although usually referred to as *Manuscrito anónimo*, contains valuable information on drinks, regional variations of common Muslim dishes, couscous, and the peculiar Iberian and Maghrabi reverence for fish.

The thirteenth-century original of al-Baghdadi's *Kitāb al-tabīkh* begins with a brief introduction in which the author discusses the wholesome pleasures of good food and the obligations of the professional cook. This is followed by a chapter on 'sour dishes', starting with a recipe for a famous dish known as *sikbāj*, a meat and vegetable stew seasoned with coriander, cinnamon and saffron, soured with vinegar and sweetened with date juice or honey, which is then brought to the table decorated with almonds, raisins, figs and a sprinkle of rose-water.

The recipe for the first dish in the initial chapter of al-Baghdadi's *Kitāb al-tabīkh* tells us much about the state of Islamic cuisine in the early thirteenth century. For example, the name *sikbāj* alone, with its unusual *-āj* ending (an Arabic transliteration of the Middle Persian *-ak*) reveals that this was a dish with origins to the east, in Iran. Indeed, medieval Arabic culinary literature is filled with Persian loan words, words borrowed when the court cuisine of Persia was adopted as suitable for the court of the newly risen caliphs, a cuisine that was then passed down through generations to later Muslim cooks. So that in the first chapter of *Kitāb al-tabīkh*, written nearly five hundred years after the founding of Baghdad, the author can still describe how to cook Persian dishes such as *zirbāj* (meat and vegetables seasoned with coriander, pepper and mastic, soured with vinegar, sweetened with sugar) and *nirbāj* (meat seasoned with coriander, pepper, cinnamon, mastic, ginger and mint, to which is added pomegranate seeds, black grape seeds and walnuts ground fine).

Beyond the seven dishes with Persian names described in the first chapter of al-Baghdadi's *Kitāb al-tabīkh*, there are also another fifteen recipes for other luxury fare, such as Ibrahim al-Mahdi's famous *ibrahimīya*, and for other sour dishes made with unusual ingredients, such as *summāqiya*, a combination of meat and root vegetables, to which is added the bitter juice of sumac berries, and *hisrimīya*, meat and eggplant soured with the juice of unripe grapes.

Aside from the sour flavour, what ties these dishes together is the complexity of their preparation. Many of the dishes have a score or more intricate steps, including the grinding of various ingredients to different levels of fineness, the straining of liquids, the careful mixing of different spices, and the addition of special ingredients at specific times in the process. Meats are always cut into medium-sized pieces (to be suitable for picking up with the forefingers of the right hand and thus conveyed to the mouth, as the Prophet had dictated), they are also usually browned in fat before being simmered in a broth. Spices are sometimes boiled in cotton bags. Pots are always skimmed of scum after the first boil, and, as with the liquids used for souring, a wide variety of ingredients, such as finely ground walnuts or chickpeas, may be added as thickening agents. And if this were not enough work for the cook, al-Baghdadi was especially fond of *kubab*, little meatballs fabricated out of minced meat and spices pounded together in a stone mortar and fried, or perhaps dropped into the boiling mixture at the right moment.

Finally, at the end of each of these recipes, special attention is paid to the aroma and visual impact of the dish as it is presented at table.

Opposite: During the first centuries
of Islam rice was most often served
as an accompaniment to the main dish.
With the rise of the Safavid and Mughal
empires, however, elaborate and carefully
prepared pilafs became the much celebrated
centrepiece of the meal. In this 16th-century
Mughal miniature a saffroned pilaf is
served with roast goose.

Rose-water was to be sprinkled on at the last minute to enhance the smell, and small pieces of fruit, or nuts, or even poached eggs, sometimes coloured with saffron, were carefully arranged on top of the finished food. Likewise, al-Baghdadi's medieval Muslim cook was reminded at the end of each recipe to 'wipe the sides of the pan with a clean cloth', for no reason other than that it will enhance the presentation.

To focus only on the elaborate and luxurious sour dishes described by al-Baghdadi is to leave out nine-tenths of the book and, by extension, nine-tenths of medieval Muslim cuisine. Immediately after the sour dishes in *Kitāb al-tabīkh* are a half-dozen recipes for the so-called 'milk' dishes, meat and vegetable stews finished with a simmer in 'Persian milk', which was probably sour yoghurt. The most important of these was *madīra*, a dish of meat, onions, leeks and spices, simmered in a pot until the water was gone and then mixed with sour yoghurt, mint and lemon juice and simmered again until thickened. It was a dish prized for its curative powers, the equivalent of a medieval Muslim chicken soup.

After the milk dishes comes a chapter devoted to 'plain dishes', simple stews of meat and vegetables or legumes which were more heavily seasoned with spices, a contrast with the sour dishes, whose primary seasonings were their vinegary sauces. It is here in this chapter that rice, the greatest of the Persian staples, makes its first appearance on al-Baghdadi's table, as part of *isfanakhīya*, a dish comprised of pieces of browned meat and pounded spinach, seasoned with cumin, dry coriander, fine pepper, mastic, little pieces of cinnamon-bark, and bruised garlic, to which near the end of the cooking is added rice. After a final period of cooking for the rice, everything is ladled out over fried meat *kubabs* and sprinkled with finely ground cinnamon. This is what al-Baghdadi considers a 'plain dish', presumably called such because it does not have a complex sweet and sour sauce, not because of its ease of preparation, nor because it lacked spice.

It is interesting to note that despite the Persian origins of many of its dishes, al-Baghdadi's cookery book does not exhibit the sort of consuming reverence for rice that one finds in later Persian culinary texts. Indeed, for late medieval and early modern Persians, rice is the greatest of foodstuffs, something to be prepared in one of four traditional methods with the utmost care, in fact, prepared with more care than is taken with meat, as rice is both more delicate and more prone to disaster. But in thirteenth-century Iraq, at least in the kitchen of al-Baghdadi, rice is simply washed and almost carelessly thrown into the pot, with only a brief caution to guard against it becoming 'hard'. So, although rice was common in the diets of medieval Muslims, and was grown throughout the Muslim world, from India to Spain, it was rarely accorded the exalted status it would later have in, say, Safavid Persia. Instead, it was treated as a staple to be mixed in the pot with spinach and meat, rather than as a saffroned dish served alone as the centrepiece of the meal.

Much more important than rice to the diets of most medieval Muslims, however, would have been bread, and presumably all of the dishes described by al-Baghdadi, even those that specifically mention rice, would have been accompanied by bread, in any of several varieties. In fact, the more varieties of bread a host could place on the table the more favourably he was judged by his guests. Naturally, the caliphs of Baghdad excelled at bringing forth the greatest variety of all at dinner time, when dozens of kinds of bread, from unleavened, paper-thin flat breads to crispy crackers and large, round loaves of pillowy white bread, made their appearance. There was a universe of bread available for baking and eating for the average Muslim city dweller, breads that could be as simple as flour and water cooked on a griddle, or as complex as that prepared according to a recipe taken from the Franks and Armenians. The latter started with a buttery yeast dough to which was added salt, lots of pepper, ginger, husked sesame seeds, hempseed, aniseed, caraway toasted with a little cumin, poppy seed, ground cheese, fresh rue leaves, saffron, pistachios and *atrāf at-tib*, a famous and expensive aromatic spice mixture concocted from at least a dozen different ingredients, including ground bay leaves, lavender, betel, cloves and rosebuds.

Following the recipes for the plain dishes in al-Baghdadi's *Kitāb al-tabīkh*, were recipes for fried and 'dry' dishes, the latter being dishes in which all of the liquid involved in cooking is allowed to evaporate. Of the recipes here, *naranjīya* is perhaps the most fanciful: a preparation of large, round *kubabs* cooked in a broth spiced with pepper, mastic, cinnamon, ginger, carrots and onions, repeatedly removed from the broth and washed with egg yolks and saffron, and then finished up with bitter orange and lemon juice, chopped sweet almonds

Opposite: Bread in all varieties, from humble rustic rounds like this one, photographed in Algeria in the 1920s, to pillowy loaves of refined white bread, have always been a necessary part of the Muslim meal.

Below: A 7th-century Syrian mosaic depicts camels laden with jars of olive oil and wine. From the earliest recorded history, the Middle East stood astride the great trade routes of the world, which insured that Muslim cuisine would develop a complexity and sophistication unrivalled in the Middle Ages.

and a little mint. The result would have looked and smelled like oranges, but tasted like fried, spiced meat.

A discussion of fried dishes, fats and cooking oils leads naturally to one of the biggest differences between the cuisine of the modern Middle East and that of the medieval Muslim world. In the modern world, the cuisine of the Mediterranean and the Middle East is closely associated with olive oil. For the medieval Muslims of Baghdad, olive oil was a thing generally too costly for everyday use as a cooking oil. It was instead most often reserved as a condiment to be sprinkled on dishes, either as a final step in cooking, or at the table. By comparison, we find in the *Manuscrito anónimo*, that the Muslim chefs of al-Andalus and the Maghreb preferred olive oil above all other fats, to the point that their Christian neighbours to the north in more temperate parts of Spain adopted it, even though they had no olive trees of their own.

Much more common for cooking in Baghdad than olive oil, even in the kitchens of the caliph, would have been *alya*, the fat rendered out of the tail of a plump sheep. Many, if not most of the recipes in al-Baghdadi's *Kitāb al-tabīkh* begin with instructions to render out tail fat in a hot pan, fat which is then used to brown meat for stewing, or as the medium for frying *kubabs*. In other, later Arabic cookery books, much space is given over to methods of clarifying, enriching, colouring and perfuming this staple, all things which would have made this humble fat suitable for even the most refined of dishes. Sesame oil was also widely employed, but although used by Muslims, and cited by al-Baghdadi as suitable for deep frying, it was much more closely associated with Jews, to the point that many claimed you could tell a Jewish household from the street simply by the way it smelled of burning sesame oil. Of lesser importance as a cooking fat was *samn*, clarified butter, which appears in a number of contexts, especially as a base ingredient for pastries and breads, and aged as a condiment, valued for its rancidity.

The matter of condiments and relishes and their rancidity is another area in which the cuisine of the modern Middle East has deviated from the medieval standard. Several of the favourite sauces and condiments of medieval Islam are conspicuously missing from the modern table. None more prominently than *murrī*, a liquid brine sauce made from rotted barley and wheat flour. The food historian and critic Charles Perry, one of the few to attempt to replicate the process of making *murrī* in modern times, compares its flavour and texture to 'soy sauce', although admittedly the soya bean plays no role in its production. *Murrī* appears in several of al-Baghdadi's recipes, always as a seasoning added during cooking, never as a table condiment.

An important variation of *murrī* that was a condiment, however, could be made by adding milk and salt to the barley at a medial stage of

Medieval Islamic cuisine was rich in condiments and relishes, and so this 9th-century Egyptian dish might have been filled with pickled vegetables, soured yoghurts, spicy pastes and *murrī*, a fermented sauce made from rotted barley, which has disappeared from modern Muslim tables.

One of the favourite dishes of Baghdadis from any era is *shabbūt*, a succulent river fish best prepared on an open fire on the banks of the Tigris immediately after capture. A 15th-century Persian miniature depicts such a scene.

the rotting process, producing *khamakh ahmar*, a cheesy substance that would usually be served spread on pieces of bread. Although al-Baghdadi gives no recipe for either *murrī* or *khamakh ahmar*, he does give the recipe for *khamakh rijāl*, a sort of cheese-like condiment made in a gourd shell. Started in the heat of mid-summer, and fed each day with fresh milk, it would be finished in late October, possibly with the addition of garlic, mint and nigella seed, or even rose leaves.

Along with *khamakh rijāl* and *khamakh ahmar*, other relishes and pickles, frequently served as appetizers, were also prominent on the medieval Muslim table, especially when simple dishes such as roast meat were served. Medieval Muslim chefs pickled a broad range of items: cucumbers, eggplants, turnips, green beans, mint leaves, even small fish and locust, were soused in spiced vinegar. Other types of table relishes were produced with vegetables like beets or pieces of gourd mixed with curds, or sour yoghurt and spices. Sour dips and sauces, some by the time of al-Baghdadi known as *sals*, a word that may actually be derived from the Romance word *salsa*, were served with slices of cold meat, fish, or cooked vegetables. Medieval Muslim cooks also smoked a number of items for the table, not just meat and fish, but even olives. By comparison, smoked items rarely appear in the diet of modern Arabs.

One of the favourite finger foods of medieval Muslims, and something also frequently served as an appetizer, was *sanbusāj* or *sanbusāk*, a little savoury or sweet pie, made from thin dough shaped in a triangle or half moon, filled with an infinite variety of substances, from meat to cheese or fruit, pinched closed and deep fried in sesame oil. They are identical in concept and etymology to samosas, the Indian fried pies, and as with many other dishes and cooking methods from both the subcontinent and Iraq, they would have had a common genesis in Sassanid cuisine. They were also perhaps the most common Baghdadi fast food, available to be purchased from street cooks anywhere in the city.

Fish, however, was not something that could be bought anywhere in the city, and was not an overly common item in the diets of medieval Iraqis. Indeed, al-Baghdadi gives only a dozen recipes for fish, five of which are for fresh fish, the others salted. Of these twelve recipes, eleven are for variations of fried fish. The twelfth is for a whole fish stuffed with a mixture of chopped walnuts, garlic, sumac, thyme, coriander, cinnamon, cumin and mastic. The outside of the fish is smeared with a paste of sesame oil, saffron and rosewater, then tied up and roasted whole on a skewer in a *tannour*, a clay oven.

The paucity of fish recipes in al-Baghdadi's *Kitāb al-tabīkh* is not unusual given the context of Baghdad, a city located hundreds of miles inland from the Persian Gulf. Ibn Sayyar al-Warraq's tenth-century cookery book, *Kitāb al-tabīkh*, only mentions three species of fish by name, the carp, the sturgeon, and the most highly prized of Tigris river fish, the *shabbūt*, valued throughout the history of Mesopotamia for its succulent, mild flesh. Modern Baghdadis love it best roasted on an open fire right by the river bank immediately after capture, and fish for it avidly with dynamite and hand grenades.

The true fish lovers of the medieval Muslim world, however, could be found in Iberia and the Maghreb, and in the Nile river valley. In the thirteenth-century Andalusi *Manuscrito anónimo* there are dozens of recipes for fish, and at least seventeen individual species, mostly saltwater varieties, are mentioned by name. In that book, fish is prepared in every way imaginable, from roasting to frying, to stewing with yoghurt. Small fish are even fried and soused in vinegar, the origins of Spanish escabeche. Likewise, fish was highly prized by the ordinary Egyptian fellaheen, who even made *madīra*, the famous yoghurt stew, with pieces of river fish instead of mutton.

Although fish was not often on the menu in Baghdad, chicken most certainly was, and al-Baghadi provides instructions, in a brief passage at the end of one chapter, for how to prepare the bird for use in many of his stews. Most often, the type of meat to be used was not specified in a recipe, it was simply 'meat', although undoubtedly mutton was the default. Yet, as we see in al-Baghdadi, chicken or lamb would be a perfectly acceptable substitute, as would kid most probably. Veal is mentioned only once in al-Baghdadi, and beef is almost never mentioned in any of the cookery books. There are, of course, many famous dishes that call for chicken exclusively, such as roast chicken stuffed with nuts, or al-Baghdadi's version of *fustiqīya*, a dish made from boiled, shredded chicken breasts and equal parts ground pistachios and sugar, one of several very sweet meat dishes that feature chicken.

Another type of sweet dish that frequently called for chicken is *judhaba*, a kind of sweetened Yorkshire pudding run amok. In his book, Al-Baghdadi provides only eight recipes for *judhaba*, and al-Warraq only nineteen, but the true number of varieties of this Muslim favourite must have been in the hundreds. The preparation began with a large shallow pan layered with bread – any type, from stale bread crumbs, to slices of leavened bread, to uncooked yeast dough, to *qatāʾif*, a type of stuffed crepe. Layered with the bread were pieces of fruit or melon, berries, nuts, eggs, honey, or syrup, in any possible combination. The whole thing was then lowered into a clay oven and over it would be suspended a chicken, a leg of lamb, or mutton. The hot fat and juices from the cooking meat would drip down onto the *judhaba* below, infusing the sweet mixture with its savoury flavour. At the end of the cooking, the pan would be inverted, freeing the *judhaba*, which was then cut into pieces and eaten with thin slices of the meat it had been cooked under. Loved by caliphs and ordinary folk alike, *judhaba* was sold by street vendors throughout the Muslim world, and few cuts of meat anywhere in Baghdad would have been roasted without a pan of *judhaba* under them.

The taste for fruit, sugar, honey and sweetened syrup was of course not limited to just meat-based dishes. There were literally hundreds of types of candies, cakes, cookies, puddings and desserts available for the sweet-toothed.

The inhabitants of Islamic Spain were famous throughout Islam for their love of fish. By the 13th century, the date of this plate, the Muslim potters of Iberia had become famous in southern Europe for the quality of their decorative glazed dishes.

Sweets and pastries were popular with medieval Muslims, as
they still are with their modern descendents. It is not surprising
that the English words 'candy', 'sugar', 'marzipan', 'sherbet'
and 'syrup' all have Arabic roots.

It is impossible to list here even the various combinations of *natif*, nougat and nut, or the varieties of *aruzzīyat*, rice and milk puddings. Suffice it to say that if it was sweet, the medieval Muslims would have enjoyed it. Among their favourite desserts were *qatā'if*, crepes stuffed with everything from fruit to nuts, and *faludhāj*, a marzipan-like confection made from ground almonds, sugar and rose-water, and *ka'k*, cakes made from flour, eggs, sugar and sometimes butter. (And here one is tempted to suggest that modern etymologists have erred in identifying the genesis of the English word 'cake' in an Old Norse word for 'lump of something', rather than in a perfectly suitable Persian and Arabic word, one which is identical to an even more ancient Sumerian word for the same thing.) Another pastry popular in both Baghdad and al-Andalus was *qanawāt*, pieces of dough made into tubes, deep fried and then filled with a variety of sweets. Some have suggested, not without justification, that *qanawāt* remained popular in Sicily after Islam was defeated there in the late twelfth century, and was known as cannoli.

Sweetness was so valued in dishes that many of the favourite pastries and candies were further drenched in honey or sweetened syrups, much like baklava is today. One such treat, which was not particularly sweet and never went out of fashion, was the Prophet Muhammad's beloved *hais*, the humble mixture of curds, dates and clarified butter. Al-Baghdadi's version is naturally a more refined, urban dish, made with dates, ground pistachios and almonds, a little sesame oil and breadcrumbs to help bind it into finger-food sized balls.

By the beginning of the thirteenth century, the two halves of the Muslim world were in political disarray. In Iberia, the Umayyad caliphate of Córdoba had fallen in the early decades of the eleventh century, to be replaced first by a score of petty kingdoms and then by a pair of North African fundamentalist theocracies, the last of which, the Almohads, was defeated by Christian forces at the Battle of Las Navas de Tolosa in 1212. Within thirty years of that defeat all of the Muslim possessions in Portugal and the Guadalquivir valley, including the great cities of Córdoba and Seville, were in Christian hands, reducing the Muslim polity to the mountainous regions around Granada. Meanwhile, in Baghdad, by the middle of the tenth century the caliphs had become mere puppets in the hands of upstart, non-Arab Muslim dynasties, first the Iranian Buwayhids and then the Turkish Seljuks. The final blow, however, was struck in 1258 when the Mongols under Hulagu Khan arrived from the east and destroyed the city in a calculated orgy of violence. Cuisines, however, are not as easily stamped out as caliphates and theocracies. Neither the Iberian Christians, with their love of the pig and the fermented grape, nor the Mongols, whose diet according to Ibn Battuta consisted chiefly of boiled horsemeat and mutton, were immune to the charms offered by the Muslim table, and many of the most famous dishes lived on in the East and the West.

In Spain, especially in the south, the modern table fairly groans with dishes that have their origins in Persia, Baghdad and North Africa, from paella to gazpacho, to albondigas, which are nothing if not al-Baghdadi's beloved *kubabs*. And although the Mongols quickly retreated back to central Asia, their legacy lived on in the Timurids, the Muslim dynasty founded by Timur, who by the first decade of the fifteenth century had conquered a swath of land from Damascus to Delhi. The children and grandchildren of Timur, unlike their Mongol forebears, wasted little time in becoming refined Muslim gentlemen, and many of them were gourmands of the first order. It was they, and their Safavid successors, who were chiefly responsible for spreading the court cuisine of Baghdad and Persia eastward into India and Afghanistan, where it survives in a host of recognizable dishes.

Of course, the cuisine never completely died in the Muslim heartland, although it did become greatly simplified, losing many of its famous sauces and condiments. Display dining and the high cuisine, however, remained the prerogatives of the ruling class, which after the Mongols left was mostly Turkish. Like the Mughals and Safavids in the east, the Ottoman rulers of Istanbul in the west were diners on a grand and innovative scale. But, for the ordinary residents of Baghdad, Damascus and the Hijaz, the years of culinary glory were in the past.

*Food and Taste in Europe in
the Middle Ages*

C. M. Woolgar

A page from the *Très Riches Heures,* a book of hours made in the early fifteenth-century for John, Duke of Berry (d. 1416), provides a vignette of fine dining in Europe during the Middle Ages. It belongs to a genre of illustrations of 'Le bon repas', celebrating hospitality and good food, and it accompanies the calendar for January, that part of the book of hours setting out the principal liturgical feasts for the month. Here it extols the festivities of the New Year, when hospitality in ducal houses was at its greatest.

The meal takes place in public in a great chamber, hung with chivalric tapestries. The chamber is not a dedicated dining area: in that period most rooms served a variety of functions. It is unlikely to have been a 'high table' in a hall since in Europe (except for England) high-class diners were separated from the lower servants of the household, who ate in their own 'low halls'. The Duke is seated at table on a banker (a bench with a back), covered with a rich textile, which goes down to the floor. He is under a canopy or cloth of estate, with his back to a fire, from which he is shielded by a fire screen. This position for the fire-place in the great chamber was quite common on the Continent, but not usually found in England. Behind the Duke, to his right, is a steward or master of the household with his rod of office. The man behind the Duke, to his left, leaning on the banker, is possibly his physician, advising him on the dishes that are set before him. Also behind the Duke is a group that has probably just come in from a cold January day, who are instructed to come closer – 'aproche, aproche' – to benefit not only from the warmth of the fire but also the Duke's general hospitality. One guest is already helping himself to a drink from the buffet.

The table, although laid with a fine diapered cloth and gold (or silver-gilt) dishes, is a board resting on trestles. Tables like this, which could be readily cleared away, were used well into the fifteenth century in northern Europe. The Duke is seated with considerable honorific space separating him from the churchman next to him. They both have either finger bowls or a dish with a pottage (thick meat or vegetable soup). On the table are two large gold or silver-gilt dishes, with birds

Fine dining at the start of the 15th century: January from the *Très Riches Heures* of John, Duke of Berry, one of the great books of hours painted for the Duke by the Limbourg brothers of Nijmegen, who had also worked for the Duke's brother, Philip the Bold, the Duke of Burgundy.

that are being carved. In front of the Duke is a series of gold dishes with silver covers, to keep the food warm. To the right is a *nef*, a great gold salt in the shape of a ship, which is well known from the inventories of the Duke's possessions and which is decorated with a bear on one end and a swan on the other (picking up the Duke's favoured heraldic motifs on the textile canopy). Elaborate salts were a hallmark of grand dining. The *nef* was a form that was used both for salts and for vessels that held alms. A small standing cup is on the table next to it. In front of the Duke stand two servants. One is a carver or *écuyer tranchant*, possibly the pantler (in charge of the pantry), with his towel or tippet over his shoulder. Another servant stands at the end of the table preparing the food of the churchman, while yet one more crouches in the foreground with a greyhound and the meat that he has cut for it. Two further small dogs are on the table. The rush matting on the floor was a common covering in rooms like this and would be replaced frequently.

The buffet in the corner, with its gold or silver-gilt vessels, flagons and drinking bowls, is among the foremost indicators of status. Its size, the number of tiers and scale of wealth displayed were keenly scrutinized. Buffets were a feature of all dining at this level, across Europe, from the Italian *credenza* to the English 'rich cupboard'. Here, a servant with a pitcher holds a bowl, while wine is poured into it from another bowl by a servant who is also holding a standing cup. Standing cups of this quality were usually intended to be shared and would have been taken round the table by servants. The servants may be taking an assay of the wine – that is testing it to make sure that it has not been poisoned or is unsuitable in any other way. Two servants have black purses suspended from their belts, both with a gold-handled implement – and this may have part of a 'unicorn's horn' set in it, used to touch foodstuffs and drink to counteract poison.

The information that we have about food and taste in the medieval period comes from a wide range of sources – not only illustrations such as the one described above, but also cookery books, domestic accounts and menus for feasts, and archaeological remains – but their survival has been patchy and varies in its coverage. The documentation is at its best between AD 1200 and 1500, primarily for the upper classes and some ecclesiastical institutions. The evidence to support a detailed analysis of gastronomic habits before the year AD 1000 is largely absent.

With the end of the Roman Empire the common perceptions that had created a widespread understanding of high culture and cuisine had been destroyed. It was more than five hundred years before there was again a similar recognition of gastronomy. The barbarian invasions of Europe brought an abrupt disjuncture with classical Roman cuisine. The influence of Apicius may just have lingered in the Italian and Iberian peninsulas, but on the whole it had to be rediscovered in the fifteenth century. What replaced it was, to judge by Christian responses, excesses of food and drink. Caesarius of Arles (*c.* 470?–542) tried to persuade his listeners from participation in heavy drinking and feasting, not only for the likelihood of consequences that might cause regret, but also because this was behaviour typical of pagans. Feasting on an heroic scale is celebrated in poetry, for example in *Beowulf.* Funerals provided a special focus. From Merovingian Gaul, notably in the first half of the sixth century, there is Christian legislation against funerary feasting. Graves – not always pagan – from the fourth to the seventh centuries AD, in Gaul and beyond, contain evidence of food that was the share of the dead on some of these occasions. Chicken and eggs, cooked with honey, along with other meats with mustard and sage, were found in two fifth-century graves under the church of St Severinus in Cologne. A sixth-century grave at Krefeld-Gellep contained, among other things, beef ribs and a large spit. From the point of view of cuisine and gastronomy, however, the evidence awaits more detailed analysis. After this period, much less complex food offerings are found in graves. Memorial feasts were to endure in the Christian calendar, for example, for saints, albeit with the participation of the dead recast in a different guise.

On domestic sites, archaeology documents the range and ages of animals consumed. In Early Saxon England, bone assemblages often contain remains of cattle and sheep slaughtered between six months and two years old, that is, prime beef and mutton. From the eighth century onwards, this evidence suggests that many animals were older at slaughter, indicating that agricultural demands had become more important than meat production. The pattern was not reversed in general until specialized dairy farming spread more widely from the thirteenth century onwards. English high-status sites, such as Ramsbury, from the seventh century and later show a greater diversity in animal bone deposits, with more than half of many assemblages made up of pork, poultry, fish and game. These sites are also distinguished by a higher proportion of beef than mutton, a pattern of consumption unlike that from urban or rural sites. As much of the beef came from older animals, it may not always have been of high quality, but this may represent provisions for retainers. Younger animals, presumably reserved for the elite, appear in the later medieval period in increasing numbers in high-status contexts, as at Guildford Castle, where a thirteenth-century level produced food remains derived from no fewer than fifteen sheep or goats, none more than a matter of weeks old. The differences apparent from archaeozooloogy underscore dietary practice throughout the Middle Ages: upper-class food was distinctive. Although it is difficult at present to describe the period before AD 1000 in terms of gastronomic experience, we can see that elite diet was both more broadly based in its constituents and more selective in the quality of some elements.

One of the earliest and continuing determinants of eating patterns was the link between diet and virtue. From at least the fourth century, Christianity promoted abstinence for its spiritual benefits. Refraining from meat and dairy fats, and hence from carnality and its associated

In a 15th-century French illumination from the *Livre des bonnes mœurs*, Greed eats and drinks by himself inside a fine castle. The meat on his plate reflects the vices of carnality, here combined with alcohol. Outside the castle, Abstinence, in his virtue, stands away from the feast, dressed in sober colours.

vices of gluttony and lechery, helped to ensure the salvation of the soul. Many devout individuals were inspired to follow ascetic paradigms for abstinence, even if secular society was more liberal. Understanding fasting is therefore essential to recognizing the possibilities for cuisine in medieval Europe. On days of abstinence, fish became the food of choice, although not the only option. The great fourteenth-century French cookery book, the *Viandier* of Taillevent, identified meat days as Sunday, Tuesday and Thursday. Domestic accounts show a pattern of fasting that was more varied. In England, by the end of the thirteenth century, a noble household would have abstained from meat on nearly half the days of the year: throughout the season of Lent, on all Fridays and Saturdays, on many Wednesdays, as well as on the day preceding the feasts of the Evangelists and the great Marian feasts, and on others on the basis of personal devotion. Additional periods were added by the most devout. Other parts of Europe had different customs. The household of Marie d'Anjou, Queen of Majorca (daughter of Charles II, King of Sicily and Count of Provence), fasted in Lent in 1340–1, but during the remainder of the year only on Fridays, although poultry and rabbits were consumed on other days. These lighter meats may have equated to fasting: in England, they were eaten alongside fish on Wednesdays by female aristocrats. The Archbishop of Arles, in 1424–30, fasted on two days each week. Elsewhere there were general waivers that permitted

In medieval Europe, it was believed that all things were composed of the four elements. The human body had four related humours – melancholic, sanguine, phlegmatic and choleric (depicted clockwise from top left in this 15th-century English medical textbook) – the individual balance of which dictated the most appropriate form of diet. Regimens that matched or complemented the individual's make up were the concern of physicians who, in the greatest households, might advise their master at table on those foods that would best suit them.

consumption of proscribed foodstuffs. Payments for the consumption of butter in Lent are said to have paid for the construction of the Butter Tower at Rouen cathedral, *c.* 1480.

Medieval diet was also influenced by humoral theory. Derived from philosophical and medical works of classical Greece, its inspiration may possibly be detected as far afield as China, as noted in Chapter 3. In the medieval West, it produced a common belief that the universe was made up of four elements, each of which had its own characteristics: fire (hot and dry), water (cold and wet), earth (cold and dry) and air (hot and wet). The human body depended for its existence on four related humours: choler or yellow bile, phlegm, black bile and blood. All things reflected these elements and humours. Medieval dietetics

matched the individual to foods with the optimum characteristics, to achieve a temperate state – warm and moist. Cooking changed a food's nature: heat dried a food; boiling, however, would moisten it. Fish were typically moist and wet – and a cook might aim to dry them to achieve a more temperate mean. Digestion was a form of 'cooking', to be conducted in a measured way to translate the food into blood or other humour: over-indulgence at the meal might produce an imbalance of humours. Late medieval medical theory considered that there were eight flavours: sweet, greasy, bitter, salty, sharp, harsh, salty like the sea and vinegary. The eight tastes were linked to humoral analysis and may underlie some of the workings of medieval cookery books.

While it is difficult to see these theories in operation, physicians in great households were expected to make this connection. In 1473, Olivier de la Marche, a master of the household of the Duke of Burgundy, wrote an account of the detailed operation of that establishment. When the Duke was at table, his physician placed himself behind the banker on which the Duke was seated, as is probably depicted in the feast of the Duke of Berry seen on p. 162. The physician surveyed the foods served to the Duke and advised which would be the most profitable to him. As well as selecting foods for their humoral properties, other items, with powers of their own that might contribute to good health, were added to what was consumed. In his *Du fait de cuisine*, Master Chiquart, the renowned early fifteenth-century cook of Duke Amadeus I of Savoy, included a recipe for a *restaurant*, a restorative dish especially designed for the sick. Jewels known for their virtue – such as diamonds, pearls, rubies and sapphires – were to be placed in a little bag of silk or linen and mixed in with the chopped capon during cooking, along with sixty to eighty pieces of gold.

By *c.* 1200, and until *c.* 1500, elite culinary tastes were remarkably consistent across Europe. Common features can be identified, although, like Gothic architecture and other aspects of medieval culture, there was considerable regional variation. We should not forget, however, that for much of the medieval period, to the mid-fourteenth century, the choices implied by gastronomy and cultured taste were not available to many in Europe.

Eating fresh food was, throughout the medieval period, a mark of status. At a period when the consumption of any meat was exceptional, Europe's elite consumed large quantities of fresh meat, even through the winter months when others, if they had access to meat, would have had preserved forms. In the late medieval period, in terms of meatstock, the north European littoral from the Low Countries through to Brittany had a predominance of cattle over other species. More pigs were kept in central France and Germany. Sheep were much more common in Britain than elsewhere in northern Europe, but were more important in the south, especially around the Mediterranean. These patterns were reflected in collections of recipes. There was little beef in French recipes, but predominantly pork and poultry, along with some selective use of the best cuts of mutton. There was at the same time a preference for young animals.

Pigs do not produce secondary products, such as wool, and they were therefore killed when they reached the optimum size for meatstock, as in this late thirteenth-century French illumination. Pork was a meat that preserved well and slaughter typically took place in late autumn, after the pigs had been fattened in the woods on acorns and beech mast.

Preparations for hunting deer: the lord and his two huntsmen discuss the report of the lymerer, with his hunting horn, who has just laid on the table the fumets he has found on his reconnaissance. In his *Livre de la chasse*, Gaston Phébus asks for a substantial meal to be laid on at this point, before the hunt begins. In this early 15th-century French manuscript of his work, the lord sits at a table, others eat off tablecloths spread on the ground and drink is kept chilled in a nearby stream.

A special place was reserved at the tables of the upper classes for the beasts of the chase. These conferred both status and distinctive flavours on cuisine. Access to these animals, particularly deer and wild boar, was increasingly restricted after *c.* 1000 with the development of hunting preserves, such as the New Forest in southern England, and parks, for example that of Roger II of Sicily at Palermo, as well as warrens for rabbits. Even among the elite, deer were not always available. In France, there must have been a predominance of small game and Gaston Phébus wrote about them at some considerable length in his *Livre de la chasse* at the end of the fourteenth century. In order to provide food – rather than entertainment – hunting was carried out by groups of specialist servants, frequently far away from the household. The venison (*venaison*, 'the product of hunting') was then butchered and often salted, either for preservation in local hunting larders or placed in barrels to be sent to the household.

Poultry and wild fowl were available in impressive quantities. Typically provided by peasant farmers (rather than the lord's own estates), there was in some places a specialist industry, with investment in, for example, the production of capons. There were also specialist providers of wildfowl and bird-catchers to accommodate the vast consumption of small birds. Some were caught, raised or maintained on estates until needed for consumption. Thus the third Duke of Buckingham (1478–1521) kept quail at Bletchingley; others had bitterns and peacocks.

In northern Europe, from the Viking period and the advent of boats suitable for deep-sea fishing, fish consumption became more marked. Eating fish, especially cod and herring, became more widespread in the decades around 1000 when it coincided with the renewed influence of the Church on dietary practices; but consuming fish, especially fresh marine fish or freshwater fish, remained closely linked to status. Fish formed a major element in upper-class consumption. Large parts of northern Europe, lying within a day's journey by pack-horse from the sea, had access to fresh marine fish. The widest range of species is found in the greatest households. An early fifteenth-century Bishop of Salisbury had, in one nine-month period, no fewer than forty-two different types of fish, crustacea and shellfish for his table. Freshwater fish were also a mark of status. Large-scale investment was made in the construction of fishponds, particularly from the eleventh century onwards; and fish from these ponds – pike, perch, tench and carp (although the last not in England until the fifteenth century) – were popular alongside

An ample bourgeois drinks wine from a glass beaker before progressing to his meal of small, roasted birds. Few wild birds were not eaten and they were also believed to bring health benefits. This illumination, probably by the Frenchman Jean Bourdichon (1457–1521), illustrates the calendar for January in a book of hours, a time of year when wild birds, flocking together, were caught in great numbers.

Fish provided a virtuous dietary alternative to meat, and freshwater fish were especially valued. The frescoes of the Chambre du cerf, in the papal palace at Avignon, decorated for Clement VI in 1343, show a team of fishermen about to take a rich harvest from an elegant fishpond using a seine-net (held by the man standing on the right); the smaller net on a pole would have been used for individual fish.

those that came from streams and rivers – salmon, trout, eels, lamprey and sturgeon.

From the ninth century to the peak levels of population in the early fourteenth century, there was an increasing dependence on cereals, with diminishing amounts of meat and dairy products available per person. Cereals were a major constituent of all medieval diets, but they were a smaller element within the diet of the elite. Manuscript illuminations show typical round loaves or rolls on most aristocratic tables. The best wheat was required to produce fine white bread – *pain de main* (literally 'household bread') or superior variants. In the greatest households, bread was either baked or bought fresh each day; but in others it was kept for longer periods, for up to a week. Older bread was sliced for trenchers (the bread on which it was customary to serve the meal), grated or crumbled into sauces to thicken them, or used by those serving the meal to prevent their hands burning on metal dishes they carried. While some might emulate the elite in their consumption of

In this woodcut of King Solomon with his wives, probably by Michael Wolgemut, c. 1491, the King follows late 15th-century custom, dining alone. In front of him is a square trencher; to his right a carver or pantler offers him food on a flat-bladed serving knife; to his left on the table is a standing salt, and a servant brings in a stack of covered dishes, to the accompaniment of music. Drink, in a flagon, is kept close at hand in a cooler in front of the table.

white bread, others relied on poorer grains, rye, barley and even oats, and some may have consumed their cereals only in pottage.

After the high point of population levels, no later than the 1320s, and the catastrophic reduction in population in the Black Death of 1348–9, the balance of diet changed. In late medieval Europe, there were proportionately many more animals per person, resulting in a major growth in meat consumption and 'carnivorous Europe' became a reality. Periods of famine and dearth persisted, particularly in Continental Europe, but after the Black Death many more people had choice in terms of their food.

The availability of dairy foods, closely linked to animal husbandry, constituted a small part of diet generally until after the Black Death. Their impact on high-class cuisine was restricted, even in England, northern France and the Low Countries, where dairy foods were more widely produced. Cheese and butter both occur as items of gastronomic importance, however, across Europe. The best cheeses were

highly valued and transported considerable distances. For at least 150 years after *c.* 1170, cheeses from Gloucestershire were taken to the Norman Abbey of the Holy Trinity at Caen, carried by the Abbey's tenants to Southampton for shipment.

Gardens, despite their appeal to the aristocracy and the considerable investment they made in them, were more important for the peasantry and monastic orders as a source for food. In France, recipe collections include leeks and cabbages, garlic and onions, with rare mentions of root crops. In England, although gardens did supply considerable amounts of produce to great households, on the whole vegetables provided flavouring rather than substantial elements in consumption. The underdeveloped nature of English horticulture is perhaps illustrated by cross-Channel trade; for example, cabbages were imported from northern France. Vegetables were more prominent in upper-class cuisine in southern Europe, both in terms of the range of produce and the quantities, and salads were also more common there. In the north there was some prejudice against these foodstuffs on health grounds, but they did appear, particularly in monasteries.

Fruit was widely available, although some kinds, such as citrus, were grown only in southern Europe. In France, grapes constituted an important flavouring as well as providing wine. They were grown on a modest scale in England in the thirteenth century, where they were used principally for flavouring, as verjuice, rather than as a sweetener. Apples, pears, quinces, medlars, cherries and a wide range of nuts were all eagerly sought after. Their ubiquity is underestimated by cookery books, largely because in the greatest households the responsibility for the supply of fruit was often not in the hands of the cook, but of a specialist fruiterer. Domestic accounts show that fruit was consumed and that, along with spices, it was readily available in chambers after the conclusion of formal meals. Raisins, dates and figs were common accompaniments to fish at the fasting seasons. Eating fruit was considered to have health benefits and it was frequently consumed by invalids.

As well as similarities in the kinds of food consumed across Europe, there were other common features in medieval gastronomy. The cooks of Paris, London, Barcelona or Rome would all have recognized *brouet* (a pottage with diced meat or fish), *blanc-manger* (a dish based on ground chicken, pork or veal, mixed with rice and other flavouring or colouring), mortress (a dish of boiled, ground pork, chicken or white-fleshed fish, mixed with almond milk, and stiffened with either egg or breadcrumbs), rissoles (chopped meat, fish or fruit, mixed with spices and flour into balls or cakes, and fried), green sauce (parsley, mint, chopped in vinegar, with other spices, thickened with bread, sometimes with egg), and a wide range of other dishes.

Medieval cookery was marked by a passion for spices and strong tastes. Spices were employed not solely for their aromatic

Opposite: A 14th-century Italian corn market: cereals provided a substantial element in diet throughout the Middle Ages, as bread, pottage, ale and beer. It was only after the Black Death that the peasantry had access to significant quantities of meat.

Below: Growing lettuce, from a 15th-century Italian *Tacuinum Sanitatis* or handbook on health. These handbooks, inspired ultimately by Arabic medical sources, examined the make up of the human and influences on health: food consumption was prominent among their concerns and southern European works described the place of salads in this overall pattern.

and digestive qualities, but also (and sometimes exclusively) for the colours they gave food. More than 70 per cent of recipes recorded in cookery books used spices, which were the hallmark of aristocratic cuisine. Master Chiquart was responsible in 1416 for making a sauce for a roast lamprey for the Duke of Savoy. He required 1 lb. of white ginger, 2 lb. of cinnamon, with grain of paradise, pepper, cloves and other spices. By 1420, when he wrote up this recipe in his cookery book, additional spices were needed, including mace and nutmeg.

Flavourings such as these probably first made a major impact in northern Europe around the time of the Crusades. They became an important feature of trade across the Continent and far beyond, some of them originating in present-day India, Indonesia and China. In the notebook that he compiled probably over the first forty years of the fourteenth century, the Florentine Francesco Pegolotti listed nearly 300 products that he classed as 'spices'. These encompassed not only what one might now consider as spices, but also nuts and fruits, such as almonds (which were commonly employed crushed, to form a milk), figs and dates, and ingredients for medicine, perfumery and cosmetics. In the Middle Ages, little distinction was made between these goods in terms of their end use (and some of these products, sweet, fruit-based confections,

Cinnamon, from Ceylon, was among the most prized of eastern spices consumed in Europe. It was described by Dioscorides in the 1st century AD, and this illustration of a spice-seller overwhelmed by his wares comes from a fifteenth-century Latin translation of his work. The sweet odour of cinnamon was especially associated with virtue: it was sometimes used as an epithet of the Virgin Mary and was employed in expensive cosmetic preparations as well as in foodstuffs.

may have been interchangeable in some settings, both as a food and as a cosmetic).

The purpose of spices in cuisine was fourfold: to change the nature of the dish in humoral terms; to alter its flavour; to dictate its colour; and to indicate the standing of the establishment in terms of conspicuous consumption. Those lower down the social scale employed fewer spices and embraced with vigour those flavourings that were also locally grown, for example, mustard, crab apples and saffron. Of the imported spices some, such as pepper, which had commanded a high price in the thirteenth century, became more commonly available as the volume traded increased.

One spice in particular – sugar – changed the possibilities of cuisine. Sugar cane was introduced to the Middle East from India in the eighth and ninth centuries, then grown in Egypt and North Africa, and, by the later Middle Ages, on the islands of the Mediterranean. The mid-thirteenth-century development on Cyprus of water power for mills to crush sugar cane transformed the volumes available in the market. It was widely traded throughout Europe by the Venetians and Genoese in the form of sugar loaves, sometimes flavoured, and it was employed to make sweet confections, often traded as boxed, candied fruits (from the Arabic 'kand', sugar, hence also Candia, now Crete), or sweet powders. In northern Europe it was in turn used to make fruit compotes and preserves.

Flavourings were also derived from fruits and these supplied some of the sour, acidic and bitter tastes desired by medieval cuisine. Citrus fruits, especially the citron and sour Seville oranges, along with pomegranates, from North Africa, Spain, southern France and Italy, made a significant impact on cookery in these areas, following Arab influences. Their presence was rare in northern Europe, except in sweet confections, such as citrinade. Staple sources of tart or acidic flavours more widely employed were wine, vinegar and verjuice, or sour ale, as well as sharp-tasting soft fruits such as redcurrants or gooseberries, green or crab apples, or bitter herbs, such as sorrel. These sharp flavours were introduced into cooking in two principal ways and in considerable quantities, as pottages or as sauces. Some of these sauces were commercially available and could be bought by the gallon. Their tastes were extensively appreciated throughout society. There was nothing unusual in the testimony of Thomas, son of William of Donnington, a witness to one of the miracles of St Thomas Cantilupe, recalling how he had set out from his Welsh village in mid-September 1305 with the intention of gathering crab apples for *salsa* (sauce). The sauces were thin and not made with fat or oil, but various thickening agents were employed, including breadcrumbs and wheat starch.

The same dish might be presented, seemingly without distinction, spiced as savoury or sweetened with sugar (or honey). Sweet or savoury spice could be applied to meat and to fish as readily as to what might now be termed desserts.

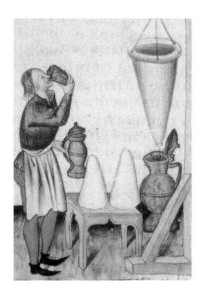

Above: Sugar had a profound influence on elite cuisine in the Middle Ages, especially in Italy, Catalonia and England. It became available in Western Europe in much greater quantities after the middle of the 13th century. This Italian illustration of Dioscorides from the 15th century shows the manufacture of conical sugar loaves.

Opposite: Lorenzo Lotto (c. 1480–1556) included this market scene in his *Martyrdom of St Barbara*, at Bergamo. The market sellers have brought vegetables, fruit and possibly bread or cakes, and eggs in baskets. This is the trade of local small-scale, peasant producers; it was important, but is not well documented.

Beyond these features, but still within this recognizable style, there were regional variations, based on the range of products available, on the kinds of seasoning and type of food preparation, and on patterns of meals. Arabic cuisine was a major influence, particularly in the Mediterranean, in Sicily, Catalonia, Spain and southern France; but it had less of an impact in northern Italy. The Italians and Catalans, like the English, were very given to sugar. Sugar was used in England to counter the force of the acidity of many flavourings, or of spices. It was employed increasingly from the fourteenth century; and then much more extensively in the period 1400–20. The link to Sicily through the Normans introduced to England dishes that had an Arab origin or theme. The use of sugar may have been one of these elements. Most English cookery books have dishes described as 'Saracen', many of them coloured red, others flavoured with pomegranate. The Arab influence was less noticeable in northern France and Germany. 'Sweet' dishes were one of the features that differentiated medieval English recipes from medieval French ones.

English cuisine used wheat starch as a thickener, another practice that distinguished it from French custom. English cookery books were also given to quirky inspirations – feats of design, use of colour, moulding of ingredients (after they had been reduced to a plastic texture) and dressing them up as other things, for example, meatballs as hedgehogs. Something similar is found in German cookery books: the *Kochbuch Meister Hannsens* of c. 1460 includes 'eggs' made from almonds and a 'roe deer' made of fish. Some of these inventions were directly related to 'subtleties', often served at the close of a course or as *entremets*, 'between courses', discussed below; but they also encompassed a range of unexpected combinations. In England, local ingredients, particularly blossoms of primrose, hawthorn, violet, peony or rose, which were used for flavour as much as for colour, produced a genre of dishes without parallel.

The use of spices in English recipes of the thirteenth and fourteenth centuries was much more restrained than in French recipes of this period. English cuisine concentrated particularly on ginger and cinnamon, sometimes with pepper but the recipes had changed significantly in this respect by the fifteenth century when the spices employed in both countries tended to be similar. Ready-prepared spice mixes, such as blanchepowder – in the manner of 'curry powder' – probably made largely with ginger, cinnamon and some nutmeg, in part led to this uniformity. Sometimes a recipe demands 'spicery', which must have implied something similar. Some spices, such as cubebs, seem not to have been used elsewhere.

French cuisine can be divided between north and south. The *brouet* or broth was particularly important in northern France. This was not a broth as we understand it today. To the liquor were added meat and fish, either ground or in nuggets, and often almond milk. The use of ground almonds in a paste, rather than milk products, was a

distinctive feature of elite cuisine. The French use of spices was more subtle than the English. In France, the *grosses espices* – ginger, cinnamon, pepper, grain of paradise – were employed in considerable quantities. Ginger was the key ingredient. Smaller quantities were drawn from what were known as the *menues espices* – cloves, galingale, nutmeg and mace. Significant use was made of mustard, but less of green herbs. Grain of paradise became very important in France in the fourteenth century, probably displacing pepper in French *haute cuisine*. By the time of Chiquart, it appeared in perhaps two out of three recipes. This usage was particularly French: around 1400 it was found in only one in ten recipes in English, Catalan and Italian cookery books. But its use in France declined in the fifteenth century and it was hardly to be found in the sixteenth. The identification with paradise was not coincidental to its success. It was commonly believed that exotic spices came from the area where the Garden of Eden had been; they and their aromas were equally prominent in accounts of the heavenly Jerusalem. The opportunity to transfer this association to one's own cooking was not to be passed by.

French domestic accounts record the consumption of raw fruit. Unlike England, however, there were few recipes in French cookery books for fruit-based dishes. Nor was there much reference to cooking in pastry cases, or pies ('coffins', in English). This was a common practice, but a straightforward one, and therefore may have been overlooked in cookery books. French cuisine equally did not make extensive use of tarts and flans that employed large quantities of eggs. These were popular in Italy and in England. One English speciality was the preparation of great cheese flans for Rogation (the three days immediately preceding the Ascension). Although it was probably more common, there are few French references to candying fruit except in the *Ménagier de Paris*, a compilation prepared in the 1390s, including recipes and menus designed to assist a bourgeois housewife.

Northern France, Burgundy and Savoy were at the centre of international culinary influence and cookery books contain an eclectic range of recipes denominated by place of origin. *Brouet d'Engleterre* or *brouet d'Allemaigne* appeared here alongside dishes from Tournai, Paris, Brie, the Bourbonnais, Poitou, Savoy and Provence. Italy featured strongly in the same way, with recipes for, for example, *leche Lombard*, and dishes from Parma, Bologna, Genoa, Florence, Pisa and Rome. These dishes may, of course, have been totally unlike those natives would have expected, much like the resemblance between contemporary *crème anglaise* and custard; but they are indicative of the cross-currents of culinary influence.

The cuisine of southern France contained distinctive elements, for example, pomegranates and citron, which also appeared in Catalan and Italian cookery books. Other characteristics included the use of oil, rather than butter, as a cooking medium, and chickpeas. More spices were used than in the north, especially ginger, pepper, mint and saffron. The typical balance of ingredients can be seen in the household of Marie d'Anjou, Queen of Majorca, who spent £243 on foodstuffs in Provence in 1340–1: £68 was disbursed on wheat (principally for bread), £55 on wine, £52 on mutton, pork and veal, fat and rabbits, £19 on poultry, pigeons and partridges; £13 on fish (only tuna is named, but fresh and salt fish in general were recorded), £9 on spices (cinnamon, cloves, pepper, saffron, mustard, vinegar, sugar and honey), £7 on eggs, £7 on fresh and dried vegetables (cabbage, leeks, spinach, root vegetables, gourds, onions, garlic, chickpeas, beans, lentils), £5 on salt and oil, £4 on fresh and dried fruit (almonds, cherries, chestnuts, figs, peaches, filberts and nuts, pomegranates), £4 on cheeses and £2 on sauces and condiments, including oranges as a sauce.

Consumption in Spain and Catalonia was similar, although the Arab influence was stronger here and there were different traditions of cooking associated with the Jewish community. There were significant contrasts between the foods of the Mediterranean south and Atlantic coast of the north, which again contrasted with the central plain. The Catalan *Libre de Sent Soví* of around 1324 was particularly strong in terms of seafood recipes. Despite its claim to have been written by the cook of Edward II of England, there was nothing English about its recipes, which have a firm base in the Mediterranean. The cuisine was also characterized by the variety of vegetables, such as asparagus. An account for three days' expenses of Alfonso II, the Count King of Catalonia, at Manresa, probably in March (Lent) 1181, included salt, vinegar, fresh fish, salt fish, oil, honey, beans, chestnuts, pepper, bread and wine, spinach, leeks and chickens. In 1184, in Provence, his agents had similar foodstuffs, this time with meats: pork and beef, rabbit, lamb, goat, chickens and partridge.

The evidence for Italian cuisine that comes from Platina – the humanist Bartolomeo Sacchi, whose work *De honesta voluptate et valetudine* (On Correct Pleasure and Good Health) was published in Rome in 1470 – at the end of the Middle Ages, includes soups, stews and straightforward recipes for fish. The pottages of northern Europe were absent. A good deal of prominence was given to vegetables and exotic ingredients, particularly oranges and dates. Sicily may have had a much spicier cuisine. Links to the Arab world were responsible for the development of desserts or sweets such as sherbet and ice cream.

From Germany across Poland to Silesia evidence for a homogenous pattern of cookery comes from cookery books of the mid-fourteenth to early sixteenth centuries. There were some influences from French and Italian cuisine, the latter probably introduced by physicians. The spices in *Daz bûch von gûter spise* (The Book of Good Food) of *c.* 1350 from Würzburg include salt, pepper, saffron, ginger, aniseed, caraway, then garden herbs. There was some use of sugar, but much more of wine, milk and vinegar. Some recipes employed multiple cooking, with food taken out of the skin or away from the carcass, cooked, replaced and cooked again. Fritters and flatcakes were favourite dishes. A late medieval cookery book from Mühldorf in the Lower Inn valley is unusual in focusing predominantly on the products of hunting and fishing, a reflection of their prominence in the local environment. The dishes from north and south Germany and Austria were broadly similar in pattern, but were distinguished by the presence of far fewer sauces than in France, more pies, roasts and soups. The great lakes of the area provided significant quantities of fish and there was printed advice on fishing in lakes, such as Tegernsee, from the late fifteenth century.

Despite these local variations, the key determinant in medieval diet was social class and connections to display and social competition. The link to display was especially apparent in the transformational qualities of medieval cooking. Through mincing, pounding and chopping, ingredients were frequently reduced to a malleable form, which might be moulded into the most fantastic shapes, sometimes regaining their former skins and plumage, or assuming old or new forms inside pastry. Colour was of particular importance, sometimes without reference to flavour, opening up realms of curious possibilities.

With much clearer direction than they give about taste, cookery books gave instructions on how to achieve visual effects. *Daz büch von güter spise* indicated that saffron, parsley, violets and cherries might be added as much for colour as for taste. Colouring beyond green and yellow came quicker to Anglo-Norman cuisine than to the French.

Norman cooking, late 11th or early 12th century, from the Bayeux Tapestry. William the Conqueror lands at Pevensey and food is prepared for a feast. 'Here meat is cooked', shows meat prepared on spits, the boiling of foods in a pot suspended over a fire, a bearded servant placing cooked food from a stove on a dish and the delivery of food and drink to a table improvised from a number of shields. A horn summons the guests to table.

The fourteenth-century Anglo-Norman *Diversa cibaria* (Diverse Foodstuffs) included indigo and multi-coloured presentations. Its first three recipes were for a Saracen dish of ground chicken, rice, almonds and sugar, which were distinguished by their colouring: blanc desire (i.e. of Syria), vert desire and [j]anesere, that is, white, green and yellow, coloured green with parsley and yellow with saffron. Pottages were sometimes 'departed': two separate, coloured pottages served in the same dish. This was also achieved with jellies and custards, such as doucet. A fifteenth-century recipe for 'colouryd sew', a dish made with ground almonds and rice as its base, spiced with white sugar, cloves, maces, cubebs and cinnamon, was to be coloured: 'And let that one part by white, the other yellow, and the other green with parsley.' The range of colouring was impressive: from red and indigo, through to green and yellow. There was a pattern to some colouring: a green sauce and/or green colouring went with many fish dishes.

Cooks were required to create the appropriate colour: green might come from parsley, but that was only one possibility. A version of the *Viandier* refers to the use of sorrel, vine leaves or buds, or even green corn in winter to achieve the same effect. Grated toast might add dark colour to a sauce; chicken livers would turn it brown; and egg yolk would reinforce a yellow colour. Extensive use was made of saffron to create a yellow or gold colour, with no intention of adjusting the flavouring. The inspiration for this colouration may have been Arab

A medieval kitchen, from a 14th-century handbook on health (*Tacuinum Sanitatis*), where offal, possibly tripe or chitterlings, is being prepared. Although a food that was commonly available to the poor, sausages, puddings and some offal dishes were also delicacies. There was a seasonal pattern to their production, most commonly falling in the winter months, coinciding with the pattern of slaughtering animals.

cuisine. 'Golden food', using gold leaf, but also generally coloured gold and eaten off coloured plates, especially gold ones, made a huge impact on the Crusaders. There was further an emphasis on the lustre of colour: this might be achieved through the use of egg glazes. Gold and silver leaf, in themselves prophylactics and of particular interest to those interested in alchemy, had similar effects.

Cooking methods in late medieval Europe did not differ significantly between countries. The most common methods were boiling, baking, roasting, frying and grilling. The late eleventh-century Bayeux tapestry depicts a great meal after the landing of William the Conqueror at Pevensey. Meat is boiled in a pot suspended over a fire; meat and fowl are roasted on spits and brought to table; and on the table there is fish. Boiling shared much with basic methods of cooking, but the great household required that it be conducted on a vast scale, with massive cauldrons. Baking, roasting and frying required a greater investment. Not all great households possessed ovens and payments were sometimes made separately for baking. Dame Katherine de Norwich, as part of the great feast held in Norwich in January 1337 for the anniversary of the death of her first husband, paid for the baking of twenty-four hens and 157 pies. In southern Europe, dry cooking of meat in an oven was much more common than in the north. Small, portable ovens were used, buried in ashes.

Eating roast foods was a sign of rank. Not only did roasting require meat of a high quality, but also lavish quantities of fuel. The household of Edward II of England was not unusual in restricting access to roasts to servants of the rank of esquire and above. Frying required additional fats (animal fats gathered in dripping pans, or the skimmings from cauldrons) or expensive oils. Only a small proportion of recipes require this technique, such as fritters, rissoles, 'crisps' and 'chawettys' (stuffed dough balls).

Most processes took place in a kitchen or bakehouse and surviving kitchens show something of the scale of the enterprise. It was not uncommon for kitchens to be detached buildings, minimizing the risk of fire, as at Glastonbury and Fontevraud. More delicate processes, for example, creating confectionary, might be performed using chafers and charcoal almost anywhere in the household. The fire risks from bakehouses, brewhouses, scalding houses (for processing poultry) and sculleries (for washing dishes and equipment) also kept them separate from the main buildings. Storage facilities were required for the pantry for bread, dairy products and table linen; and for the buttery, for ale and wines. It is not until the fourteenth century that there is good evidence for the laying down of wine, as opposed to drink for consumption in the short term. Larders were required for meat and fish, for both the storage of dry goods and for the processing of wet items. Wherever possible, stock and fish were kept alive for as long as possible to ensure that food was at its most fresh. Local pastures were

¶ Le liure de taillevent grant cuy sinier du Roy de France,

¶ On les vend a Lyon/en la maison de feu Barnabe Chaussard/pres nostre dame de Consort.

The title page of a late 15th-century edition of the *Livre de Taillevent*, now known as the *Viandier*, with a woodcut vignette of royal dining, printed at Lyons by Barnabas Chaussard. Although styles of dining and cuisine were to change, at least twenty-five printed editions of this work are known to have been published between 1486 and 1615, testimony to its popularity.

needed for cattle and sheep, fishponds for freshwater fish, and a reliable packhorse route for the supply of fresh, marine fish.

European cuisine was led by its cooks, but most remain largely unknown. They were among the most highly paid of domestic servants, frequently remembered in their master's will. Like most servants in the great household, men constituted the majority. It is possible to describe something of the careers of those at the highest echelons. Typically they learned their trade through experience on the job. The best were described as 'master', which may reflect a formal apprenticeship or a general level of recognition. Guillaume Tirel, known as Taillevent, is famous for the cookery book named after him. Even though the recipe collection now known as the *Viandier* of Taillevent was circulating before Tirel was alive, that it should have been identified with him speaks of his importance. He was possibly of Norman origin and is first recorded in 1326 as a child of the kitchen of Joan of Evreux, wife of Charles IV of France. He served in a series of other ducal or royal households: in 1346 and 1349, as 'ame queu de bouche' of Philip VI, cook for the king's personal food; as *écuyer* (squire) and cook to the Dauphin of Viennois; in 1360, as cook of the Duke of Normandy, the future Charles V; in 1368, as cook and sergeant of arms to the King; and in 1373 and 1377 as first cook of the King. He remained in royal service under Charles VI (r. 1380–1422), an *écuyer* of the kitchen in 1381, first *écuyer* of the kitchen of the King in 1388, and *maitre des garnisons*, responsible for the bulk purchasing, literally the 'catering', for the King's kitchen in 1392. He died *c.* 1395, aged about eighty-four. His career shows the breadth of a cook's activities, responsible not only for the kitchen, but for selecting and organizing supplies. In some households this was an administrative position and those who served might move to other departments to perform other organizational tasks. But in Tirel's case, his professional culinary expertise was to the fore. Another professional chef was Pierrot, the French cook of Henry VII of England. He had been cook to the King of Castile; he was in Henry's service from 1505, receiving the substantial wage of 20 marks a year (£13 6s. 8d.), along with cash rewards, the same rate as the King's surgeon. He may be synonymous with the 'French pasteler', the pastry cook, who received 10s. reward at Easter 1508.

In the late fifteenth century, according to Olivier de la Marche, the cook for the Duke of Burgundy was carefully selected from the *écuyers* of the kitchen, 'for it is not a common estate or office, it is a subtle profession and costly.' Like most household officers at this level, the cook had to swear an oath and give surety before his appointment was confirmed. There were three cooks for the Duke's own food, serving in rotation. If no cook were present, the servant in charge of the roasts was next in importance, although the pottager had a claim, for he was closely aware of the Duke's taste and the style of flavouring that the cook selected to suit his appetite. All provisions were to be taken before the cook, who was to choose what seemed best for the Duke himself. Seated in the kitchen, with a great ladle, the cook was to taste the pottages and *brouez*, and to chase children out of the kitchen. The cook looked after the spices acquired by bulk provision (*garnison*); the controller released to him other spices, such as sugar. He was allowed personally to bring food before the Duke, especially if it were the first occasion in the year that a foodstuff, such as fresh herring or truffles, had been served.

The Duke's kitchen establishment was substantial, at least twenty-five men, with children (without wages). The *hateur* looked after the roast, the *potaigier*, all the pottage ingredients, such as beans, peas, wheat, parsley and salt, with spices supplied by the cook. The Duke's saucerer looked after the ingredients for the sauces, including essential components for an acidic taste, the verjuice (*verjus de vin*) and corn-based vinegar (*verjus de grain*). The saucerer had assistants to help make the sauces and valets to clean the dishes. When the meats for the Duke were ready to serve at table, the saucerer gave the sauces to the pantler in covered dishes. The saucerer was to be in the room when the Duke ate. Other kitchen servants looked after the cauldrons, kept the door, provided wood and charcoal, and cleaned pots and equipment. The children carried out low-level tasks, turning spits, plucking the fowl and cleaning the fish, giving them to those who were to prepare them.

Beyond the kitchen, other sections of the household were responsible for food. The fruiterer took care of fruit of all kinds: pears, apples, cherries and grapes, dried plums, capers, figs, dates, raisins, nuts and filberts. The fruit, after it had been washed, was served in silver vessels and brought before the Duke by the fruiterer himself. The Duke's chamberlain received from the spicer the *épices de chambre* – the

In the great psalter prepared for Sir Geoffrey Luttrell of Irnham, Lincolnshire, *c.* 1320–45, a sequence of illuminations shows preparations in the kitchen for a meal served to the lord. At the table on the left, a cook chops roast piglet and poultry; at the second table, prepared sauces are poured into saucers from distinctively shaped sauce-bottles; and the meal is then taken to table.

Above: A child licking a wooden spoon after eating from a clay pot: a detail from a carved and painted reredos showing the family of St Anne, Voyri, Finland, c. 1500.

Opposite: A drinking scene – the filling of jugs or flagons – from the cycle of frescoes in the Oratory of St John the Baptist at Urbino, painted by the borthers Lorenzo and Jacopo Salimbeni in 1416. Although some wines were traded over considerable distances and fetched high prices, local wines in Italy were consumed in much greater quantity and drunk by all. In northern Europe, wine was an elite drink; ale was drunk by others, although in the later Middle Ages in the Low Countries the brewing of beer, with hops, made a more durable product and one of some distinction that could be marketed more widely.

mixtures of spice, sweet confections and dragées that were eaten in the chamber, as an aid to digestion.

With the food prepared, when was it consumed? Lunch (*prandium*) was the main meal of the day – and for many it may have been the first meal. The timing varied: in a large establishment both lunch and supper were sometimes eaten in shifts, drawing out the process. As part of a display of conspicuous consumption the meal could, even without this, take a great deal of time. In the fifteenth century, in England, when mechanical clocks were in common use in aristocratic households, lunch was eaten from about 10 a.m. onwards. In some establishments, especially ecclesiastical households or those with a particularly religious inspiration, this was the only meal that was eaten on a Friday. It was usually eaten later on these days, probably in imitation of monastic custom, postponing all food until after Vespers, the time of which was commonly advanced to the middle of the day so that food could be eaten earlier. Supper (*cena*) was eaten in the late afternoon, where clocks were used, between 4 p.m. and 6 p.m., and was a less substantial meal.

Breakfast was reserved for the elite in the great household. In many cases it consisted of little more than bread, but by the start of the sixteenth century it was a larger meal. The fifth Earl of Northumberland (1478–1527) and his wife expected to have in Lent bread, beer, wine, salt fish, smoked herring, salted herring and a dish of sprats. Out of Lent they also had a dish of butter and, as a variation from salt fish, a dish of buttered eggs. On flesh days chine of mutton or beef was substituted. Their children had chicken or a broth of boiled mutton bones. Other occasions for consumption included formal drinkings in the afternoon and sometimes in the morning. In England, the day concluded with a formal ceremony called 'all night', at 7 p.m. or 8 p.m. onwards, at which bread, wine and ale were issued for the evening and placed in chambers.

The structures of lunch and dinner were similar across Europe, although not everything happened in a uniform way. In late medieval England and France food was delivered to table in courses. In England there were rarely more than three courses; in France four or more were not uncommon in the service of the highest aristocracy. Within each course numbers of dishes were brought to the table together, paralleling in some ways the later *service à la française*, differing in that each course had a structure of its own.

In France, the roast was the pivotal point of the menu. Before it, there were frequently either one or two courses. Medical advice divided fruits into those that should precede a meal and those that should conclude it; meals sometimes started with, or were preceded by, small quantities of fruit, sausage or pudding, and pâtés. The first course proper typically was boiled beef and usually another boiled meat, either mutton or pork, sometimes with poultry. Heavily salted dishes, particularly those derived from salted foodstuffs, appeared in this course; and in France, too, there were some salads

Previous page: John of Gaunt dines with the King of Portugal, from a late 15th-century copy of Jean de Wavrin's *Chronique d'Angleterre*, prepared in Flanders for Edward IV of England. It shows a meal in a great chamber. Note the canopy over the King and the banker on which he is seated, along with the honorific space either side of the King. On the table are round loaves, metal trenchers, salts and knives. The food is delivered straight into the room from a serving hatch where the cook or saucerer would add the final sauces.

and accompanying vinaigrette dishes. This course was the place where the pottages were most commonly served.

The next course typically contained roast meats, accompanied, in France, by dishes of salads and sauces, and thickened pottages, such as *blanc-mangers* and gravies. A further course might consist of poultry and wild birds, other products of hunting, and sometimes fish (the tendency in France to have meals containing both meat and fish was greater than that in England), and a whole variety of dishes, from fritters to tarts. The final service, the 'issue' or *boute-hors* – called the 'void' in England – marked the removal of tablecloths and boards, and was a course in itself, often containing the fruits best eaten as digestives, followed by wine, typically spiced, like hippocras, as well as by plates of spices.

In England, each course consisted of a mixture of the different foods. Pottages commonly appeared at all courses, as did roasts, poultry and wild foods, subtleties and desserts. Salads and vegetables were usually absent. One pattern was to employ boiled meats in the first course, along with sauces and salted foods; roasts and baked meats in the second; and fried meats in the third; but equally often they were mixed without distinction. The week of feasting that accompanied the enthronement of Archbishop Neville of York in 1465 indicates the latter pattern. The first course on the first day brought a range of foods including brawn with mustard, furmenty (a dish of wheat boiled in milk, seasoned with spices) with venison, spiced venison, boiled meats (beef, pork or mutton), pheasant, roast swan, gannets and gulls, capon 'de haut grece', roast heron, pike, fritters, baked venison and a custard.

Two further aspects of the meal deserve special mention. Entremets, or *interfercula*, were literally items served between the courses to cover a break in the service of food and to allow dishes to be cleared. There was no fixed point for them in French meals and sometimes they came with each course. They were usually smaller items, perhaps like hors d'œuvres – in England they were occasionally referred to as 'served out of course', which has much the same meaning, and were sometimes called 'subtleties'. Across Europe, they gained a life and extravagance of their own; they could be as much political statements as food in the great, set-piece feasts of the period. In 1416, the feast to mark the elevation of Savoy from a county to a duchy had as the principal entremets a representation of the new duchy – a great model in pastry like a relief map. An entremets might even make no pretence at edibility and could be a table piece, such as a fountain.

In the late medieval period there is occasional mention of the 'banquet'. This appears first as the last course at major festivities. In the fifteenth century, it designated a cold buffet, a regular evening meal at the French court. In the Low Countries in the sixteenth century it comprised cold dishes such as salads and jams. In England, it was another term for the service of spice and wine that occurred at the 'void', or at the conclusion of a major festivity, not necessarily a meal. In this way, at the extravagant entertainment arranged in Westminster

Hall in 1501 to mark the marriage of Catherine of Aragon with Prince Arthur, the banquet concluded the pageants and dancing, with spices and wine brought in by more than 200 nobles, knights and squires, along with the Yeomen of the Guard. It was only at a much later date that 'banquet' came to mean a celebratory meal as a whole.

Elaborate ceremonial and considerable resources were devoted to ensuring food reached the plates of the diners in a manner that gave consumption its most conspicuous effect. Olivier de la Marche's description of the elaborate arrangements for public dining made for the Duke of Burgundy allows us to see the quasi-liturgical movements of servants, kissing towels, the exact and elaborate ritual that went with dining at this level and which must have prolonged the meal considerably. After the tables had been set up and covered with cloth, the butler brought into the chamber the alms *nef*. In it were the silver trenchers – used for setting out the slices of bread on which the food would be served – along with the small salt and another small *nef*. A piece of 'unicorn horn' to assay the Duke's food was also brought in the *nef*. The saucerer next brought in the verjuice, which, along with the other sauces, was assayed by the pantler. The pantler stood in front of the *nef* and served the Duke. At the main meal, he served the Duke twice, on each occasion from twelve or thirteen dishes; at supper, he served once. With his knife, the pantler took salt from the large salt and placed it in the small one for the Duke's immediate use.

The carver, or *écuyer tranchant*, also stood at the table before the Duke. When all the dishes were on the table, the *écuyer* was to

A set of two different sizes of knife, and a larger, flat-bladed serving knife with a rounded end used for transferring food to the plate of the diner (as in the woodcut of King Solomon dining, p. 173), made in Milan, c. 1460. Knives like the eight smaller ones are to be found on the table of the King of Portugal (pp. 190–91). These items were intended for display and came with highly decorated handles.

uncover them and to place them in front of the Duke one after the other. He had discretion to present to the Duke the dishes as they arrived, the pottages before the main dish, and the eggs before the fish. The carver placed pieces of boiled and roasted meats in the alms *nef*. After the concluding grace, the almoner took up the alms *nef* to distribute its contents and the table cloth was then removed.

At this point, wine was commonly served, with spices on elaborate pieces of plate. On her death in 1359, the goods of Queen Isabella, daughter of Philip IV of France and widow of Edward II of England, included four spice plates, a large one of silver enamelled at the base and on the circumference with the arms of France and England, and two smaller ones with the same decoration. Among the table equipment were eight silver plates for fruit, a great silver dish *pro interferculis*, a series of nine other great dishes, presumably for serving, all close to 4 lb. of silver, with fourteen dishes about half their size, and more than 170 dishes about half that size. There was a silver tureen (*cacabus*), weighing more than 6 lb., a great silver spoon for vegetables and a silver skimmer, weighing together more than 2 lb. There were two large silver chargers and forty-seven silver saucers (for holding sauces); a range of cups and beakers (*bekeritz*), goblets and two nuts, probably coconuts worked into cups. Amid the silverware was a gold cup for the Queen and gilt saucers.

Isabella's scullery and saucery had a quantity of spoons and six silver-gilt forks for apples. Forks were very rare in medieval Europe and were almost always associated with sticky and sweet confections. Spoons were everyday utensils: even wealthy peasants had silver spoons. Knives, however, offered more possibilities for display, as carvers and pantlers offered and presented meats.

By the late Middle Ages, there was a common perception across Europe of an elite cuisine. A lot of evidence suggests its power as a model for consumption, especially after the Black Death. Wealthier peasants kept freshwater fish; poor chantry priests invested in spices for the great festivals; the diet of Benedictine monasteries came to resemble that of the upper classes generally, as far as it was possible to negotiate that within the Rule; urban cookshops might offer bitterns, herons and pheasants and roasts, purchases for guild feasts, along with humbler fare. Many others were involved in the production of specialist food products. Some areas of Europe were renowned for the cheese they produced, centuries before Pantaleone da Confienza complied his *Summa lacticiniorum* of *c.* 1475, surveying dairy products. Taxation records show that the inns of the port of King's Lynn, *c.* 1290, had among their possessions hams with a value four times greater than those owned by peasants in rural villages. Preserved pork featured in the earliest domestic accounts. Other products of the preservation process, such as sausages and puddings, or the *mortadella* of Platina, also appeared in aristocratic establishments, even if they may more commonly have been eaten elsewhere. Special preparations might extend to fish: fish *confit* appeared in a late fourteenth-century cookery book from Languedoc. Veal, a by-product of regimes of dairy farming, was supplied by specialists to both the aristocracy in Italy and in England; capons 'de haut grece' were fattened by peasants; others caught and kept wild birds, managed freshwater fish in ponds, or were expert at catching them in streams. While a trout might fetch 1od. in fourteenth-century England, two to three days' wages for an unskilled labourer, it was more likely to be sold than to be eaten; but the market into which it could be sold was very much wider after the middle of the fourteenth century. After the Black Death labourers demanded – and obtained – higher quality foods; in England, sumptuary legislation of 1363 attempted to restrict the types and amounts of foodstuffs the lower classes might consume, a sure sign that their choices and aspirations had widened.

In the late medieval period, when there is detailed evidence for consumption in aristocratic circles, it is possible to observe a number of dietary changes taking place. Principal among these is a shift to lighter meats among the high aristocracy: while their retainers might still consume vast amounts of beef and mutton, their masters ate more poultry, birds and young animals, such as veal or suckling pig. In England there was a marked decline in pork consumption at this level. Fish, the mainstay of consumption on fast days, were purchased in smaller quantities from the mid-fifteenth century. The Reformation would diminish further the cultural impetus for fasting in Protestant countries. The Renaissance recovered classical notions about cooking and reworked the connection between dietetics and health. Platina's *De honesta voluptate* was intended for the new Roman Academy and advocated an Epicurean approach, a course between the poverty of fasting and the perils of gluttony. It had close links to the *De re coquinaria* (On Things Pertaining to Cookery) of Apicius. Marsilio Ficino's *De vita triplici* (Three Books on Life) of 1489 overturned common practice in its advice against the consumption of fish and dairy foods. New foods from the Americas would alter the possibilities for cuisine and changes in manners would gradually alter the setting for consumption and the place of cooks. By 1600, some aspects of medieval *haute cuisine* would have looked distinctly old-fashioned, but others would not have seemed at all unusual.

GVSTVS

6 NEW WORLDS, NEW TASTES

Food Fashions after the Renaissance

Brian Cowan

From the sixteenth century onwards, it has often been said that three great modern inventions had inaugurated an important break with the past. The invention of gunpowder, the compass and the printing press in fourteenth- and fifteenth-century Europe had combined to lay the groundwork for the discovery and even conquest of many 'New Worlds' in America, Africa and Asia, as well as the competition between states and ideologies that exploded so violently in the early modern wars of religion between Protestant and Roman Catholic Christians.

These three great inventions also transformed the food culture of early modern Europe. The printing press allowed for the widespread publication of cookery books, dietary advice manuals and even gastronomic philosophy. The combination of overseas travel enabled by the compass and the amplified deadly force made possible by gunpowder shaped the rise of early modern European empires across the globe. This expansion of European political, military and economic power also introduced Europeans to many new foods and culinary influences from abroad. Simultaneously, the nation states that forged these empires developed an ever more self-conscious sense of national identity which was increasingly understood in terms of distinctive national cuisines.

For these reasons, a set of paradoxes lay at the heart of early modern European culinary experiences. The food culture of the period can be understood as perpetually torn between pressures to maintain continuity in the face of revolutionary changes, as well as being divided between common cosmopolitan tastes shared by European elites across the continent and a growing sense of urgency behind defining national differences in terms of rival cuisines. On the one hand, the sophisticated intellectual culture of humanism struggled to maintain and revive the culinary and dietetic legacies of classical antiquity. On the other hand, the 'modern' pressures for change were irresistible, particularly as access to, and knowledge of, new foods and new cooking techniques increased. This chapter explores these paradoxes of early modern food culture by examining the two most important influences on European understandings of food between the age of Columbus and the age of the French Revolution: humanism and mercantilism.

The intellectual culture of humanism had a substantial influence on early modern understandings of food. Beginning in *quattrocento* Italy, humanist writers undertook an attempt to document and preserve the culinary genius of classical antiquity in order to provide greater benefits, understood both in terms of good taste as well as healthier dietary practices, to contemporaries. Although profoundly conservative in their intent, these humanist culinary writings opened up a range of debates regarding what foods should or should not be eaten, how they should be eaten, how often they should be eaten, and in what combinations or with what seasonings and spices. The resulting debates settled nothing and in fact did very little to revive ancient cooking practices or classical tastes in food. Paradoxically then, humanist culinary conservativism set in process a major revision of European taste.

The so-called first 'modern' cookery book was written in late fifteenth-century Italy by the 'eminent Maestro Martino of Como' (*fl. c.* 1450), who had cooked for the Cardinal Trevisan, Patriarch of Aquileia as well as at the court of the Dukes of Milan, and was entitled the *Libro de arte coquinara* (Book of the Art of Cooking). What made this work modern was less its particular contents or its culinary worldview, all of which would have been quite familiar to late medieval cooks and courtly gourmands, than its afterlife. Martino's book, which was something more like a practical manual for courtly cooks, was adopted almost wholesale by the humanist writer Bartolomeo Sacchi (1421–81), who wrote, as was the custom, under the Latinate *nom de plume* of

Previous page: The artichoke enjoyed great popularity in early modern European courtly feasts and gained a reputation as an aphrodisiac. It appears at the centre of this illustration of 'Taste' by the French artist Abraham Bosse for a series on *The Five Senses* (c. 1635) and artichoke hearts featured as a luxury dish in early modern French writings on cookery, such as La Varenne's *Le Cuisinier françois* (1651).

Above: Detail from a 15th-century fresco by Melozzo da Forlì showing Pope Sixtus IV appointing Bartolomeo Sacchi, called Platina, as director of the Vatican Library. Platina is the kneeling figure and author of the immensely popular *De honesta voluptate et valetudine* (1470), a work that attempted to celebrate both gastronomic pleasure and dietetic healthiness.

'Platina'. Platina's own work, the *De honesta voluptate et valetudine*, a treatise 'on correct pleasure and good health', borrowed the content of most of Martino's recipes and added to them further medical and moral commentary derived from ancient authorities such as Apicius, Pliny and the ancient Greek medical writer, Galen (129–200). The result was an immensely popular book that fulfilled the function of a practical cookery book, a dietetic guide for good health and a philosophy of eating. Although the word 'gastronomy' was not commonly used in European languages until the nineteenth century, the notion that a philosophy of eating well was a task worth doing was articulated with growing enthusiasm by humanist writers such as Platina and his later imitators.

Platina's *De honesta voluptate* was originally composed in manuscript form around the year 1465, but it soon found itself caught up in the changes inaugurated by the printing press. It was first published in Rome in 1470, in Florence in 1472 and in Venice at around the same time, and in several subsequent editions. By 1505, his work had been translated and adapted into French as *Le Platine en françoys*. Another collection of Martino's recipes by Giovanni de Rosselli (1513) was translated into English as *Epulario, or the Italian Banquet* (1598). Henceforth Platina's book in all its various guises would take its place as one of the most important works on food in early modern Europe.

What did humanists such as Platina have to say about food? The first thing to notice is that they tried to balance both dietetics, the science of eating for good health, with gastronomy, the art of eating well for pleasure and as a sign of cultural refinement. The very title of Platina's work combined a concern for dietetic healthiness (*valetudo*) with a celebration of gastronomic pleasure (*voluptas*). It is fruitless to try to distinguish between guides to healthy eating as opposed to gourmet celebrations of good-tasting food in these writings.

Like humanist culture itself, humanist cuisine was cosmopolitan. Humanist recipes came from a variety of different national sources and were shared and spread internationally. Martino's recipes include dishes identified as being variously Catalan, French, Papal and Saracen in origin. In Platina's revision of Martino's recipe for Catalan *mirause* or half-roasted poultry, he added even more generously the comment that 'the Catalan race…is indeed distinguished and considered not much different in talent and physical form from the Italian level of skill.' Platina's comments on the Catalan manner of preparing a partridge (roasted quickly, with salt, spices and citrus juice) are even more telling: 'My friend Gallus frequently eats this food, although he is a bitter enemy of the Catalonians, for he hates the race of men, not their dishes.' The gastronomic mind of Renaissance humanism was open to culinary influences from just about any culture, be they allies or enemies.

This may explain the continued presence of Arabic dietetic and culinary preferences in early humanist food writings. Platina was

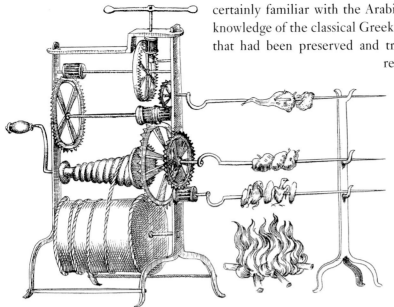

certainly familiar with the Arabic tradition and indeed much of his knowledge of the classical Greek and Latin texts relied upon editions that had been preserved and transmitted by Arabic scholars. The recipes found in these texts continue to recommend substantial quantities of spices such as saffron, pepper and cloves, as was common in Arabic and indeed in medieval European cooking. Condiments that would be considered by moderns as distinctly savoury or sweet were considered together as similar sorts of seasonings. The concept of a 'dessert' as a sweet dish separate from the main meal did not yet exist. Sugar was an omnipresent flavouring in Renaissance cookery. Platina remarked that 'nothing given us to eat is so flavourless that sugar does not season it.' Martino consistently recommended flavouring his foods with sugar, almonds and spices, and his sauces included the raisins, prunes and grapes that were commonly a part of Arabic cooking practices. Martino's recipe for marzipan (*marzapane*) as a sweet-filled pastry or calzone (*caliscione*) was similar to Arabic practices. There was no attempt in these works to purge the kitchen of foreign influences, although calls to do so would become more frequent in the seventeenth and eighteenth centuries.

There *was* an attempt to reconcile modern cooking with the recommendations of the ancient authors whose works were held in such high esteem by humanist writers. Classical authorities on cooking, diet and natural history such as Apicius, Galen and Pliny are cited relentlessly. But even here, one finds a remarkable flexibility towards the authority of antiquity in practice. Foods or recipes were not simply rejected if they could not be supported by ancient authority. More often than not, they were assimilated into a sort of neo-classical dietetic system whose principles remained wedded to the Galenic humoural paradigm but whose practice remained open to debate among the learned. Platina's commentary upon Martino's recipe for blancmange (*cibarum album*), another sweet dish of Arabic origin which had no classical precedent is telling: 'I have always preferred this to Apician condiments, nor is there any reason why the tastes of our ancestors should be preferred to those of our own, for even if we are surpassed by them in nearly all arts, nevertheless in taste alone we are not vanquished, for in the whole world there is no incentive to taste which has not been brought down, as it were, to the modern cooking school, where there is the keenest of discussion about the cooking of all foods.' Good taste here is not defined exclusively in terms of ancient

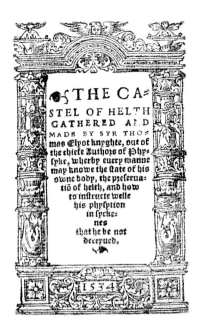

authority, indeed the ancients' taste can even be surpassed by modern cooks who have learned their lessons well. In this way, the cuisine of Renaissance humanism furthered innovative debate about the role of food in the social order by spurring a dialogue between contemporary 'moderns' and the established wisdom of the ancients.

The primary justification for post-Renaissance food writing was that a healthy diet was good for you. A proper understanding of how food worked to nourish the body would lead to healthier lives for all and thus a happier, more prosperous society. This dietetic rationale was the primary justification for taking up the topic of writing on food at all. The titles of English dietetic manuals in this genre offer a clue to their purpose: Thomas Elyot's *Castel of Helth* (1534); Andrew Boorde's *Compendyous Regyment of a Dyetary of Health* (1542); Thomas Cogan's *Haven of Health* (1584); and Thomas Moffett's *Health's Improvement* (1655) are all typical examples of this style of writing.

Moderation and frugality in eating were constantly advised in these works. Yet a tension remained in certain texts between the obvious admonitions towards frugal consumption and the lavish detail accorded to describing how best to prepare particular dishes. This is especially evident in works such as Platina's, which combined medical advice on proper diet with practical advice on how to prepare favoured dishes. Platina began the eighth book of his treatise, which was devoted to the various condiments that could be used to enhance the flavours of foods, with a typical warning that these condiments should not be used for 'luxury, lust and intemperance', a set of vices that he thought prevailed particularly in Rome and other Italian cities, so much so that the citizens

Above: Thomas Elyot's *The Castel of Helth* (1534) was an immensely popular work of dietetics in English. Sixteen editions were published in the 16th and 17th centuries. The book made ancient Greek and Latin medical and dietary teachings accessible in the vernacular and popularized the Galenic theory of the four humours for Renaissance readers.

Right: Medieval admonitions against gluttony, such as found in this image of a glutton's sickness by James le Palmer (*c.* 1360–75), continued to resonate with Renaissance and early modern food writers. Platina advocated the 'pleasure which derives from continence in food' and recommended 'moderation and frugality' in eating to his readers.

were dangerously obese and yet so sated that their appetites could be stimulated only by artificial means. He then continued on to enumerate and expound upon the delights of sixty-two various condiments, although the pies and rolls that he lists at the end of the book might be considered complete dishes in themselves rather than condiments *per se*.

The rationale behind the medical advice offered regarding the benefits or hazards of consuming particular foods was derived almost primarily from Galenic physiology, a medical model that had never fully disappeared since antiquity but was now revived by Renaissance humanist writers with great vigour. In this system, as discussed in chapters 3 and 5, the human body was understood to be comprised of four basic fluids or 'humours': blood, phlegm, black bile and yellow bile or choler, each of which possessed two basic properties, being either hot or cold and either wet or dry. Foods too possessed these properties and anything eaten or drunk could thus affect the humoural complexion of anyone who ate them. Galenic dietetics then was the science of balancing the humours within the body by regulating one's food consumption.

Dietetic concerns could rule out certain foods as dangerous to consume. Platina noted that the properties of mushrooms were cold and damp 'and for this reason have the force of poison' and his commentary on Martino's recipe for eel pie could not have induced many of his readers to try it: 'When it is finally cooked, serve to your enemies, for it has nothing good in it.' In general, meats and fish were considered to be more nourishing and healthier than fruits and vegetables in this dietetic regime. It was also important to regulate *how* one ate as well as what one ate. For example, Platina counselled that vegetables should not be eaten after consuming fruit because digestion is hampered by eating so many cool and damp items at once.

The power of Galenic dietetics was that the system was infinitely flexible. Every person's body has its own complex set of humours and properties which must be balanced by various different dietary combinations. Supposedly 'dangerous' foods such as melons or mushrooms could be improved by 'correcting' their corruptive possibilities with other foods or spices. It is hard to find total agreement in these dietetic texts on any one right way to prepare or improve foods, but the organizing principles and possibilities of Galenic dietetics provided the playing field in which Renaissance debates about healthy eating took place.

Dining etiquette was also a major concern of humanist cuisine. A substantial amount of Renaissance food writing took place in a courtly context: the works were written by authors who either already possessed or sought patronage from a princely court. Courts had the monetary means to afford the often expensive and lavish dishes praised by humanist writers and they also sought the cultural capital that accompanied fine dining, so the court became the primary focus for the humanists' attempted reformation of the table.

In Christoforo di Meissisbugo's 1549 woodcut of a Renaissance kitchen, the roasting, preparation and preservation of meats figures much more prominently than does the cooking of fruits and vegetables. Poultry and game meats are at the centre of this kitchen's activity, while the vegetables are consigned to a few baskets in the margins.

Proper etiquette and settings were part of the Renaissance 'civilization of the table' that transformed elite dining habits in the early modern era. Note the tablecloth and the elaborate plate settings in this detail from Kaspar van der Hoecke's *Lazarus and the Rich Man's Table* (1648).

This Dutch knife and fork set, with handles in walrus tusk representing allegorical figures for Hope, Charity and Justice (1761), exemplifies the long-term triumph of the knife and fork as the mainstays of European tableware. The fork was introduced in 14th-century Italy, but it was not fully accepted at European tables until the later 17th century.

Platina and later writers assumed that any proper banquet would include several courses, although the particular order and composition of these courses remained subject to debate and local variation for centuries. Platina thought that herbs and vegetables (*herbis et holeribus*) were appropriate before serving a main course or courses with meat and/or fish. After that, a final course should consist of foods conducive to proper digestion. For Platina, this included fruits such as apples or sour pears, or perhaps a bit of hard cheese, which was thought 'to seal the stomach and stop vapours from seeking the head and brain'. This last course was not considered a dessert, but it did bring closure to a formal meal.

It remained customary until the later seventeenth century to serve many different kinds of dishes simultaneously, so that a proper succession of 'courses' must have often been difficult to discern at many dinners. Samuel Pepys (1633–1703) thought of this sort of dining as the norm in Restoration London and when he did on occasion experience a meal consisting of several distinct courses, he called this dinner 'in the French manner'. Seventeenth-century English commentators also viewed the 'dessert' as a dangerous French innovation. Curiously, French food writers at the same time still thought it was customary for them to serve several dishes simultaneously as well and thought it necessary to defend the practice against criticism. By the age of Louis XIV (1643–1715), national differences were being more stridently mapped onto culinary practices, at least in the minds of the moralists who saw fit to comment on these matters.

Even more important to Renaissance writers on culinary courtesy was the regulation of table manners. The table became an important site of social discipline for humanist advisers to their courtly advisees. Desiderius Erasmus's (d. 1536) instructional manual *De civilitate morum puerilium* (1530), a book 'on good manners for boys', articulated proper table manners for elites throughout Europe. Within less than a decade, it had been translated from its original Latin into English, German, French and Czech. Works such as this tried to displace the focus of table sociability away from the food itself, for an overt demonstration of one's hunger was thought to be rude, and towards good fellowship and edifying 'table talk'. Hence Erasmus advised: 'It is neither polite nor safe to drink or speak with one's mouth full. Continuous eating should be interrupted now and again with stories.'

Erasmus also offered his readers practical advice such as this: 'It is boorish to plunge your hands into sauced dishes. You should take what you want with a

Abraham Bosse's engraving (1633–34) of the feast of the
Chevaliers of Saint-Esprit with Louis XIII at the head illustrates
the courtly dining etiquette of the 17th century. A large number of
dishes have been served for the diners simultaneously, while the
diners themselves have been lined up on either side of the King's
table, which remains the focus of attention at the head and
centre of the dining hall.

knife or fork; nor should you select from the entire dish as epicures do but should take whatever portion is in front of you.' The fork was a rather rare item even at princely dinner tables in the sixteenth century. The first recorded notice of a fork appears in fourteenth-century Italy, but it was really only in the sixteenth and seventeenth centuries that the fork became a standard item at elite tables. Even in the later seventeenth century, commentators noted that the English do not use 'forks but fingers' and even at the court of Versailles, a place that was thought to have established the highest standards of elite etiquette in Europe, the Princess Palatine reported how Louis XIV did not approve of forks when his grandson adopted the custom.

Along with the introduction of proper dinnerware, such as forks and knives appropriate for the table rather than the combat field, came the notion that places at the table should be laid properly. Platina advised that tables should be set according to the season: flowers should be placed on the table and the dining room in spring, while in the winter 'the air should be redolent of perfumes'. Napkins and tablecloths were also part of the necessary setting because, he noted, 'if they were otherwise, they would arouse squeamishness and take away the desire to eat'. Renaissance notions of civility found an ideal space in which they could be articulated at the dinner tables of the European aristocracy as well as anyone else who wanted to be associated with this new civility of manners.

Seating was strictly regulated at elite tables. Great households in late medieval and Renaissance England commonly maintained both a chamber usher and a marshal for the dining hall, both of whom were responsible for placing guests at the table in their proper place and with due courtesy. Servants and guests of insufficient standing in the social order were not welcome at the same table as elites. As early as the fourteenth century, the architecture of dining arrangements in aristocratic great houses had changed to accommodate a separate dining chamber, distinct from the old medieval great hall, for the lord and his immediate family, so that they could eat privately.

Despite the efforts of humanist food writers to emphasize the importance of good taste and good society at the tables of Renaissance courts, it is clear that the princes of the day still valued magnificence and ostentatious display at their meals. Feasting lavishly was a central element of the conspicuous consumption that defined court society.

Martino's cookery book included a recipe entitled 'how to dress a peacock with all its feathers, so that when cooked, it appears to be alive and spews fire from its beak.' This choice dish was also included in Platina's *De honesta voluptate*, where he added the comment that peacocks and suchlike edible birds 'are more delicious than others and more suitable to the tables of kings and princes than the lowly and men of little property'. The consumption of magnificent fowl and large game birds was always popular at Renaissance courts, despite the

Overleaf: The Biblical marriage feast at Cana at which Jesus turned the jugs of water into wine was often used by Renaissance painters as an occasion to illustrate contemporary dining practices, such as in this painting (c. 1561–70) by a Greco-Venetian artist in imitation of Tintoretto.

The peacock features prominently in this detail from *The Allegory of Senses: Hearing, Touch and Taste* by Jan Brueghel and Hendrick van Balen. Peacocks were a major element in elite banquets from classical antiquity until the Renaissance. Cicero thought it was daring to hold a feast without one; thirty peacocks were served at a banquet given for Catherine de Médicis in 1549; but the arrival of the New World turkey gradually displaced the peacock at European dining tables over the course of the 17th century.

growing concerns by dieticians that these foods were difficult to digest and should be avoided.

The Renaissance emphasis on magnificent dining must also account for the continued attraction of using liberal amounts of spices for altering not only the taste, but also the appearance of foods. A golden or reddish hue was particularly valued; hence the enduring popularity of saffron in Renaissance recipes. Diego Granado's *Libro del arte de cocina* (1599) recommended the use of saffron specifically because 'it has the colour of gold'.

The expense involved in preparing meals was also meant to be conspicuously displayed at Renaissance feasts. Platina complained of the high cost of obtaining lamprey for his meals because 'entrenched gourmands [*delicatissimum*] vie amongst themselves when the prices of things increase'. Lavish dining was one of the major outlays of an early modern court. In the first fifty years of the sixteenth century the Este family's court in the Italian city of Ferrara consumed 900 tons of wheat, 100 tons of pulses, 9,000 hectolitres of wine, 60 tons of beef and veal, 40 of fish, 15,000 fowls, 6 tons of salted meat, 4 tons of cheese, 1,400 kilograms of butter and more than 1,000 kilograms of ricotta cheeses.

An elaborately dressed swan dominates the left side of this painting of a kitchen interior by David Teniers the Younger (1644). As with the peacock, swans were prized as feast birds. In 1555, the French naturalist Belon thought it a 'French delicacy, eaten at public feasts and in the houses of lords,' but it too gradually lost favour to the more easily reared New World turkey in later centuries.

All of this was to be eaten by ducal courtiers whose numbers comprised of anywhere between 550 and 750 people. When the English King Charles I's mother-in-law, Marie de' Medici, visited his court in 1639 and 1640, her entourage was given a monthly allowance of £1,600 for food expenses alone.

As the dinner table took on greater importance for Renaissance elite society, the social role of the cook should have increased proportionally as well. The cook had a reason to stake a claim as a professional and highly valued member of court society. Like other skilled workers at the Renaissance courts, such as painters and builders, cooks

performed primarily manual labour and this was thought to be demeaning to the prestige of their trade. But all of these workers sought to edify their labour by claiming that the manual execution of their work was merely the last step in a highly intellectual and civilized profession. In this contest for dignified recognition, the support of humanist intellectuals was crucial. Platina certainly emphasized both the civility and the science of cooking. A good chef, he argued 'should lack all filth and dirt and know in a suitable way the force and nature of meats, fish and vegetables so that he may understand what ought to be roasted, boiled or fried. He should be alert enough to discern by taste what is too salty or too flat.' Platina singled out his friend Martino as a perfect example of the civil cook.

These images of a female and a male cook by Martin Engelbrecht (c. 1735), from a collection of engravings of artists and artisans, demonstrate the continued association of cooking with manual labour in the early modern era. The culinary arts never achieved the status of fine or liberal arts such as painting and sculpture.

The continued professionalization of cooking is evident from the account by Michel de Montaigne (1533–92) of a conversation he had with an Italian chef who had been brought to France by his patron the Cardinal Giovanni Caraffa (1476–1559), the future Pope Paul IV. This cook gave Montaigne 'a discourse on this science of supping [*science de gueule*] with a grave and magisterial countenance, as if he were speaking of some grand point of theology. He unravelled…the rules regarding sauces…[and] the different salads according to their season.' But Montaigne's wry final comment on this cook's praise of the science of cooking reveals that at the end of the day the philosopher had not been persuaded: 'all this bloated with grand and magnificent words, such as one might use in describing the government of an empire.'

The 'science of supping', it seems, was not yet worthy of the grand and magnificent words appropriate for politics or moral philosophy. Renaissance cooks were far less successful than Renaissance painters in their bid for recognition of the dignity of their labour. Martino aside, very few early modern cooks made a name for themselves and received recognition for their achievements by either the humanist intelligentsia or courtly elites.

Even in the seventeenth and eighteenth centuries few cooks managed to establish themselves as recognized professionals, and cooking itself was never elevated to the status of a liberal art. No academies of cooking were established by early modern states, nor were the culinary arts considered to be an appropriate object of study for early modern intellectuals. The early modern 'science of supping' lacked a figure such as Giorgio Vasari, whose *Lives of the Artists* (1550) did so much to establish a canon of important Renaissance visual artists and artistic achievements, and set painting in particular on the road to recognition as a liberal art. In this respect, Platina's *De honesta voluptate* remained an important but ultimately rather lonely book in the wider intellectual culture of Renaissance humanism. Platina's praise for the civility of the cook's trade would not translate into further respect for cooking as a profession for another two hundred years. Only in the eighteenth century, as we shall see, did the work of the chef emerge as a recognized profession.

If the culinary legacy of Renaissance humanism was complex and often contradictory, that of early modern mercantilism was much more obvious. European voyages of discovery to the 'new worlds' in the Americas, Africa and Asia brought European travellers, merchants and imperial administrators into direct contact with new foods and new culinary practices in these places as well. The growth of international trade and intercultural contact entailed by these new encounters made Europeans aware of many new foodstuffs and consumables, and the desire to profit from this expanding overseas trade encouraged the exploration of new markets.

Many of the standard items found on European tables today were unknown until the early modern voyages of discovery. The potato, the tomato and American corn (maize) were all introduced to Europe in the sixteenth century, but these foods did not meet universal acclaim upon their first reception in Europe and did not really become widely consumed until the nineteenth century. Potatoes were discovered by Spanish conquistadors in Peru in 1539 and by the later sixteenth century they were known and consumed in Spain, Italy, Britain and central Europe, but not in great quantities. The potato would not become a European dietary staple until the eighteenth century, when the plant's caloric potentials for supporting large numbers of people very cheaply was increasingly exploited by the growing population of western Europe. Speaking of the tomato, or the 'love apple' as it was first called in English, John Hill noted in his gardening manual *Eden* (1756–7) that 'few eat this, but it is agreeable in soups. Those who are us'd to eat with the Portugese [Sephardic] Jews know the value of it.' Sauces for pasta or other dishes made with a tomato base would not be common in Europe until the 1830s. Both potatoes and tomatoes fell under the suspicion of dieticians because of their supposed similarity to the poisonous nightshade plant family. Maize was one of the first foods from the Americas to be added to the European diet: Columbus encountered it on his first transatlantic voyage and it was being cultivated in Iberia, southern France and northern Italy by the early sixteenth century. It did not become a major cash crop however. Peasants were more likely to

Above: The oldest depiction of the potato appears in this watercolour by an unknown artist (c. 1588). Potatoes were brought back from the New World to Europe by the 1550s and were first harvested in Spain and Italy, but with little success or enthusiasm. By the 18th century, attitudes had changed and both the Swedish and the Prussian governments began to encourage potato cultivation as a means of feeding their growing populations.

Opposite: This fanciful depiction of a Turk, a Chinese man and a Native American with their respective drinks on the title page of Philippe Sylvestre Dufour's *Traité nouveau & curieux du café, du thé, et du chocolat* (1671) reinforces the exotic associations that Europeans continued to draw between coffee, tea and chocolate and their foreign countries of origin.

cultivate maize in their own gardens or plots for personal use as the new crop was not yet subject to the same tithe and tax levies that applied to their staple wheat crops.

Other new foods, such as the turkey and particularly the 'new hot drinks' of early modernity – coffee, tea and chocolate – were assimilated into the European culinary repertoire with remarkable rapidity. Simple contact with new worlds of foods from overseas did not automatically lead to acceptance and assimilation into European dietary habits, however. Many foreign and exotic products which were very popular in non-European cultures were encountered by Europeans in the post-Columbian centuries of discovery and yet they failed to make an impact on the old world. The betel nuts which were, and remain, popular among the populations in the Indian Ocean world were rejected by Europeans despite the attempts by certain enthusiasts to promote their domestic consumption. In the 1660s, the English merchant and Royal Society Fellow Daniel Colwall thought that betel nuts might find an enthusiastic reception at home, but he turned out to be quite wrong.

What accounts for the different ways in which these new foodstuffs were received in the age of the voyages of discovery? Here again the dietary influence of humanism may provide some guidance. The resistance encountered in Europe to the introduction of exotic new foods discovered overseas can be attributed in some respects to the stubborn conservativism of early modern culture, both elite and popular. Novelty was by and large not a valued quality in the societies of this period: innovations, particularly in social customs such as eating and drinking, were thought of as potentially dangerous threats to the established social order. By setting up the works of classical antiquity as established authorities, Renaissance humanism participated in this sort of early modern conservativism and it is easy to agree with J. H. Elliott's observation that 'in some respects the Renaissance involved, at least in its earlier stages, a closing rather than an opening of the mind. The veneration of antiquity became more slavish; authority staked fresh claims against experience.'

Yet there is also a sense in which humanism opened the door for a select number of new food products. Galenic dietetics as a medical worldview could be extremely capacious. New foods and drinks could easily be fit into the Galenic paradigm of humours, properties and degrees. Those new products which could be understood within this Galenic system as possessing particularly beneficial, or even medicinal, qualities were most likely to find acceptance in the European diet and this was indeed the way in which most of the new and exotic foods of the post-Columbian age of discovery found legitimacy. Of course, this process was easiest for foods that were already very similar to longstanding elements of the European diet. Thus both guinea fowl, introduced in the early sixteenth century from West Africa, and the American turkey were

quickly and enthusiastically praised by Renaissance dieticians and banqueters alike.

The most strikingly innovative new consumer products of the early modern era, tobacco, coffee, tea and chocolate, were all introduced first as medicinal products and they were all quickly slotted into the prevailing Galenic medical paradigm. Once understood in this way as legitimate additions to the *materia medica* of orthodox physicians, these new exotics were able to work their way into the dietary routines of early modern Europe, and within decades of their introduction they had become wildly successful. Tobacco was encountered by Columbus on his first voyage to the Americas and was being imported and later even cultivated in parts of Europe by the latter half of the sixteenth century. Another Native American product, chocolate had also found its way to Spain by 1544, when a delegation of Mayan nobles brought the drink as a gift for King Philip II, and a transatlantic trade in the commodity was underway by 1585 when the first shipment of cocoa beans was dispatched from Veracruz to the port of Seville. Coffee was already being consumed in the Ottoman Empire when Columbus stumbled upon the Caribbean islands and by the end of the sixteenth century it had been introduced to Italian consumers in Venice; by the mid-seventeenth century it would be available in English, French and Dutch cities as well. Along with coffee, Turkish sherbet was also introduced to western Europe in the seventeenth century.

The relatively rapid rise and acceptance of these new exotics led some observers to marvel at the accomplishment. Royal Society Fellow John Beale thought that expanding the horizons of the English diet was an integral part of the new scientific programme for the reconquest of nature inaugurated by the works of Francis Bacon. In 1659, he remarked on the remarkable success of coffee, tea and tobacco, and marvelled that 'smoke is become an aliment entertainment, and the meanes to sustaine the livelihood of many millions, and many newly planted nations. In this I see the Mystery of Gods providentiall expedition in increaseing knowledge, commerce, and mutuall accommodations, all over the world.' Some of the earliest and most enthusiastic proponents for the adoption of such new consumer habits as smoking or drinking caffeinated beverages came from the international community of intellectuals who had an interest in the natural sciences. Today, we would consider them scientists; in the seventeenth century, these people called themselves 'virtuosi' and their interests ranged from the natural sciences to the fine arts.

The new science of the seventeenth-century virtuosi encouraged an interest in novel foods and drinks. Their wide-ranging curiosity about the natural world led them to attempt to understand such recently discovered commodities as tobacco, chocolate, coffee and tea.

The new 'hot drinks' of coffee, tea and chocolate were quickly assimilated into European dining customs. Ralph Leake's silver chocolate cup (c. 1685), on a stand that also acts as a lid, is an early example of a European table product designed to accommodate the drinking of a new beverage. In François Boucher's painting, *The Afternoon Meal* (1739), hot drinks are at the centre of a new afternoon domestic ritual. In 18th-century 'polite society', the taking of coffee, tea or chocolate was dominated by women.

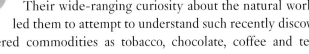

Jan van Grevenbroeck's later 18th-century drawing of Italian noblemen in a café illustrates the widespread success of coffee drinking in eighteenth-century Europe. Introduced to European societies in the middle of the seventeenth century, coffee drinking had become widespread throughout the continent in the eighteenth century, so much so that it had come to be seen as a daily necessity for many.

Their familiarity with the Galenic medical model offered them a language in which they might explain the health benefits of the new exotic commodities. In addition, the knowledge gained by the innovative practices of experimental science bolstered the claims of the virtuosi to have discovered important new additions to a healthy diet and lifestyle. Coffee in particular benefited from an almost immediate association with numerous curative properties but also as a means to promote sober and civil society, rather than drunken carousing, in public houses. Most of the extravagant claims in support of the new exotics were gradually dismissed or ignored by future generations: fewer and fewer people would concur with Edward Pococke's 1659 endorsement of an even older Arabic belief that coffee drinking offered an effective cure for smallpox or the measles, but by that time, the coffee-drinking habit had already been well established as customary and the need to argue for its legitimacy had long passed. The novel had become familiar and the exotic had been domesticated.

Along with the introduction of the new commodities, the rise of overseas empires in the early modern period also transformed the culinary uses of older foodstuffs. Perhaps the most remarkable change of the period took place with regard to the role of sugar, which had always been a part of European cooking, but used much as any other spice. Sugar was ubiquitous in medieval food and even Renaissance cooking approved of its liberal use. Platina lamented that the ancients had no knowledge of sugar and said that it could spoil no dish. In 1560, the French King Henry II's physician wrote that 'it hardly needs to be pointed out how many condiments and foods to which [sugar] is added.' Over the course of the seventeenth century, the role of sugar in the European diet would change dramatically.

The main reason for this transformation was the rise of colonial plantations in the West Indies. Although sugar cane had long been grown in the Iberian islands of the eastern Atlantic and it was transported by both the Spanish and the Portuguese to their New World colonies in the sixteenth century, the development of colonial slave societies by the British, the French and the Dutch in the seventeenth-century Caribbean enabled the production of refined sugar on a hitherto unprecedented scale. The British islands of Jamaica and Barbados and the French colonies in Saint Domingue (Haiti), Guadeloupe and Martinique all became large-scale sugar producers and they were widely understood to be among the most valuable of all European colonies in the Atlantic world. In the eighteenth century, sugar consumption exploded. Per capita consumption of sugar in the British Isles grew from perhaps 4 pounds per year around 1700 to about 18 pounds per year in the first decade of the nineteenth century. Sugar had been transformed from an elite luxury condiment that graced the tables of Renaissance princes to an everyday sweetener that was used to supplement, and increasingly to replace, the staple foods of commoners.

The success of sugar in Europe was built upon the exploitation of slave labour in the Caribbean. As such, it offers perhaps the most direct example of the ways in which mercantilism altered the European dietary heritage. A few dissenting voices against the rise of sugar were raised when the plantation economy and its accompanying slave societies were in their infancy. The vegetarian and anti-slavery writer Thomas Tryon (1634–1703) thought that the new slave-based sugar plantations were not worth the pain and suffering they brought to the African workers who worked them. But Tryon's was a lonely voice in his day.

The dramatic growth of sugar production and consumption after the mid-seventeenth century enabled the articulation of a rather new distinction within the European understanding of food taste, namely the difference between 'savoury' and 'sweet'. Although fundamental to modern taste, the salty and the sweet had been intermingled in medieval and Renaissance cooking, but with the ever-increasing quantities of sugar now available on the market from the later seventeenth century onwards it was possible and desirable to distinguish between

The making of sugar from sugar cane is depicted in this engraving of 1570 by Philipp Galle after Jan Stradanus. Sugar began as a luxury product in medieval Europe, but with the expansion of sugar-cane cultivation westwards to Atlantic islands, such as the Canaries and ultimately the Caribbean, and with the addition of slave labour, it could be produced in substantial quantities.

the two. Hence one of the odder consequences of the Caribbean sugar revolution was that sweetness was increasingly relegated to fewer dishes, although a much greater amount of sugar was now used in those dishes that were thought of as 'sweet'. Sweetness was used more intensively, but less extensively, in recipes and elite cooking.

The sweet/savoury distinction brought an end to the older tradition of strong flavoured, deeply spiced sauces and condiments that had been the hallmark of European elite cuisine for centuries. A new cuisine would be born in the middle of the seventeenth century, one which claimed to pay more respect to the intrinsic flavours of the foods eaten. These claims were first articulated in France, and it was this new culinary tradition that would become the basis for classical French *haute cuisine.*

Another consequence of the rise of sweetness was the invention of the 'dessert' as a sweet dish that would customarily follow a main course or courses of savoury foods. At the beginning of the seventeenth century, the notion of a separate 'dessert' course was viewed with some scepticism. The English writer William Vaughan declared in his *Naturall and Artificiall Directions for Health* (1600) that the 'desert' was a French innovation and unnatural. Things had changed in the later part of the century, when it became increasingly common even in England. Pepys remarked upon being served dessert at a dinner in July 1666 without any notice that it might have been unusual. Thus although main courses were still served together, the closing or dessert course was a seventeenth-century development.

The invention of the dessert also gave rise to new culinary skills. R. Campbell's 1747 *London Tradesman*, a guide to the various occupations of Londoners, mentioned a new trade, that of the 'confectioner' whose duties he described equivocally:

> The confectioner is a sweet-tooth'd tradesman: He makes all manner of sweet-meats, preserves all manner of fruit, and is the architect of a dessert. He builds walls, castles, and pyramids of sweet-meats and sugar-plumbs.
> He is a Proteus in his kind, he disguises many things; he makes sour things sweet, and sweet things sour; he coveres the products of summer, and the hottest season of the year, with artificial frost and snow, and delights the eye as much with the arrangement of his pyramids as the taste with the delicious flavour of his wet and dry sweet-meats. It requires no small knowledge to compleat a confectioner; though I never esteem him one of the most useful members of society.

The new culinary art of confectionary reached its apogee in the last decades of the eighteenth century, when the rococo aesthetic of excess perhaps encouraged the most imaginative uses of sugar paste for

decorative dishes. Rather than Martino's flaming peacock, the aristocratic tables of enlightenment Europe preferred elaborately decorated desserts. The Italian food writer Francesco Leonardi (*fl.* 1740–1800) reminisced in his *Apicio Moderno* (The Modern Apicius), first published in 1790, upon the old regime masterpieces of Italy's best confectionary artists who brought their 'immense genius and a fertile imagination to the creation of the most beautiful works of decoration, some of which represented the greatest actions of distinguished men or remarkable events from the history of nations…nothing that the very best drawing, architecture and good taste could contribute to such efforts was neglected…to make the dessert a joy to behold.'

The new trends in European tastes were perhaps best exemplified by the more prosaic habit of adding sugar to the new exotic drinks of the seventeenth century: coffee, tea and chocolate as well. Each of these drinks is rather bitter when drunk alone and none of them had been drunk with sugar in their original cultural context. Native American chocolate, Middle Eastern coffee and Chinese tea were all served unsweetened when they were 'discovered' by Europeans. Within decades of their introduction into Europe, it became common for these drinks to be sweetened with sugar from the Caribbean plantations.

The classical French dessert was dominated by pyramids of confectionary such as in this 1791 engraving. François Massialot's often reprinted *Le Confiturier royal* was first published in 1692 under the title *Nouvelle Instruction pour les Confitures* and it established the confectioner's art as a complementary specialization found in classic French *haute cuisine*.

Maize was the staple crop of Native Americans when they encountered European colonists in the 16th and 17th centuries and it was gradually assimilated into the diets of European creole societies in the New World as well.

As well as bringing new foods and new tastes to Europe, the overseas empires brought Europeans and their tastes to the new worlds. The planter and colonial societies in the Americas, in particular, established a consciously European cuisine in their new environs, although in practice this was in fact more a hybrid between European and Native American practices than a complete transplant of old-world ways of eating. The traditional European staple, wheat, often would not grow in the New World and in these colonial societies it was replaced by 'Indian corn' or maize, which had also been an essential crop for many of the Native American populations. British North American colonists quickly took to eating Native American dishes such as succotash (a thick bean and maize soup), Indian (maize) pudding and ryaninjun (a bread made with rye and maize), although these dishes carried little cultural prestige due to their Indian origins.

In other respects, European colonial societies were able to replicate older dietary habits and customs with greater ease. The feasting culture of aristocratic great houses was adopted with particular gusto in the planter societies south of the Chesapeake. William Hugh Grove, an English gentry visitor to early eighteenth-century Virginia was impressed by the abundant food supplied to the tables of Virginian planters. 'The gentry at their tables have commonly five dishes or plates, of which pigg meat and greens is generally one, and tame fowl another. Beef, mutton, veal and lamb make another. Pudding, often in the mid[dle], makes the fifth. Venison, wild fowl, or fish a fourth. Smal[l] beer made of molasses, with Madera wine [and] English beer [is] their liquor.'

A major difference between the dining customs of the colonial plantation manors and the medieval and Renaissance great houses upon which the former were modelled was the foundation of the plantation society upon forced slave labour and racial discrimination rather than the feudal model of class hierarchy and reciprocal obligation that bound the lord of a manor to his peasants. The bonds of charity, which had been so important a glue in maintaining the social fabric of the medieval manor, did not extend to the slave societies of the New World. The contrast between the slave's diet and that of his master's table could not be more clear, as J. F. D. Smyth's 1784 description of a colonial Virginian plantation demonstrates:

> [The slave] is seldom allowed time enough to swallow three mouthfuls of hominey, or hoe-cake, but is driven out immediately to the field to hard labour; at which he continues, without intermission, until noon…about noon is the time he eats his dinner, and he is seldom allowed an hour for that purpose. His meal consists of hominey and salt, and, if his master be a man of humanity, he has a little fat, skimmed milk, rusty bacon, or salt herring to relish his hominy, or hoe-cake….It is late at night [if there is work to

CUISINIER FRANÇOIS

La Varenne's *Le Cuisinier françois* (1651) initiated a new and very popular style of food writing in Europe. Thirty editions were published within the next 75 years and translations into English, German and Italian soon followed. La Varenne's example was widely imitated by later writers and it established French as the dominant language of European culinary discourse.

be done in the tobacco houses] before he returns to his second scanty meal.

The rise of slave societies in the European New World transformed the eating habits on both sides of the Atlantic. On the one hand, the quintessential inventions of the baroque and enlightenment eras, coffee, tea and dessert confections were all enabled and enriched by the growth of sugar plantations and their phenomenal productive capacities. On the other hand, these innovations and new delicacies were only made possible by the cruelest exploitation of human labour hitherto devised by European society.

At the same time that sweetness was transforming European diet more generally, another revolution in elite cuisine began to take shape in the age of Louis XIV. The first sign of this revolution appeared with the publication of a book entitled *Le Cuisinier françois* in 1651. The author was a man named François Pierre (*c.* 1618–78) but he was better known by his pen name 'La Varenne'. Despite the availability of the printing press and despite the precedent set by Platina, very few cookery books had been published anywhere in Europe up to this moment. Most food writing in the Renaissance took the guise of medical and dietetic advice and it offered very little practical advice on how to prepare foods. La Varenne's book was different. *Le Cuisinier françois* was almost wholly devoted to food and, even more so, to cooking and preparing food in a way that would make it as delicious as possible.

Unlike Platina's book and the many works that followed it, *Le Cuisinier françois* made very little attempt at justifying itself as a dietetic manual. La Varenne's printer made a hasty gesture in this direction in his introductory advice to the reader when he declared that 'it is sweeter by far to make according to one's ability an honest and reasonable expense in sauces, and other delicacies of meats, for to cause the life and health to subsist, than to spend vast sums of money in drugs, medicinal herbs, potions, and other troublesome remedies for the recovering of health.' But La Varenne's book was not really about how to improve one's health by adjusting one's diet. It was a cookery book and it was perhaps the first European cookery book almost entirely dedicated to the task of instructing its readers how to cook food.

Le Cuisinier françois is often thought to epitomize the birth of classical French *haute cuisine* and there is something to be said for this view. La Varenne's recipes put great emphasis on sauces and reductions and his cooking makes heavy use of fats such as butter and cream in his dishes. La Varenne's cookery book has liberal recommendations for including mushrooms, lard, butter, truffles, pepper and vinegar in its recipes. Although his recipes listed far fewer spices than those of his predecessors, he did continue to include old spice standards such as saffron in several of his dishes. La Varenne would later be criticized by his French successors for this excessively 'Arabic' influence on his

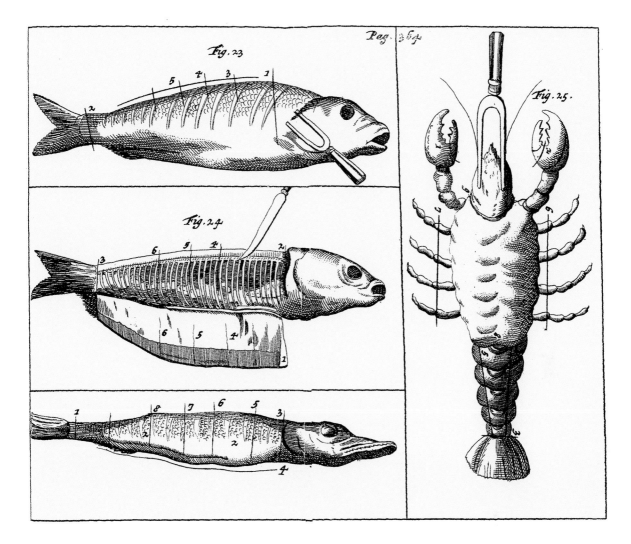

A page from La Varenne's *Le Cuisinier françois* (1651), showing different cuts of fish and lobster. Unlike most Renaissance dietary treatises, La Varenne's work focused in great detail on how to prepare and cook food. It marks a radical break with the pretensions to health and medical advice that guided earlier European food writing. La Varenne paved the way for modern European gastronomy.

cooking, but his *Cuisinier françois* marks a notable turn away from the older culinary traditions of liberal spicing.

La Varenne's recipes offer an excellent example of the mid-seventeenth-century elaboration of the sweet/savoury distinction: his book does not mention desserts or sweets, save for a short section on preserves. This is a work devoted to the salty, fatty dishes of the main courses. The dessert would be the province of a book that acted as a sort of sequel to La Varenne's, Jean Gaillard's *Le Patissier françois* (1653), another work that claimed to be the first of its kind.

At the heart of La Varenne's cooking is the sauce. He does not devote a separate section to sauces but he includes them in his recipes throughout his book. The first recipe in the book is for his broth stock (*bouillon*), which later forms the basis for over sixty of his soups. According to La Varenne, the French cook should aspire at all times to achieving a '*haut goût*' in his sauces, although he never precisely defines what he means by this supposed 'top taste'. However, one can infer from his recipes and later tradition that he sought to prepare highly reduced and flavourful sauces which would complement the natural flavours of each dish. His recipes recommend the slow cooking of meats in liquid as a means of procuring stock as well as preparing a dish. After La Varenne, sauce rather than spices would be the central element of most European *haute cuisine.* Francesco Leonardi's late eighteenth-century pronouncement that 'a tasty and delicate sauce is the soul of any excellent food' succinctly encapsulated the culinary spirit of classical French cuisine.

Perhaps the most important sauce in La Varenne's work is the ragout, a manner of preparing a strongly seasoned sauce to accompany almost any food, but in the *Cuisinier françois*, the ragouts were recommended almost exclusively as accompaniments to meat and fish. The 'ragout' was defined for English readers in the 1653 English translation as 'any sauce or meat prepared with a *haut goust*, or quick or sharp taste.' As with sweetness, spiciness was being intensified in certain preparations such as sauces or ragouts, while it was made less extensive in general cooking.

The *Cuisinier françois* introduced a whole new culinary language to its readers. The English version's 'table of hard words' introduced new terms of technique such as 'fricasseé [*sic*], defined as 'frying with a sauce'; 'farce', or 'anything made up for to stuff any meat with'; and even 'to stove or soak', which La Varenne said was 'to cause to boile very softly before or over the fire, that so the juice or liquor may be imbibed, or drunk in by degrees, to the end that the potage or sauce may be well allayed.' Also introduced were new or rare foods such as 'andouilles' – 'great guts of pork, or beef, filled up with thin slices of tender meat, or small guts of pork well seasoned' – or new ingredients such as 'moriles' and 'trouffles or truffles' – both 'a kind of excellent mushrums'. The glossary in the early editions of La Varenne was rather short and left much to be desired, but an important new step in the development of an independent field of culinary discourse had been taken here. After La Varenne it would be customary for food writers, especially those concerned with cookery books and cooking manuals, to develop their own specialized, and almost always Francophone, vocabulary for discussing the techniques of, and naming the ingredients in, their dishes.

La Varenne's new culinary vocabulary and his reduction-based cooking were both immensely successful and his work loomed large in subsequent culinary debates in the later seventeenth and eighteenth centuries. Some of his terms, particularly the 'ragout' and the 'fricasseé' struck a chord with diners as well as cooks throughout Europe and they became standard terms of cooking which remained untranslated from their original French. Terms of this sort also struck a chord with literary wits, for whom this new brand of elite cooking seemed suspiciously overwrought and pretentious. Particularly in England, the term 'ragout' became a sort of Grub Street code word for sophisticated nonsense. In the prologue to her play *Love's Contrivance* (1703), Susanna Centlivre satirized the 'modish kick-shaws' (a vulgar Anglicization of the French *quelques choses*') on offer at London's elite taverns such as

Pontack's, Locket's and Brown's, in which Francophile beaus devour 'famed ragouts' and 'new invented sallad', all with 'pretensions to regale the palate'. More morbidly, Jonathan Swift's *Modest Proposal* (1729) suggested that the children of Ireland could 'equally serve in a *Fricasie*, or a *ragoust*' for the pleasure of English palates.

Despite these anxieties in other countries about the creeping hegemony of French cuisine, Parisian publishers continued to produce the most important and innovative European works on cooking in the later seventeenth and eighteenth centuries. Nicolas de Bonnefon's *Les Délices de la campagne* (1654) quickly followed La Varenne's work. In the 1660s, the first culinary encyclopaedias were published with titles such as *L'Escole parfait des officiers de bouche* (1662) and *L'Ecole des ragouts* (1668). The famous *Cuisinier royal et bourgeois* (1691) by François Massialot (1660–1733) also included large plates folded into the text in which elaborate table settings were detailed. This explosion of French culinary writing in the late seventeenth century helped construct something like a field of literary discourse about cuisine for the first time in European history. Within this new field, debates about proper cooking would erupt in print and be rehearsed back and forth from one author to the next.

The haughtiest tone was struck by the author known only by his initials as L.S.R., whose *L'Art de bien traiter* (1674) denounced previous food writers for their 'antique' and 'rustic' ways of cooking. He deplored the 'abundance of ragouts' and the 'confused mixtures of diverse spices, the mountains of roasts, the successive services of *assiettes volantes*,' which characterized the cuisine of past times and insisted instead that an excellent and elegant meal should be judged by its 'exquisite choice of meats, the finesse with which they are seasoned, the courtesy and neatness with which they are served, their proportionate relation to the number of people, and finally the general order of things.' Even, and perhaps especially, La Varenne came in for particular scorn here. L.S.R. condemned many of La Varenne's recipes, particularly those preparations that seemed too close to peasant or 'Arabic' cooking. 'Arabic' here works almost as a synonym for the heavily spiced and flamboyant dishes of medieval and Renaissance elite cuisine. This desire to break with past traditions would continue through the rest of the eighteenth century and ultimately lead to the announcement in the 1730s of a '*nouvelle cuisine*' or a '*cuisine moderne*'. The substance of this 'new' eighteenth-century cooking was in fact less novel or less modern than its rhetoric proclaimed, but the claims to novelty and the culinary supremacy of these new dishes marked the emergence of a new way of thinking about food. Cooking was now a competitive field in which successive chefs could contend for supremacy by constantly attempting to supersede one another's recipes, and the ultimate announcement of one's innovative recipes would be made in print.

La Varenne succeeded in the later seventeenth century where Platina had failed two centuries earlier: he initiated a serious debate on how to cook and eat well which would be taken up and developed by successive writers in perpetuity. Cuisine became a legitimate field for debate. This allowed for the further development of cooking as a dignified profession and the development of food writing as a distinct and internationally recognized literary domain. By the early nineteenth century, the literary articulation of these various notions of eating well began to be understood by the name of 'gastronomy'.

It is perhaps ironic that the relatively unlearned La Varenne should succeed where the erudite humanism of Platina had failed, but the reasons for the success of gastronomic discourse in the later seventeenth century rather than in the Renaissance have more to do with the timing than the content, let alone the actual taste, of this cuisine. Whereas Platina articulated his Latinate philosophy of eating well in a courtly context in which feasting was still evaluated primarily in terms of quantity and magnificent display, La Varenne published his work in the vernacular at a time when the print trade had expanded to service a much larger body of readers. He wrote at a point when Latin was losing its international literary prestige with relation to other European vernaculars and he had the good fortune of writing in French, the one vernacular that was quickly replacing Latin as the *lingua franca* of European elites. Writing when he did, La Varenne was able to reach a far larger audience than Platina and yet do so with the prestige of writing in a language that was fast becoming recognized as the first vernacular among equals in the European literary field. The fortunate, albeit paradoxical, combination of mass appeal and snobbery that would characterize Francophone culinary writing is perhaps elegantly captured in the title of Massialot's *Cuisinier royal et bourgeois*. It was possible to have it both ways, both snobbishly royal and popularly bourgeois, in the post-La Varenne culinary field.

Fortunes also improved for the food workers who prepared the meals to meet this new interest in culinary matters. Professional cooks remained servants in princely and aristocratic households and unlike most of the cooking in the homes of the middle classes or labourers, elite cooking was a job for men. A clear sign of the growing prestige of cooking for elites was that the work was seen by the later seventeenth century to require not just manual skills, or 'mechanick arts' in the parlance of the day, but an intellectual ability and a 'good taste' which was akin to the tastes of elites themselves. Vincent La Chapelle (*fl.* 1733–36), who served as cook for various European elites including the Earl of Chesterfield, the Count of Montijo and the Prince of Orange, insisted that good cooking required a command of the 'rules' of cooking in his *Modern Cook* (1733), as well as an ability to know how to innovate upon past practices: 'A cook of genius will invent new delicacies to please the palates of those for whom he is to labour; his art, like all others, being subject to change.' La Chapelle proudly, albeit

In the 18th century, aristocratic feasts often included elaborate table settings and decorations. Several courses were still served at once and ample room was accorded at each table for attentive service. Elite dining of this kind also remained a sort of spectator sport, as evidenced by the large number of onlookers in a 1707 engraving of a dinner in Paris for the Duke of Alva and the Prince of Asturias.

falsely, announced that his own work was wholly original, 'the whole being the result of my own practice and experience.' Although about a third of his recipes were directly plagiarized from Massialot's *Cuisinier royal et bourgeois*, it is significant that La Chapelle felt it important and dignified to assert the novelty and originality of his recipes.

The development of professionalized cooking was not universally welcomed. Particularly because the international language of elite cuisine was quickly established as French, some resistance to the new cuisine appeared on nationalist grounds. Campbell's *London Tradesman* (1747) complained that 'in the days of good Queen Elizabeth, when mighty roast beef was the Englishman's food; our cookery was plain and simple as our manners; it was not then a science or mystery, and required no conjuration to please the palates of our greatest men. But we have of late years refined ourselves out of that simple taste, and conformed our palates to meats and drinks dressed after the French fashion.' Despite his evident distaste for this overly sophisticated form of cuisine, Campbell grudgingly recognized that the modern cook's trade required a distinct set of skills including 'a distinguishing palate' as well as a command of 'the whole mystery of mixing and disguising everything that comes under his hand' and he noted that these cooks could expect to earn anywhere from five to a very respectable fifty pounds per year, 'according to the rank of his master'. Cooking as a potentially lucrative profession had arrived.

By the eighteenth century then, cooking had developed into an autonomous field, now distinct from the medical practice of dietetics, with a language of its own and a growing sense of professional identity. As was the case with the wider European republic of letters at this time, the universal language for culinary discourse was French and even in terms of personnel, French chefs found their way into employment in elite households throughout Europe based on the sense that French cuisine was synonymous with good taste.

French cuisine did not extinguish all other forms of cooking in the age of enlightenment, indeed its grandiose pretensions more often than not provoked a reaction against it, but it did come to dominate European thinking about cuisine in the period in a way that no other national cuisine was able to do. Hence was born the particular and peculiar association between French cuisine and European *haute cuisine*. This association has survived in many respects until the present day and has been perhaps even more resiliant than the associations between Francophone philosophy and literature and European 'high culture' that were also established in the century before the French Revolution.

in **MAGGIs Suppen**

W. BRAND
BERLIN

MAGGIs SUPPEN
35 Sorten

7 THE BIRTH OF THE MODERN CONSUMER AGE

Food Innovations from 1800

Hans J. Teuteberg

Eating, a basic element of human life, is a hugely complex activity. It not only involves innate biochemical processes, but is also a cultural phenomenon. Every day, humans must quite literally 'incorporate' food, and, in contrast to animals, who simply follow their instincts in their choice of foods, people are confronted by a vast array of determining and sometimes even contradictory factors, of which they may be conscious or unconscious.

This chapter looks at how one of these factors, technical progress, which is intricately bound up with industrialization and urbanization, has had a lasting impact on the culinary culture of the last two hundred years. As there has never been any unified European cuisine I shall take as my examples the German-speaking regions of Central Europe, whose political borders have often changed throughout history, but whose traditional cultures have remained broadly consistent. New tastes radiated from here to the rest of Europe, and vice versa, and in many ways what happened in these countries can be seen as representative of the general transformation in the processing, preparation and appreciation of food in the nineteenth and twentieth centuries. If we are to understand the nature of these changes, we must first look briefly at nutrition before the industrial age.

Until the middle of the nineteenth century, the situation in the German-speaking regions north of the Alps, as in many other parts of Europe, was just as it had been in previous centuries: famines and rising food prices were part of everyday life and the quest for one's daily bread was the top priority in the struggle for existence. Thus people would sit at table, thank God for what they were about to receive, and ask for his blessing. Most of the population lived on grain, which would be eaten in the form of thick porridge or thin soups, mixed with water or milk, pancakes, bread, rolls, dumplings, noodles and, on rare festive occasions, pastries and cakes. The popularity of cereals lay in the fact that grains could be kept for long periods without losing their flavour, and all kinds of meals could be produced from them.

Convenience foods date back more than a century. In the late 19th century, the Swiss miller Julius Maggi realized that women working in industry no longer had time to prepare and cook nutritional meals for the family. He created pea and bean powders that could make nourishing soups, swiftly followed by meat bouillon cubes, sauces and flavourings which saved time in the kitchen. The products of his Maggi company (now part of Nestlé) contributed a great deal to the improvement of taste.

In Europe from the Middle Ages until the Second World War it was family custom to say grace before meals, as depicted in this detail from a painting by Mary Evelina Kindon from c. 1900. When a child came late, he or she was made to feel ashamed by standing in the corner and having to say grace alone. Today, people merely wish each other 'bon appetit'.

All the different varieties of cereal contained large amounts of carbohydrates, mostly in the form of starch and so provided the daily quota needed for energy, but they did not contain adequate quantities of some essential amino acids. As these were highly concentrated in peas, beans and lentils, a mixed diet of cereals and pulses provided a much better source of vegetable protein. But even this diet must have been lacking in important vitamins and trace elements, as has been demonstrated by sample analyses. Vegetable oils and animal fats contributed very little to the daily requirement for energy, but they contained additional vitamins. Meat, fish, butter and eggs were rare pleasures, which were mainly confined to festive occasions or Lent. It is likely that the necessary amount of fat was hardly ever available to the poorer classes, and this would also have had a profound effect on the taste of their daily meals. Food derived from animals was always extremely expensive, and consumption of it was directly dependent on income and social status. Among the poor, only peasants with cattle living in the rich pastures near a river, or the marsh and mountain regions, and fishermen in the coastal areas had substantial amounts of animal protein at their disposal. Strangely enough from our point of view, it has been statistically shown that until the late nineteenth century, people living in the countryside consumed on average less meat than those living in the town. This is because the few cattle that were available for slaughter were sold at urban markets; meat dishes were for those of a higher social status.

By comparison with today, the consumption of fresh fruit and vegetables was also minimal until the 1860s. This was because vegetables did not have much flavour without other foods and, like fruit, were not really filling; if they were not washed, they often caused stomach problems, as the bacterial causes of such illnesses had not yet been discovered. These vegetables were generally preserved, and that meant not only a loss of water, but also a loss of taste and vitamins. Scientists only established their nutritional value much later, as is indicated by cookery books from 1920 onwards. Instead, pre-industrial food contained a great deal of roughage, much of which was hard to digest and, because there were so few spices and seasonings, distinctly lacking in flavour. Tropical cane sugar had been known in Europe since the crusades of the late Middle Ages, and it was also grown in Sicily and Madeira; since the fifteenth century it had been used alongside honey in court kitchens and rich patrician households to make some sweets for the dessert, but it was so expensive that it rarely found its way into the diet of ordinary people. Not until after 1800 did German beet sugar provide a cheap new source of calories as well as a vast extension to the range of tastes available to the general public. It is also important to note that until the end of the nineteenth century the majority of country-dwellers fed themselves, while people in the towns tended to buy their food from peasants in their immediate neighbourhood, so that there was very little variety

In the pre-modern era the provision of flour and bread was an essential element of daily life, as illustrated in this 19th-century German painting. With urbanization, the traditional custom of baking bread at home came to an end, but sometimes continued in the countryside until the early 20th century. Nowadays, Germany alone has more than 1,000 different kinds of bread.

in their meals. The content was determined by the seasons and the produce of the region.

To sum up, food prior to the industrial age was more or less deficient by modern standards, difficult to digest, often poorly prepared, inadvertently or deliberately adulterated, and it made the consumer susceptible to diseases that could lead to death. The high mortality rate particularly of small children was to a large extent due to inadequate and unhygienic food. As a result of poor nutrition, individual productivity at work was also relatively low.

There is, however, a lack of data concerning consumer habits prior to 1850, especially in relation to people in the country, as the food they produced and ate remained independent of cash income and market prices. But experts are agreed that 'ordinary' people around 1800 must have spent on average 70 to 80 per cent of their income on food alone. There is a good deal of evidence that luxury foods played little part in most households, and even then they were often consumed only in mixed or substitute forms. The low standard of living led to food being evaluated firstly by its capacity to fill the stomach, how much could be used without waste, the ease with which it could be prepared (utility value), and its cost (exchange value); secondly, for its social prestige value, and only finally its taste and nutritional value.

The transition to the modern diet initially came about in some regions through the expansion of rural trade and industry, which led to an increasing use of money in everyday life. Colonial coffee, like tea and cocoa, had originally been a luxury drink for the aristocracy and the wealthy bourgeoisie, but from 1770 even this became available to ordinary people, though only in much diluted or substitute forms. This hot black drink with a bitter taste worked as a stimulus in the morning, and with 'coffee bread' it began to replace the old and less tasty beer and flour-based soups at breakfast time. The growing demand for bread led to the construction of large steam-driven mills, and millet, oats and buckwheat gave way to the consumption of rye and wheat as the most favoured cereals. Oats were the biggest losers, being relegated to mere cattle fodder. In the remoter rural areas such as the Alpine valleys, however, traditional cereal-based snacks continued to be common right through to the early twentieth century.

Another far-reaching development was the increased cultivation of potatoes. Although this South American tuber had reached Germany via Seville and the Spanish Netherlands as far back as the early sixteenth century, at first it was only of marginal importance as a botanical curiosity and used later only as cattle feed or as sustenance for the very poor. It only began to be cultivated locally in what had traditionally been cereal-growing regions when the great famines of 1770–1 and 1816–17 induced some state governments to recognize its nutritional value, and they encouraged the initiatives of enlightened 'experimental economists' to start large-scale production. And so this unassuming, long-despised vegetable now became a staple food for the common people in many German, Austrian and Swiss regions. One great advantage for the poorer classes was that the potato – unlike other vegetables – required only tiny quantities of fat, cream and salt to accompany it. It could be prepared quickly as a main dish in many different ways, was far more easily digested than pulses, was filling and, thanks to its neutral taste, ideal as an accompaniment to various other dishes. Moreover, the potato fed more people on less acreage in comparison to grain. By 1846–47, the potato was so popular as a main dish that two crop failures following the potato blight led to the last great famine in Germany to be caused by nature. By 1850 the potato had become one of the major foods of Central Europe. Its triumphant progress was halted only where particularly tasty flour-based meals were integral to regional identity. Even today, the 'dumpling line' between north and south Germany (the latter area traditionally consumes dumplings) can be seen if you examine restaurant menus.

The third vital change in food habits was the increasing consumption of spirits. Back in the seventeenth century, peasants had already begun to distil it from the residue left by wine presses, cereals and different fruits. Around 1800, chemists discovered that the cheapest drinkable spirit could be made from potatoes. When country folk got to hear of this new source of income, the 'spirit bug' spread as rapidly as potato growing. The potato, which because of its high water content could not be stored for too long, could now be transformed into a highly profitable, extremely tasty and durable product with the aid of relatively simple apparatus. Even the remains from the process of distillation could be used to feed the pigs. Supported by favourable taxation, 'potato schnaps' (hard liquor) began to take over from home-brewed, bottom-fermented dark beer, which could not compete in terms of alcoholic strength, taste or price with the new drink. Not until

und abends Kartoffeln

In Central Europe during the 19th century the potato became the second main food staple after bread. For a long time, a dish of a herring with potatoes in their skins, as shown in this 1935 poster, was popular in ordinary households in north Germany. Since the arrival of the consumer society in the 1960s, industrial potato products that use fat, such as chips, have improved the taste of the potato.

the late nineteenth century were the great breweries able to find new techniques and sales methods and, with their lighter 'lager' beer, extend the taste range and reconquer the market. In the ancient wine-growing regions on the Rhine, Mosel and Danube, however, old habits died hard, which was partly due to the fact that in these small firms the work was done by hand and could not be mechanized.

Until the middle of the nineteenth century, none of these food innovations could on their own put an end to the undernourishment that typified the pre-industrial age. Only certain fundamental political, socio-economic and technological structural changes were able to bring about the beginnings of modern eating habits. First of all, in the wake of liberal agricultural reforms after the Napoleonic Wars, there was a swift and lasting increase in agrarian production. This state-led 'Agrarian Revolution', based on models of English and Scottish 'gentlemen farmers', entailed more systematic rotation of crops, artificial

Beer was for centuries the most popular beverage in Europe north of the Alps. During the Industrial Revolution the many types of home-brewed dark ale were superseded by the new light-coloured beers of the big brewery companies. But the old beer-drinking customs remained such as raising the glass to somebody and singing the beer songs, and the pub and beer gardens continued as places to meet and to imbibe. A painting by Edmund Harburger from 1890, entitled *The Empty Jug*, captures the drinker's perennial search for one drop more.

fertilization, new agricultural tools and machinery, and intensified cattle farming. Other factors included the peasants being freed from the old feudal system, and land being redistributed and privatized. The cultivation of fallow, wild and waste land made it easier to grow plants for fodder, and hence to rear cattle. The provision of natural dung for the fields was no longer the main motive for raising cattle – on the contrary, the land now served as a means of supplying rapidly increasing quantities of meat. The rise in living standards meant that consumption of animal products now outstripped that of vegetables. The most rapid increase in demand was for pig meat: not only could practically every part of the pig be eaten, but it was also the cheapest animal to raise and to feed; bacon, ham and all sorts of sausages kept well and were as tasty as fresh meat.

New forms of transport such as the railways and steamships had expanded since the 1830s, and they too played an important role in raising the standard of nutrition and in opening up new potential for the development of culinary culture. So it became possible to carry foodstuffs as a staple commodity from remote rural areas that had surplus production and also from overseas into the spreading cities, where demand was now mushrooming. The invention and spread of the electric telegraph and a series of international trade agreements also facilitated the long-distance transportation of ordinary and luxury foods. Various factors led to a lasting reduction in the price of grain as well as to a lessening of seasonal fluctuations. Among these factors were lower freight charges, the introduction of national corn exchanges and the expansion of trading networks. The abolition of the age-old protectionist grain duty was particularly important in putting an end to the exorbitant price rises that took place whenever there was any kind of disaster.

Last but not least, results obtained from research into the physiology of nutrition found their way into the industrial and commercial processing of food. New methods of preservation made the consumer largely independent of fluctuations in the harvest, and for the first time in history brought about mass production. Legislation against food adulteration raised the quality of meat, flour and drink. The considerably lengthened storage times and free competition between different suppliers also made it possible for food to be distributed over a far wider area. The introduction of modern methods of advertising, establishing new connections between producer and consumer, put much greater emphasis on the taste and the nutritional value of products than had ever been the case in pre-industrial times. The far-reaching structural changes that took place within a single generation during the nineteenth century also fundamentally changed the eating habits of the industrializing nations of Europe, which were now once and for all freed from the periodic famines imposed by nature.

From that time onwards, there was a rapid growth in population, as a result of the falling death rate, though birth rates initially remained unchanged at the pre-industrial level. At the same time, there was an acceleration in the growth of the cities, as more and more people flocked to them from the countryside. Food production, despite the much-discussed and pessimistic theories of the English demographer Thomas Robert Malthus (1766–1834), not only rose proportionately, but also improved in terms both of quality and, especially, of taste.

If one leaves aside temporary price rises, differences according to social class, income or regional preferences – all of which may distort the general trend – it can certainly be said that the basic supply of foodstuffs in the developed areas of Central Europe underwent a substantial improvement prior to the First World War. The fear that food could run out faded within just a few decades. The decisive breakthrough from the old European world of shortages to the modern, industrial consumer society can actually be measured statistically:

1. The average yearly consumption per head of most basic foodstuffs has continuously risen right through to the

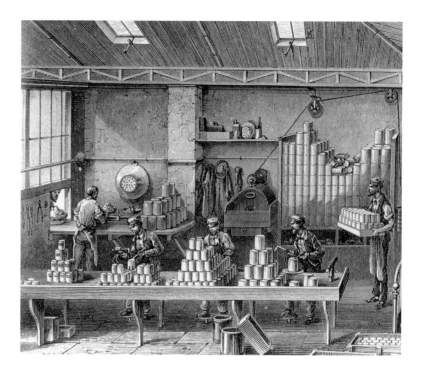

Methods of preserving food were rather limited in earlier times. A revolutionary change occurred in the 19th century with the invention of tinned food. It was now possible to eat any food at any season. The picture shows the canning process in one of the new factories in about 1860. It was around then that the military authorities began to be interested in this technical innovation.

end of the twentieth century, if we discount the two world wars and the subsequent periods of austerity.

2. By contrast with the rising standard of living, the percentage of the average income spent on food has continuously fallen.

3. The food consumed by the lower classes of society increasingly contained a greater number of calories, and especially of protein and animal fat, as can be seen from household budgets as far back as the late nineteenth century.

***

The rapid growth of urban populations during the second half of the nineteenth century necessitated changes in the food-supply system. Above all, it was a question not only of bringing far greater quantities of food from the distant areas of production, but also of ensuring that these were not ruined during transport, marketing and storage. There was therefore a massive leap forward in techniques of preserving and packing food products. For many centuries, people had dried, smoked and salted food, or placed it in vinegar, olive oil, alcohol or honey to extract the water and the harmful bacteria and thus prolong its edibility. In the late seventeenth century, the invention of a pressurized steamer (ancestor to the pressure-cooker) led to heat sterilization and vacuum sealing being discussed and tested as a new method of preserving food, initially with no success. It was not until 1809 that a Frenchman named Nicolas-François Appert, who was personal master chef to a German prince, demonstrated the first practical means of doing this, which was radically improved on by the Englishman Peter Durand in 1810 who replaced Appert's glass bottles with tin-plate containers, leading the way to the modern tin can. After Louis Pasteur had demonstrated the way micro-organisms worked during the process of fermentation, and had proved that these were killed by heat, many European countries saw a big surge in the commercial production of what initially were expensive preserved fruits and vegetables as well as cream. But it was only after the invention of cold-rolled sheet tin, tinning by electrolysis, and an automatic tin-closing machine that from the 1930s such preserves could really be mass-produced. Herein lay the secret of how to capture the seasons in a sealed container and to conquer nature's organic barriers to preservation without the loss of taste that had marred all previous attempts.

A no less significant symbiosis between nutrition science and the developing industrial technology can be found in meat extracts. Around 1800, after much debate about the usefulness of gelatine in treating the sick, French chemists evaporated meat soup into a purée from which they made 'bouillon bars', which could be used as ship provisions or as tonics for patients during convalescence. In 1847, in the context of his research into the function of muscles, the leading German chemist Justus Liebig was the first to make meat extract (*extractum carnis*) the subject of a theoretical scientific treatise. His student Max Pettenkofer, after various experiments, sold small amounts of powder from beef extract through an apothecary. In 1863, Georg Christian Giebert, an engineer from Hamburg who had been involved in railway projects in South America, and two Belgian wholesalers from Antwerp, established Liebig's Extract of Meat Company in Fray Bentos, Uruguay. Liebig himself was not associated with the firm, although they used his signature as a trademark. Once all the fat was removed, the evaporated brown meal was packed in tins, in which it could be preserved for long periods, and then, with the help of advertising, it was sold all over the world. Liebig's Extract of Meat, although initially rather expensive, pointed the way to the modern soup industry.

The manufacture of ready-to-cook 'soup rolls', 'meat soup capsules', 'Gusto' seasoning, and stock cubes by the Swiss miller and corn merchant Julius Maggi after 1891, and that of soups made from pulses and other vegetables by the former hawker Carl Heinrich Knorr in Heilbronn, constituted the first competition in this industry, with a veritable 'soup war' breaking out between Maggi and the British-Belgian Liebig's company over the merits of their meat-extract supplements. They were, however, faced with even more competition from a business established by the Scotsman John Lawson Johnston, who had gained a contract to supply the French army with cans of beef in 1871, but found that cows were in short supply after the Franco-Prussian War. His product, known originally as 'Fluid Beef' and later

The Liebig Extract of Meat Company, founded in 1863, was the first enterprise to produce a cheap but nutritious alternative to meat. By 1875, the factory at Fray Bentos in Uruguay was processing the meat of 150,000 cows each year.

Above: By the turn of the 20th century, by-products from the Chicago slaughterhouse and meatpacking company Armour & Co. reached around the world. This advertisment for the Extract of Beef dates from 1899.

Below: Leibniz-Keks, a type of butter biscuit, were first invented for travellers by Hermann Bahlsen, a merchant from Hanover, in 1891. Success was aided by stylish packaging that ensured the biscuits stayed fresh for a long time. The biscuits were named after the philosopher and mathematician Gottfried Wilhelm Leibniz, a famous resident of Hanover, and are still available today, including chocolate-covered varieties.

Opposite: Originally called Johnston's Fluid Beef, Bovril was the product of a company formed in 1889. By the time this poster appeared in the early 20th century, the product was selling as far way as South Africa and South America.

named Bovril, was not an evaporated meal but a liquid from squeezed beef. It was a food aimed primarily at sick people. In a big advertising campaign he claimed it to be fifty times more nourishing than Liebig's Extract of Meat, but this was denied by other chemists. After the turn of the century, many similar products came on the market, mainly from the English-speaking world, with Armour's Extract of Beef from Chicago being the best known, thanks to extensive advertising.

There are many other examples of how chemistry influenced the food industry, with particularly beneficial effects on the flavour of foods. Hermann Bahlsen, son of a merchant from Hanover, worked in a sugar factory in London and learned how ship's biscuits were made; these could be kept for long periods, were easily digestible and tasted good. He hit on the idea of manufacturing a sweet biscuit that would keep well and would serve as a little snack for travellers. In 1891, he produced his first Leibniz-Keks; Keks was an adaptation of the English word 'cakes'. The mysterious packaging, with the ancient Egyptian sign of TeT (meaning eternal life) and an elaborate graphic design, helped to ensure the success of his first German biscuit factory. The firm of Bahlsen is still going strong today.

Intensive study of the baking process also led to a company taking out a patent in 1898 on the production of a particular malt extract, which not only accelerated the fermentation of yeast dough, but also gave a brand-new flavour to cakes and pastries. As a result of the huge demand for this product, the newly founded parent company Diamalt GmbH in Munich was soon opening affiliated companies elsewhere. Even before that, in 1891, the Bielefeld chemist Dr August Oetker packaged the baking powder Backin in small bags and advertised it through special 'Oetker schools', demonstrators and 18.5 million copies of his cookery book. It was no longer necessary to use yeast to bake a cake and baking powder also made it possible to use smaller stoves suitable for urban households. Thus he laid the foundations for the modern, huge Oetker diversified company, still involved in food products but also banking, construction and shipping.

More intensive cattle farming meant increased milk production, with a resultant growth in butter and cheese consumption in Germany from 6 kg per head per year in 1860 to 11.6 kg in 1910. Dripping and beef fat also remained popular for cooking, but as the population grew faster than fat production, prices rapidly rose. It was therefore inevitable that the food industry began to look for cheaper substitutes. In France, in the 1860s, in response to a contest sponsored by Emperor Napoleon III to develop a butter substitute, the chemist Hippolyte Mège-Mouriés, after much experimenting, came up with a substance made from beef fat and milk, which he called 'margarine'. His patent was established in 1869 but he was unable to exploit it because of the Franco-Prussian War, and he sold it to the Flemish butter traders Anton Paul Jurgens and Simon van den Bergh who in 1871–73 founded the first margarine factory in the world in Brabant. Just one year later,

the first German margarine factories opened, and by 1885 there were no less than forty-six. Margarine production took a major step forward with the discovery of a process for hardening oil. This made it possible to use oily plants such as copra, sesame and palm nuts, and also groundnuts and soya beans. The consumption of butter rose from 200,000 tonnes to 470,000 tonnes between 1897 and 1913, but at the same time margarine consumption rose from just 90,000 tonnes to 200,000 tonnes. Germans consumed about a third of the world's margarine. The breakthrough to mass consumption had therefore also taken place before the First World War. It must be said, though, that the success of this 'artificial butter' probably had more to do with its cheapness and massive advertising campaigns than with its taste.

Owing to their relatively high cost, some tinned vegetables (green peas, beans, asparagus, gherkins and mushrooms) and peaches, pineapple, pickled fruit and fruit in rum were available only in small quantities until mechanization made it viable to produce more. The biggest success of all was jam: thanks to favourable taxation and an international sugar agreement, the price of sugar beet fell drastically and production rose accordingly. As well as the traditional, rather sour plum pap that had always made at home, there was now a vast range of new, sweet and attractive spreads, with the first factory being built in Lübeck as early as 1845. The fruit and vegetable exchange founded in Hamburg in 1899 showed just how swiftly demand had risen for fresh raw materials. The first commercial production of mushrooms began around 1880. Apples especially had been exported in small quantities to Scandinavia, and from around 1900, apart from various preserved fruits, fresh bananas and oranges were sold by auction in Hamburg and transported, sometimes in refrigerated lorries, to all the major cities in Central Europe.

The industrial processing of meat had also initially encompassed the more expensive, luxury kinds of meat, including roast venison, game, ragouts and fricassees. From the USA, corned beef, corned pork and boiled pork found their way into tins that were cheap enough to appeal to the masses, but the German meat-inspection law passed on 3 July 1900 banned their importation from Chicago for hygienic reasons, after German food analysts had taken a closer look. The German meat industry, which began in the 1860s and, unlike the family butchers, used machines such as cutters, mincers and bacon slicers to cut up the meat, had its first major success not with imitating these American preserves but with tinned sausages. In 1895, the master butcher Friedrich Heine from Halberstadt packed some of his so-called 'boiling sausages' in airtight tins, and he was already selling 1,500 of them a day by 1900. Other butchers soon followed to produce this first kind of fast food and in particular the 'Frankfurter' proceeded to conquer the world, also known in the US as the 'hot dog'. Those butchers and farmers who embraced the new industrial technology soon realized that the airtight containers allowed for a mild degree of pickling, which enhanced the

When the mechanical meat-cutter was invented a wave of canned 'corned-beef' came to Europe from the USA. However, the Germans preferred their own tinned 'boiled sausages', or Frankfurters, made at plants such as this one, photographed in the 1920s. Sold in airtight cans, in the United Sates these sausages were the forerunners of the famous 'hot dogs'.

flavour expected of the finest meat products. The commanders of the Prussian army noticed these innovations and established two canning factories of their own which, from 1870 onwards, processed meat as well as vegetables and pulses, and the troops were also supplied with Erbswurst, tablets of soluble pea soup in the form of a sausage, for iron rations.

There was an equally dramatic development in the fish-preserving industry although this was less rapid and varied between the different European nations. For centuries, people living inland had only had access to dried, smoked or occasionally pickled sea fish, but after the 1880s the English style of trawler, with new haul nets and processing on board, together with central fish auctions and rapid rail transport in cold storage wagons, made sea fish available in the cities. Building on the traditional smokeries on the Baltic coast, various small-scale fish-processing plants sprang up. There were several obstacles to overcome, however. Experiments with heat sterilization had shown that several kinds of fish lose their consistency and taste. Other tinned fish could not be stored much longer than before and had to be consumed as 'half-preserves'. Sardines in oil, fully sterilized by a new Spanish method, were imported and became the first mass-market product. It would only be with 'full-preserves' that the fish industry could achieve independence from the seaonal nature of the fish hauls, so the fish factories began to process the sprat, which like the sardine could fit in a tin. However, the hauls were too small and irregular for large production. It was, therefore, the smoked and fried herring which gave rise to

The fish-preserving industry, which came into being through new fish trawlers, rational processing on board and fish auctions, facilitated the sale of seafood to inland towns. By 1900, the German fish factories were mainly processing the popular dried or smoked herring for the urban market. The more luxurious tinned sprats, or the more expensive fish such as salmon and sturgeon, were sent by direct mail to the consumer or delicatessens, hence the need for special posters such as this one, which dates from the 1930s.

the first brand names of the German fish-processing industry, which then centred on the fishing village of Schlutup near Lübeck and later in Altona next to Hamburg.

By 1900 there were about 450 fish-processing plants in Germany, which by 1914 had risen to 650. Compared to their European neighbours, Germans still consumed relatively little fish per person per year, but the average consumption of fresh, smoked and pickled sea fish and of tinned fish – later boosted by recommendations from food experts – rose substantially from 2.7 kg (1850) to 10.9 kg (1975), and more recently to 15.3 kg (2001). As cookery books show, the herring was always the most popular fish, used in many variations.

As far as drinks are concerned, one immediately thinks of the great breweries which towards the end of the nineteenth century, as we have seen, replaced local production and especially home-brewing. There were many contributory factors to this development: scientific research into fermentation, with the aid of the microscope; advances in brewing technology; new malting processes; the use of steam power for energy; automated cleaning and filling of new beer bottles; new tops; improved cooling and transport facilities; the new liberal trading regulations, which in 1873 put an end to brewing privileges that had been granted since the Middle Ages to one particular house; and last but not least, the general adoption of the Bavarian bottom-fermented method of brewing. With the need for more and more capital investment, the number of small breweries rapidly dwindled after 1871, and output came largely from breweries that were joint-stock companies, such as Schultheiss (Berlin), Dortmunder Union, Löwenbräu and Spaten (both in Munich), and Beck (Bremen). In 1913, the market leader, Schultheiss, had 11 breweries, 4 malt houses and 135 distribution centres, and at that time it was probably the biggest lager brewery in the world. These giant companies made Germany into one of the leading exporters of beer. Average yearly consumption at home went up from 6.8 litres per person (1875) to 117 (1900), before gradually decreasing to 51.3 (1932), rising again to 70.1 (1938), falling to its nadir of 28.8 (1946), but then rising steeply to 150.8 (1976). These statistics, however, do not show that now, as in the past, there are huge regional differences, which may well be linked to the very different tastes of the various beers.

Germans are not only heavy beer-drinkers but also great coffee-lovers. In 1979, out of an average total of 663 litres of fluid consumed by each person in the Federal Republic, 187.8 litres were real coffee, even eclipsing beer. News of this 'heathen, Turkish drink' had reached Europe as early as the sixteenth century, through Venetian traders, and in the late seventeenth century – as in France and England – the first coffee houses opened in Vienna, Hamburg and Leipzig. However, 'coffee circles' only came down gradually from the royal and aristo-cratic houses to the wealthy bourgeoisie in the towns. Before it became a nation Germany had no colonies of her own and had to import coffee beans as a luxury. The 'common' people, and especially those in the country, had to make do – as already mentioned – with coffee substitutes, and chicory in particular. Production of these substitutes had soared since the blockades imposed by Napoleon's Continental System in 1806, and was boosted by the number of large factories manufacturing Malzkaffee (a substitute made from barley malt), which improved the taste, as well as by a greater demand for healthier, caffeine-free coffee in the context of the quest for a more natural lifestyle. Until the early twentieth century, pure coffee remained a luxury, mainly because it was so expensive, and it was only after the Second World War that it became an everyday drink. Although in earlier times there were specialist coffee firms in Hamburg and Bremen, and in 1887 the Hamburg Coffee Exchange established a futures market, most of the raw coffee beans – mainly imported from Brazil and Guatemala – were exported again after roasting.

Like coffee, cocoa was initially a luxury and for a long time did not feature in the ordinary consumer's daily diet. Germans first heard about it in 1644, through the translation of a piece written by the Spaniard Antonio Colmenero de Ledesma, but it was only used for medicinal purposes. In the late seventeenth and eighteenth centuries, hot liquid 'chocolate' was tried out in courtly circles, and sugar bakers (confectioners) began to make chocolate cakes. It was not until 1756 that

By the First World War the big German breweries were catering to an enormous domestic market as well as regularly exporting their product elsewhere. An Art Nouveau poster from 1904 advertises the Italian sales agent for a German beer.

Opposite: Coffee consumption began to increase in Central Europe as elsewhere in the late 18th century, but for a long time most ordinary households could afford only various kinds of cheaper substitute coffee. Until the mid-1950s pure bean coffee was a semi-luxurious beverage reserved for festive occasions, a visit to a coffee house or a country inn with an open-air 'coffee garden'; this one in Potsdam was photographed in 1930. It is only in the last fifty years that 'real coffee' has become a drink consumed on a daily basis.

Below: At the time this poster appeared in 1906, the Dutch firm Van Houten was the largest manufacturer of cocoa drinks and dark, bitter-tasting table-chocolate, in contrast to the Swiss producers who made sweet-tasting milk chocolate. Chocolate had evolved from being an expensive status symbol in the 18th century to a quite normal daily morning drink for children or a nice gift.

the first German chocolate factory opened in the tiny Westphalian principality of Lippe. In neighbouring Prussian and Hessian states, however, the import of cocoa, like that of real coffee and tea, was either heavily taxed or forbidden altogether. But then pioneers such as the English firm of Cadbury began to mix cocoa powder with wine, beer or sugared water, and the Dutch botanist C. J. van Houten extracted cocoa butter, which he was able to use separately. It was, though, the abolition of high import duties and the falling price of cocoa, together with the introduction of steam-driven machines, that eventually set in motion the first industrial production of chocolate in the 1830s.

In 1863, Daniel Peter, son of a Swiss butcher, married the daughter of François-Louis Cailler, founder of the first chocolate factory in Switzerland, and he came across the new children's food that was being made from thickened milk and flour by his neighbour in Vevey, the chemist Henri Nestlé. He hit on the idea of mixing Nestlé's milk product with chocolate powder, thereby overcoming the problems others had found if normal milk was used, and in 1875 his milk chocolate for drinking appeared, followed by eating chocolate in the 1880s. In 1899, during the Boer War, the British army included it in their provisions, and its transition from a snack for the rich to an everyday treat was complete. The foundations had now been laid for the worldwide success of the Swiss chocolate industry (Tobler, Lindt, Cailler, Kohler, Peter), much of which was later to come under the umbrella of Nestlé. The firm of Van Houten, which had been the first to market soluble cocoa powder for children, did like Nestlé a great deal to popularize this sweet food through copious advertising in family magazines. Among those who profited from these innovations was Franz Stollwerck, a manufacturer of cough-drops, chocolate and marzipan in Cologne, who in 1871 had the idea of installing vending machines in

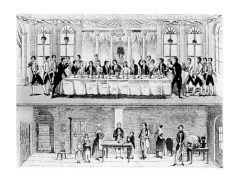

Above: Until well into the 20th century lower-class households, particularly in the countryside, preserved the traditional pattern of master of the house, his wife, children and any servants sitting together at the table to eat a meal, often from a common dish or pan. In wealthy, urban middle-class homes the social separation of the classes had been established earlier: the servants sat downstairs to take their meal and the bell became the means to communicate. An engraving from about 1840 compares the dining arrangements of different social classes.

railway stations, so that travellers could put a coin in a slot to take out small wrapped bars of chocolate and little bags of sweets – one of the earliest forms of self-service. As the industry developed, the ever-increasing assortment of confectionery followed two main paths: the cheap, mass-market products that could be bought in the ubiquitous kiosks and other snack bars, while the more expensive gourmet items in their luxurious packaging were to be found in the inner-city delicatessens.

***

Between the late Middle Ages and the industrial era, methods of cooking – boiling, frying, baking, drying – changed as little as the tools that were used. For centuries, the open fireplace was the centre of family life, not only for the preparation of meals but also as the sole source of warmth and light. Only castles, manor houses, monasteries and, later, palaces had larger separate kitchens with masonry outlets for the smoke, because there were so many people to be catered for in such places. In urban upper-class houses, following the model of the great Italian trading cities during the Renaissance, there were different sections for masters and servants, as was also the case in the country houses of the aristocracy. Later, in two-storey townhouses, chimneys were built that could be linked to the parlour stove upstairs as well as to the cooking stove in the kitchen below. People now had a cosy room where they could both eat and warm themselves and the kitchen was a separate area used only for preparing food and for the domestic staff to eat in. This social segregation in upper middle-class homes took place only gradually, between the late seventeenth and early nineteenth centuries. In most lower-class households, especially in the country, the

Below left and above: The traditional open fire-place was replaced by the iron cooking stove in the second half of the 19th century. The new 'rational stove' prepared hot water and divided the glowing coal fire from the ashes, so the preparation of meals became quicker, cleaner and easier. It also had the advantage that several cooking-pots or pans could be heated at once.

old multifunctional living-room persisted until well into the twentieth century, with the traditional rural table arrangements – everyone sitting at their allotted place and eating out of a common bowl. It was not until urbanization and the construction of large tenement blocks in the cities that the lower middle classes and the working classes had separate kitchens, although they were still mainly used as a kitchen-living room.

The emergence of the kitchen as a place just to prepare food accelerated technological developments. Ovens made of cast-iron and brass burned coal instead of wood, and they had an ingenious system that combined cooking and water heating. This 'thrifty stove', which was based on British and American inventions, revolutionized the centuries-old methods of cooking, and in its way was just as important as the almost contemporaneous invention of the steam engine. The gas stove, which gradually took over in the period 1880–1930, was in the long term superior to the coal-burning stove in three ways: it was quicker, it did not leave any ash, and it allowed precise temperature regulation, which meant a considerable saving of energy. Initially, the experts had to allay the fears of the housewife that the gas might ruin the taste of the food. The electric cooker, which came later and reduced the source of the heat to a single ring, was simply a logical continuation of this development, and it came into common use during and after the 1930s. With the introduction of separate top and main ovens, fan ovens and infra-red grills, the electric cooker has evolved still further, with the ceran hotplate being the very latest invention.

The electric cooker was only one aspect of the electrification of the kitchen. As early as 1900, the Swiss were making the 'Caldor' electric water heater, and in 1910 the Württembergische Metallwarenfabrik in Stuttgart produced a similar machine. After the First World War, bachelors were treated to single hotplates, electric pans and immersion coils, while housewives revelled in pressure cookers (predecessor of the microwave, which took over in the 1980s), electric kettles, hot-water tanks and toasters. With economic recovery after the Second World War, in the mid-1950s, came many more electric machines for mixing, making coffee, opening tins, cutting bread and grilling, all of which made life in the kitchen much easier.

The new coal, gas and electric stoves required suitable utensils, and so the metal industry came up initially with flat-bottomed iron pots of various sizes, and also heat-resistant ceramic pottery ware. The most popular model, however, was the enamel pot, which combined all the advantages of iron and glass. It was acid-resistant and easy to clean, as well as being virtually unbreakable. Nonetheless, it is clear from catalogues, advertisements and handbooks for restaurants around 1900 that these, and the heavy, sooty copper and cast-iron pots, gave way to thinner, more hygienic white tinplate vessels and then – from the mid-1920s – to those made of the even lighter and easier-to-handle aluminium. This new, rust-free metal was also particularly suitable for cups and plates, insulated containers and screwtop bottles, all of which enabled people to take hot food and drinks from home to work. The industry devised a huge variety of new pots, kettles and casseroles for

The first workable electric cooker, an important technical development after the gas stove, originated in the United States – one of the first was shown at the Chicago World's Fair in 1893. By the 1920s mass-production had started using the assembly-line model of the automobile factories. In Germany in the 1930s the electric cooker slowly started to replace the gas stove, but it was not until the 1950s that it became standard kitchen equipment.

The Frankfurt Kitchen, the first fitted kitchen to be made in any quantity, was installed in about 10,000 flats built by the Frankfurt Municipal Building Department. Designed by Grete Lihotsky in 1926–27, it was totally prefabricated and aimed at maximum efficiency, drawing on texts such as *The New Housekeeping: Efficiency Studies in Home Management* by Christine Frederick. The kitchen came in three different sizes but all of them were resonant of the compact ships' galleys and kitchens of the railway dining cars of the period.

different forms of cooking, as well as cake tins, cutters for meat, sausages, bread, vegetables and fruits and more spoons to ladle, stir and to taste, and, especially with the aid of electrolysis, produced rust-free, nickel-plated cutlery. By 1900, the utensils used in an ordinary, middle-class kitchen were an astounding advance on those used in 1800 and 1850.

With industrialization and urbanization, more and more women, attracted by rising wages, began to get jobs outside the home, which led to a shortage of servants and stimulated the rationalization of housework. Improved working practices were now essential. In the United States, Frederick Winslow Taylor's ideas of scientific management were adapted to the working processes in the kitchen. The ship's galley and the American railroad dining car were the models for redesigning furniture and equipment, in order to simplify procedures and shorten the time required for housework. The idea was to put together systematically the work tools and the work place. Women's magazines and housekeeping advisers were full of praise for this 'new household of efficiency'.

The 'New Kitchen', constructed as a proper workplace, was soon being manufactured everywhere. The first German to take it up was the carpenter Friedrich Poggenpohl, whose company was founded in 1892 in the Westphalian town of Herford, where there was already an established furniture industry. His kitchen furniture had flat, hygienic surfaces, and facilities for storage, cleaning, preparation and cooking were kept strictly apart. He divided the old kitchen dresser into two sections, which fitted onto one wall to save space. A wide work surface was situated directly below a tilt window, which gave good ventilation. The oven was at the same height as the work surface. Previously, up-market kitchens had been designed with an eye to aesthetic appeal, whereas now the focus was on practicality. The housewife had to do less bending and moving around, and preparing meals was easier and quicker. The kitchen was no longer an unimportant backroom but a proper workplace on a par with the other rooms in the house. After the First World War, the white-painted, enamelled fitted 'compact kitchen' became all the rage in the industrialized countries of Europe, and particularly in urban middle-class homes. Connection to water supply, drainage, gas and electricity systems and the introduction of refuse collection were additional, external factors that helped to promote this drive to modernization, although kitchens in rural regions had to wait a long time before these technical advances reached them.

***

All the German-speaking, Central European states that underwent industrialization during the nineteenth century experienced similar changes in the nature of their basic foods, leaving aside the obvious regional and social differences. Consumption of pig meat and beef rose steadily per head per year from 1850 until the end of the twentieth century, whereas demand for the tender, expensive veal remained the same, and that for mutton and goat actually suffered a relative decline. On average, over the long term, milk, cheese, butter and eggs, offal, animal fats, wheat flour, and especially fresh fruit and vegetables, also became increasingly popular. The consumption of potatoes and rye flour (as the main ingredient of bread) initially went up a great deal, but around 1900 began to decrease. The earliest and most drastic fall was that of the pulses, which had been so much in demand throughout the centuries, whereas tropical fruits from the southern hemisphere – bananas, oranges and so forth – and also poultry rose sharply, and after the Second World War the annual growth rate of consumption per person actually exceeded that of sugar in the previous century. Overall, this meant that from about middle of the nineteenth century onwards, there was a measurable shift from vegetable to animal nutrition, and consequently a greater intake of animal protein and animal fats with a simultaneous reduction in carbohydrates. Filling, indigestible and boringly routine foods were now replaced by meals that were easier to digest, more satisfying and, above all, tastier and more varied. They were not served merely to fill a space, but also to give pleasure to the senses.

Housekeeping courses for girls and young women began in Germany in 1889 on a voluntary base, and were extended to primary school girls in 1908. These women were photographed in about 1900. For girls who had left school, particularly those from working-class families, private cooking courses were established by churches and charitable societies. After the First World War housekeeping became a branch of study in vocational schools.

Of course, inevitably, the poorer, lower echelons of society had to make do with the inferior cuts of meat and the cheapest fruits and vegetables. Often they were compelled to use substitutes because of the sheer cost of foodstuffs: instead of sugar they bought the by-product treacle, and for butter they used dripping, vegetable oil or margarine, while the bitter root of chicory, roasted grain or malt replaced pure bean coffee. But even these substitutes led the way to the higher quality foodstuffs, and they certainly helped to put an end to old eating and drinking habits and to open the door to modern nutrition. Many food innovations were already apparent in the 1880s, and the socio-economic, technological, political and legal roots of our consumer age can be traced back to that period. The quantitative and qualitative revolution in nutrition from the late nineteenth century was for a long time concealed by major regional and social differences as well as by political upheavals, but the huge structural changes in the food industry that led to our modern mass consumerism were both cause and consequence of the much-discussed modernizing processes that came with urbanization and industrialization.

Changes in the preparation of food in the kitchen and meals on the table are best documented by cookery books. From the late Middle Ages until the nineteenth century, these dealt only with the eating etiquette of the aristocracy. The chief priority was to display as many lavishly prepared dishes as possible. The first signs of an urban 'bourgeois cuisine' were not to be seen until around 1800, when a new 'gastrosophy' or 'science of the stomach' manifested itself in the form of cookery books that combined culinary advice with literary reflections on the taste and the development of gastronomy in general. Increasingly numerous collections of recipes, known as 'husband's fare' (Hausmannskost), were no longer aimed exclusively at the professional chefs of the court but set out to give domestic advice to middle-class housewives and their daughters. There were also recipes for festive occasions, but the authors were more concerned with new *cuisine bourgeoise* – rational and economic meal preparation with tasteful variations was now the main point. French *haute cuisine* still dominated noble households and restaurants until German unification in 1871. The meal as a spectacle and as the gourmet dinner for a small group of the aristocracy was now joined by meals consisting of plain, nutritious regional dishes, traditionally prepared, in which taste was all-important.

The huge popularity of this middle-class cooking can be seen from the success of the *Praktisches Kochbuch für die gewöhnliche und feinere Küche* (Practical Cookery Book for Plain and Fine Cuisine) written by Henriette Davidis, daughter of a Westphalian parish priest; it was first published in 1845, was reprinted in countless revised editions through to the end of the century, and was still known to subsequent generations right up to the present day. Katharina Prato's *Süddeutsche Küche* (South German Cuisine), published in Graz in 1858, was another classic work on bourgeois cuisine, and went through more than seventy editions. It is interesting to note that the author, herself a member of the Austrian aristocracy, never once used the term 'Austrian cooking' or 'German cooking' but, like other books on the same subject, simply gave a detailed description of regional dishes. At the end of the nineteenth century, special books were produced to cater for rural households, and so it may be said that this form of culinary literature provided an accurate reflection of all the different German, Austrian and Swiss-German gastronomic cultures. Although the top restaurants always liked to include French dishes on their menus, for the sake of prestige, they stuck mainly to those from the *cuisine bourgeoise* with regional or local connections.

This trend towards the pleasures of regional cooking was partly connected with the growing need for orientation in an increasingly confused world, where geographical and social mobility as well as nationalism and internationalism left people searching for an identity of their own. Eating and drinking were an ideal vehicle for the expression of such a localized identity. It was no coincidence that in the nineteenth century over 5 million Germans emigrated to the USA for economic reasons, but took with them their mothers' recipes, which for a long time continued to mark out their cultural identity. In the course of generations, the German language may have been lost to them, but the old cookery repertoire persisted for an astonishing length of time.

The same phenomenon is to be observed today in Turkish families that have migrated to Germany.

***

In the second half of the twentieth century, eating habits changed, though not so radically as a hundred years before at the height of the Industrial Revolution. The most important technical advance was undoubtedly the introduction of refrigerated and frozen foods into daily life. This innovation in fact had a long prehistory. The use of ice to cool drinks, meat and fruit had been a familiar means of preservation in Europe ever since antiquity, and edible ice as well as ice-cooled fruit juice had been known since the late seventeenth century, but otherwise it played no significant role. Not until the eighteenth century were 'ice houses' built in England's North American colonies, in order to prevent expensive meats from rotting during the long hot summers. Plantation owners were prepared to invest a great deal of money in this system of refrigeration, and so a new 'natural ice' industry sprang up, transporting evenly cut blocks of ice by clipper as far afield as Central

Ice houses and ice cellars existed on country estates in the pre-industrial era to store ice that was used in preserving food. In the late 19th century special ice cars on the railways and on the streets brought ice from frozen lakes to the growing cities, where breweries, slaughterhouses and fish traders, as well as dairies, ice-cream parlours and restaurants used it. There was, however, a growing interest in, and much experimentation with, artificial cooling machines, such as this freezer and ice house from 1875.

Carl von Linde's invention of an economical ice machine in the 1870s ultimately led to the domestic refrigerator, first developed in the United States. The American 'fridge' began to be exported to Europe during the 1920s but it was only after the Second World War, at the time this poster was produced for the American Gibson Refrigerator Company, that sales began to take off.

and South America. Dairies and meat factories in the USA took advantage of this technology to set up 'ice cars' on the railways and in the streets, while in Europe the English herring-fishers profited from it by sending their fresh fish inland or to Billingsgate, the fish market in London. When the modern German deep-sea fishing industry began in 1885 on the North Sea coast, again it was not long before 'ice works' were built in the ports. There were special 'fish-cooling' trains that took the catch from the fish-auctions directly to the city markets. After the First World War, in Berlin alone there were 200 ice dealers with 400 wagons, supplying dairies, slaughterhouses, breweries, restaurants, butcher's shops and even refreshment kiosks with these much sought-after blocks.

On the large German estates, 'ice cellars' and 'ice pits' had been in existence at least as long as they had in the UK and USA, and were used for preserving game among other things. Between 1860 and 1870, private houses in the cities began to become interested in 'portable ice cellars'; this was a time when local products were no longer sufficient and there was greater dependence on food shops, which meant keeping larger stocks at home. There was also greater demand for quality and freshness. The first industrial attempts at making 'ice boxes' and 'cooling cupboards' smelt bad because of the melting ice, were full of mould, and needed constant cleaning, and they failed to replace the old pantry.

The technological breakthrough began with the invention of artificial cooling, which has a long prehistory. The French engineer Edmond Carré succeeded in creating in 1859 an ice machine, after much experimentation. He used condensed ammonia as a coolant, and in 1862 his refrigerator was on display at the Universal Exhibition in London. However, as his 'freezing apparatus' took two hours to produce 1 kg of artificial ice, his invention – like many other attempts to construct similar cooling machines – attracted no interest from private consumers. Carré's improved invention succeeded only with the construction of a special refrigerator ship, which from 1877 began the transport of frozen meat and opened a new trade with Argentina, Australia and New Zealand.

A huge leap forward was taken in the 1870s by a professor of mechanical engineering in Munich, Carl von Linde, whose new compression principle made the ice and cooling machines far more efficient; his first commercial refrigeration system was patented in 1873. By 1896, there were 2,756 of these cooling machines being used in 1,659 businesses worldwide – most of them in breweries, meat factories, ships and dairies, especially in the USA, Germany, England and Austria. It was Linde's success that finally led to the construction of a smaller, more practical refrigerator. Even before 1914, delicatessens, ice-cream parlours, cafés and restaurants had begun to use these artificial coolers, although they were still not to be found in ordinary private households. This development only came about when houses were

In the late 1950s the first big supermarkets opened in Europe. The provision of cool cabinets and frozen food revolutionized both shopping habits and taste, so that people did not have to shop everyday and yet could still eat something of quality.

connected to the electricity supply, and when mass-production techniques taken over from the American automobile industry brought down the originally high cost of manufacture.

It is not surprising that the first modern refrigerators all came from the USA. In 1930, only 0.6 per cent of all German households possessed a refrigerator, which was then regarded as the height of luxury. By 1960 the figure had crept up to 3 per cent, but with the change in production techniques, the figure shot up to 86 per cent in West Germany in 1969. One year later, refrigerators with freezing compartments came on the market. It is no coincidence that at this time consumption of frozen goods in West Germany leapt almost tenfold from 22,100 tonnes to 218,992 tonnes. Simultaneously, supermarkets and their frozen-food sections arrived, together with self-service, ready-cooked meals that could even be delivered to people's homes, and in due course the now ubiquitous microwave. The establishment of this cold chain, which preserves for relatively long periods the taste, quality and freshness of foods that in the past had been easily spoiled, must rank alongside the invention of the tin can as one of the turning points in the history of human nutrition.

Since the middle of the twentieth century, it can be said that the age-old problems of hunger and storage have finally been solved in Europe, and with the relative prosperity of our present-day society, the modernization of gastronomic culture has moved in totally different directions. The food industry is now going to ever greater lengths to cut down the work involved in washing, peeling, skinning, pip-removing, filleting, mixing, spicing and cutting up; the housewife and cook are even relieved of the necessity to buy the ingredients and put the meal together. These new convenience foods are one more form of 'rationalization', built on the many processes and pieces of equipment developed in earlier times.

Nowadays there is an increasing emphasis on foods and meals that aim to fit in as precisely as possible with particular consumers, health-risk groups, or changing circumstances. In the nineteenth century, Henri Nestlé manufactured foods especially designed for infants, and then there were diet foods for sick people; today there are foods made specifically for old people, pregnant women, sportsmen and so forth, as well as fast foods and slow foods. There are more and more Italian, Greek, Turkish and eastern dishes coming on the market. This trend towards functionalism has been on the increase for the last few decades and it is connected with efforts to reduce intake because of obesity and other health-related problems, as well as with the modern quest for the slim figure that represents the current ideal of physical beauty.

The hugely intensified expectation of tastiness and pleasing appearance that typifies our post-industrial gastronomic culture is clearly expressed in packaging design. Around 1900, most shops and market stalls sold their foods loose, as in previous centuries, or, if necessary, in paper bags or baskets. But since the advent of plastics in the early 1960s, almost every item is wrapped in as attractive a package as possible. All kinds of packing materials have not only facilitated the movement of goods from producer to market, as well as the convention of self-service, but have also contributed enormously to maintaining freshness, hygiene, taste and smell. Colourings and taste enhancers developed in laboratories are designed primarily to stimulate the appetite (not to be confused with biological hunger) of the consumer, and hence increase the marketability of the product.

The increased emphasis on organic foods since the 1980s can be seen as a reaction to the ever greater technical and economic rationalization of the industry. Following on from late nineteenth-century reforms in health and lifestyle, the Green movement aims to keep food as free as possible from all artificial, chemical additives, and to promote natural methods of production through an alternative form of agriculture. This new trend in favour of organic foods, which has a great deal in common with the older movement of vegetarianism, is different from other new nutritional concepts in that instead of aiming to extend the range of available foods and flavours, it seeks to free nature from technology and industry, in order to preserve its non-renewable resources. In the context of gastronomic culture, this means no less than reverting to a lifestyle of the past. Under the influence of various revelations concerning the doctoring of food, these new, natural products achieved sales amounting to 2 per cent of the entire German food market in 1999, but despite intensive support from the government, this figure only slightly increased to 2.6 per cent in 2004. Opinion polls on what people regard as the most important thing about their food have elicited the same answer as in the past from the vast majority of Germans: 'It's got to taste good!'

***

Since the late eighteenth century, gastronomic culture has vastly expanded under the influence of technology, and from this development we might briefly draw the following conclusions: the foods that humans eat are first and foremost products drawn from the natural resources available and from basic transformations of those raw materials. At the same time, because of the processing that is generally necessary prior to consumption, foods are subject to rational procedures of technical production and economic distribution. Finally, they are also bearers of a culture that is dependent on materials but is inspired by the mind. A meal as a complete social phenomenon regularly links nature, culture and the human body; external objects and inner, mental perceptions. Taste provides a kind of catalytic bridge and an ever-changing guide for each link in the food chain. Somewhere along the evolutionary way, human beings lost their instincts when it came to the daily satisfaction of hunger and appetite, and since then food has become primarily an expression of each individual culture, needing to be learned anew from birth and passed on from generation to generation.

It is clear that over the last two hundred years, the radical restructuring and modernization of food culture has completely changed all the values involved. Food is no longer assessed according to the degree in which it assuages hunger, or symbolizes social prestige, and not even the price is now a major factor; what count above all are taste and health. Members of our modern consumer society want to know precisely what their food contains, what new tastes they can experience, and what advantages and disadvantages they can expect in relation to their bodies. The growing interest in food is also connected with the fact that apart from the qualities of the product, we are also concerned about the effects food production is having on the environment. The various qualities are therefore linked to a more general context that is quite independent of our own nourishment and our subjective tastes. In this respect, food may be seen as a vehicle for the promotion of extremely controversial economic and social reforms. Once, there were similar, overriding connections between food and magic, myth and religion, but these have long since faded into the background or disappeared altogether, to be replaced by scientific knowledge and a new, secular view of the world.

8 CHEFS, GOURMETS AND GOURMANDS

French Cuisine in the 19th and 20th Centuries

Alain Drouard

Impossible to define taste. Anyone who tries, fails.... So what is taste? What is this strange thing which, as we have just seen, can and does exist beyond morality, reason, courtesy, progress, truth, reality, shame, consciousness, reconciles itself to savagery, consents to bestiality, accepts sodomy and, with all the powers to be evil, forms part of the beautiful?

Victor Hugo, *Proses philosophiques,* 1860–1865

Since the beginning of the nineteenth century, French cuisine has emerged as a system of relationships between three groups who all depend on one another: the cooks – both at home and in the restaurant – the gourmets, and the consumers.

At the start of this period, most of the chefs came from the great houses of the *ancien régime* that fell during the Revolution. Some, like Antoine Beauvilliers (1754–1817), worked in restaurants, and others went into domestic service, such as Antonin Carême (1783–1833), the most famous of all the nineteenth-century chefs. He specialized in pâtisserie, which he considered to be a branch of architecture, and saw himself as a culinary artist, an inventor, a creator. Chef to Talleyrand, he subsequently worked for Tsar Alexander and George IV of England, before ending his brief career with the Rothschilds. He was, above all, a great theorist and classifier, and to him we owe a number of important works, including *Le Pâtissier royal parisien* (1815), *Le Pâtissier pittoresque* (1815), *Le Maître d'hôtel français* (1822), *Le Cuisinier parisien* (1828) and *L'Art de la cuisine française* (1833). Carême was an admirer of the eighteenth century, when the great French cuisine had been born, and he wanted not only to continue this tradition but also to introduce reforms. He got rid of '*jus noirs*', strong spices, and used

Previous page: Born in 1926, Paul Bocuse is the most famous French chef in the world and in the years 1970–80 was leader of the pack in the field of *nouvelle cuisine*. He is seen here in the kitchen of his restaurant near Lyons.

Above: Antonin Carême (1783–1833) began his training with pâtisserie. Inspired by the architecture which he studied in books at the Bibliothèque Nationale, Carême's *pièces montées* and spun-sugar creations in the form of pavilions, rotundas, temples, towers and ruins justified the title of one of his books on pâtisserie, *Le Pâtissier pittoresque*.

the condiments we tend to use today: salt, pepper, thyme, bay leaf, parsley. He revived the concept of fine dishes without meat, which came back into favour when Napoleon restored the period of Lent. In his reformist zeal, he also classified recipes, and rejected some existing combinations of foods:

> What is more ridiculous and absurd than, for example, seeing pike and carp *à la Chambord* served with side dishes composed of calf's sweetbread covered in streaky bacon, then young pigeons and cock's combs and kidneys? It is so easy to change this old custom through the infinite variety available to us through working with fillets of fish such as sole, trout, whiting, salmon, etc., and serving them *en escalopes*, *en attereaux* [on a skewer], *conty*, *aux truffes*, *en quenelles truffées*, or *aux champignons*.

Even though in Carême's eyes cuisine and gastronomy were closely linked, and the chef was 'a gastronome by taste and by profession', culinary literature – the work of the chef – was not to be confused with gastronomic literature. The latter, which came into being after the French Revolution, was 'the work and the province of gourmets and those who write well', by which he meant doctors, lawyers, novelists, poets, journalists and songwriters. Aimed at a bourgeois audience that included many of the *nouveaux riches* who were ignorant of etiquette and table manners, such literature set out to teach these people the necessary codes of gastronomic courtesy and propriety.

The term 'gastronomy' first appeared in 1800, in the title of a poem by Joseph de Berchoux (1775–1838). The noun 'gastronome' dates from 1803, and the adjective 'gastronomic' from 1807. 'Gastronomy' made its entrance into the *Dictionnaire de l'Académie française* in 1835. However, rather than referring to the art of fine food, it was then a means of acquiring and gaining recognition of one's social status.

According to Alexandre-Balthazar-Laurent Grimod de La Reynière (1758–1838), famous as the author of the *Almanach des gourmands* (1803) and a *Manuel des amphitryons* (1808), gastronomy was a means of legitimizing the new social hierarchy that had emerged from the French Revolution. Son of a *fermier général* (tax farmer) and born during the *ancien régime*, Grimod wanted to help the new ruling classes acquire the customs and manners of the old. 'The upheaval that took place in the distribution of wealth – as a necessary consequence of the Revolution – having placed that wealth in new hands, and with the minds of most of today's rich people turning towards purely animal pleasures, we have thought it might do them a service to offer a sure guide to the most solid of their most cherished affections.'

Above: The tasting panel was instituted by Grimod de La Reynière during the First Empire. In the course of their weekly meetings at Grimod's mansion on the Champs-Elysées, the well-informed gastronomes tasted fine foods from various suppliers. The products that were considered the best after due deliberation, benefitted from being publicized in the *Almanach des gourmands*, the ancestor of today's gastronomic guides.

Below: A male and female cook stare at each other across a stove. In the 19th century there was an intense rivalry between men and women in the market for culinary work. The chefs claimed the monopoly of *haute cuisine* and wanted to confine the women to the domestic kitchen.

For Grimod, gastronomy brought together the old ruling class (the aristocracy) and the new (the bourgeoisie), by subjecting both to the same laws: 'The practice of this art (cutting up meat), so indispensable to every *maître de maison* anxious to prove that he was not born yesterday, adds greatly to the pleasure of fine food, to the visual impression and even to the true bounty of a feast. These elements having been lost during the revolutionary turmoil, we have sought to bring them back into focus.' Prefiguring the gastronomic guides of today, Grimod also introduced the concept of the tasting panel, and he published the resulting judgements in his *Almanach des gourmands*.

The other founding father of gastronomy was Grimod's contemporary, Jean-Anthelme Brillat-Savarin. Born at Belley, east of Lyons, on 2 April 1755 into a family of lawyers, he began his career in 1779 as a local magistrate and became a deputy in the States General in 1789. He was elected mayor of Belley and commander of the National Guard, but after the fall of the Girondins in 1794, he went into exile in order to escape from the revolutionary tribunal. He went first to Switzerland, then via the Netherlands and England to the United States. For two years he earned his living playing the violin in the John Street Theater orchestra in New York. In 1796, under the Directory, he was allowed to return to France and resume his career, ultimately becoming a counsellor in the Court of Cassation, a position he held until his death on 2 February 1826. He had caught cold while attending mass on the anniversary of Louis XVI's death, just a few weeks after the anonymous publication, at his own expense, of the work that was to make him famous: *Physiologie du goût, ou méditations de gastronomie transcendante: ouvrage théorique, historique et*

MÉDITATION XX.

De l'influence de la diète sur le repos, le sommeil et les songes.

Un dessert sans
fromage est une belle
à qui il manque un œil.
BRILLAT-SAVARIN.

Above: One book, *Physiologie du goût*, was enough to secure the international reputation of Brillat-Savarin. Divided into meditations like the poetry of Lamartine, the work begins with twenty famous aphorisms reminiscent of the 'Elements of Gourmet Manners' in Grimod de La Reynière's *Manuel des amphitryons*. In the 19th century Balzac celebrated its merits but there was no shortage of detractors: Carême, Monselet and above all Baudelaire, who called it 'a tasteless brioche'.

Opposite: 'Town of the mouth', Lyons owes its reputation as the gourmet capital to the produce of its *terroir* and the riches of the neighbouring areas of the Rhône valley. The work of great chefs as well as women – the famous 'Lyonnaise mothers' – the cuisine of Lyons is a rich one, symbolized by the heavy use of onions.

à l'ordre du jour; dédié aux gastronomes parisiens, par un professeur membre de plusieurs sociétés littéraires et savantes (The Physiology of Taste).

Brillat-Savarin defines gastronomy as a science of synthesis, embracing all the disciplines connected to human nutrition: 'Gastronomy is the analytical knowledge of everything related to man's eating. Its aim is to ensure the preservation of mankind by means of the best possible nutrition. It achieves this aim through firm principles that guide all those who research, provide or prepare those things that can be converted into food. And so it is this that in all truth motivates the farmers, the winegrowers, the fishermen, the hunters and the vast family of cooks, whatever the title or qualification used to describe their work on the preparation of food.'

Brillat-Savarin refers to physiology, a science then very much in fashion. He seeks out the physiological elements of taste in order to improve them:

I myself am not only of the opinion that without the participation of the sense of smell there can be no true sense of taste, but I am also inclined to believe that the senses of smell and taste in fact are a single sense, for which the mouth is the laboratory and the nose the chimney, or to be more precise, for which one serves to taste the tactile bodies and the other to taste the gases….One eats nothing without smelling it with a greater or lesser degree of awareness; and for unknown foods, the nose always fulfils the function of an advance guard who cries: who goes there? When one blocks off the smell, one paralyses the taste….

According to Brillat-Savarin, gastronomy should bring together pleasure and good health, and the enjoyment of food is no longer a sin: 'We have begun to separate gourmandise from gluttony and greed; it has come to be regarded as a penchant that one can enjoy, like the social qualities that are pleasing to the host, profitable to the guests, and useful to science, and gourmets are placed alongside all others who have a particular object of predilection.'

From the beginning of the nineteenth century, the works of both gastronomes and food-loving writers played a major role in defining and promoting 'French' cuisine, whether it was *grande cuisine, cuisine bourgeoise,* or *cuisine de province. Grande* or *haute cuisine* was that of the great Parisian restaurants; it was an 'art' and a 'science', celebrated by all. It was 'gastronomy'. *Cuisine bourgeoise,* also known as *cuisine de ménage* or domestic cooking, was woman's work, done every day at home in the kitchen and lacking the prestige of Parisian *grande cuisine. Cuisine de province* was considered closer to nature, but it referred to that of provincial towns and was not the same as *cuisine paysanne.*

Opinions and judgements were not without some ambivalence: on the one hand, critics considered the 'dishes cooked in the country' to be of inferior quality to the masterpieces of Parisian cuisine, but on the other hand the same writers did not hesitate to praise the simple, fresh and good cooking that was to be tasted in the provinces. Thus Stendhal writes: 'There is only one thing I know that is extremely well done in Lyons: one eats superbly there – in my view, better than in Paris. The vegetables in particular are prepared divinely. In London I learned that they grow twenty-two species of potato; in Lyons I saw twenty-two different ways of preparing them, and at least twelve of these are unknown in Paris.' Balzac tells us that provincial life is so boring that the only pleasure people have there is eating: 'In the provinces, the lack of things to do and the monotony of life encourage the mind to engage on the subject of cuisine.'

In seeking to define 'French' cuisine, gastronomes did not confine themselves to distinguishing between Parisian 'gastronomy' and provincial 'fine food', or to highlighting diversity and richness. They also joined in debates that caused a great stir within the culinary profession concerning what constituted national cuisine and national dishes. At the end of the nineteenth century, there was general agreement that the *pot-au-feu* qualified as the *potage national*.

Shortly afterwards, in 1927, Curnonsky (1872–1956) – the acknowledged prince of gastronomes – drew attention to the vital role of sauces in the definition of French cuisine: 'Sauces are the finery and the honour of French cuisine; they have helped to achieve and ensure its superiority or, as was written in the sixteenth century, its *préexcellence* that is disputed by nobody.' Curnonsky also extolled the combination of dishes and wines as another basic feature of French cuisine: 'Our sublime wines of France are the only ones on the planet that one can drink while eating.' According to him, there was not *one* French cuisine, but at least four:

A stew of meat and vegetables, the *pot-au-feu* has existed since the Middle Ages and for a long time has been considered the national dish of France. The recipes are numerous and varied. In the north of France beef is used, south of the Loire other types of meat are added such as pork, veal, ham and bacon, as well as cabbage. *Poule-au-pot* is a chicken-based version.

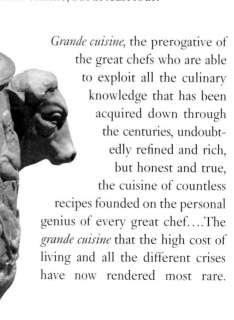

Grande cuisine, the prerogative of the great chefs who are able to exploit all the culinary knowledge that has been acquired down through the centuries, undoubtedly refined and rich, but honest and true, the cuisine of countless recipes founded on the personal genius of every great chef....The *grande cuisine* that the high cost of living and all the different crises have now rendered most rare.

Cuisine bourgeoise, the pride of our ancient families. Meticulous, thorough, and lovingly prepared, the cuisine that is best enjoyed as a paying guest. The cuisine of our fine *cordons bleus*, who know that the preparation of a good meal demands a kind of piety, that time has no respect for anything done without it, that things must 'taste of what they are', and that nothing can replace butter...unless it is good fat and olive oil. *Cuisine régionale*, that incomparable cuisine which incorporates the diversity of our thirty-two provinces and centuries of experience, and which has created five thousand local dishes, the entire repertoire of which you will find in the *Trésor gastronomique de la France*. And finally, *cuisine paysanne*, the cuisine that one might call *impromptue*, improvised in a flash with poultry from the henhouse, fish from the nearby river, rabbit from the hutch, vegetables from the kitchen garden, fruit from the orchard.

Although they needed gastronomes in order to make themselves known, chefs never ceased to question the competence of the critics to judge their work. Carême was the first to cast doubt on those who dared to criticize him or even to discuss his cuisine. On the subject of the *pot-au-feu* he writes:

this is the principal food of the nation's working class: they deserve to have something done to improve their food. The culinary writers of our modern times have assumed the same disdain for the humble *soupe grasse* and have not bothered to analyse it theoretically; but on the other hand, they see no shame in writing that no one in the *grandes cuisines* knows how to make a good bouillon, although they do not suggest any new procedure in order to put that right – if such a thing actually exists. O ignorance! What darkness surrounds you! And yet how proud you are! But your efforts will be in vain; it will be of no avail for charlatanism to seek to impose itself on the public, for among the culinary practitioners are men brave enough to unmask it publicly and to avenge our science by working honourably for the gastronomy of the nineteenth century.

The restaurant boom coincided with the birth of gastronomic discourse and literature. Originally, the word 'restaurant' did not mean an establishment where food was served, but, as discussed in Chapter 9, it referred to the refreshing or 'restorative' soups served by caterers who, from the end of the eighteenth century, were called *restaurateurs*.

Overleaf: Entitled *Preparations for the Pot-au-Feu*, this painting was once attributed to Chardin. The ingredients depicted include leeks, parsnips or carrots, a big green cabbage, a piece of beef, perhaps a shank, and a garlic bulb. The copper cooking pot, with its iron handle implies lengthy cooking over a chimney hearth, suggested here by the dark background of the painting.

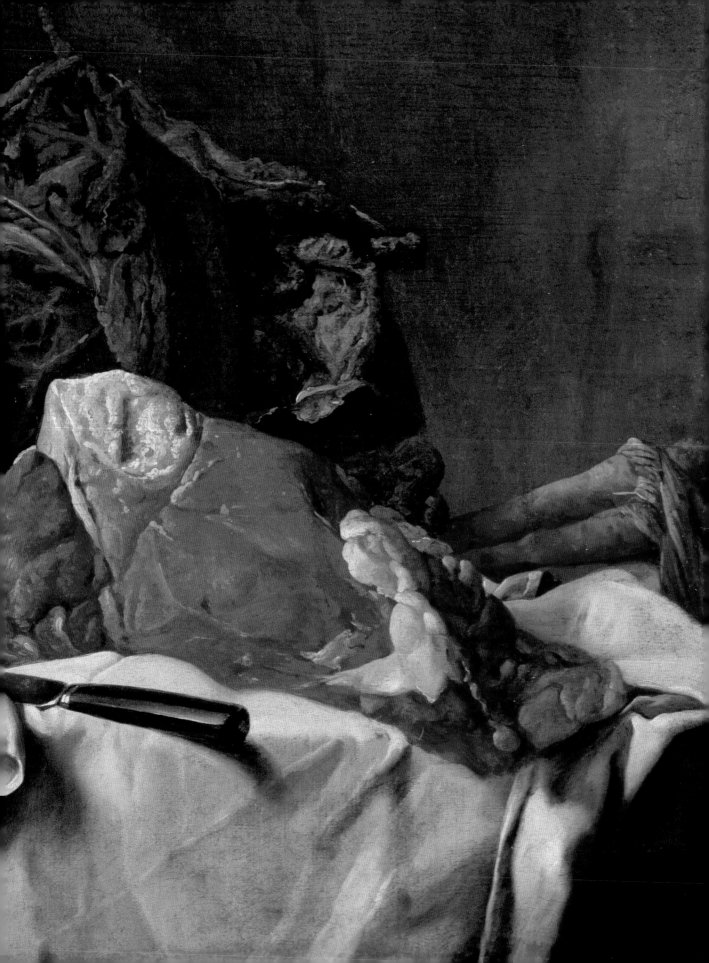

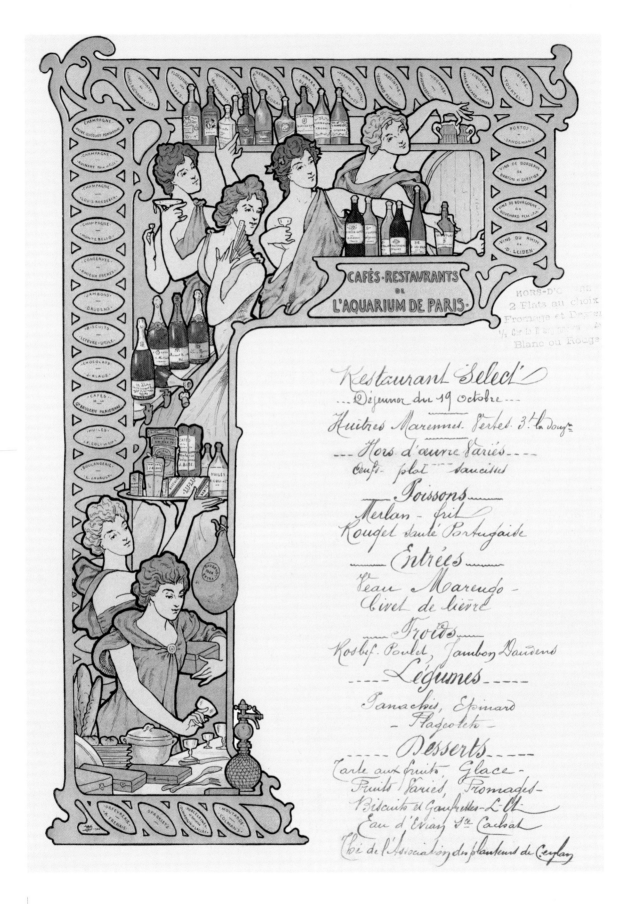

CAFÉS-RESTAURANTS
DE
L'AQUARIUM DE PARIS.

Restaurant "Select"
...Déjeuner du 19 Octobre...
Huîtres Marennes Vertes 3 fr la douz.
--- Hors d'œuvre Variés ---
Œufs plat saucisses
_____ Poissons _____
Merlan Frit
Rouget sauté Portugaise
_____ Entrées _____
Veau Marengo -
Civet de lièvre
_____ Froids _____
Rosbef Poulet, Jambon Daudens
----- Légumes -----
Panachés, Épinard
- Flageolets -
----- Desserts -----
Tarte aux fruits Glace -
Fruits Variés, Fromages -
Biscuits et Gaufrettes L. U.
Eau d'Évian Ste Cachat
Thé de l'Association des planteurs de Ceylan

Restaurants multiplied in Paris in the first few decades of the nineteenth century as a bourgeois clientele took to the idea of sitting at individual tables and consuming a variety of dishes, chosen from a list complete with prices. Prior to the Revolution, there were less than a hundred restaurants in Paris, but by 1804 the number had increased five or sixfold. In 1825 there were nearly a thousand, and in 1834 over 2,000. The word 'restaurant', in the sense of an eating establishment, entered the *Dictionnaire de l'Académie française* in 1835, and the restaurateur was defined by Brillat-Savarin as follows: 'He whose business consists in offering the public a banquet which is always prepared and whose dishes are served in portions at a fixed price on demand from consumers.'

As restaurants multiplied, so they diversified and changed their locations. The earliest – Les Trois Frères Provençaux, Véfour, Véry – were concentrated around the Palais-Royal. During the first half of the nineteenth century, the most famous – La Maison Dorée, Le Café Anglais and Le Café de Paris – were situated on the boulevards, and by the end of the century the main area was the Champs-Elysées. The hierarchy of restaurants echoed the hierarchy of society. At the head were the great *à la carte* restaurants serving *haute cuisine* to a wealthy clientele – these were relatively few in number. Then came the fixed-price restaurants, catering for the 'average' purse. But there were also other kinds of establishment, such as the *bouillons* which entertained the less well-off. Brasseries appeared during the Second Empire, but spread rapidly after the Franco-Prussian War of 1870–71 and the loss of Alsace-Lorraine. Beer and Alsatian dishes were served there. Countless bars, 'wine merchants' and cheese shops offered food and drink to the poorer classes, while the poorest of all went to the so-called *gargotes*, which were cheap eating places serving low-quality food.

Dining out became a common custom, and restaurants were extremely popular. According to Jean-Marc Vanhoutte, 'in Paris during the first half of the nineteenth century, out of a population of 800,000, 60,000 went to a restaurant every day. If one includes the *gargotes* and the taverns, 100,000 Parisians dined there daily.' By 1903, to meet the needs of such a vast clientele, Paris had 1,500 restaurants, 2,900 hotels, 2,000 cafés and brasseries, and finally – a staggering figure – 12,000 wine merchants, three-quarters of whom also served food.

In the nineteenth century, Paris was the gastronomic capital of France, containing the finest restaurants and the best food. It was in Paris that new recipes and dishes first appeared, often boasting misleading names that suggested provincial or regional origins they never had. There was sauce Mornay (a béchamel sauce with added egg and grated cheese) created by Voiron, chicken Père Lathuille (chicken with potatoes, artichokes and onions), the Henri IV casserole which originated at Chez Magny, entrecôte Bercy, sauce Choron (a béarnaise sauce with tomatoes) created by the chef at the restaurant Voisin. Béarnaise sauce itself is said to have originated at the Pavillon Henri IV in Saint-Germain-en-Laye. That is also reputed to be the birthplace of soufflé potatoes, introduced at the inauguration of the Paris to Saint-Germain-en-Laye railway line in 1837. Sole normande came from Le Rocher de Cancale, and sole Marguery from Chez Marguery. Lobster *à l'américaine* made its debut at Noël Peters's restaurant in the passage des Princes, and lobster Thermidor was created by the chef Léopold Mourier at the Café de Paris, when Victorien Sardou staged his play *Thermidor* (1891).

The inventiveness of the chefs fitted well with the appetites of nineteenth-century diners, or at least those who could never stop talking about fine food and who made themselves out to be gastronomes. There were panels of tasters, journals and magazines such as *Le Gourmet*, *Le Gourmand*, *La Salle à manger*, *La Gazette*

This caricature goes beyond the traditional tension between thin and fat people which runs through history to mock the 19th-century gourmands and their consuming passion for the delights of the table.

A painting of 1766 by Michel-Barthélémy Olivier depicts one of the famous suppers with musical accompaniment held by the Prince de Conti, cousin of Louis XV, in his palace at the Temple in Paris. Throughout the 19th century the supper was the most fashionable and social event for the privileged classes.

gastronomique, *L'Almanach de la table*, and 'literary dinners' such as those given by Madame Sabatier and the '*dîners* Magny' – all of which bore witness to this bourgeois passion for fine food, which was mainly indulged in during the evening.

The rhythm of mealtimes changed during the nineteenth century. Dinner tended to be put back to the evening, which affected the other main meals: lunch, which expanded, and supper, which remained the focal point of high-society life. As early as 1808, Grimod de La Reynière noted: 'Since people started dining in Paris at five, six or seven o' clock in the evening, lunch has become a real meal, and in many houses it differs from dinner only through the absence of soup and the compression of three courses into one, albeit somewhat ambiguously, for coffee and liqueurs are generally also served.' Supper, which made its comeback after the Restoration of 1814, was served late, after the theatre. It was eaten either in a restaurant or at home, and it was the time for gourmet food as well as for ceremonial and social events.

***

Comestible.

Truffe noire (Tuber cibarium).

39

Comestible.

Truffe blanche (Choiromyces maeandriformis).

Above: There are many varieties of truffle, a fungus that grows underground. Symbol of rich cuisine, it appeared on opulent tables in the 19th century. Brillat-Savarin called it the diamond of cuisine – a black diamond. Chefs of the grand restaurants use truffles copiously in their dishes, garnishing game, fish and pâté de foie gras with them. They are also used in sauces such as sauce Périgueux, which accompanies filet of beef.

Right: Christened 'the cardinal of the seas' by the critic Jules Janin, and featured by this title on the menus of the great restaurants of the 19th century, the lobster was ideal for decorative grand cuisine. The methods of preparation are numerous: grilled, à la mayonnaise, à l'américaine, Thermidor, Newberg, and so forth.

The century after the French Revolution was, in Charles Morazé's phrase, the period of the 'triumphant *bourgeois*'. This new ruling class used cuisine to demonstrate its power and its role in the governance of the country. If, as Balzac wrote in *La Cousine Bette* (1847), 'the table is the surest thermometer for gauging the income of a Parisian family', then spending money on food was also a way of satisfying the passions. One might say that food was the real delight of the bourgeoisie, even more than sex, although Balzac associated the two in his *Cousin Pons* (1847): 'The luxury of the table is indeed, in this sense, the courtesan's one competitor in Paris, besides representing in a manner the credit side in another account, where she figures as the expenditure.' In *Splendeurs et misères des courtisanes* (1847), he describes the reception given for Esther by the banker Nuncingen in a box at the Théâtre de la Porte Saint-Martin:

> This box, like Chevet's dainties, is a tax levied on the whims of the Parisian Olympus….Nuncingen had provided three services of plate, and the best – plates, dishes and all – was of chased silver gilt….As to the linen, Saxony, England, Flanders and France vied in the perfection of flowered damask….The dishes were so highly spiced as to give the Baron indigestion, on purpose that he might go home early.

Dishes are identified with money, and appetite with lust. In *Le Père Goriot* (1835), Vautrin says: 'Such is life. It is no cleaner than a kitchen; it reeks like a kitchen; and if you mean to cook your dinner, you must expect to soil your hands.' At a supper given by Nana in Zola's eponymous novel of 1880 the restaurateur Brébant – who also catered for people in their homes – began with asparagus purée Comtesse and

Boilly's gourmand is seated – alone – before three dishes symbolic of *haute cuisine* and *grande cuisine bourgeoise* of the 19th century which he is getting ready to eat with rapture: crayfish, roast turkey and vol-au-vent. The painter is caught between admiration and criticism of this solitary pleasure. In this period, Brillat-Savarin wrote that greed 'when it is shared, has more influence on happiness than one could find in a marriage.'

consommé à la Desclignac, followed by rabbit caul with truffles and gnocchi with parmesan; the next two courses were Rhine carp à la Chambord and saddle of venison à l'anglaise; there were three entrées: chicken à la Maréchale, fillet of beef with sauce ravigote, and escalopes of foie gras; next came mandarin-orange sorbet; there were two roasts, one hot and one cold, and two entremets: ceps à l'italienne and croustades of pineapple Pompadour; and finally desserts. The meal was intended for twenty-five but eventually consumed by more than thirty.

Cuisine bourgeoise blossomed in the nineteenth century but it is important to stress that, like the bourgeoisie itself, it was far from uniform. Just as we can distinguish between the upper, middle and lower bourgeoisie, it is possible to identify different *cuisines bourgeoises* as well a *cuisine parisienne* and a *cuisine de province*.

At the top is the *grande cuisine bourgeoise*, to use André Guillot's term, inspired by the *haute cuisine* of the aristocracy and at its best on a par with that. Classified by Carême at the beginning of the nineteenth century, and redefined by Escoffier a century later in his *Guide culinaire* (1903), this luxurious, sumptuous and decorative cuisine used and combined in complex, sophisticated ways the rarest and most expensive produce – truffles, foie gras, fillet of beef, pheasant, woodcock, salmon, lobster – for the delectation of a wealthy and privileged clientele of noblemen, bourgeois businessmen and people of independent means, all eager to become gastronomes.

The work of chefs in bourgeois homes as well as those in the great restaurants and hotels, this cuisine was to be found in the menus of dinners and receptions which followed a fixed order and very strict principles, as described by Gustave Garlin:

Always try to ensure that at a dinner there is no mixing of two butcher's meats, or at least of two white meats. That no garnish resembles an entrée, even if it is in an hors-d'œuvre.

That a somewhat spicy dish should be tempered by one that is less spicy.

That a cold entrée should at least freshen hot entrées (aspic or mayonnaise).

That a fish, if it is represented in a hot hors-d'œuvre, should not have any counterpart, even as a cold roast, with the exception of oysters, which do not exclude having a fish entrée.

It is the same with roasts, entremets, two forms of poultry, two forms of game, two forms of fried food....

If a vegetable is part of a garnish, it must not reappear as an entremets. The same applies to noodles, macaroni and lasagne.

If a sweet such as a bavarois, jelly or fruit salad is on the menu, it should be accompanied by a biscuit, a sponge cake or a small dry cake, even if it is only the traditional wafer.

With hot desserts, there is no need for any accompaniment.

Jules Grun's painting of 1913 captures the end of an evening meal in good society. By this period, dinner was the most important meal of the day and in general lunch was quite frugal. Supper, long the favourite of the aristocracy, tended to exist only among the demi-monde.

Ice cream should have nothing in common with other desserts, except that it can also be presented with wafers and petits fours.

The order of dishes laid down for the menu has remained the same for a very long time: Soup, cold hors-d'œuvre, hot hors-d'œuvre, relevé (remove), entrées, roast, punch, salad, entremets, ice cream, dessert, coffee.

The names of *grande cuisine* dishes sometimes referred to the Court or to the aristocracy – à la Reine, à la Royale, à la Dauphine, Soubise, Condé, Maintenon – and sometimes to regions – à la Lyonnaise, à la Bordelaise, à la Provençale, à la Périgueux, à la Montpellier, so long as the appellation was not too far-fetched.

The best *cuisine bourgeoise* was inseparable from the table, décor and setting so well described by Plumerey, senior member of Talleyrand's household and also chef to the Comte de Pahlen in the first half of the nineteenth century.

The setting follows just one principle that applies from the furnishing of the dining room to the centrepiece: simplicity and harmony between all the main parts. The cloth must be very white; it is the heart of the décor; today it is decorated with graceful designs and covers the table two-thirds of the way down the legs. The dining room is spacious: in winter it must be heated by stoves. The heat is gentle, uniform, regulated by a thermometer hanging in the centre of the room.

The dining room is situated to the north if possible; it is cool in summer; its length is greater than its width. A beautiful dining room is built of marble or stucco, with parquet or mosaic flooring covered in winter by a rich carpet and left bare in the summer; a moquette runner is laid behind the guests in order to conserve the carpet....
A beautiful chandelier hangs down from the ceiling, and *étagères* with mahogany consoles are all round the table....

The table is mahogany, the extensions are oak...its width is measured according to what is to stand in the middle, that is to say the salver, the centrepiece, the candelabra, the dessert, the serving dishes....

All the plates are set straight and evenly spaced; the knife, spoon and fork are on the right; the spoon, placed a little further apart, allows one to see the coat-of-arms and numbers engraved on the fork.

Each guest has four glasses of very fine crystal; this is pure light: one glass for Madeira, one for champagne, one for Bordeaux. Glasses for Rhenish wine are kept on a salver. They are not put on the table to start with….

The order of dishes is very precise:

After dinner has been announced in the salon, all the entrées are placed under cloches; all the servants, wearing white gloves, take up their posts; with napkins draped over their hands, they stand behind the chairs. When everyone is seated, a lacquer screen is put in front of each door, so that it can keep out any draught without impeding the service.

When the maître d'hôtel removes the cloches, which he hands to the servants in attendance, the oysters and cold hors-d'œuvres are taken round and offered. These are followed by the soups and the hot hors-d'œuvre: these are served while the fish are being cut up and garnished with sauces; next come the larger items – the sautéed entrées and the other entrées, and lastly the cold entrées. The second course is laid out in an area adjacent to the dining room; it keeps its heat as it is placed on stoves.

The large items, roasts and entremets are carried to the maître d'hôtel, who puts them on trolleys; one by one he removes the plates from the first course. The second course is served immediately; the roasts are taken to be cut up. During this time, the vegetables are presented to the guests; the roasts are cut piping hot, and the salads are next to arrive; then it is the turn of sweet entremets; before the latter are served, all the salt cellars and hors-d'œuvre are removed; plates are made ready for cheese….

Glasses and dessert plates and carafes of iced water are placed before the guests….The first items to be offered are fresh compotes and pineapple; sweets come next; the rest of the dessert proceeds with four dishes.

The maître d'hôtel immediately presents the guests with two sorts of ice cream; after these, the guests are given palate-cleansers…(three-quarters of a glass of lukewarm water with two or three drops of mint in each glass). Coffee and liqueurs are taken in the salon; they are offered by the maître d'hôtel accompanied by a servant….

The order of the dishes goes together with the order of the drinks:

The wines offered at a dinner like the one I have just described must be of top vintage, fine and delicate. This is the order: after the soup, dry Madeira or sherry; with the first entrées, Sauternes or champagne frappé; then Bordeaux, Château Margaux or Château Laffitte; during the roast, Rhenish and champagne…. Dessert wines must be of exquisite quality; the most

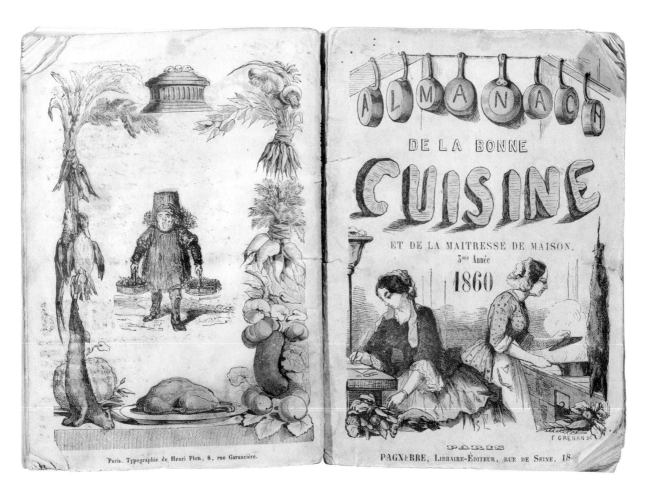

Paris. Typographie de Henri Plon, 8, rue Garancière.

PAGNERRE, LIBRAIRE-ÉDITEUR, RUE DE SEINE, 18.

In the 19th century, household cooking and *cuisine bourgeoise* were not in conflict. Although the recipes were often identical, the housewife prepared the meal alone, whereas the middle-class lady of the house and the 'grande dame' had at their service a cook or cordon-bleu chef. Cookery books, such as the *Almanach de la bonne cuisine et de la maîtresse de maison* of 1860, contributed to women's culinary education at this time.

highly esteemed are Malaga, Malvoisie, Constance and Ténériffe.

Haute cuisine was the province of men while this *cuisine bourgeoise* was for women, consisting of dishes that were cooked slowly over a long period, and left to simmer. It was the work of female chefs who could create 'masterpieces' without ever having learned the culinary arts. In *Within a Budding Grove* (1919), Marcel Proust describes the famous recipe for *boeuf carottes* devised by Françoise:

> The cold spiced beef with carrots made its appearance, couched by the Michelangelo of our kitchen upon enormous crystals of aspic, like transparent blocks of quartz.
>
> 'You have a first-rate cook, Madame,' said M. de Norpois, 'and that is no small matter. I myself, who have had, when abroad, to maintain a certain style in housekeeping, I know how difficult it often is to find a perfect chef. This is a positive banquet that you have set before us!'
>
> And indeed Françoise, in the excitement of her ambition to make a success, for so distinguished a guest, of a

dinner the preparation of which had been sown with difficulties worthy of her powers, had put herself out as she no longer did when we were alone, and had recaptured her incomparable Combray manner.

'That is a thing you don't get in a chophouse, not even in the best of them: a spiced beef in which the aspic doesn't taste of glue and the beef has caught the flavour of the carrots. It's admirable! Allow me to come again,' he went on, making a sign to show that he wanted more of the aspic. 'I should be interested to see how your chef managed a dish of quite a different kind; I should like, for instance, to see him tackle a *boeuf Stroganoff*.'

Curnonsky was always full of praise for women who cooked by instinct, without ever having learned to do so. The widow Marie Chevalier Coutance was the Curnonsky family chef for forty-one years: 'I remember her as a large French countrywoman and one of the most perfect *cordons bleus* that I have ever known. She had not learned to cook either in schools or through books. She knew it from birth and ancestrally, and she did it like her mother, her grandmother, her great-grandmother and her great-great-grandmother, like twenty generations of good housekeepers. She brought to the task the qualities of her origins and her people: restraint, taste, integrity, patience and simplicity.' This feminine cuisine was 'simple, straightforward, clear in taste and never aimed at effect....A tranquil and well-prepared cuisine, a cuisine of *cordon bleu*.'

One rung lower in the culinary hierarchy were *cuisine bourgeoise et ménagère* and *cuisine ménagère*, which catered for the lower middle and working classes. Taught in the context of home economics, *cuisine ménagère* was basically the same as *cuisine bourgeoise*, and the recipes were often identical, but they had different contexts: the housewife would prepare the meals on her own, whereas the *bourgeoise* or the *grande dame* would have cooks and *cordons bleus* to help her.

The 'triumphant' bourgeois, the gourmands and the gastronomes constituted only a small minority of the French population. In the cities, particularly Paris, hunger was endemic for a long time, although the poorer classes no longer starved. Several surveys of the eating habits of the working class in the second half of the nineteenth century and the early twentieth century showed that the total expenditure on food by the workers in Paris represented roughly half of their income. A quarter went on solid food, and a quarter on drink. The staple food was always bread, which was accompanied by soup. Town-dwellers ate more meat than country-dwellers, but meat – and especially beef – was expensive. After 1870, horsemeat often replaced beef on working-class tables. For most people, bread was sacred, soup was essential, potatoes were the vegetable saviours, wine was a much sought-after drink, pork was a gastronomic treasure, butcher's meat an almost unobtainable luxury, and cake the only real dessert.

Bread was always the first item on the table and on the list of culinary expenses. Around 1850, according to Claude Thouvenot:

> A well-off farmer spent twice as much on his bread as on his meat, about a quarter of his annual budget…he took the raw materials from his fields, and made it on his farm. He had the oven, as much wood as he liked, free labour, and time was of no consequence….Bread was eaten at all meals and in all forms, plain with a glass of brandy, first thing in the morning, by threshers, wine-growers and farmers; with homemade cheese or smoked bacon, for a snack in winter and in summer. Workers rubbed garlic on it or spread it with salt. Women cut it into thin slices to put in all their soups. Children with toothache chomped on wet crusts. Toothless old men were fed on bread soup, often thickened with potatoes. On coming home from school, children ate it with fromage frais, and later, moistened, with caster sugar.

The bread eaten in the country was generally brown, almost black – rye, or mixed wheat and rye, baked in the family oven. The white bread made by town bakers did not come into vogue until the end of the nineteenth century. Along with bread there was the ubiquitous soup. Every province had its own favourite: in Lorraine it was bacon soup and *potée* (boiled meat and cabbage); in Béarn, *garbure* (cabbage and confit of goose); in Flanders, turnip soup; in Limousin, chestnut soup.

The monotony of the daily diet was only rarely broken – at weddings or village festivals. Meats, patisseries, good wine and sometimes champagne, coffee and the local liquor would figure on the menu at celebrations and family gatherings. The meats would come from rabbits, cocks, pigs and calves slaughtered the previous week. Beef was the highlight, to be savoured. Wine, from the family cellar or often purchased in vats of 250 litres, washed down the feast, and the tarts and gateaux baked in the family oven sweetened it.

In the nineteenth and early twentieth centuries the expression *cuisine française* covered a whole range of cooking styles, both in terms of the social categories catered for and the many regional variations, such as Alsace, Lorraine, Brittany, Normandy and Provence, but it was also used to designate the cuisine exported abroad by French chefs, from Carême in the early nineteenth century to Escoffier at the beginning of the twentieth. Known as 'the chef of kings and the king

Auguste Escoffier (seated on the left) at a Parisian café in 1921 shortly after his retirement at the age of 74 at the end of one of the longest and most glorious careers in the history of cuisine. Ambassador of French cuisine, he had been made a chevalier of the Légion d'honneur by President Poincaré in 1919.

of chefs', Auguste Escoffier (1846–1935) worked with the great hotelier César Ritz, and ran the catering at the Savoy and the Carlton in London. He organized the great teams that worked in the kitchens and, at the end of his life, he boasted that he had placed 2,000 chefs around the world. In 1912, he launched the Ligue des Gourmands and the menus he devised, the *Dîners d'Epicure*, were served to hundreds of guests in several European cities.

At the end of the First World War, French cuisine found itself in trouble. *Haute cuisine* had practically disappeared. Many chefs had been killed or wounded, and there was a shortage of staff and apprentices. Families were employing fewer and fewer domestic servants and housework became more onerous. With the development of home economics, in which the first courses were held in 1923, new inventions began to enter the kitchen. One of the most important, the refrigerator, made its appearance in the homes of well-off families, and it became commonplace after the Second World War.

There were so many changes that some critics took up the old refrain, speaking of the 'decline' of French cuisine. The chefs mobilized their forces to defend themselves and to attack the gastronomes, whom they called *culinographes*. An article in *La Revue culinaire* of April 1923 proclaimed: 'The *culinographes* are the wasps that buzz round chefs.

In their new writings, the subject has not changed: "French cuisine is dying! French cuisine is no more!" An absurd theme, and how wrong they are!'

In fact, the menus became simpler and garnishes became dishes, as *La Revue culinaire* remarked in 1925:

> Seasonings and preparations have become simpler, which is an advance; nowadays there is no attempt to disguise the flavour of a dish by means of condiments which now seem to us to be heterogeneous; on the contrary, one seeks to respect the true flavour, to accentuate it, to augment it by ingredients chosen with discernment. Just as they have abandoned complicated preparations, the chefs of today have rejected sumptuous, pompous, pretentious presentation….The cuisine of today seeks to be simple, which does not exclude elegance or good taste – in all senses of the term.

Although the disappearance of *socles* (decorative plinths, often carved from lard), already underway before the war, accelerated the end of decorative cuisine, the 'modern' style proposed by Escoffier during the 1920s was nonetheless a rich form of *cuisine bourgeoise.*

This cuisine was as successful in Paris as it was in the provinces, thanks to gastronomic tourism. It was in fact a period in which regional cuisine was celebrated as an integral part of the gastronomic heritage of France. In 1927, Pampille alias Marthe Daudet published *Les Bons Plats de France, cuisine régionale.* Earlier, Curnonsky had launched a fashion for gourmet tours, which he called *gastronomades,* and which facilitated the discovery of good restaurants in the provinces.

After the Club des Cent, founded in 1912, several gastronomic societies, associations and clubs were formed between the wars, in response to a threat which Curnonsky described as follows: 'At the beginning of this century, the eminent and age-old superiority of French cuisine was threatened by two scourges: the snobbery of anonymous, cosmopolitan cuisine which permeated all the luxury hotels and caravanserais in the universe, and the outdated taste of that complicated, over-elaborate cuisine that likes to disguise flavours and aromas and present under bizarre and pretentious names dishes in which chemistry mingles with conjuring.'

After the Club des Purs Cent and the Académie des Psychologues du Goût, founded in 1922, other societies were formed, including the Association des Gastronomes Régionalistes (1923), the Académie des Gastronomes (1928, founded by Curnonsky to defend 'the traditions of French cuisine'), the Cercle des

Gourmettes (1929), and the Association des Gastronomes Amateurs de Poisson (1937).

Chefs such as Alexandre Dumaine, Fernand Point and André Pic represented and expressed the success of this *cuisine bourgoise*. At the Hotel de la Côte d'Or in Saulieu, Burgundy, Dumaine (1895–1974) – who was awarded his third Michelin star in 1935 – created an Escoffier-inspired *grande cuisine d'hôtel*, as exemplified by the following menu:

> *Hors d'œuvres variés, beurre*
> *Truites de la Cure à la façon des meuniers*
> *Feuilletté de queues d'écrevisses*
> *Petits pois à la française*
> *Poularde de Bresse rôtie*
> *Pâté de gibier en croûte*
> *Salade de saison*
> *Fromages*
> *Entremets*
> *Corbeille de fruits*

At La Pyramide in Vienne, south of Lyons, another starred chef, Fernand Point (1897–1955), served a *grande cuisine de maison bourgeoise: brioche de foie gras, filet de sole napolitaine, poularde de Bresse à la crème, glaces, friandises.* André Pic (1893–1984) – also starred by Michelin when he was at the Auberge du Pin in Saint-Peray – offered his clients in Valence, where he moved, *chausson aux truffes, ballottine de pigeons farcis et truffés, terrine de bécasse, poularde à l'ancienne*, and his famous *gratin de queues d'écrevisses.*

André Guillot, another great *bourgeois* chef, said that the same cuisine was served to families:

> Normal menus at lunchtime consisted of a *farinade* [dish made of flour and eggs] or a fish, a dish of meats garnished with several garnishes, a vegetable, an entremets.
>
> In the evening, two soups, a *farinade* or fish, a dish of meat or poultry, generally fairly light, a mixed salad and an entremets. Main meals rarely departed from this number of dishes. At grand dinners, there were two soups, a fish course, an entrée with garnishes, a vegetable, a mixed salad, an entremets and Chester cakes [a type of cheese savoury].
>
> Although most houses had adopted the simpler form of menu, there were some where the ancient rules were still upheld in a modified fashion: two soups, a remove, two entrées, a roast, two vegetable entremets and a dessert entremets. This was the menu at the home of

Comte Boni de Castellane, Baron Rothschild and various other houses.

After the rationing and shortages of the Second World War, the French went back to this *cuisine bourgeoise* for a time, but at the end of the sixties, by which time the consumer society was in full swing, it had both reached its peak and begun its decline in the turmoil of 1968. It was in this context that *nouvelle cuisine* came on the scene.

The expression *nouvelle cuisine* first made its appearance in an article by Henri Gault entitled 'Vive la Nouvelle Cuisine française', published in 1973 in the monthly magazine *Gault et Millau.* Its advocates, the journalists Henri Gault and Christian Millau, presented it as a 'reaction against the appalling dogmatism that was prevalent', repeating at every opportunity that they were not its inventors: 'We have suggested the formula, and it has caught on like a superb mayonnaise, but that's all. The rest – that is to say, the most important thing – is the business of the chefs themselves. We are and we remain observers.' So what was it that they observed?

Haute cuisine was in a rut, bogged down in its dogma and its recipes. 'Alas,' wrote Robert Courtine (1910–98), alias La Reynière, who was in charge of the food section of *Le Monde*, 'there are hardly any new dishes to be found in the honours lists of the chefs, and it is more likely to be in families that housewives, allowing free rein to their imagination, "invent" new and original dishes.' The cuisine and the reputation of the great restaurants rested on a limited repertoire of recipes, such as *gratin de queues d'écrevisses, tournedos Rossini, sole Dugleré.* In Paris, people went to La Mère Michel to eat *poisson au beurre blanc*, to La Tour d'Argent for *canard au sang*, Chez Lasserre for *cassolette de filets de sole.*

In the 1960s, the cuisine of many restaurants had barely changed since the end of the Second World War. Hygiene and refrigeration were far from prevalent, and nobody bothered much about the freshness of products, as sauces were used to mask the taste of the food. 'Ready made' was also common practice – the basic sauces were prepared in advance, and some dishes were pre-cooked, so that they could be served as soon as the customer ordered them.

The inspiration for *nouvelle cuisine* came to the two journalists during a meal cooked by Paul Bocuse (b. 1926), before he was awarded his third Michelin star in 1965: 'He wanted to feast our eyes and feast our stomachs: crayfish soup, bass *en croûte*, etc. It was perfect, but we had not been given any sort of shock.' Nonetheless, the two friends decided to return that evening to the Auberge de Collonges au Mont d'Or, Bocuse's restaurant near Lyons: 'Paul Bocuse served us a simple salad of French beans with tomatoes.

Magnificent, the scent of the garden, an unforgettable flavour. Next he brought us red mullet, lightly cooked. Once again we were overwhelmed with forgotten scents. We had just discovered *nouvelle cuisine*. It already existed, we had encountered it, but we didn't yet know that we had.'

After Bocuse, they went in search of other chefs who were offering *nouvelle cuisine* without knowing it. At Roanne, north-west of Lyons, the brothers Jean and Pierre Troisgros served them frogs' legs *aux herbes*. 'They rolled them in flour, but with incomparable lightness, and the fresh herbs were applied at the very last moment.' Christian Millau spent a week in the kitchens of the Troisgros brothers, and saw that there was nothing ready made, everything was prepared on the spot. This was 'cooking without a net'. Shortly afterwards, he went to see Michel Guérard in Asnières, then Alain Chapel, Alain Senderens, Jean Delaveyne, Roger Vergé, Denis, Paul Manière – and noticed that: 'The *nouveaux cuisiniers* had in common the banishment of tired culinary practices, such as the same old bases, sauces mixed with flour, dishes prepared in advance before becoming the walking wounded of the reheating process, false appearances, destroyers of taste, and a hundred other routine ways of murdering good produce under the pretext that our fathers did the same, and our grandfathers too.'

'Lightness' was to be celebrated as one of the key features of this new cuisine. In 1976, Michel Guérard published *La Grande Cuisine minceur*, and then it was André Guillot's turn, with *La Vraie Cuisine*

Maxim's, the most fashionable restaurant of the Belle Epoque,
took its name from the head waiter. The 1900 décor is the work
of the architect Louis Marnez and the sequence of rooms is
decorated with paintings of nude women. The mahogany
panelling is adorned with vegetable motifs in copper.
A stained-glass roof plays with the colours and the light.

légère, published in 1981. André Guillot was one of the pioneers of this lighter form of *grande cuisine*:

> In fact, following the thoughts and ethos of my old mentor M. Fernand Juteau, I think I performed the work of an innovator by *abolishing* as from 1947:
> a. roux sauces
> b. the abomination that is *sauce à l'espagnole*
> c. vol-au-vents and *bouchées à la reine*, a ritual for a century which I have replaced with *feuilletés* (true puff pastry can only be light. The expression 'light puff pastry' used by some people is therefore a tautology)
> d. overloaded menus. My formula was: a single dish (but large), preceded by something small, pleasant and original, with a light dessert afterwards. I also advised having a single wine in harmony with the main course.

Alex Humbert at Maxim's was one of the chefs who had anticipated this movement with his saddle of lamb *Callas* and the baby vegetables that came in with *nouvelle cuisine*. Stuffed with a julienne of truffles and mushrooms, the lamb was simply roasted; the sauce was the *jus* obtained from deglazing the stock, together with a little bit of veal stock and sherry; the garnish consisted of asparagus spears and potatoes *parisiennes*.

Raymond Oliver, who came from a family of restaurateurs in Langon, near Bordeaux, was one of the exponents of *cuisine de marché*. Proprietor of the Grand Véfour in Paris, he introduced personal dishes into his menu – egg Louis Oliver, pigeon Rainier III. He was France's first TV chef, thanks to a programme called 'Art et Magie de la cuisine', which he hosted with Catherine Langeais from 1953 onwards, and he was one of the first French chefs to abandon his stove and take himself abroad, notably to Japan, whose culinary aesthetics also found their way into *nouvelle cuisine*.

A state of mind? A movement? A trend? A shift of attitude? It is only possible to understand *nouvelle cuisine* by looking at the dependent and interdependent relations that developed in this period between three separate groups: the chefs and cooks, as they rose up the social ladder, the new media and a new clientele. The emancipation of chefs from their status as employees and servants had begun before the Second World War, when several famous chefs established themselves, at their own expense, in Paris and the provinces: the Bises in Talloires, André Pic in Valence, Alexandre Dumaine in Saulieu, Fernand Point in Vienne. But even at the end of the Second World War, the majority of restaurants were not owned by the chefs. Things began to change in the 1950s, and the trend accelerated during the sixties and seventies. The chefs who were now proprietors put their own names on the façade: the Auberge de Collonges au Mont d'Or became Chez Paul Bocuse.

They also freed themselves from the supervision of the maître d'hôtel, and introduced plate service, which reduced the role of the staff to that of 'plate-bearers, whose actions are limited to a beautifully coordinated lifting of the silver cloches that cover the dishes'. Paul Bocuse succinctly described his role in the social rise of the chef: 'I took the chef out of the kitchen.' There was a seductive charm in this formula. The *bande à Bocuse*, which in 1970 became the Association de la Grande Cuisine Française, brought together – around Bocuse himself – all the main exponents of *nouvelle cuisine*: Pierre and Jean Troisgros, Michel Guérard, the Haeberlin brothers, Charles Barrier, Louis Outhier, Pierre Laporte, René Lasserre, Roger Vergé and Raymond Oliver.

The *Gault Millau* guide and monthly magazine sought to take the place of France's leading food guide – *Michelin* – and to make its own contribution to the renewal of French cuisine. The two journalists toured the country in search of restaurants worthy of attention. Their criteria had nothing to do with the location, the décor or the quality of the crockery, but were based solely on the taste, presentation and imagination of the chef. They graded the restaurants by their own standards and took no notice of what other guidebooks had to say. Their independence of mind encouraged many others to take the plunge and to try out these controversial new places. As a result, *nouvelle cuisine* spread throughout France.

The 'new' cooks and chefs, as well as the new media, were now targeting a new clientele, a social group that was expanding in a more industrialized, more prosperous France: middle and senior management. This section of consumer society had different values and found slimness, lightness, healthiness, pleasure and originality appealing.

What were the basic features of *nouvelle cuisine*? In their inaugural article of 1973, Henri Gault and Christian Millau set out the 'ten commandments':

1. Reduced cooking times for fish, seafood, game, veal, green vegetables.
2. New use of produce. Cookery should use market fresh, high-quality ingredients.
3. Reduce the number of items on the menu. A shorter menu means: 'less expenditure on stock, a more inventive cuisine, greater freshness, less routine, everything prepared to order. And a felicitous end to the custom of leaving sauces stewing in a double boiler – that glory of the pre-war era.'
4. *Nouvelle cuisine* chefs are not 'systematically modernist'.

5. *Nouvelle cuisine* chefs have no objection to new cooking techniques or new materials: 'Their ovens are new and clean and have easily controllable temperatures. They work in a less stifling atmosphere, without unbearable odours, in a space that is bright and roomy; they use mixers, ice-cream makers, automatic rotisseries, potato peelers, waste-disposal units. They take extra care with frozen foods....Lastly, they experiment with methods of cooking and warming that would bring a shudder to the old-school chef, who would do well to go and taste Paul Bocuse's red mullet microwaved in its own juices.'

6. *Nouvelle cuisine* is opposed to the hanging of game and, consequently, the 'spices that conceal the disgusting fermentation have disappeared from its repertoire.'

7. *Nouvelle cuisine* seeks to do away with rich sauces, 'heavy' sauces, those 'terrible brown and white sauces, the *financière, grand veneur, béchamel* and *mornay* which have murdered so many livers and concealed so much tasteless flesh.' It follows that 'jellied meat, veal stock, red wine, Madeira, blood, roux, gelatine, flour, cheese, starch are not on the authorized list. But of course chefs do continue to use *sauce fumet*, cream, butter, pure juices, eggs, truffles, lemon, fresh herbs and peppercorns, and they give pride of place to light sauces, sauces which blend together and are uplifting, leaving the mind clear and the stomach light.'

8. *Nouvelle cuisine* does not ignore nutrition. It favours methods of cooking such as steaming, poaching, grilling and roasting.

9. *Nouvelle cuisine* is concerned with aesthetics – the design of the plate and the appearance of the dish – but within limits (though these may not be respected).

10. Finally, *nouvelle cuisine* seeks to be 'inventive' and creative. This creativity manifests itself firstly in the accompaniments to the main dish, which need not always be the same: 'They do not consider it to be sacrilege if mutton is not paired with beans, lobster with rice, sole with steamed potatoes, veal with spinach, steak with chips; nor must fish always be accompanied by white wine, or foie gras by truffles.' But chefs can and should look further afield, for this is a key principle of *nouvelle cuisine*. 'Anything goes', for better or for worse. Not so far away from the spirit of 1968, with its slogan 'It is forbidden to forbid.'

Nouvelle cuisine associated and combined ingredients in ways that had never before been attempted. Michel Guérard proposed a seafood *pot-au-feu* – first cousin to that of the meat of the land. Alain Chapel included in his menu a '*pot-au-feu* of woodpigeon with star anise and herb ravioli'. Jacques Manière offered steamed cuisine in his restaurant Le Pactole in Paris. The chefs of the *bande à Bocuse* did not take long to achieve recognition in France; in 1965, Paul Bocuse was awarded his third Michelin star, to be followed in 1967 by the Haeberlin brothers at L'Auberge de l'Ill in Alsace, and in 1968 by the Troisgros brothers in Roanne and Charles Barrier in Tours. In the early 1970s, the same accolade was earnt by other chefs in the *bande*. This new breed of French chefs not only went out of the kitchen, they also went out of the country, exporting *nouvelle cuisine* to all parts of the world. Paul Bocuse was one of the first to go to Japan and the United States, and was soon followed by other members of the *bande*.

The corollary of all this success, however, was that imitators, attracted by the lure of fat profits and a rapid rise to glory, reproduced feeble copies of the recipes of the pioneers, claiming to be creative artists themselves. The opponents of *nouvelle cuisine* were quick to lambast these derivative dishes. Jean Ferniot railed against '*les coquilles Saint-Jacques à l'orange...*; vanilla sweetbread; potted herring with chicken livers; pigeon with honey; a terrine of chanterelles accompanied by pumpkin sauce; lamb with fromage frais and ginger; foie gras and melon; sweetbread and oysters; *ragoût* with *coquilles Saint-Jacques* and pigs' trotters...'.

Courtine, alias La Reynière, writing in *Le Monde* in 1986 was scathing about what he called 'L'Assiette aux leurres' (the Plate of Illusions): 'Others rely excessively on this device, initially amusing and baptised *nouvelle cuisine* in order to reduce the portions and to serve a carrot (in strips, it is true, not to mention in leaves or in whistles – *sic* !) at the price of caviar. Light cooking, they murmur....Alas! The lighter it is, the heavier the bill!'

In fact praise and criticism both went to excess. But without really being a *new* cuisine, *nouvelle cuisine* did exercise a profound influence on several generations of chefs and consumers. The emphasis on the quality and freshness of the ingredients contributed to defining the basics of a new form of gastronomy, and its promotion of a 'cross-fertilization' of tastes and flavours paved the way for the world cuisine and fusion cuisine of today.

Through the centuries, French cuisine appeared to be something varied but national, which proclaimed its pre-eminence loud and clear over the cuisines of other countries. After the early nineteenth century, this diversity diminished, and the beginning of the twentieth century saw the demise of *haute cuisine* as defined by Carême, and – more recently – of *cuisine paysanne*. Even if this 'country' cuisine has now been restored to favour everywhere, those who were its pillars – the countryfolk themselves – have virtually disappeared. *Cuisine bourgeoise* stood the test of time rather more successfully: after absolute dominance in the nineteenth century, it only began to crumble during the last third of the twentieth century, when it was supplanted by *nouvelle cuisine*, which was pre-eminent for about twenty years before it, in its turn, faded.

Globalization together with the industrialization of food production and the evolution of cooking and preservation techniques (microwaves, vacuum-packing, induction, deep-freeze) have changed the nature of the art, both for chefs and for consumers. Raw or fresh produce is no longer prepared on the premises except in truly gastronomic restaurants, where some chefs even go so far as to grow fruit and vegetables in their own gardens. The agriculture and food industries have penetrated most kitchens, public and private, and food is now frozen, vacuum-packed, precooked, wrapped, sliced and portioned out.

There are other changes that have also affected how and what we eat. In private homes, preparation time has continued to shrink over the last few years, the average meal now taking about thirty minutes. At the same time, mothers no longer pass their knowledge on to their daughters as they used to in the old days. With ready meals and take-aways now standard fare during the week, cooking is no longer a daily

Nouvelle cuisine stressed the importance of presentation and the aesthetic of the plate while playing with colours and the shape of vegetables. Sometimes to the detriment of the portions...

domestic activity but more of a leisure pursuit reserved for the weekend or holidays. And this is how it is now taught: more and more adults are attending cooking lessons and culinary circles.

If we are to believe Alain Ducasse, the most starred French chef, the current direction of French cuisine is to be found in the luxury industry. Following the example of *haute couture*, which cannot exist without its off-the-peg derivatives, modern gastronomy can only survive by developing a strategy that embraces originality, creativity, and various by-products. His creations are labelled – there is an Alain Ducasse trademark. As for the by-products resulting from the 'calculated diversification of activities', they range from publishing books and training through to setting up new establishments.

Nowadays, most award-winning French chefs are simultaneously 'creators' in their starred restaurants and consultants, not to mention those who are employed by the food industry itself. When they devise and give their names to vacuum-packed or frozen dishes for general distribution, are they – as they claim – really contributing to the 'democratization' of *grande cuisine*?

One thing is certain. While *grande cuisine* is inaccessible to the vast majority of the population, there has never been a wider gap between the words that describe French gastronomic excellence and the culinary practices of the French people themselves, most of whom consume daily the products provided for them by the food industry.

9 DINING OUT

The Development of the Restaurant

Elliott Shore

People in the Western world have eaten away from home for centuries, but the restaurant as opposed to the inn, foodstand or other modest convenience or necessity, has existed for merely 250 years. The restaurant began, and remained for about its first century of existence, as an exclusive place for the wealthy, which served – in London, Paris, New York, Berlin – an international more-or-less French cuisine with little variation. Even as the restaurant started to become more accessible to a varied clientele, the uniformity of the offerings remained fairly constant for another century. It is only in the last fifty of those 250 years that we can start to speak of the move towards the phantas-magoric array of food, of atmosphere and of styles of service that have made the restaurant such a successful and ubiquitous feature of the culture of taste.

Naturally, long before the modern restaurant was born in the mid-eighteenth century, there were many occasions to dine, or at least to eat, while travelling or during the urban workday. Travellers had to eat some place, after all, and in medieval and early modern Europe pilgrims, students, emissaries and soldiers thronged the roads and had some expectation of being fed. The first restaurants were in China. Marco Polo describes the multi-faceted restaurant culture of Hangzhou in 1280 – one that was already about two centuries old – which had familiar elements of contemporary restaurants: waiters, menus, banquet facilities, along with some aspects of a sexual market and meeting place that would make at least a brief appearance in the restaurant culture of the West.

A restaurant is a destination in itself as a place to eat, rather than (as with an inn) a place of local gathering or traveller's refuge that also offers food. Within the restricted opening hours of the establishment, a restaurant offers a variety of dishes, more so than is the case with an inn. Thus most restaurants do not open for breakfast and those that do, outside of hotels or modern-day inns, specialize to some extent in this meal, but the meals they do serve have more options than traditional inns could provide. At a restaurant one eats what one desires from an often extensive menu. During most of its history, the restaurant has offered meals served by a waiter whose job is limited to this (so he is not doubling as an innkeeper, ostler or bartender). Rather than gathering

A motley gathering at a table d'hôte. This engraving after a painting by A. Perez, from the *Illustrated London News*, may romanticize the meal somewhat, but the diner in the centre does seem to be tucking it away better than his companions. This kind of meal, served at a set time for a set fee, both preceded and persisted after the invention of the restaurant.

Previous page: Ever on the lookout for customers, this waiter scans St Mark's Square in Venice from the Caffè Florian, a scene that would not have been much different when the café first opened in 1720. Unlike a true restaurant, this kind of establishment was limited in its offerings, but it did provide a respite and a place for its clientele to socialize.

with the other lodgers at an inn or guesthouse, the clientele of a restaurant come with their friends, sit apart from others, and pay for a specific meal when they are finished.

Certain facets of restaurant dining now seem so natural or automatic that it is worth noting that they are based on culturally and historically specific rules and expectations. Once having chosen not to dine at home, one might plan ahead and decide to go at a particular time to a certain restaurant, but the decision to go out could as easily be made on the spur of the moment. Even with a reservation, unless the restaurant has certain specialties (Joe's Stone Crabs in Miami Beach or a Brazilian *churassceria*), usually a decision about exactly what to eat has not been made in advance. Even going to a restaurant renowned for a certain food, one's partner might want to eat something else (hence steakhouses offer fish of a sort, and sometimes vegetarian options). Even if arriving a few minutes late, the diners still expect the food to be ready for preparation (or reheating) when ordered, and cooked, or at least plated, once the guests are seated. A plate with the food ordered is set before each diner, or served from a plate set on the table. The party has a general idea of what this will all cost, depending on the category of the restaurant, the nature of the ingredients, whether or not wine or spirits accompanied the meal, and how many courses were consumed. When it comes time to settle up, a bill arrives listing the dishes ordered, with prices that agree (one expects) with those stated on the menu.

Although these expectations might not explicitly occur to someone routinely dining in a restaurant, they are established characteristics that have defined the institution since it sprung to life fully formed in the 1760s in Paris. No such institution was available in the West before then. Away from home or the court, one might have an array of dining choices, but none would include the attributes of what would be considered a restaurant. It was possible to eat at what was called a 'table d'hôte' where there was a fixed eating time and everyone dined together. Food was placed on the table and the guests could partake of what was brought. If you came late, you probably did not get the choicest of morsels. A fixed price was set for the pleasure of dining at table, whether you were hungry or just wanted a little something. Many a table d'hôte had regular customers, but it was also an institution that made provision for travellers, as long as they could show up on time. An example of the table d'hôte is Simpson's Fish Dinner House, which opened in 1714 near the Bank of England and served a meal called a fish ordinary – a dozen oysters, soup, roast partridge, three more first courses, mutton and cheese – for two shillings.

A coffeehouse, or a café, was also not a restaurant in the modern sense because it did not have an extensive selection of cooked foods made for the diner and ordered from a menu. The Caffè Florian in Venice, which still plies its trade to tourists in St Mark's Square, opened in 1720 and has been in continuous operation ever since, but its menu is limited to pastries and snacks to accompany caffeinated beverages. Another alternative for the traveller was to dine at an inn where he was lodging. Here it was not so much the time that was fixed as the choice of what to eat. Whatever had been cooked that day would be what was offered. Inns tended to have a reputation for a certain conviviality of a low sort and for terrible food, as Cervantes, for example, reminds us in *Don Quixote*:

> They set the table at the door to the inn, to take advantage of the cooler air, and the host brought him a portion of cod that was badly prepared and cooked even worse, and bread as black and grimy as his armour; but it was a cause for great laughter to see him eat, because, since he was wearing his helmet and holding up the visor with both hands, he could not put anything in his mouth unless someone placed it there for him, and so one of the ladies performed that task.

Later, at another inn, Sancho asks what is to be had for dinner. The innkeeper tells him he can serve anything he likes. A request for roast chickens is met with the unfortunate news that all of the chickens have been eaten by hawks. The second choice of pullets is also unavailable, all the pullets having been sent to the city. Veal, kid, bacon, eggs… all evoke a similar regretful negative response. Sancho finally exclaims:

> 'My God…why don't you just get down to it and tell what you've really got, and stop all this scurrying around.'
> The innkeeper said:
> 'What I've really and truly got are some cow's feet that look like calves' hooves, or a couple of calves' hooves that look like cow's feet, and they've been cooked up with chickpeas, onions and bacon, and they just sit there, saying "Eat me! Eat me!"'

It was possible in the large cities to do considerably better than these impoverished alternatives. In Paris particularly it was possible to acquire the equivalent of modern takeaway meals. The typical kinds of foods that one would eat for dinner – sausages, soups, poultry – had separate guilds of caterers. These establishments provided food to take away or eat immediately, but only the kind of food that conformed to the caterer's licence. To this day in Spain bakeries that make cakes and pastries (not bread) are traditionally open on Sundays and also on that particular day provide rotisserie chickens for after-church meals.

The scholar Rebecca L. Spang has helped us to understand that the first restaurant was an establishment named after a particular type of food, a bouillon 'restoratif'. The restaurant served a healthful hot broth that was supposed to soothe and 'restore' the body. The first restaurant provided both food and a place to eat it that promoted health. Mathurin Roze de Chantoiseau opened his Parisian establishment in 1766 with the claim that he would serve broth made from a nutritious extract of meats and vegetables, a claim that was based on the quasi-scientific ideals of the Enlightenment, the movement that among its many projects purported to apply reason to such problems as curing the ailments of intellectuals and artists. The impetus for such frugal and healthful dining in Paris might have been a reaction against the elaboration of French cuisine in the first half of the eighteenth century. The shift between ostentatious, baroque and innovative tastes and a reaction in the direction of (supposedly) classical purity was not new.

Drawing on Epicurus as well as an aesthetic of simplicity and delight in the best basic ingredients, the Renaissance humanist Platina had argued in the late fifteenth century for a return to eating in moderation, away from heavy sauces that masked the nature of the foods served in noble households. His teachings seemed to have spurred a return to meals with a good deal of variety where people ate lightly. Much of this would be familiar to certain tendencies and teachings today: the exaltation of simplicity and authenticity, as in salads dressed with oil and vinegar, good bread, grilled fish, lamb or veal or poultry instead of beef or mutton, all served in their own juices, not with heavy overlays of sauce, and simple desserts. In essence, having the foods themselves do the work of pleasing the palate and reflecting their own origins. The response to what was considered excessively heavy, complicated food would be lighter food that was closer to its origins. This pattern would reassert itself several times through the next 250 years.

The other innovations of the restaurant followed swiftly. Within a few years the restaurant became a privileged site of supposedly healthful eating in the new style (which included, but was not limited to, the original restorative broth). The distinctive practices of ordering from a menu, paying only for what was ordered, sitting at a small table with friends, and having a choice of times available were quickly developed. Dining with acquaintances in public encouraged the notion of eating not simply as a matter of health, but also an expression of taste and specialization.

The entire set of practices characteristic of the 'true' restaurant can be seen best at La Grande Taverne de Londres, which opened in Paris in 1782, and was, in the words of Jean-Anthelme Brillat-Savarin 'the first to combine the four essentials of an elegant room, smart waiters, a choice cellar, and superior cooking.' Its owner, Antoine Beauvilliers, had been the pastry chef for the brother of the king before going into business on his own. He is the classic example of a restaurateur who brought to the bourgeois table the style and bearing that previously only the aristocracy had enjoyed, or at least certain elements of that style. He and a number of other ex-employees of the nobility opened restaurants at the Palais-Royal, which became the centre of the new world of the restaurant. Among these new restaurants were some known for certain specialties or attributes: Balaine's Rocher de Cancale for fish, or the Café Mechanique, where the kitchen was below the diners and the food was sent up mechanically through the hollow pedestal of the tables, or Henneveus, where the fourth floor was given over to private rooms.

This last characteristic of restaurants, offering opportunities for intimate and perhaps illicit meetings, was important in their earliest days but is no longer integral to their meaning or function. The *cabinets particuliers* provided a programme of which eating formed only a part. Objects of many stories, the private rooms in Parisian restaurants offered a new venue for encounters between men and women not married to one another who could meet in a public place but a private space, more elegant and less stigmatized than a brothel. Private rooms flourished in Parisian restaurants for at least the first half of the nineteenth century, and they fulfilled a number of social functions

The meal is not the main course at this lunch in a private dining room. Note the casual way in which the coat and hat are thrown over the chair and the almost complete absence of food on the table. Will the waiter actually return with any? Champagne seems to be the only necessary precursor. Throughout the 19th century many restaurants offered private rooms for private matters.

in addition to serving as places for sexual meetings. Some of the more discreet Parisian restaurants maintained separate entrances, so that the couples did not have to traverse the public space in order to reach their rendezvous, but private rooms also allowed for political groups, for spies, for people who needed a space outside of the home to meet, but for whom public meetings were interdicted by French law. But despite the pleasures of the flesh and the stimulation of political discussion, the private room of a restaurant was a locale for the delectation of food.

In addition to La Grande Taverne de Londres, three other early Parisian restaurants embodied the style of French restaurant that was to set the world standard: Les Trois Frères Provençaux, Véry's and the Grand Véfour (this last surviving to this day). These three epitomized what would become – for all of the world – the meaning of the French restaurant, and became tourist destinations for the curious who were in Paris to taste what the cultural capital of the West offered. They were nearly as important in the imagination of those who never ate there as for those who dined in them regularly.

The restaurants projected a certain image of familial intimacy and refinement at the same time. The owners of Les Trois Frères Provençaux, founded in 1786, were actually unrelated but married to three sisters. From their native Marseilles they brought to Paris a splendid recipe for the Provençal brandade de morue (puréed salt-cod). It was the first stop in Paris for many foreigners on the nineteenth-century grand tour, especially for Americans, who admired its furnishings as much as its food and who perhaps felt it easier to experience France in a way that seemed to demand less advance preparation than did visits to historic sites and museums. This one establishment so embodied the notion of the French restaurant that it was imported to the first world's fair in the United States, the Centennial Exposition in Philadelphia in 1876, where the American author William Dean Howells lamented, after dining at the temporary branch: 'When I think of it, I am ready to justify the enormous charges at the restaurant of the Trois Frères Provençaux (so called because each of the Brothers makes out his bill of Three Prices, and you pay the sum total), as a proper reprisal upon us; but I would fain whisper in the ears of those avengers that not all Americans are guilty.'

We have been left a detailed description of La Grande Taverne de Londres by Francis William Blagdon, from *Paris As it Was and As it Is*, published in London in 1803, which encapsulates how contemporaries thought about the classic French restaurant:

> On the first floor of a large hotel, formerly occupied, perhaps, by a farmer-general, you enter a suite of apartments, decorated with arabesques, and mirrors of large dimensions, in a style no less elegant than splendid, where tables are completely arranged for large or small parties. In winter, these rooms are warmed by ornamental stoves, and lighted by *quinquets*, a species of Argand's lamps. They are capable of accommodating from two hundred and fifty to three hundred persons, and, at this time of the year, the average number that dine here daily is about two hundred; in summer, it is considerably decreased by the attractions of the country, and the parties of pleasure made, in consequence, to the environs of the capital.
>
> On the left hand, as you pass into the first room, rises a sort of throne, not unlike the *estrado* in the grand audience-chamber of a Spanish viceroy. This throne is encircled by a barrier to keep intruders at a respectful distance. Here sits a lady, who, from her majestic gravity and dignified bulk, you might very naturally suppose to be an empress, revolving in her comprehensive mind the affairs of her vast dominions. This respectable personage is Madame Beauvilliers, whose most interesting concern is to collect from the gentlemen in waiting the cash which they receive at the different tables.

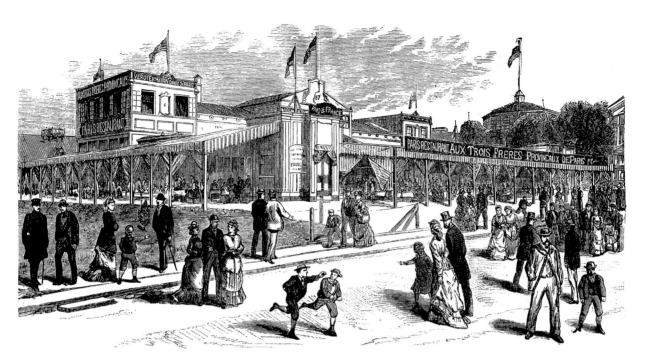

The French Restaurant is depicted here as luxury export product. World's Fairs of the 19th and early 20th centuries would introduce millions to the industrial, cultural and social characteristics of foreign lands. One of the first of the great French restaurants, Les Trois Frères Provençaux, was recreated at the Centennial Exposition in Philadelphia in 1876.

In this important branch, she has the assistance of a lady, somewhat younger than herself, who, seated by her side, in stately silence, has every appearance of a maid of honour. A person in waiting near the throne, from his vacant look and obsequious carriage, might, at first sight be taken for a chamberlain; whereas his real office, by no means an unimportant one, is to distribute into deserts the fruit and other *et ceteras*, piled up within his reach in tempting profusion.

We will take our seats in this corner, whence, without laying down our knife and fork, we can enjoy a full view of the company as they enter. We are rather early: by the clock, I perceive that it is no more than five: at six, however, there will scarcely be a vacant seat at any of the tables...

Good heaven! the bill of fare is a printed sheet of double *folio*, of the size of an English newspaper. It will require half an hour at least to con over this important catalogue. Soups, thirteen sorts.—Hors-d'œuvres, twenty-two species.—Beef, dressed in eleven different ways.—Pastry, containing fish, flesh and fowls, in eleven shapes.—Veal, amplified into twenty-two distinct articles.—Mutton, confined to seventeen only.—Fish, twenty-three varieties.—Roast meat, game, and poultry, of fifteen kinds.—Entremets, or side-dishes, to the number of forty-one articles.—Desert, thirty-nine.—Wines, including those of the liqueur kind, of fifty-two denominations, besides ale and porter.—Liqueurs, twelve species, together with coffee and ices....

Remark that portly man, so respectful in his demeanor. It is Beauvilliers, the master of the house: this is his most busy hour, and he will now make a tour to inquire at the different tables, if his guests are all served according to their wishes. He will then, like an able general, take a central station, whence he can command a view of all his dispositions.

…Observe the cleanly attention of the waiters, neatly habited in close-bodied vests, with white aprons before them: watch the quickness of their motions….An establishment, so extremely well conducted, excites admiration.

Aiding the development of the restaurant as the hallmark of French culture was the emergence of a nascent publicity industry that would help enshrine classic examples of the institution. Guidebooks, listings and reviews of restaurants abounded. As was the case with the 'restaurant' itself, we can name the person who set this machinery in motion: the Parisian lawyer and gastronome Alexandre-Balthazar-Laurent Grimod de La Reynière, who published the *Almanach des gourmands* in 1803, the same year that Blagdon's description of La Grande Taverne de Londres appeared. Twenty years before he had staged a strange and ornate spectacle to which twenty-two notables were invited to dine in a stage-set atmosphere, observed by hundreds of spectators who were moved through the gallery of the room as they gawked at the proceedings below. Odd in appearance (he wore gloves to cover the mechanical metal fingers with which surgeons had replaced his webbed hands), Grimod in the first decade of the nineteenth century developed the preconditions for what constituted true gastronomic spectacle, the nexus of cuisine and atmosphere characteristic of the modern restaurant. A great establishment had to satisfy taste but also to fulfil fantasy and desire. Grimod helped to fix in the minds of his readers the restaurant as a place apart, with its own rules, where learning to read the menu and to order the right foods and wines developed into an act of taste that would take an effort to perform correctly. The client as well as the waiter had to obtain a degree of expertise.

The French restaurant soon became a fixture not only of Paris but of international sophisticated culture, a major export product of France. In some ways, the French restaurant becomes truly French in its exportation to other countries, most notably to England. La Grande Taverne de Londres paid homage to French fascination with English public houses, and French food, prepared in London restaurants by chefs trained in Paris, complemented this act of trans-Channel fascination. Rules Restaurant, founded in 1798 and still thriving, seems to be London's oldest. Started as an Oyster Bar, it claims to have served over the more than two centuries of its existence classic British dishes such as jellied eel and steak and kidney pie, but it developed in a milieu where French food was the standard.

Fine French dining could be found in London hotels by the 1820s. The foremost example was the Saint James, presided over by a student

An illustration of costumes of cooks from different eras, from a book by one of the first great French chefs, Antonin Carême, *Le Maitre d'hôtel français* (Paris, 1822). Carême had a European-wide reputation and clientele: he confected Beef Stroganov and Charlotte Russe for Tsar Alexander I, oversaw the banquet for 1,200 guests that celebrated the restoration of the French monarchy in 1815 for Louis XVIII, and worked for both Talleyrand and the London banker Baron de Rothschild.

of the Parisian restaurateur Carême. The grand development of hotel restaurants would swell after 1890 throughout the capitals of the Western world, but the restaurant that would embody the notion (indeed, its telegraphic address was 'Restaurant, London') was the Café Royal, which opened in 1865. But if the definition of the French restaurant was extended from the original healthful soup establishment to become a world model of elegance, richness and style, the kind of broth that would give birth to the restaurant was still simmering: the restaurateur Déharme in Paris claimed in 1803 that his stockpot had not been off the fire for eighty-five years and that he had rendered in that time 300,000 capons.

The quality of the ingredients in the US was excellent, but the development of a restaurant culture took a bit longer. As Brillat-Savarin had experienced in 1794 when he lived in the United States, American food was abundant and even, on occasion, delicious:

One fine day in October, 1794, therefore, with a friend, I set out with the hope of reaching the farm of Mr Bulow, five mortal leagues from Hartford, before night....After our return from walking we sat around a well-furnished table. A superb piece of corned beef, a stewed goose, and a magnificent leg of mutton, besides an abundance of vegetables and two large jugs of cider, one at each end of the table, made up our bill of fare....The turkey, which was our only roast dish, was charming to the sight, flattering to the sense of smell, and delicious to taste. Therefore, until the last fragment was eaten, there were heard around the table, 'Very good'; 'Exceedingly good'; 'Dear sir; what a nice piece.'

New York could boast of one of the first true French restaurants outside of France. Its founder was the retired sea captain Giovanni Del-Monico, born in 1788 in the Swiss canton of Ticino. His schooner carried tobacco from Cuba to Cadiz, then wines to New York and lumber back to Cuba. He stayed in New York after 1824, setting himself up as an importer and rebottler of wine, and changed his name to John. His brother Pietro, who was a pastry chef in Berne, would become Peter in New York in 1826, when he and his family joined his brother. This wealthy pair (they possessed about $20,000 in capital) first opened a café and pastry shop that, as the story is told, the sign painter spelled out as Delmonico, and the family used that form of the name from then on. From a small shop with a few pine tables serving coffee and cakes to the model for all of the nineteenth-century restaurants in the US was a step of only four years. By 1830, they opened the first real restaurant in the United States at 25 William Street and the next year they called their nephew Lorenzo to join them: this establishment introduced French cuisine that employed American-grown ingredients that were not widely used before and delivered this cuisine with care and attention to each individual diner. Endive, aubergine and artichokes in such dishes as 'Chicorée au jus', 'Aubergine farcie' and 'Artichaux à la Barigoule' were among the three hundred and seventy-one selections on the eleven-page menu of 1838. It became an important place for businessmen to gather for an elegant luncheon. For almost a century the various incarnations of Delmonico's set the standard for sophisticated dining in the United States.

Self-promotion may have been one of the most important innovations that the Delmonicos employed to reach and secure the restaurant's place in New York's economy and high society. Opening their new building at the corner of Beaver and South William Streets in 1837, John Delmonico welcomed almost the entire press corps of New York to a preview dinner while standing between marble pillars that he claimed to have imported from Pompeii to grace the front of this new establishment. The press notices he received for this event were entirely favourable. The restaurant was built according to classic lines, with three floors of dining, the third floor reserved for private dining rooms. The cellar supposedly held 16,000 bottles of wine. The

restaurant had cost the unheard of sum of $100,000 in a city that had just become the largest in North America. But the key to its success was undoubtedly the food and its preparation.

The Delmonicos used good basic ingredients and the latest French cooking and presentation techniques to teach Americans about taste. They were the first to employ a side-by-side translation of the menu in French and in English as they eased their adopted countrymen into the world of fine dining. Like many of the immigrant groups who came to the United States, the Delmonicos kept in touch with Europe, devouring the latest cookery books and importing what they could not reproduce from local ingredients. Samuel Ward, a New York gourmet, reported: 'Today a new *aide cuisinière* brought the last inventions of the Rocher de Cancale, the Trois Frères Provençaux, and the princely laboratories of Talleyrand – tomorrow, a new invoice of pâtés of Strasbourg, Toulouse or Angoulême, or the arrival of a Clos de Vougeot or Chambertin, unscathed by its then supposed enemy, the sea.'

Following his clientele uptown with successive moves, Lorenzo Delmonico and subsequent generations of the family would develop the restaurant to its greatest reach at four locations in Manhattan. They employed Charles Ranhofer, a French-born and trained chef, from the 1860s to the 1890s, except for a short interruption in the late 1870s. He began his American career at Maison Dorée, the only New York rival of Delmonico's in the second half of the nineteenth century, and then presided over the finest restaurants in the country, published an all-encompassing cookery book and was the first to achieve what can be considered the status of celebrity chef in the United States. He invented Baked Alaska to commemorate the purchase of that territory, was involved in the creation of Lobster à la Newberg, and taught the next generation of American chefs. He was an early member and president of the Société Culinaire Philanthropique, the oldest association

Charles Ranhofer, born in 1836 in St Denis, came from a long line of French chefs. Both his father and grandfather were well known and his career began in Paris at the age of twelve. Ranhofer made his name in the United States as an authority and an autocrat in the kitchen, insisting upon absolute control over every aspect of the meal. He was an innovator to the very end: in *The Epicurean*, a work of more than a thousand pages and 3,500 recipes, he mentions the 'alligator pear', or, as it is now better known, the avocado, which he introduced to New Yorkers in 1895, just as his career was nearing its end.

of chefs, cooks and pastry chefs in the United States, founded in 1865 by a group of French chefs for the promotion of French cuisine in the United States and still very much in existence. Delmonico's first real rival did not spring up until 1890, when Louis Sherry, a confectioner, opened a restaurant and hotel at Fifth Avenue and 37th Street in New York City. Eight years later, he moved Sherry's to Fifth and 44th Street, where he would oversee some of the most lavish dining events of the opulent period that preceded the imposition of the first income tax, America's entry into the Great War, and Prohibition (the outlawing of wine and other alcoholic drinks).

If we return to London, the first true restaurant was arguably the Café Royal, but before it opened in 1865, the private clubs in London had already welcomed French cuisine beginning in the early nineteenth century. Like their French counterparts of the mid-eighteenth century, by 1800 the British upper middle class had few places to gather in public. Public houses – pubs – were ubiquitous but not for the middle or upper classses. As the nineteenth century wore on and the commercial classes attained both more leisure and a desire for elegance, wealthy people abandoned pubs, which had never really featured food in any case. Clubs would play an increasingly important role through the century and not just in London: there were more than a hundred clubs with a total of sixty thousand members in New York in 1886. In London, the clubs employed French chefs and were so important that only with the opening of the Café Royal was there a public establishment that might be said to fulfil the expectations of the elite for French cuisine, prepared by French professionals in sumptuous surroundings, where the leading lights of London's aristocracy were willing, even eager, to gather to eat and to be seen.

There were three parts to the Café Royal: the Restaurant, the Grill Room, and the downstairs Domino Room, which became the Brasserie. Its proper name was the Café-Restaurant Royal, which it was christened two years after it first opened its doors in February 1865 as the Café-Restaurant Daniel Nicols. M. Daniel Nicolas Thévenon and his wife Célestine arrived from France in 1863, after their wine business collapsed. He combined three shops on Glasshouse Street

This view of the kitchens of the Reform Club of London is from 1841, when the new clubhouse was built, a time when private clubs were more ubiquitous than restaurants as the places where the upper middle class would dine. Formed in 1836, the Reform Club, which brought together liberal politicians (250 members of Parliament were among the first thousand members) instructed its architect Charles Barry to pay particular attention to the preparation of food by designing the kitchens to the specification of its chef, Alexis Soyer. Soyer is credited with such innovations as cooking with gas, variable temperature ovens and cold-water-cooled refrigerators. These kitchens were so famous that they became a tourist attraction.

with 68 Regent Street, where the Café had a plate-glass window with a highly polished brass sill jutting forward at the base. White raised letters, stuck to the glass pane, advertised *Spécialités de la Maison.* In the shop-window there was an exciting display of *glace* dishes on ornamental pedestals, salads of many hues, and game in season.

Two future kings of England, Edward VIII and George VI, ate lunch there together; Winston Churchill waited there to be called by the prime minister; James McNeill Whistler and Gustave Doré preceded him there, but the most celebrated habitué was Oscar Wilde. At the beginning of his Café Royal period, Wilde ate and drank frugally in the Grill Room with his artist colleague Whistler, drinking a cheap claret with his meals. Wilde and Whistler had a falling out and Wilde's luncheons became the place to be, overtaking Whistler's Sunday-morning breakfasts. 'He overfed like a schoolboy in a tuckshop with an unexpected sovereign in each hand,' wrote his biographer Arthur Ransome. According to Guy Deghy and Keith Waterhouse, Wilde became the consummate gourmand, who would confer with the chef before each course and drank the most exquisite wines in the cellar. Wilde was not the only person to overeat there – the son-in-law of the founder Nicols (now styled De Nicols) was the most afflicted:

> Every day Georges Pigache travelled from Surbiton to the
> Café Royal, where he had made the kitchens his special

The Café Royal in London, where the worlds of bohemia and respectability meet in this detail from a work by Sir William Orpen of 1912. In addition to Wilde and Whistler, Aubrey Beardsley, Max Beerbohm and Augustus John were regulars. The restaurant expanded again in the 1920s to include large ballrooms that hosted wedding receptions and debutante cotillions. The Grill Room closed in 1951, but in 1971, Le Relais du Café Royal reopened at 68 Regent Street under the guidance of George Mouilleron.

study. This enthusiastic interest in food increased his girth to such an extent that one morning the family coachman and groom found themselves unable to coax his bulk into the De Nicols carriage, which was to take him to Surbiton station to catch the London train. After much deliberation it was decided that a phaeton, with a considerably wider approach, should be ordered from the local livery stables, and this became Pigache's regular means of transport between his home, near Regent House, and the Surbiton Station.

There remained the tricky question of manoeuvring the Pigache circumference into the railway carriage. The phaeton-type open carriages having gone out of use in George Stephenson's lifetime, the London, Brighton and Chatham Railway Company had no answer to this problem. But after much thought, the stationmaster at Surbiton detailed a working party of three hefty porters to haul Georges Pigache into the railway carriage every morning, and to extract him thence every night....[When] he died...the banisters had to be removed from the staircase of his home, Vine House, before his body could be carried down.

Even as London and New York completed and extended the reach of the restaurant, Paris remained its epicentre. Just a bit more than a half century after the English observer Blagdon described the early restaurants of Paris, the American traveller James Jackson Jarves saw the same three establishments through his own spectacles: Véry's, Trois Frères Provençaux and Véfour's still stood at the top of the list. 'These are the places to test the renown of French culinary art, and the depths of your purse.' The middle classes were now a new audience for the restaurant, and several establishments sprung up at mid-century: the Tortoni, the Café Riche, the Maison Dorée and the Café Anglais. It was in these newer restaurants that the Parisians ate, leaving, according to Jarves, the grand establishments for the foreign tourists:

> To see the French eat one should visit the restaurants of lesser magnitude and fame, particularly of a Sunday, where the rush to dinner, as no one dines that day under his own roof, is absolutely fearful to a lover of a quiet meal. Infants, dogs, and nurses, all have a seat that day, and the amount consumed would indicate considerable preparatory fasting....A family enters, consisting of father, mother, maiden sister, two children under five years of age, and a dog. All the tables are filled. They turn to go out. The restaurateur rushes forward, intercepts their retreat, and promises a table 'toutsuite'. He sees one party have called for their bills, hands them their change, and plumps the newcomers into their warm seats, with an array of broken bread, dirty glasses and all of the debris of the previous meal before them. Once seated, with bonnets and hats hung up, they are considered as fish fairly hooked. The 'garçon', with a dexterity and rapidity peculiarly his own, whisks away the soiled table-cloth and dishes, and in an instant has replaced them with snow-white linen and porcelain. Now commences the 'tug of' eating. Each member of the party, except the dog who gravely occupies his chair, too well bred to manifest impatience, plants a napkin under his or her chin, of the dimensions of a moderate-sized table-cloth. The females pin the extremities to each shoulder, so that in front they have much the appearance of being in their shrouds. The 'carte' is studied, orders given, and content

A Sunday family lunch in Paris around 1860. At this restaurant, the dog does not have his own chair, but he does have a place at the table. The bustle and sheer exuberance of life that this colour lithograph (after Henri Bonaventure) evokes stand in stark contrast to the more formal nature of the dining experience in the classic French restaurant. Getting the waiter's attention, then as now, can be a fraught exercise with unexpected results.

Louis Ober was born in Alsace in 1837, came to New York with his parents in 1851 and moved around various cities in the eastern United States plying several trades until he landed in Boston. In the mid-1870s, he opened his restaurant, which was so successful that it was remodelled in 1886 in the opulent style, much of which is still evident today in the combined Locke-Ober. The original Restaurant Parisien was a classic French restaurant, with private rooms on the upper floors in which women were welcome, but the main floor of the Locke-Ober restaurant was restricted to men until the 1970s.

and pleasure reign. At these family feasts children are literally crammed, indulged with wines and all of the delicacies called for by adult taste, their parents delighted in proportion to the quantity they consume. Eating, under almost any circumstances is to the looker on a vulgar operation…. The waiter has a dozen calls at once – the same dish perhaps ordered dressed in a dozen different modes – he is to remember each mode and each table – to supply every change of course, omitting nothing required, and at the end of the meal he has to recall every dish, the quantity and the quality – and there may have been twenty different articles called for at one table – that the 'addition' may be made out. What wonder then, if in the confusion of orders, he at times mistakes his napkin for his handkerchief, and unconsciously wipes the perspiration from his brow, performing with it the next instant the same service for your plate, or rushes in from the 'cuisine' with six dishes piled pyramidically in his hands, a roll of bread under each arm, and the latest called for 'addition' between his teeth.

The restaurant had changed dramatically in the first fifty years of the nineteenth century as the classic dining experience remained more or less constant. New publics, new foods, new parts of the western world developed restaurant cultures that both accorded with what had become in the first half of the nineteenth century a grand tradition and set out on other paths, like those of the Sunday diners in the less grand restaurants of Paris. In San Francisco in the Gold Rush year 1849, Norman As-Sing opened Macao and Woosung, the first Chinese restaurant in the United States, at the corner of Kearney and Commercial Streets, while in the same year, a restaurant along classic French lines, the Au Poulet d'Or, which quickly became known as the Old Poodle Dog to non-French speakers, opened for business. The Old Poodle Dog was a French restaurant on three floors, the main dining room for family dining, the second floor for conducting business in relative privacy and the third floor reserved for more private matters. Macao and Woosung provided the city with a place where politicians and police could gather under the guidance of an important ethnic politician. In the US, the restaurant took on local colour, local foods and local traditions while the larger cities all developed some kind of French restaurant, with a few still functioning in more or less their original form in the early twenty-first century. Boston still has five restaurants from the nineteenth century: The Union Oyster House from 1826, Durgin Park, another fish establishment of 1827, the Parker House Hotel from 1854 (home of the standard American dinner roll), Jacob Wirth's, 1868, a German-American eating establishment, and finally Locke-Ober, an amalgamation of Restaurant Parisien, owned by an Alsatian, Louis Ober, with retired Maine sea captain Frank Locke's

'Wine Rooms', in 1894. Philadelphia also retains Bookbinder's, one of its oldest restaurants, founded in 1865, whose reputation was built on nearby sources of fish and seafood. New York still hosts The Old Homestead, a steakhouse established in 1868, which functioned for a long time, as did its many New York imitators, as a convivial club where men enjoyed what was reputed to be their favourite repast.

American innovation in restaurant design, purpose and patronage can be seen in the golden age of the railroads, which ingeniously elaborated on both luxury and convenience. Two developments between 1868 and 1872 were central to the provision of something more than mere rudimentary food on the long cross-country routes that had just been completed. To the sleeper cars that he had built in his company town south of Chicago, George Pullman added an opulent dining car, providing a plush mobile restaurant for wealthy travellers, staffed by professional waiters and chefs who made use of the local food products they found along the way. For those whose pockets were not as deep or

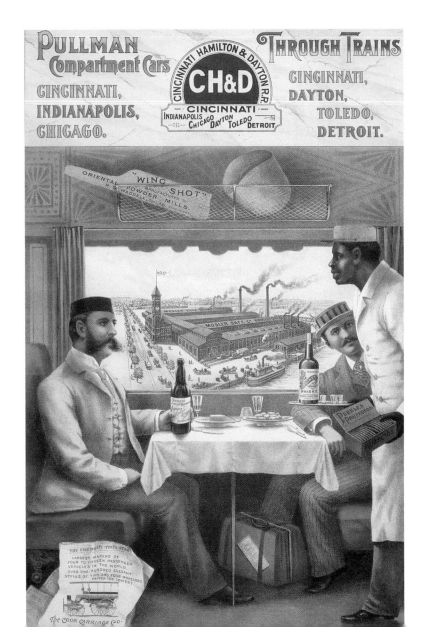

The automat was as famous as the New York skyline. Exactly a decade after its introduction in Philadelphia, the first Horn & Hardart automat opened on Broadway between 46th and 47th Streets, and by the 1920s became a fixture of popular culture. The façade of an automat was reproduced in the 1932 Broadway musical *Face the Music*, for Irving Berlin's celebration of the automat, 'Let's Have Another Cup of Coffee'.

who preferred to eat while not in motion, the alternative was a chain of restaurants affiliated with railroad lines, the Harvey House. A native of England, Fred Harvey joined with the just-launched Atchison, Topeka and Santa Fe Railway in 1870 to offer a prototype that would be often imitated later in the United States: good food served quickly at reasonable prices in clean, moderately elegant restaurants. It is possible that in the Harvey Houses strung along the line, the first women worked in restaurants, serving the patrons with their food.

Convenience and speed were considered important outside of the world of the railroad as well. The first self-service restaurant, the New York Exchange Buffet, developed in 1885, directly across from the Stock Exchange, cutting down on the time needed away from the trading floor. By 1888, the first food chain began, also in New York, under the brothers Samuel Shannon and William Childs, and grew to more than one-hundred restaurants by the 1920s. The Childs' formula was akin to the Harvey House, emphasizing hygiene and low prices: all white furnishings, waiters dressed in white from head to toe, and scrupulously fresh food. At the Chicago Columbian Exposition in 1893, John Kruger opened a self-service restaurant based on the idea of the Swedish *smorgasbord*, which he called a cafeteria, while in Philadelphia in 1902 the new century opened with a German import that epitomized the mechanization and industrialization of the restaurant: Horn and Hardart's automats. At these self-service restaurants, the food was obtained from coin-operated, food-dispensing machines where glass doors set in polished metal frames opened at the insertion of a five-cent coin. The ideal for busy, urban office workers was speed, cleanliness and technology – the furnishing of food that seemed never to have been touched by human hands.

Thus by the end of the nineteenth century, what constituted a restaurant was changing – some of the first characteristics of the mid-eighteenth century, such as waiters and bills at the end of the meal, would transform themselves into self-service and paying a cashier. What remained constant was the notion of consumer choice from an extensive menu, and a fairly extensive selection of times when food was available.

The middle of the nineteenth century marks the beginning of restaurants that catered to the middle and working class. Certain of the basic (or at least original) defining characteristics of the nineteenth-century restaurant were often missing from such establishments, however, as they were almost always self-service and the food was not necessarily cooked to order. A cross between the cafeteria of 1893, a tavern and a take-out shop, we have a marvellous description of one such place from a novel written at mid-century in German in Philadelphia by an anonymous German-American. The tavern is run by an Irishman, serving German food to men and women, black and white, in a rickety building on the southern outskirts of the city:

Upon entering the front room, which was really the dining room, one was taken aback by the extraordinary fittings of the restaurant: the buffet table was filled with the richest selection of dishes, exactly like that of the fashionable restaurants of Chestnut Street. The only difference was in the kind of foods, in the bowls in which they were kept and in the art and manner in which they were dispensed. In two rows, one behind the other, stood twenty large, big, shiny red clay pots and in each one was stuck a large tin ladle. In one was pickled pigs' knuckles, in another giblet stew, in a third pork and sauerkraut, in a fourth white beans, in a fifth yellow pea soup, the sixth apple butter, the seventh mashed carrots and potatoes, in the eighth plum jam and in the others marinated oysters, fish and meats of most different kinds, fried liver and potatoes boiled in their skins, and on top of that 'Fruchtkuchen' ('pies') of all possible combinations.

These dishes weren't just for those sitting in the restaurant or for the regular customers. They were intended much more for those outside customers, who came in with tin or earthenware dishes and for one, two, three, four, five or six cents – the amount didn't differ depending on whether it was the midday or the evening meal – to take the food home. The eat-in guests could dine and sup for the same prices receiving what they paid for on a tin plate. A large ladleful was normally reckoned at one cent and so on in that proportion. Noteworthy in regard to the food at Clapmann's tavern was that in spite of the Irish origin of the innkeeper, almost all of the dishes were and tasted 'German'.

The food in US restaurants in the middle of the century was indeed often influenced by German immigrants, as ethnic styles of eating began to become defined as separate from the dominant cuisine of each regional section of the country. The German presence in American cuisine is seldom explicit (there are few avowedly German restaurants left, perhaps four in all of New York, for example), but from the style of barbecued beef and sausage in Texas to the cuisine of the Pennsylvania Amish, it nevertheless persists.

The pioneer of what might be called fast food (as opposed to quickly prepared but complete meals on the Harvey House model) was the English fish and chips establishment. This famous working-class meal or snack started out as two separate fried dishes sold on the street. The fish seller was an itinerant who hawked his fish and bread for a penny at the pubs, or sold from a stall. The chips sellers sold to the very poor, often from the front room of a home to people who either ate them in a back room or took them away, like the fish, wrapped in newspaper. When the two dishes were joined together is unknown, but

You can almost smell and taste it! Long a feature of British seaside resorts, such as Llandudno in North Wales, the fish and chip shop can now be found where the British holiday abroad, particularly the Mediterranean coast of Spain. Despite competition from other, more recent fast-food outlets, the fish and chip shop is still the UK market leader in cheap meals.

THE END OF A PERFECT DAY!
AT LLANDUDNO

Two views of the Restaurant Kempinski in the Leipziger Strasse, Berlin. Above, the kitchens in 1913 (where up to 250 chefs were employed at once), and on the right, the restaurant with diners in 1917. Opened in 1889, Kempinski's became the largest restaurant in Berlin. But it did not remain so for this was only the first incarnation of the large-scale Kempinski restaurant empire: the second was on the Kurfürstendamm (now rebuilt as the Hotel Bristol), and the most glorious was called the Haus Vaterland on Potsdamer Platz (heavily damaged in the Second World War). Under one roof there were 12 restaurants, a huge café (with 2,500 seats) and a movie theatre – all told a capacity of 8,000 with more than one million visitors a year. The restaurants were themed: here a Spanish Bodega, there an American Wild West Bar. The entire chain was confiscated from its Jewish owners by the Nazis in the 1930s.

Joseph Malines is generally credited with having opened the first true restaurant to serve fish and chips in London in 1864. New technology played a major role in the development of this staple of British working-class cuisine, which flourished in the second half of the century. North Sea steam trawlers brought huge hauls back home with fish packed immediately on ice the moment it was caught, and new kinds of cooking oils were both cheaper than such things as lard and reached a higher temperature without burning to create the crisp texture that is part of the appeal of the dish.

Germany and Italy show a similar pattern to Britain and the United States: the restaurant was first imported from France through the introduction of *grande cuisine* by chefs trained in Paris and then the middle-class and lower-class versions of the restaurant followed in the latter half of the nineteenth century due to the rise in the urban population and the influence of technology. Germans took the word 'restaurant' into their language after 1850, and it was used to designate establishments that followed the example of the Café Royal or Delmonico's. Previous German terms referred to inns or taverns and they were superseded, at least in legal terms, by the words *Gastwirtschaft* or *Gaststätte*, for those restaurants that would develop for the middle class. After 1840, Berlin, Hamburg, Frankfurt am Main and Munich would all boast well-known restaurants, many of them connected to the rise of the luxury hotel, a phenomenon that helped to make the classic restaurant an internationally familiar institution. But the most striking developments in restaurants in Germany were not at first related to hotels. They are those of the Kempinski family which began to develop in Berlin in 1872, when they started to sell sandwiches and hard-boiled eggs in tasting rooms in the cellars from which they conducted what was then their principle business, the sale of

Hungarian wines. The enterprise grew in the first third of the twentieth century into three major mass and luxury restaurants. The flagship would by 1913 serve luxurious eight-course dinners (or half-portions for half the price) to 10,000 diners a day.

It was in the world of hotels catering to an increasingly international set of wealthy travellers that the original restaurant achieved its fullest form. Near the end of the nineteenth century, a group of what can without anachronism be called celebrity restaurant chefs and hoteliers became the guardians of the world of restaurant cuisine, an important facet of social distinction. The Waldorf-Astoria Hotel opened in 1893 in New York, two years later, the Palace Hotel in St Moritz, then in 1897 the Vier Jahreszeiten in Hamburg, the Naples Grand Hotel Excelsior and the London Connaught Hotel all welcomed their first guests. In the following year, the Ritz opened in Paris under the greatest celebrity chef of all, Auguste Escoffier. But if any one institution set the international standard for restaurants after the turn of the twentieth century, it was the Savoy Hotel, opened by Richard D'Oyly Carte in 1889. The great hotelier César Ritz came to be its manager and he brought with him maître chef Auguste Escoffier and Louis Echenard, a master of wine, as maître d'hôtel.

What the Savoy, the Ritz, the Waldorf-Astoria and the numerous other grand hotels, many of which became part of the kingdom over which Ritz presided, had in common was the same elite but extensive clientele. The idea behind the creation of these extraordinary palaces was to establish a place to eat and to be seen, and to hold parties that would in many ways be similar to the events that the wealthiest nobles or merchants would have held in their own homes or great houses before the end of the nineteenth century. In fact, many of the hoteliers and their great chefs either made their

Above: The scale of the operations in the large hotel restaurants at the turn of the 20th century is only partly revealed in this set of storage shelves for tableware at the Ritz in London. The extraordinary achievement in these establishments was the feeling that the individual diners and their companions were somehow the sole object of attention at the meal, so that the work of hundreds of hands, the precise carrying out of dozens of processes, the availability of specialized serving dishes for each course, stayed behind the scenes.

Opposite: The Savoy Hotel in London in 1889, the year it opened – the grand hotel in its full service glory. The success of the Savoy Theatre inspired Richard D'Oyly Carte to build this hotel to host the audience after the show. It took five years to complete, had full electric lighting and extraordinary public spaces. The dining room witnessed a long list of dishes created by Escoffier for the female guests who were welcomed there. They included poularde Tosca for the great Australian singer Dame Nellie Melba for her title role in the Puccini opera, as well as potage Miss Betsy, filets mareille Olga, fraise Sarah Bernhardt and bombe Miss Helyette.

names as caterers to the wealthy and/or continued to provide the service of their restaurants and hotels to their famous guests at their various homes.

The grand hotel restaurants were huge operations that relied on the newest kinds of industrial efficiencies of the dawning of the twentieth century. Escoffier was famous for the order in his kitchens, for the control of the dish from the stove to the table, ensuring that it arrived piping hot. At the Savoy, the scale of the enterprise was such that it provided its own power and water, and roasted its own coffee. Escoffier created dishes for Sarah Bernhardt, Lily Langtry, Dame Nellie Melba and the Prince of Wales, later Edward VII, so that this era of opulence before the First World War saw the mixing of performing and political celebrities with culinary celebrities. The Savoy sparkled with glittering parties. One of the most famous was the Gondola dinner, hosted by champagne millionaire and Wall Street financier George Kessler in July 1905. Venice was recreated in the old forecourt, lit by 400 Venetian lamps; there was a silk-lined gondola decorated with 12,000 fresh carnations; a five-foot birthday cake; and arias were sung by Enrico Caruso. Royalty patronized the Savoy in such numbers that the special bell heralding their arrival had to be abandoned, and by 1914 the Savoy Grill had established itself as a rendezvous for leading stars, impresarios and critics.

The cult of the 'Maître D' was linked in many ways to the cult of the celebrity chef and international fame. Oscar Tschirky of the Waldorf-Astoria Hotel in New York was the original or at least emblematic high-profile maître d'hôtel, known for coddling famous favourite patrons and snubbing the less-than-glamorous: for half a century after 1893, he determined who was and who was not to cross his famous (or infamous) red velvet rope barrier. Trilingual himself, from the German part of Switzerland, he hired only waiters who also spoke impeccable English, French and German so that the international visitors would feel at home and be understood.

It was the partnership of the hotelier and the chef that cemented the notion of the grand restaurant, which was carried into the twentieth century, and nowhere was that collaboration more perfectly matched than in the talents of Ritz and Escoffier. Their common goal was the marriage of fine cuisine and fine service: the perfecting of how the food was prepared and the elegance with which it was served. The formula of delicacies and spectacle was reproduced throughout the world. From Rome to New York, from London to Budapest, the same dishes (involving lobster, caviar, rich sauces, flambé preparations) and the same punctilious (if to some intimidating) service were presented. Dining in the restaurants of grand hotels became something akin to a spiritual experience for generations of the powerful who

Charles Rennie Mackintosh's Willow Tea Rooms in Glasgow in 1905. This is a view of the ladies front tea room, looking towards the lunchroom and tea gallery at the back of the building on Sauchiehall Street, from which the Willow Tea Rooms got their name: the Celtic meaning of Sauchiehall, 'a boggy place full of willows'. The grand feature of this room is the wrought-iron flower holder perched atop a wooden structure: the four customers who sat beneath it could feel enclosed while in a very public space.

had conquered the financial, political or artistic worlds. César's wife Marie Louise Ritz describes the ceremony of Crêpes Suzette:

> The hush that descends upon the waiters as they gather like acolytes round the blue flame, the deft gesture of the sacerdotal maître d'hôtel as he pours the rich liqueur into the copper dish, the aromatic smoke which rises suddenly, fills the onlooker, the prospective diner, with a feeling of proper respect, and he tastes the first mouthful with something like religious fervor. In the matter of wine the same thing holds good. The shape and size and fineness of the glass, the manner of the waiter as he

pours the wine, all contribute to the ultimate enjoyment of the taste.

The restaurants that these two men developed abolished a number of earlier traditions and brought about a revolution in tastes throughout the West. Elegance was to be based on simplicity and the lack of extraneous details. Escoffier banished garnishes that were not edible and broke with the Victorian partiality for monumental forms of food presentation. He simplified menus and sauces so that entrées no longer looked like Greek temples: food was to look like food. Marie Louise Ritz linked this change to the attention now, for the first time, paid to the preferences and tastes of female diners who were increasingly influential as the restaurant ceased to be a species of men's club.

Women were not only dining in restaurants but also beginning to own and operate them. Over a twenty-year period, Kate Cranston, wishing to combine modern interiors with light refreshment, commissioned Charles Rennie Mackintosh to design or restyle rooms in all four of her Glasgow tea rooms. At the Willow Tea Rooms at 217 Sauchiehall Street, Mackintosh created a *Gesamtkunstwerk*, of which the Room de Luxe was the main attraction with its silver furniture and leaded mirror friezes. In contrast, at Ingram Street Mackintosh produced a Chinese Room using a series of vertical and horizontal lattice-style screens, designed to reduce the height of the ceiling and to increase the room's intimacy; he also used vibrant colours and introduced plastic design elements. By the end of the nineteenth century, the dining experience was becoming increasingly aesthetic.

At the beginning of the twentieth century, the classic French restaurant still held sway as the standard. Although many of the first great generation had disappeared – such as Rocher de Cancale, the Trois Frères Provençaux and the Café Véry – the next wave of temples of cuisine took their place: Voisin's, Paillard's, the Tour d'Argent, Durand's, Henri's and the Ritz. When Lieut.-Col. Newnham-Davis, an English restaurant critic, was asked in 1903 where he might choose to dine, he answered: 'Breakfast chez Henri at the Gaillon, dine at the Ritz, and sup at Durand's.' At the Tour d'Argent, which began numbering consecutively its famous pressed ducks in 1890, the act of eating its signature dish enrolled the diner in a solemnized history of fine dining. But there was also a new idea on the horizon, embodied by Maxim's, where the food took second place to the culture of celebrity and society. Music-hall stars, ballerinas and other members of the entertainment world, many of whom would arrive at the restaurant only after midnight, were, along with their wealthy patrons, the main attraction of the restaurant.

Although the classic restaurant would endure and thrive throughout the twentieth century, the world of the restaurant would encompass new foods, publics and presentation that expanded in every direction until by the beginning of the twenty-first century, in many

The scene at the Tour d'Argent in 1890 shows Frédéric Delair, the owner, who introduced the custom of numbering what would become the restaurant's signature dish. Delair found the recipe in an old cookery book and brought it back into fashion. Caneton Tour d'Argent consists of two-courses: first the breast is cooked in port, cognac and the essence of pressed duck carcass. Later, the legs are presented in a rich sauce. Delair still appears on the postcard guests take home as a souvenir of the visit. Each duck is numbered, and a record is kept of who ate it and when. The 500,000th duck was consumed in 1976, the millionth in 2003.

parts of the West, dining out is more prevalent than eating at home. The ethnic variety of cuisines and their delectation by those not belonging to the cuisine's cultural tradition, described in Chapter 10, has its origins in the early twentieth century. Lieut.-Col. Newnham-Davis in his *Gourmet's Guide to London* (1914), in addition to reviewing Simpson's in the Strand, the Ritz and the Café Royal, offers sympathetic reference to more eclectic, or at least not easily categorized places such as Romano's, whose chef, in addition to having mastered French cuisine, 'had an open mind with regard to the cookery of other nations. The *mouzakkas*…from his kitchen are the best I have eaten outside of Bucharest. He makes a groundnut soup…[from] Nigeria…quite admirably, and Romano's is the only restaurant I know of in Europe where one can eat a Malay curry cooked as it is cooked in Malaya.' At Goldstein's, our critic wonders how anyone could eat the entire panoply of dishes at this kosher restaurant as he praised the kugel, the pickles, corned beef and almond pudding, 'one of those moist delicacies that I thought only the French had the secret of making.' He praises also a Chinese restaurant and those Italian restaurants in Soho that 'jostle the French restaurants in every street'.

If the ethnic restaurant represents variety and a degree of adventure, restaurant chains simultaneously expanded, offering identically reproducible buildings with identical menus. As has been remarked, these were already developing in the United States in the 1870s, with the Harvey Houses and the Childs restaurants in New York City. In London, the Lyons chain of restaurants started from a catering business run by the Salmon and Gluckstein families in 1887 and diversified into tea rooms and middle-class restaurants. Postwar Britain, after rationing was finally ended, turned to fast food and in the 1950s, Lyons and their Wimpy hamburger chain became the largest producer of food in Europe.

Here we see the waitresses at a Lyons Corner House, London, on the first day of opening, 1 March 1939. The Corner Houses dated back to 1909 and they lasted until 1977. They were large buildings with as many as five floors, the ground floor of which was a food hall with counters for delicatessen, sweets and chocolates, cakes, fruit and flowers. They were full-service establishments that could include hairdressing salons, telephone booths and theatre-booking agencies. On the upper floors were various themed restaurants. The Corner Houses were for a period open 24 hours a day, and at the height of their popularity they had staffs of up to 400.

Restaurant chains that began in the later nineteenth century were not restricted to middle-class and working-class restaurants. The Ritz-Carlton empire at its height had grand hotels not only in London, Paris and New York, but also in Budapest, Rome, Naples, Buenos Aires, Evian, Lucerne, Rapallo, Boston, Philadelphia and Atlantic City. Nevertheless, it was food for the masses that made the chain such a ubiquitous part of the twentieth century, harking back to pre-restaurant days in eighteenth-century Paris: limited menus offering specific foods prepared and made available to take away by caterers. By the late-twentieth century the restaurant had in many ways escaped the definition with which we began this chapter. One would not always be served, not always presented with a bill at the end of the meal, nor would the food necessarily be cooked exclusively for a specific customer. One might not even sit down, either alone or with anyone else. The restaurant had become an all-encompassing notion of eating out.

Many of those foods that would be the centrepiece of the chain restaurants of the twentieth century began their lives as 'ethnic' food, an idea that would link the production and consumption of foods in Europe and the United States with members of immigrant groups from Southern and Eastern Europe or from Asia, Africa and Latin America. One need only think of pizza or tacos or gyros. Or even, as in the case of the hamburger in the United States, an outgrowth of German-American cooking. The hamburger started out in the United States on the first printed menu at Delmonico's in 1836 as one of the most expensive dishes, 'hamburger steak'. One account has the sandwich by that name invented at a county fair in Wisconsin in 1884; another claims it was invented in 1891 at another county fair, this time in Ohio; and a third creation myth moves the story to the East Coast in New Haven, Connecticut, when, in 1900, Louis Lassen served grilled ground beef between two pieces of toast at the Louis Lunch, a still-thriving establishment with all of three seats. The hamburger chain restaurant began in 1921 in Wichita, Kansas, with five stools and one store, which by 1964 grew into the White Castle System, with 100 'outlets', as they would be called, in eleven metropolitan areas across the United States. But the more important moves were made in the 1950s, when McDonald's and Burger King started to change the food industry along industrial production lines that would make them the world's largest and second largest food-service companies.

As the restaurant became ubiquitous, eating and working in these establishments became issues for government regulation, union organization and increasing specialization. The restaurant industry emerged, and with it educational institutions such as the Culinary Institute of America (1946), but also McDonald's training centres, both teaching chefs with a military-like precision appropriate to the now segmented and regimented techniques of an increasingly standardized restaurant cooking. With restaurants in every conceivable setting, from sports stadiums to convention centres, to beaches and rest stops on highways, the restaurant became a unit in a vast skein of commercial enterprises. The democratization of eating out led not only to vast chains serving identical, portion-controlled meals in themed restaurants whose largest costs were in advertising, but it also had the contrary effect of developing an appreciation for a less predictable cuisine, the rediscovery of local cooking, regional dishes and the joys of the small restaurant, where the service might not be up to the ceremony of the Ritz, but the

In the United States, diners grew out of the 19th-century lunch wagons, which were usually stationed at a busy downtown intersection. At the end of the 19th century, discarded horse-drawn trolleys were refashioned at very low cost into lunch wagons; right after the First World War, the first diners were fabricated. In the 1920s, diners were placed mostly at factory gates or at street-car stops. The move to the nation's highways did not really begin until the 1930s. This example is near Poughkeepsie, New York.

essential nature of the experience returned to concentrate on the taste of the food. In the United States, the roadside diner, the soda fountain, the crab shack and the country inn nurtured a newly rediscovered respect for the oldest tradition of the restaurant, as a place to get clean, wholesome, good food in pleasurable surroundings. In Britain and Europe, the café, the bistro and the out-of-the-way restaurant in a small provincial town became again the place for the spirit to be restored.

In some ways, the two movements – towards standardization and towards local authenticity – found themselves in alliance. In the development of the restaurant industry, Jacques Pépin, who would emerge in the late-twentieth century as an advocate of artisanal cooking, made his start in the United States helping Howard Johnson's, a once huge chain of restaurants, to develop a menu and with it a reputation for wholesome, inexpensive meals. Nevertheless, reliance on foods available regardless of seasons, innovations such as frozen foods, long-distance food transport, industrialized agriculture and high-density artificial livestock rearing have created a technological triumph, a series of actual and impending ecological problems, and a degeneration of taste, an obliviousness to what food really is and how it should be experienced. At the same time, there is a growing cultural resistance to the trends towards homogeneity, artificiality and standardized and unseasonal variety. The Slow Food movement, the rediscovery of regional cuisine and a desire for real food, as well as the survival of certain traditions of elegance, give ground for hope in the evolution of the restaurant and in the future of taste.

The New Landscape for Gastronomy

Peter Scholliers

Picture a group of well-off Westerners around a nicely set table in a fancy Ethiopian restaurant in north-west London in the year 2000. It is their first East African meal. It took a while before they decided to visit this restaurant, but an enthusiastic review and reasonable prices convinced them. The *doro wot* and *kitfo* are served to the diners who instantly comment on the look, colour and aroma of the dishes. One of them knows about the food, and he gives some explanations and comparisons with Maghrebi and European cuisines. His companions closely watch their friend (who becomes the guide) taking the first mouthful. Some of them may discretely sniff at the dish and hesitatingly taste the sauce. Giggling, comments and questions to each other accompany this. Then, reassured, the entire party starts eating while still making remarks and comparisons with familiar food. One, however, cannot swallow the spicy, raw minced beef (*kitfo*), muttering something about unsafe raw meat and hunger in Africa. After a strong coffee, the party leaves the place quite pleased with the new culinary encounter. In the following days they tell friends and colleagues about their Ethiopian experience, some quite enthusiastically but others very casually. One diner puts a favourable review on the Internet.

As this little scene indicates, there are Ethiopian restaurants in Europe that cater to a European clientele, but it essentially shows that our reasonably affluent contemporaries are interested in new food, hesitate when confronted by it, try to classify it within familiar food categories, wish to be reassured about what they eat, reflect about food, and finally swallow it (or not). In any case, the visit to a restaurant is a pleasant occasion and opportunity to talk about food, spread culinary information, and express emotions and opinions.

The scene, in fact, reveals two basic attitudes towards new foods and tastes: fascination and distrust, what the sociologist Claude Fischler and the psychologist Paul Rozin call the 'omnivore paradox'. Physically, humans need food diversity, hence they have a biological inclination towards food innovation. Furthermore, they may appreciate new foods and tastes for social and cultural reasons. But at the same time they are also prudent, conservative and fearful about unfamiliar food, because it threatens customary categories, orderings and sentiments about food. In this chapter I shall explore the tension between

Fancying or fearing the new, a group of diners eating *injera* (spongy, sour flatbread that is used to scoop up meats and vegetables) in an Ethiopian restaurant, Washington, DC, 2001. There was probably an astute guiding diner not only showing the way to the restaurant but also how to approach this new eating experience.

acceptance and rejection of new foods, tastes and foodways since 1945. I shall do so from a European perspective, but developments elsewhere will inevitably be part of the discussion.

What is served in the Ethiopian restaurant, and what people generally eat, is the outcome of changes in a long chain, including agriculture, agribusiness, trade, retailing, mediating agents (such as dieticians and the mass media), cooking, presentation and, finally, waste disposal. In focusing on two important questions, I hope to cast light on the complex changes of each link in the food chain since 1945: *where* have we obtained our food and *what* have we eaten in this period? Prior to that, I shall deal with the shift in the meaning of food, and tackle the economic, social and political changes that affected food, tastes, cooking and eating.

Since the Second World War, changing economic, social, cultural and political circumstances have altered the quantity, price, choice and status of food. People, however, do not just experience these influences: they co-create them by their expectations, language and expenditures. There is an intimate and mutual influence between changes in the wider world and changes at home. The anthropologist Sidney Mintz characterized these respectively as 'grand' (or external) and 'daily life' (or inside) changes. He puts the initial emphasis on the grand changes, and asserts that daily life follows these. I would place greater stress on the interaction between the two.

For many years social and life scientists have studied how societies tend to react to food and culinary innovations, concluding that food fulfils many purposes besides pure biological ones. Interest in, or rejection of, new foods and tastes may be the consequence of social structure, the formation of identity, sublimation, frustration, social aspiration, cultural snobbery, or anxiety (to name just some). Thus, on each occasion that people eat, nibble or drink, there may be impulses besides merely satisfyinig the appetite. Surely, when people ate, nibbled or drank in the Renaissance or the Victorian age, they too did so for reasons other than pure bodily purposes. The essential point, however, is that 'secondary meanings' of eating have been more prominent in the twentieth century, which, in general, has led to increasing fascination for, and declining distrust of, new foods and tastes. Social psychologists label the latter as 'decreasing neophobia', linking this to changing preconceptions about new foods in which information, tasting and memory seem to be decisive.

This change may be interpreted in a purely materialistic way that relates to economic and social changes. Bodily needs (connected with work, transport and housing comfort) became less imperative for a growing number of people throughout the world after 1945 and, particularly, after 1975 when there was expanding employment in service industries. Using Marxist terminology, the social psychologist Leon Rappoport refers to this change as the loss of the 'use value' of the body in favour of the 'exchange value', with the body gaining symbolic meaning and being valued for its aesthetic function rather than for its physical strength. Together, the changing economic, social, cultural and political circumstances increasingly offered people new foods and tastes to be utilized in a social, cultural and psychological way much more than before 1945. Above all, this implies that people had a much wider food choice by which they could express their aspirations, extricate themselves from frustration, hope to undo worries, or manifest their joys (and all this individually or collectively, premeditatedly or spontaneously). Thus, there was a socio-cultural and psychological cause as well as a purely materialistic reason for the change in the significance of food. Choice, diversity and innovation became crucial to many people. It is a historian's job to study *when* these notions were applied and to *whom*. Some researchers, such as John Urry, situate the big change in the 1980s with the advent of the post-modern or 'post-Fordist' consumer and diner, who eats according to mood, time, environment, cravings, peer group and aims. Post-modern food consumers take novelty for granted as familiar, expected and even hoped for. This type of diner is opposed to the modern consumer prior to, say 1980, who would seem more amenable to the will of the producers.

There have, of course, always been new foods and flavours. For example, the coming of the potato to Spain in the sixteenth century, and its slow but compelling diffusion throughout Europe in the eighteenth century, which caused the invention of new dishes and tastes, and which provided the hungry masses with much needed calories (see Chapter 7). Consider, too, the introduction of spices, coffee, tomatoes and cocoa into Europe, the diffusion of bananas from Southeast Asia to Africa and South America, or the spread of beet sugar and Pilsner beer from Europe all over the world. All of these innovations in different places and times, and with various causes, have provoked substantial changes of diet and taste. On each occasion, the introduction, acceptance and diffusion was a specific process. Often a small group of mostly rich and fashionable urban dwellers took the lead, followed by early and late adopters, and finally by laggards. Naturally, opponents may have resisted the new taste altogether. For the historian Werner Sombart, writing in 1912, luxury, or conspicuous consumption, was one of the engines of capitalist long-term growth. In this process, he mentioned the late eighteenth-century ballrooms, hotels, restaurants and pastry shops, all places of fancy eating and drinking. During the second half of the twentieth century, food innovations (as shall be shown below) were not the exclusive preserve of an elite, but extended also to the rank and file that used food (and consumption in general) to express hope, ambition, frustration or enjoyment. Innovative consumption by the masses was not so much the engine of post-1945 capitalist growth as its precondition. This implies the training of the consumer, operating, for example, through advertisements and peer-group pressure.

MORRELL

Fragrant, sizzling sausage
says "come-and-get-it!"
And when it's Morrell Pride
Sausage, there's no doubt
of its quality and flavor.
Made only from choicest pork,
and seasoned just right.
This is a product we are
proud to label Morrell Pride.

PRIDE

MORRELL PRIDE BREAKFAST
SAUSAGE LINKS... delicious
blending of pure pork and
mild seasonings in handy
can for year-round use.

MORRELL PRIDE PURE PORK SAUSAGE... everyone likes that tasty, all-pork flavor. Buy the links—
or the ready-to-slice roll that makes perfect patties.

SAUSAGE

JOHN MORRELL & CO. SINCE 1827
OTTUMWA, IOWA   SIOUX FALLS, S. D.

| Pork Beef Lamb Ham Bacon Sausage Canned Meats

There are abundant signs and codes in food advertisements,
which aim not only at selling products, but also at modelling
the consumer. John Morrell's 1950s advertisement for meats and
sausages is full of eye-catching, aggressive reds. The company
was founded in England in 1827, and became one of the largest
producers of processed meats in the USA.

This, however, does not automatically imply the manipulation or deception of consumers, as some critics believe. Consumers use food consumption for their own ends.

To discover when and why and which groups welcomed or rejected various food innovations in the post-war period is an ambitious research programme and hardly any actual investigation has been done in this field. Specific data, such as the thriving sugar consumption in Sweden in the 1960s, or the huge interest in *nouvelle cuisine* restaurants in the UK during the 1970s, imply much about preferences. The way that people perceived, described, reacted to and thus fashioned such changes is particularly interesting. This is complex, as the following examples show, with a stress on the socio-pysychological element. The historian Michael Wildt emphasized the desire of the West Germans to return to 'normality' as soon as possible after the war. Food played a central role in this longing, which involved a wish to re-connect Germany to the world. Hence the West German fascination for foods and tastes from around the globe. Whisky, for example, was extremely popular in the 1950s along with pineapples, cheese crackers and candy bars. Women's magazines published many articles about Chinese, French, Italian or Hungarian food (see below). For West Germans, normality has implied affluent and innovative eating since the 1950s.

This contrasts with the Italian diet during those years when Italy, too, was going through an economic miracle with strong growth rates. Many Italians, however, viewed affluent food with some distrust and even anxiety. New tastes, ingredients and foodways, often connected with Americanization, were countered by a (re-)invention of culinary traditions. The rising purchasing power could not wipe out the decades of food austerity that had been promoted by the Fascist regime since the 1920s. As a consequence, until the 1990s, Italians tended to eat familiar foods and not to experiment.

The way French housewives viewed their mothers' cooking skills also reveals attitudes about food innovations. Asked whether they cooked as their mothers did, 65 per cent replied 'no' in the 1960s, clearly expressing an aspiration to change the cuisine. When this question was asked again in the late 1990s, only 45 per cent said 'no', revealing a trend towards tradition (albeit a very recent one). The sociologist Jean-Pierre Poulain explains this as opposition to the housewife model in the 1960s, and as opposition to industrialization of the food chain in the 1990s. This leads us to the 'grand' changes.

It is of course impossible to tackle all of the recent grand changes in the food chain, but some key factors should be mentioned. One is productivity and its companion competitiveness. Because of ongoing mechanization and higher efficacy in agriculture, industry, services, trade and retailing, the output per employee and per hour has risen tremendously in the twentieth century. The Dutch wheat yield serves as an example. Wheat production rose from 2 tons per hectare around

1900 to 8.5 tons today, with particular growth in the 1960s (accompanied by immense ecological problems due to vastly increased fertilization). Today, Europe produces about 3,300 kilocalories per person and per day, taking all food together but excluding imports. Per capita requirements of Europe's ageing population may be estimated at about 2,100 kcal per day. As a result, Europe exports food (or destroys it), and the governments of the EU countries largely subsidize agriculture. Cheap Western food exports have the consequence of hindering the expansion of agriculture in Africa and Latin America.

Agricultural improvements have been introduced in many countries around the world and have caused ecological imbalance, changing landscapes and bitter competition with loss of income on the one hand, but generally increasing food intake, cultivation of new crops and growing trade on the other. The most far-reaching consequence has been the increasing food availability in terms of diversity and quantity. The Food and Agriculture Organization (FAO) estimates a growth of available kcal per person and per day, for example, at 60 per cent in Algeria and 48 per cent in China between 1970 and 2000. This must not make us forget, of course, the grave deterioration in the situation in some countries, particularly in Africa. The percentage of undernourished people in Central Africa increased from 30 in 1970, to 36 in 1985 and 55 per cent today.

The productivity rise led to falling prices, which eventually caused fundamental shifts within the food hierarchy. Up to the 1960s, the rise in productivity benefited mostly traditional foods, leading to standardized, cheaper staples that depressed markets. Plain household bread, for example, became much cheaper, and therefore lost its

Where old meets new: the traditional baguette produced in an industrial bakery in Reims, France, in 2005. In the 1990s, industrial bakeries all over the world started to produce more diverse and tasty products.

The ability to 'control the cold' led to intercontinental transport of frozen and chilled food, and to the installation of refrigerators and freezers in many kitchens. In the 1950s, fish and vegetables were frozen, and sold in the new supermarkets. In the 1990s, full meals were prepared, as on the assembly line shown here, and then frozen, ready for heating in a microwave oven.

traditional high status. Then, in the 1970s, other bakery items were produced in large, modern plants, such as the baguette, croissant or wholemeal bread. In the 1990s, more diversified production in smaller units offered an alternative to the bland taste of mass-produced bakery items, still at a relatively low price. But the effect of the rise in productivity was not limited to bread. It became more profitable to produce (and trade) meat, milk or deluxe fruits than to till the land for grain. The competitive logic of the system required more efficiency and productivity. The once very costly chicken that appeared on the table of the prosperous in the West, for example, made a festive (i.e. unusual) dinner for the masses in the 1950s, it became a Sunday dish in the 1960s and a daily food in the 1980s. At first consumers rejected the cheaper chicken because of its bland taste, and it was only after the re-introduction of traditional breeding techniques around 1960 (accompanied by marketing and public-relations campaigns) that the factory-chicken was accepted. Generally, the rises in productivity have influenced the price and status of virtually all food products. Nowadays, the price of food still matters, but less than it used to do. This is illustrated by the fact that today the average household in Western Europe spends merely 15 per cent of its total expenditure on food, as against 50 per cent or more before 1940.

Other productivity increases apart from agribusiness inputs have affected the food chain too. Suffice it to mention the transport revolution (e.g. airlifting), the instant-meal revolution (e.g. ready-made dishes to be heated in a microwave oven), and the cold revolution (e.g. refrigerators). Moreover, the growth in productivity (along with changes in the labour market, industrial relations and state interference) encouraged a rise in wages and profits. Generally, the purchasing power of wages rose between 1950 and 2000 as never before in history and, most crucially, for long periods it did not fall or stagnate, although the growth tapered off in the last part of the century. From about 1950 to 1985 there was a continuous, reassuring rise in purchasing power. Western Europe's real gross domestic product (GDP) per head rose by 4.1 per cent per year between 1950 and 1973 and by 1.8 per cent between 1973 and 2000 (Eastern Europe reached respectively 3.8 and 0.4 per cent). These global data hide of course local miracles and disasters. For example, French economists refer to the 'trente glorieuses' when alluding to the boom years 1946–73, while Russia's GDP shrank by almost 6 per cent per year between 1988 and 1998.

Claude Fischler claims that the food chain is caught in a permanent upgrading of quality and price (the latter in relative terms), because of the ever-rising productivity, falling prices, shifts among commodities, and the search for profit through the launch of new products. As a consequence, refined products tend to replace more simple ones. This turns luxury consumption very gradually into mass consumption. After 1945 a much larger proportion of the European population had the opportunity to participate in food and taste innovations. The wider access to once-luxury foods has induced some historians to label the post-1945 period as the era of democratization. I prefer to use the term 'commercialization', meaning consumers increasingly depended on market relations to obtain food. This is the second grand change that needs to be addressed.

Evidently, food production for the market is not new. With the spread of industrialization and urbanization throughout the world, a growing number of people visited markets and shops (instead of producing their own food, or bartering for it), but this consumption remained an essentially local phenomenon. Close contact between producer and consumer led to the furnishing of locally produced food, except for some expensive items that arrived from distant shores. It meant hardly any advertising, no marketing, little state control and almost no interference by scientists, dieticians or lobby groups. In the last quarter of the nineteenth century this started to change and the distance between producer and consumer grew, with more intermediaries and supra-regional actors appearing, leading in turn to an increasing choice of foods. In the twentieth century big food enterprises emerged. These organized production and distribution in a radically different way, using an innovative image as their trademark.

Danone is an example of this commercialization. Established in Barcelona in 1919, the firm produced a new product that was sold by local pharmacies: yoghurt. It was promoted as a traditional Bulgarian preparation assuring a long and healthy life. A modern factory opened in 1923, producing 1,000 pots per day for sale all over Spain. In 1928, the enterprise moved to Paris, where a modern plant was opened. Fruit and a sweetener were added to the yoghurt, which gave the healthy product an additional image of pleasure and delight. This was a clever move and sales increased among the better-off Parisian consumers. After the war the plant was modernized, producing up to 200,000 pots per day in 1960, and diversifying the product, ranging from 'velouté' in the 1960s to 'light' and 'bio' in the 1980s. This turned yoghurt into a mass consumer item that is eaten throughout the day. Obviously, the 'yoghurt chain' has become longer and more complex: before the consumer buys yoghurt, it has been conceived, produced, controlled, packaged, advertised, shipped, distributed, analysed, tested, recommended and criticised.

In 1993, Danone bought the former state-owned dairy manufacturer Serdica in Bulgaria and turned it into a highly modern unit, providing this market (after all, the cradle of yoghurt) with Danone products. This is an example of a third grand change of the post-1945 period, internationalization (or, as some would assert, globalization). International trade, investments and migration had developed long before 1940 but in the second half of the twentieth century there was an accelerating increase of trade, as well as an ever-growing number of migrants and travellers. The annual growth rate of world trade reached 3.4 per cent prior to the First World War, boosted to 7.9 per cent between 1950 and 1973, then slowed down to 4.3 per cent between 1973 and 1990, to reach a 6.9 per cent growth in the 1990s. Products from distant places appeared in markets all over the world.

Coca-Cola (now one of the biggest firms in the world) is an example of internationalization. During and immediately after the war, Coca-Cola travelled along with the US soldiers. In the USA this gave the drink a patriotic image and elsewhere Coca-Cola became a synonym for liberators and heroes. Plants were established all over the world, with some exceptions, such as China and the USSR. Sales boomed. Advertisements, marketing and promotional prices helped the introduction of the drink, but in most countries people, and especially the young, longed to buy a Coke. Yet opposition was fierce and appeared in different forms. In the 1950s, Communist parties in the West viewed Coca-Cola as the icon of capitalism, newspapers published alarming articles about the loss of European (drinking) culture, urban legends surfaced about impotence or teeth falling out and Ministers of Health warned against the health consequences of over-consumption. Nonetheless, the 'forbidden drink' became part of a youth or counter-culture in many countries. In the 1960s and 1970s, competition (with Pepsi-Cola, juices and other

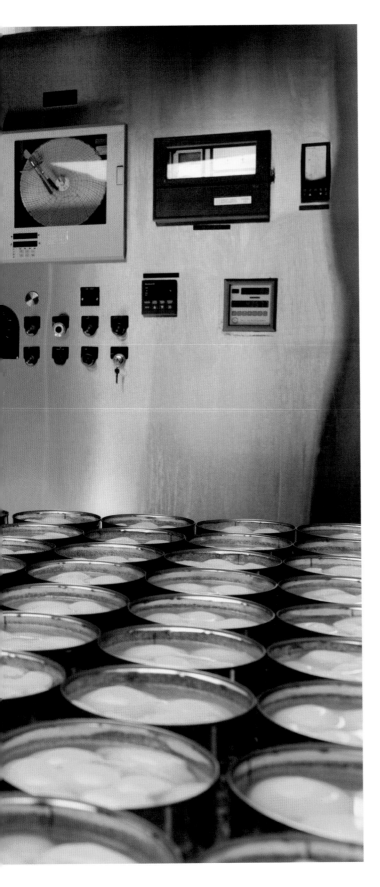

The preparation of fruit for yoghurt in 1998. This is hypermodern food processing where hygiene, efficiency, mass production, low cost and innovation are guiding principles. The addition of fruit to yoghurt in the 1930s proved to be a stroke of genius, changing the status of yoghurt from a medical product to one connected to delight and pleasure.

The advertisement "Coca-Cola goes along" was launched in 1939 and was used throughout the 1940s. 'See that every man in uniform gets a bottle of Coca-Cola for 5 cents wherever he is and whatever the cost to the company', was the credo of Robert W. Woodruff, president and brilliant PR man of the Coca-Cola company. He internationalized the drink 'that no one needed'.

soft drinks) became keener, which resulted in the launching of new types such as Diet Coke, Cherry Coke and, in 1985, New Coke (the latter fiasco now considered the marketing blunder of the century). After the fall of the Berlin Wall in 1989, Coca-Cola victoriously entered Central and Eastern Europe, the former Soviet republics and China. Still, the global, customary availability of Coke is recent. In the UK for example, soft drinks accounted for only 6.4 per cent of all drinks in 1970, whereas this share rose to 20 per cent in 1995. This 20 per cent represented 145 litres of soft drink per year and per person. In 2004, this quantity rose to 230 litres or an increase by almost 60 per cent compared to 1995.

Yet internationalization of the food chain, and of taste, was not only a matter of big international corporations such as Danone and Coca-Cola (or Nestlé, Macdonald's or Unilever). Migrants from Asia and Europe to the Americas, or from Africa and Asia to Europe, carried with them recipes, traditions and ingredients. Harvey Levenstein noted that initially in the USA most immigrants wished to adapt to an American style of food and often turned away from their own food (Italian migrants tended to be an exception). Immigrants to Europe behaved differently, by cherishing their traditional food-ways, possibly because of the more homogeneous societies in which they found themselves. With the massive migrations of the 1960s, 'ethnic' shops and markets appeared, to be followed by inexpensive restaurants that were aimed at the immigrant community. European-born diners soon visited these modest places, which had adapted food to local taste (for example, a reduced use of garlic or strong spices). In the Netherlands, the number of Chinese-Indonesian restaurants increased rapidly in the period around 1960. Cheapness, simplicity, take-away facilities and of course novelty were among the reasons for their success.

The attraction of 'ethnic' food and restaurants the world over is connected to the growth in international tourism beginning in the 1950s and the breakthrough of mass tourism around 1970. Americans discovered French cuisine on their tour of Europe in the 1950s, although they were not always enthusiastic (snails!). Western European tourists in the 1960s visited France, Italy, Greece or Spain, hoping to find their familiar cuisine with just a tiny exotic trait (steak with sauce provençale, frites). It was only in the 1970s that 'genuine' ethnic cuisine became more appreciated, finding its way into travel guides, magazines and recipe books. A study of exotic recipes in women's magazines in France and West Germany between 1930 and 1990 shows that Germany was more open to foreign recipes than France throughout the period (respectively 30 and 14 per cent of the total recipes). In particular, the study shows that interest in exotic dishes grew significantly in Germany around 1970 but in France only around 1980.

With the rise in productivity, commercialization and international-ization, many new tastes travelled around the world, arriving in particular in the prosperous West. Nowadays, kiwifruit, mango, lime, guava, lychee, papaya, passion fruit, pomegranate, dill, avocado, coriander, tarragon, cardamom, ginger, cinnamon, cumin, saffron, tequila, sake and many more spices, drinks, fruits and vegetables are routinely available in European shops. Of course, most of these had long been known in Europe, but although they were mentioned in the foreign section of most cookery books in the 1960s, they could be found only in ethnic shops or expensive delicatessens. Today, exotic fruits and vegetables are available throughout the year so that fresh strawberries (or for that matter papaya) can be bought at Christmas time for a reasonable price.

There are other grand changes that have contributed to forming new food attitudes, which can only be touched on here. For example, women's increased participation in the paid labour force, greater life expectancy, the shrinking average household size, the collapse of the Communist bloc and the rise in educational standards. Suffice it here to link the effects of productivity, commercialization and

When supermarkets were first introduced, they offered a totally new way of shopping with self-service, trolleys, check-out points, background music and the opportunity to buy in bulk. Now, supermarkets such as this Carrefour outlet at Corbeil-Essonnes in France are responding to changing tastes and a more discerning public, offering fresh fish, displayed here as in a traditional fish shop.

internationalization to people's daily lives, by looking at the composition of family expenditures.

Around 1890, the German statistician Ernst Engel posited a social 'law': the higher the family income, the lower the share spent on food. In France in 1950, for example, the share of food reached 42 per cent of the average total family expenditure, which was five to ten per cent less than the proportion prevailing in the first half of the twentieth century. Such an average was common in most West European countries in the 1950s. Fifty years later in France, this share had dropped to 14 per cent, with a rapid decrease between 1950 and 1975 (minus 19), a much slower fall from 1975 to 1990 (minus 4), and a slightly bigger decline from 1990 up to 2005 (minus 5). Overall, this decrease by almost 30 percentage points within fifty years opened the way to other consumer expenditures such as household appliances, transport or leisure. In the USA in 1988, the proportion of income spent on food reached 15 per cent, which slowly reduced to 13 per cent today. Tellingly, the highest income class in the USA now spends 11 per cent on food, whereas the lowest income group spends almost 18 per cent, a rise of 1.5 per cent compared to the 1990s and an indication of the widening gap in equality in the USA. Something similar occurred in Europe during the 1990s. In Western Europe, the food element of total spending decreased gradually in this period, but in Eastern Europe this share tended to fluctuate greatly but with a generally upward trend. In Romania, for example, the proportion rose from 49 per cent in 1990 to 52 in 1993 and 58 in 1996.

Equally big changes occurred in expenditure on particular foods. In Belgium, for example, meat was 22 per cent of the food budget of the average working-class family in the late 1920s, and this rose to 26 per cent in the late 1940s, to 31 per cent around 1960, and to 36 per cent in the early 1970s. Today, it represents less than 30 per cent of the food budget, mirroring the reduced status of meat, together with the recent increased consumption of fish in working-class households. Household bread (made of wheat) formed 12 per cent of the working-class budget in the 1920s, but only 10 per cent in the late 1940s, while other bakers' products did not amount to 1 per cent in the 1920s, but 4 per cent twenty years later. Today, household bread accounts for barely 3 per cent of working-class spending on food, with other grain products such as croissants and pastries taking a similar share. These changes reveal a process of substitution whereby 'higher-margin items' replace certain standard food products. Already in the early 1950s, a Belgian observer noted that working-class households bought pastries, croissants or currant bread, which only the bourgeoisie could afford before the war. Other examples of upgrading are the partial substitution of whole milk by yoghurt and cheese, the replacement of potatoes by crisps and other potato products (often frozen), or bottled water taking the place of tap water.

For centuries, people all over the world have tilled the land and raised animals to obtain their own food. Many still do. In some parts of Asia self-produced food forms up to 30 per cent of total food consumption, and this proportion is expanding slightly in Africa and Latin America, driven by declining incomes and increasing market prices. Yet in many so-called developing countries rapid urbanization is forcing a turn to 'ready-made' food, such as bread and pasta, giving greater emphasis to market exchange and less to own-grown and traditional foods. Nonetheless, even in some advanced market economies, such as France, the rate of self-production of some food items remains high: in 1990, one quarter of the total number of potatoes consumed was self-produced, just as in 1970. For selected items, such as poultry, self-production is now rising again.

Before the war and up to the 1960s fresh food was obtained at markets, with special sections (or days) for vegetables and fruits, fish and meat, and dairy products and poultry. Bread could be bought at the baker's, milk and dairy products at the creamery, and dry goods (coffee, spices, sugar and the like) at the grocer's. Shoppers were generally loyal to their retailers whom they trusted and from whom they could obtain credit. In some countries, consumer co-operatives and chain retailers had developed from the 1880s onwards, offering various food types within one store. Chain stores (with central distribution and multiple

The fall of a modern food icon: Ronald McDonald after an apple attack somewhere in France in the late 1990s. To many French (and Europeans), 'Macdo' is the symbol of bad eating (too fat, too sweet, too fast), and should be opposed (by Slow Food, the *terroir* and authenticity). In fact, all that McDonald's did was to make more efficient the production of long-existing snacks.

stores throughout a region or country) were particularly successful. Food was promoted by means of advertisements for specific brands, with simple messages.

In the 1960s, shopping was revolutionized; not only the form and organization of stores, but also the entire act of buying, incorporating the way food was perceived, presented and promoted. The emergence of national and international brands meant that advertisements acquired a global range and messages became more complex. For example, up to the early 1920s Coca-Cola promoted its drink by referring to good digestion, but increasingly, and after 1950 almost exclusively, by mentioning sociability and happiness. A 1948 advertisement depicted a smiling man holding a bottle of Coke, with the caption 'Hospitality in your hands'. Hidden persuaders (from the title of Vance Packard's influential 1958 book) became common in the 1960s, when advertisers not only wanted to announce products but also to create an image and a meaning for the product and, by extension, for the buyer. Shifts in food publicity reflect the changing significance and perception of food: from pure nourishment to hedonism (or self-fashioning), dieting and issues of status.

This overabundance of signals, some assert, has provoked a bio-cultural and social crisis. In the 1960s, social critics analysed advertisements to condemn the consumer society with its rapid innovations, standardization and multiplying of mass goods. For example, Theodor Adorno, Herbert Marcuse and Jean Baudrillard denounced the fabrication of false needs by the 'culture industry', the media and the non-stop stream of publicity. According to them, this fabrication was aimed at preventing critical thinking in order to integrate all social classes into the capitalist system. Beginning in the late 1950s and continuing to the present, these critics connected with, and influenced, students' movements that were antipathetic to mass consumption. Beatniks, hippies, punks and antiglobalists rejected the affluent consumer society for social, ecological and aesthetic reasons, often advocating food alternatives including raw, organic or meatless diets. They protested against genetically modified food and were highly critical of ready-made meals (sometimes referred to as 'plastic food'), in some countries going as far as attacking McDonald's fast-food outlets from the 1980s onwards.

The 1970s' political critique of developments in the food industry led direcctly to the establishment of the Slow Food movement in Italy in 1986. Today, Slow Food includes thousands of members in more than forty countries. The movement aims at opposing the 'global standardization of the world's food', by promoting diversity, authenticity and ecological gastronomy. Initially, left-wing young people provided the ideological basis, but soon larger groups were involved. Interestingly, in opposing the efficiency, internationalization and commercialization of the modern food industry (symbolized by McDonald's), this movement should be considered as innovative, not conservative, stimulating interest in local recipes, products, flavours and techniques. Nonetheless, the Slow Food movement has been criticised for its invention of tradition and authenticity, which historian Rachel Laudan sees as 'culinary Luddism'. She welcomes fast and processed food that provides a much safer diet than ever before. Fast-food stores now stress the quality and safety of their products.

Slow Food is just one of the latest critiques of consumer society. After the war consumers' organizations were set up that did not reject innovations concerning (food) consumption, but instead wished to monitor and guide the development of mass food production and distribution. These organizations had a normative, ethical basis. In the Netherlands, for example, the Consumers' Union aimed at maintaining the quality of food by carrying out comparative tests. The Union started with some hundreds of members in 1953, attained 25,000 members around 1960 and an astonishing 275,000 by 1970. By then, the Consumers' Union had become an effective lobby group that could influence producers, retailers, the government and international bodies. Similar organizations existed in many other countries.

In 1970, the American photorealist sculptor Duane Hansen created the *Supermarket Shopper* as a critique of consumer society. With the growth of the supermarket since the 1950s, the (full) trolley has spread all over the world. Other artists, as well as social critics, considered the trolley as an icon of mass consumption. Indeed, the supermarket represents the most radical change in the history of food purchasing. Its most decisive characteristics are mass sales and self-service; the aim was to lower costs by reducing the number of shop assistants and to increase sales by offering piles of mostly cheap goods. The consequence was that the organization and the outlook of the store changed totally. Diverse types of food were sold, foods were packaged (introducing standardized quantities and forms), brands predominated, the central check-out counter was installed, bargains were regularly offered, fluorescent tube lighting appeared, and shoppers were entertained with music and free tasting. Supermarkets introduced new fruits (kiwi, mango), frozen foods (pizza) and mass-produced ready meals (pasta, curries). All this changed the significance of food shopping: buying was represented, and often experienced, as entertainment.

In the late 1950s, the head of Belgium's first supermarkets believed that his stores would serve democracy by allowing all people to acquire all possible goods (and thus counter the appeal of Communism). Initially, however, shoppers would need to find their way to and within the new stores. This took about a decade, huge PR campaigns and education of the shoppers. In the late 1950s, for example, an advertisement explained the use of the trolley to Belgian customers. Looking at the sales figures of all forms of retail outlet in Belgium up to 1965, supermarkets had only modest success, but between 1965 and 1970 sales boomed, leaving other retailers' growth rates far behind. Britain had

Supermarkets turned into hypermarkets in the course of the 1980s: gigantic outlets, owned by multinationals, supplying an ever-increasing flow of food, often at discount prices. ASDA, started in the UK in 1965, was bought by Wal-Mart, the world's largest retailer, in 1999. The picture shows the innumerable row of check outs at the ASDA store in York, England in 2004.

taken the lead here: from 175 supermarkets in 1958 to 1,366 five years later was indeed an astonishing performance. By 1973, supermarkets had achieved the dominant position in Europe's food retailing, supplying both rural and urban dwellers with homogeneous food products.

The latest novelties, such as convenience foods (frozen and ready-made dishes), healthy food ('bio' and 'light') or exotic foods were available at the supermarket. Certainly, these products were sold elsewhere too, but not as generally as through supermarkets. Moreover, these stores introduced totally new techniques, such as scanning technology at the counter, which anticipates shoppers' habits by, for example, offering particular foods at specific moments during the day. Initially, a supermarket chain offered a uniform set of foods in each of its outlets, but since the 1980s a 'customization' of branches has appeared, taking into consideration the specific shopping habits of the neighbourhood. This is differentiating within massification.

Supermarkets introduced the so-called convenience foods on a large scale. These ready-made meals or parts of meals (vegetables and fish have been most successful) hardly need any preparation in the kitchen, particularly with the microwave oven, and they provide the store with a higher profit margin than it would achieve by selling the individual ingredients. Expansion was sensational. In France, for example, sales of frozen fish grew by no less than 53 per cent between 1969 and 1971, which may be linked to the spread of the refrigerator with built-in freezer and new handling techniques of freshly caught fish. In both cases, prices diminished in no time. This development towards convenience food was not in itself new, since canning and drying had been introduced much earlier (see Chapter 7). With frozen foods, however, the choice and taste of ready-made meals expanded. Moreover, new preparation and packaging techniques kept the ready-made meals fresh for a longer period. When some chefs traded their name and reputation in selling their ready-made meals through supermarkets, the scepticism about these dishes disappeared totally and success was spectacular. In 2000, for example, the Brussels chef Pierre Wynants (who had had three stars in the Michelin guide since the 1980s) started preparing meals for the supermarket chain Delhaize; it had sold 50,000 ready-made units in 1991 but was selling 8 million in 2004, of which some 2 million were signed by Wynants. As early as 1975, Paul Bocuse and Gaston Lenôtre had linked their names to Berlin's KaDeWe department store.

The ready-made meal in the supermarket, with the resulting elimination of food preparation, represents nearly the final step of the total commercialization of the food chain, with the elimination of food preparation; only the heating, the serving and the cleaning up remain. The single ready-made meal leads to the individualization of eating and, as some sociologists assert, to the end of the family meal with effects on the structure, timing and significance of daily meals. The final step of this process is the elimination of every activity by the diner except eating, which means the absolute dependence on the market for obtaining food. This includes the world of eating out, which illustrates one of the grand changes of the post-1945 period, the *total* commercialization of the food chain.

Most statistics about family expenditure on dining out indicate a significant increase all over the world. In Belgium for example, the average household (headed by a wage earner) spent less than one per cent of total expenditure on eating outside the home in the 1950s, which rose to 3 per cent in 1960, 4 per cent in the late 1970s and 5 per cent in the 1990s. Belgium held a modest place within Europe, though, where the 25 EU countries averaged 9 per cent in 2003. Spain took the lead with almost 20 per cent, followed immediately by Greece and Ireland where eating out boomed in the 1990s. In both countries, this increase contrasts with, and accompanies, the gradual reduction in the spending on food as a proportion of the total. This rising percentage spent on eating out represents immense and thriving amounts of capital and jobs, but hides a huge turnover of businesses. In the USA and the UK, however, the share spent on eating out of the total family expenditure remained stable between 1960 and today (6 and 3.5 per cent respectively). Nonetheless, also in both countries the share of eating out in total food spending doubled between the early 1960s and the mid-1990s. In short, since the Second World War people have become much more dependent on total commercialization for obtaining food.

Dining out, however, is not a new phenomenon and, moreover, it has many aspects. In Victorian London, for example, there were more than ten specialized forms of eating out in places other than the standard inns, cafés and restaurants, including peddlers of soup, fried fish, cakes and baked potatoes. In mid-nineteenth century Paris, some carpenters spent up to 30 per cent of their total budget on midday meals. This was probably an exception, however, that can be explained as a business expense. In the course of the twentieth century, and especially after 1945, more and different forms of eating out appeared. Snack bars, counters, delicatessens, inns, pubs, cafés and restaurants already existed, but they multiplied, specialized and expanded. Fast-food chains are probably the best example of this phenomenon. McDonald's worldwide development dates from the 1970s, an example of the total commercialization of the food chain, internationalization and increasing productivity and efficiency. In addition, the provision of meals for school students and cafeterias for people at work expanded greatly in many countries between 1950 and 1990. In the UK in 1995, spending on meals outside the home was divided as follows: 50 per cent in restaurants, 15 per cent in take-away restaurants, 22 per cent in snack bars and fast-food outlets, and 13 per cent in schools and business enterprises.

Dining away from the house has a venerable history linked traditionally to work (as illustrated by the Parisian carpenter). A crucial difference with the past, however, is that after 1945 eating out was given new significance by the general public, the media and the chefs. It became a social activity linked to pleasure. More people than ever before considered a meal out as a convivial, joyful occasion, which applied to teenagers in a McDonald's as well as to gourmets in Bocuse's sophisticated restaurant. Of course, both groups could have had myriad reasons for dining out. Overall, when asked in the late 1990s about their feelings concerning their most recent restaurant meal, 80 per cent of British respondents replied that 'they liked it a lot'. Looking at statistics in several countries, the big growth in restaurants started in the 1970s, with a decisive breakthrough in the 1990s. Single young urban professionals discovered the pleasures and meanings of the restaurant in the 1970s, whereas other groups, such as working-class families, followed in the 1990s. Culinary discourse attests to this general interest with the publication of hundreds of books, the making of popular television programmes with celebrity chefs and, recently, the outburst of food pages on the Internet. Yet detailed family expenditure broken down by income group, age, region or composition indicates large differences. In the USA in 2003, for example, a single male or female with the highest income spent $3,680 per year on outside food, whereas a family of four of the same income group spent $4,353 (or $1,140 per person), which represents respectively 62 and 50 per cent of all food expenditure.

The fact that millions of people all over the world zealously started to visit restaurants in the 1970s puzzled sociologists. In 1989, Joanne Finkelstein denounced the 'uncivilized sociality' of dining out because of its artificial atmosphere. With her claim that diners would search for personality and stylish identification but in fact would adhere only to false conventions, Finkelstein started what is still an ongoing debate among sociologists about the nature of (post)modern dining out. One explanation for its immense success (next to increasing purchasing power, social demarcation, a search for stimulation and the like) may be the search for what might be called food confidence. Restaurants are reviewed in food and travel guides, newspapers, magazines and on the Internet. This creates trust (and gurus), which people badly need in times of food scandals and genetically modifed foods if they wish to experience new foods. And since 1970, most of them did.

As we have seen, since 1945 the growth in productivity in agriculture and services has led to the upgrading of the diet, while commercialization and internationalization have meant the global availability of food and tastes. People spend a shrinking share of their total budget on food, they shop at supermarkets, and they rely increasingly on eating away from home and convenience food. But what does this mean in terms of the daily menu, people's eating preferences and changing food aesthetics?

Macro-economic data on food intake provide some answers. Based on British surveys of household food consumption, Christopher Ritson and Richard Hutchins proposed a general division of the post-war period. This includes war-time austerity and rationing in the 1940s, the return to pre-war diets in the 1950s, rapid changes driven by growing income in the 1960s, changes due to price instability in the 1970s, and, finally, a consumption revolution in the 1980s and 1990s. Altogether, this chronology seems to fit the West and, increasingly, many other countries in the world. I would place a revolution in the 1970s, though, because of the very drastic changes in this decade that outweigh any earlier or (so far) later change.

The intake of some food items per person in Britain illustrates this. Beef consumption, for example, rose gradually in the 1950s to overtake the pre-war level and peaked in the mid-1960s. The 1970s showed sharp oscillations, but a clear fall set in after 1979, and the average in the 1990s reached half the 1960 quantity. A similar picture emerges for mutton. Pork and bacon, on the contrary, show a gradual rise since the mid-1950s up to 1980, but then they join the declining consumption of other meats. This represents something of a poignant change. Meat was highly valued for a long time and it functioned as a clear marker of social boundaries. It kept this significance until the 1970s, and its fall since 1980 demonstrates a radical change for which the increase in the 1980s and 1990s of poultry and ground meat (for hamburgers, meatballs and the like) could not compensate. Neither could fresh fish: consumption fell constantly between 1960 and 2000. Considering the fact that meat (and to a lesser extent fish) made up the core of the traditional British diet, it appears that the typical meal was loosing its appeal.

Pertinent differences appear when data of beef consumption are considered according to class, age or region. French statistics show that between 1960 and 1990 all the social categories lowered their beef consumption, but employers and white-collar workers took the lead and farmers and blue-collar workers lagged behind. Changes occurred around the 'key year' 1980. Young people and people living in bigger cities lowered their beef consumption to a larger extent than elderly people and those living in the countryside. Undoubtedly, this was partly because younger people tend to be more interested in food novelties than older people who prefer familiar dishes, mealtimes and ingredients.

British average consumption of wheaten bread, potatoes, eggs, full-fat milk, oranges, sugar and butter diminished. In most cases, consumption had risen into the 1970s, but then a change occurred, with abrupt falls within a few years (for example, butter fell by 30 per cent between 1975 and 1979). Equally, the 1970s meant the sudden growth of consumption of juices, processed vegetables (including potatoes), frozen fish, cooked poultry, some fruits and wholemeal bread. The case of fresh fruit is telling: its consumption rose after 1945 to reach about 550 gm per person and per week in 1960. This remained stable up to 1978, but then rapid growth set in, which brought consumption to about 790 gm or 45 per cent more. Bananas, stone fruit and grapes became especially popular, whereas the consumption of apples declined.

Obviously, the 1970s were a crucial moment in the history of the British diet, when everything seemed to get into motion. All in all, energy intake from household food and drink diminished gradually from the 1980s, to reach 2,090 kcal per person per day in 2003. In that period it was estimated that the energy intake from food eaten out was slightly increasing (reaching roughly 210 kcal per person per day in 2003). This has resulted in a diminishing total energy intake since 1990.

'Fat Britain: Tackling the Obesity Epidemic' announced the *Daily Mail* in May 2004, emphasizing the distressing rise in British obesity figures of both children and adults. Similar alarms could be read in most European newspapers. Eating too much of the wrong types of food and not taking enough exercise were cited as the causes of the fact that 21 per cent of women and 17 per cent of men in Britain were reported to be clinically obese in 1998 (as against 8 and 6 per cent in 1980). The contradiction between these data and the declining energy intake may be explained by the fact that the quantity of food eaten away from the home is highly underestimated, and by sharp social and geographical differences (generally, overweight people are to be found among lower income groups). Governments launch campaigns, doctors warn against health problems, economists deplore the elevated daily cost and sociologists try to get hold of the cultural context. 'Fat people are more fun' read the message on a T-shirt of an overweight girl who clearly had not the slightest problem with her body. This was an American girl, and obesity used to be considered a particularly American problem. It is not anymore, and the number of obese people is rising all over the world (in 2004 about one third of adults in South Africa, Hong Kong or Morocco were considered overweight).

Most of the above refers to British data, and Britain is not representative for Europe. Comparing the UK to, for example, Italy reveals many differences. Both countries faced austerity after the war. Despite Italy's economic miracle in the late 1950s, the Italian diet remained caught in a combination of past traditions of frugality with food innovations (see above). This resulted in more-of-the-same well into the 1990s. Consumption of beef and pork, for instance, rose constantly between 1950 and 1990, with a marked increase for beef in the early 1960s and for pork in the late 1970s. Austerity was even mirrored in recipes up to 1970. Nonetheless, developments that have occurred in Britain appeared sooner or later, and to a lesser or greater extent, in other parts of Europe. From the 1950s, Coca-Cola, *nouvelle cuisine*, fast-food outlets and supermarkets gradually infiltrated almost every corner of Europe.

Social scientists have examined general consumption trends, wishing to discover different types of food preferences. Based on an international questionnaire about such preferences, Klaus Grunert et al., for example, classified types of food consumers in Denmark, France, Germany and the UK as: Uninvolved, Careless, Conservative, Rational, Adventurous, Hedonistic, Moderate and Eco-healthy. Each type has different interests, aims and thoughts. The Uninvolved, for instance, do not care about quality, freshness or preparation but are great fans of convenience food. The Conservative consumers distrust novelties but care about good quality, local ingredients and grandma's recipes. The Eco-healthy show great attention to health and organic food, without caring much about gastronomy or tradition. The Rational consider prices, nutritional information and cooking methods, but are not particularly adventurous. Apart from the fact that such information is crucial for those involved in marketing, I should emphasize that all the types within this scheme are sensitive to food innovations in one way or another (health and functional or pharma-food, convenient food, gourmet eating out, *terroir* food and so on). Moreover, these types seem to me anything but fixed, meaning that a Conservative consumer, for example, may become Careless or Adventurous during a special occasion (maybe easily accommodating to this new category). In addition, all categories show various amounts of distrust with regard to specific food innovations, for instance the Traditional vis-à-vis convenient food, or the Eco-healthy with regard to fast food. The classification, moreover, makes me wonder about the origin and the size of the categories. Surely, gourmets existed in the 1920s, just like health devotees or rational consumers. It is, however, difficult to assess the shift in importance of these categories, but they at least show that food consumers are still caught in the omnivore's paradox between novelty and tradition.

The latter has been emphasized in the research undertaken by the sociologist Alan Warde who has introduced an historical dimension into attempts to learn about present-day food trends. Based on food recommendations and recipes in British women's magazines in the late 1960s and early 1990s, he found 'four antinomies of taste': health and indulgence, economy and extravagance, convenience and care, and novelty and tradition. He argues that these antinomies 'comprise the structural anxieties of our epoch: they are parameters of uncertainty, apt to induce feelings of guilt and unease', thus joining with Fischler, Ulrich Beck and others. The pair novelty-tradition is of particular interest. Warde found, perhaps to his surprise, that the appeal to novelty has declined between the late 1960s and the early 1990s (from 43 to only 22 per cent of references). Conversely, the appeal of tradition had augmented (from 14 to 25 per cent). 'Tradition' referred to diverse forms, among which were familiarity, longevity and (most importantly) *authenticity*. Crucially, the content of what 'tradition' was, has altered. For example, the *real* Italian cuisine was much more present in the 1990s than previously, and the recipes mentioned the words authentic, traditional or genuine. This is an example of an 'invented tradition', which turns it into a novelty: the (re-invented) old becomes the new. Warde concludes that the curiosity for unfamiliar food was greater in the 1960s than in the 1990s (according to recommendations in women's magazines). He does not comment upon this finding very much, but I wish to stress this curiosity for novelties in the late 1960s, which preceded the great mutation of British food consumption in the 1970s.

Warde's interest is more with recent developments. Next to the concern with traditions, he stresses the curiosity for the new, albeit under the form of (or with gestures towards) the old. In short, messages about old and new are mixed, leaving the shopper, cook and diner with a measure of ambiguity and anxiety. From an historical point of view, however, it is doubtful whether people in Europe in the late 1960s were perfectly at ease with the many changes of their time, which clearly were as important, if not more, than changes after 1980. The accumulation of constant and rapid food changes prior to 1970 caused great anxiety indeed, to which social critics and critical consumers testified abundantly.

I have suggested that, in general, food and taste developments since 1945 could be divided into two periods, with the 1970s as the dividing decade. Up to the 1970s food consumption developed very much according to pre-1940 norms and aims, with rapid growth in the consumption of familiar products. The period 1945–75 could be labelled the 'meat years', in that meat consumption all over Europe reached very high levels. This mass consumption of familiar food was, however, accompanied by an explicit desire for novel food, unfamiliar ingredients, new flavours, unaccustomed dishes and culinary adventure. The immense interest in *nouvelle cuisine*, the exotic recipes in cookery books and the acceptance of ethnic restaurants during the 1960s and 1970s testify to this.

In the 1980s, a new food regime appeared that seemed to be the opposite of the previous one. Food and taste novelties were widely available. Supermarkets became loci of innovations, offering food and drink from all over the world and throughout the year. Very diverse restaurants appeared in virtually every European town. The oversupply of novelties, in practice and in discourses, seemed to have contributed to feelings of insecurity in the 1980s and 1990s, which in turn caused new interest in traditional foodways. The Slow Food movement, the interest in the authenticity of the *terroir* and the continuance of the timeless *haute cuisine* testify to this.

This is, inevitably, a broad sketch, and it is clear that neophilia existed in the 1950s just as neophobia persists at present. The two are present at all times. Without doubt, some people (and indeed whole groups and regions) would not recognize themselves in my survey. Perhaps my two food regimes, with the rupture in the 1970s, are entirely artificial. Yet it would be foolish to deny the mutations in our foodways since 1945. The 1970s were crucial in this process, with the sensational increase in purchasing power, the fast growth in world trade, the rapid breakthrough of supermarkets and the wide interest in exotic foods and places (so far unparalleled in history, so it seems). Those were also the years when criticism of how food is organized and consumed was radical, loud and effective. It made clear that food novelties may be unavoidable (in the shop), but they are not inevitable (in the home). Consumers may choose.

Food retailing is now an international operation. Western hypermarkets have moved into the immense Chinese market: after Carrefour and Wal-Mart, Tesco, the largest retailer in the UK, bought a stake in the Chinese Hymall chain of stores in 2004. The Happy Shopper store in Tianjin (the fourth metropolitan area of China, with over 10 million inhabitants) offers fresh frogs, grubs and turtles.

FURTHER READING

INTRODUCTION
A New History of Cuisine

Adrià, Ferran, *Los secretos de El Bulli: recetas, técnicas y reflexiones* (Madrid, 1997)

Albala, Ken, *Eating Right in the Renaissance* (Berkeley and London, 2002)

Belasco, Warren, 'Food matters: perspectives on an emerging field' in Warren Belasco and Philip Scranton (eds), *Food Nations: Selling Taste in Consumer Societies* (New York and London, 2002), pp. 2–23

Bourdain, Anthony, *Kitchen Confidential: Adventures in the Culinary Underbelly* (New York and London, 2000)

Chen, Patrizia, *Rosemary and Bitter Oranges: Growing Up in a Tuscan Kitchen* (New York and London, 2003)

Classic Russian Cooking: Elena Molokhovets' A Gift to Young Housewives, trans. Joyce Toomre (Bloomington, 1992). Reviewed by Tatyana Tolstaya in *New York Review of Books*, 21 October 1993, pp. 24–26

Davis, Mitchell, 'Power meal: Craig Claiborne's Last Supper for the *New York Times*', *Gastronomica*, 4:3 (2004), pp. 60–72

Franey, Pierre, *60-Minute Gourmet* (New York, 1979)

—, *More 60-Minute Gourmet* (New York, 1981)

Greico, Allen J., 'Food and social classes in Medieval and Renaissance Italy' in Jean-Louis Flandrin and Massimo Montanari (eds), *Food: A Culinary History from Antiquity to the Present* (New York, 1999), pp. 302–12

Hess, John L., and Karen Hess, *The Taste of America* (New York, 1977)

Kuh, Patric, *The Last Days of Haute Cuisine: The Coming of Age of American Restaurants* (New York, 2001)

The Jackson Cookbook (Jackson, Mississippi, 1971) with an introduction by Eudora Welty

Laurioux, Bruno, *Une histoire culinaire du Moyen Âge* (Paris, 2005)

Lubow, Arthur, 'The nueva nouvelle cuisine: how Spain became the new France', *New York Times*, 10 August 2003 (section 6), pp. 38–45, 55–57

Macfarlane, Alan, and Iris Macfarlane, *Green Gold: The Empire of Tea* (London, 2003)

Metcalfe, Gayden, and Charlotte Hays, *Being Dead is No Excuse: The Official Southern Ladies Guide to Hosting the Perfect Funeral* (New York, 2005)

Mintz, Sidney W., *Tasting Food, Tasting Freedom: Excursions into Eating, Culture, and the Past* (Boston, 1996)

Morton, Timothy, *The Poetics of Spice: Romantic Consumerism and the Exotic* (Cambridge, 2000)

Nestle, Marion, *Food Politics: How the Food Industry Influences Nutrition and Health* (Berkeley and London, 2002)

Pomés, Leopoldo, *Teoria i practica del pa amb tomàquet* (Barcelona, 1985)

Reichl, Ruth, *Comfort Me with Apples* (New York, 2001 and London, 2002)

Revel, Jean-François, *Culture and Cuisine: A Journey through the History of Food*, trans. Helen R. Lane (Garden City, New York, 1982)

Strong, Roy, *Feast: A History of Grand Eating* (London, 2002 and New York, 2003)

Trillin, Calvin, *American Fried: Adventures of a Happy Eater* (New York, 1979)

Zubok, Vladislav, and Constantine Pleshakov, *Inside the Kremlin's Cold War, from Stalin to Khrushchev* (Cambridge, Mass., 1996)

1 HUNTER-GATHERERS AND THE FIRST FARMERS
The Evolution of Taste in Prehistory

A thorough introduction to world prehistory can be found in:

Scarre, Christopher (ed.), *The Human Past: World Prehistory & the Development of Human Societies* (London, 2005)

An equally thorough introduction to archaeological method can be found in:

Renfrew, Colin, and Paul Bahn, *Archaeology: Theories, Methods and Practice*, 4th edn (London, 2004)

The following works provide a more detailed insight into some of the techniques used in reconstructing past diets:

David, Nicholas, and Carol Kramer, *Ethnoarchaeology in Action* (Cambridge, 2001)

Davis, Simon J. M., *The Archaeology of Animals* (London, 1987)

Dincauze, Dena F., *Environmental Archaeology: Principles and Practice* (Cambridge, 2000)

Wilkinson, Keith, and Christopher Stevens, *Environmental Archaeology: Approaches, Techniques and Applications* (Stroud, 2003)

About hunter-gatherer lifestyles:

Kelly, Robert L., *The Foraging Spectrum: Diversity in Hunter-Gatherer Lifeways* (Washington, DC, 1995)

Panter-Brick, Catherine, Robert H. Layton and Peter Rowley-Conwy (eds), *Hunter-Gatherers: An Interdisciplinary Perspective* (Cambridge, 2001)

An overview of the origins of farming:

Smith, Bruce D., *The Emergence of Agriculture* (New York, 1995)

Good collections of archaeological papers on food consumption:

Miracle, Preston, and Nicky Milner (eds), *Consuming Passions and Patterns of Consumption* (Cambridge, 2002)

Pearson, Michael Parker (ed.), *Food, Culture and Identity in the Neolithic and Early Bronze Age* (Oxford, 2003)

Works referred to in the text:

Atkins, Robert C., *Dr Atkins' New Diet Revolution* (New York, 1992)

Brain, C. K., *The Hunters or the Hunted* (Chicago, 1981)

Lewis, Meriwether, and William Clark, *The Journals of Lewis and Clark*, abridged with an introduction by Anthony Brandt and an afterword by Herman J. Viola (Washington, DC, 2002)

Marcy, Randolph B., *The Prairie Traveler* (Bedford, Mass., 1993; originally published 1859)

2 THE GOOD THINGS THAT LAY AT HAND
Tastes of Ancient Greece and Rome

Bober, Phyllis Pray, *Art, Culture, and Cuisine: Ancient and Medieval Gastronomy* (Chicago, 1999)

Brothwell, Don, and Patricia Brothwell, *Food in Antiquity: A Survey of the Diet of Early Peoples* (Baltimore, 1998)

Curtis, Robert I., *Ancient Food Technology* (Leiden, 2001)

—, *Garum and Salsamenta: Production and Commerce in Materia Medica* (Leiden, 1991)

Dalby, Andrew, *Siren Feasts: A History of Food and Gastronomy in Greece* (London, 1996)

Dalby, Andrew, and Sally Grainger, *The Classical Cookbook* (London, 1996)

D'Arms, J., 'Control, companionship and clientela: some social functions of the Roman communal meal', *Echos du Monde Classique / Classical Views*, 3 (1984), pp. 327–48

Davies, R. W., 'The Roman military diet', *Britannia*, 2 (1971), pp. 122–42

Flandrin, Jean-Louis, and Massimo Montanari (eds), *Food: A Culinary History* (New York, 1999)

Frayn, Joan, 'Home-baking in Roman Italy', *Antiquity*, 52 (1978), pp. 28–33

—, 'Wild and Cultivated Plants: A Note on the Peasant Economy of Roman Italy', *Journal of Roman Studies*, 65 (1975), pp. 32–39

Frost, Frank, 'Sausage and meat preservation in Antiquity', *Greek, Roman and Byzantine Studies*, 40 (1999), pp. 241–52

Garnsey, Peter, *Famine and Food Supply in the Graeco-Roman World* (Cambridge, 1988)

—, *Food and Society in Classical Antiquity* (Cambridge, 1999)

Gowers, Emily, *The Loaded Table: Representations of Food in Roman Literature* (Oxford, 1993)

Grimm, Veronika E., *From Feasting to Fasting: The Evolution of a Sin* (London, 1996)

Harcum, C. G., 'Roman cooking utensils in the Royal Ontario Museum of Archaeology', *American Journal of Archaeology*, 25 (1921), pp. 37–54

Katz, S. H., and M. M. Voigt, 'Bread and beer: the early use of cereals in the human diet', *Expedition*, 28 (1986), pp. 23–34

King, Anthony, 'Diet in the Roman World: a regional inter-site comparison of the mammal-bones', *Journal of Roman Archaeology*, 12 (1999), pp. 168–202

Meggitt, J. J., 'Meat consumption and social conflict in Corinth', *Journal of Theological Studies*, 45 (1994), pp. 137–41

Murray, Oswyn (ed.), *Sympotica* (Oxford, 1990)

Purcell, N., 'Wine and Wealth in Ancient Italy', *Journal of Roman Studies*, 75 (1985), pp. 1–19

Serjeantson, D. and T. Waldron, 'Diet and crafts in towns: the evidence of animal remains from the Roman to the post-Medieval periods', *British Archaeological Reports*, British Series, 199 (1989)

Sirks, Boudewijn, *Food for Rome* (Amsterdam, 1991)

Whitehouse, D., G. Barker, R. Reece and D. Reese, 'The Schola Praeconum I: the coins, pottery, lamps and fauna', *Papers of the British School at Rome*, 50 (1982), pp. 53–101

Wilkins, John, David Harvey and Mike Dobson (eds), *Food in Antiquity* (Exeter, 1995)

Younger, William A., *Gods, Men and Wine* (London, 1966)

Primary sources:

Apicius, *The Roman Cookery Book,* trans. Barbara Flower and Elisabeth Rosenbaum (London, 1958)

Athenaeus, *Deipnosophistae,* trans C. B. Gullick, Loeb Classical Library, 7 vols (Cambridge, Mass., 1927–41, 1971)

Galen, *On Food and Diet,* trans. and notes by Mark Grant (London and New York, 2001)

Homer, *The Iliad,* trans. Robert Fagles (New York 1990)

—, *The Odyssey,* trans. Robert Fagles (New York 1996)

Oribasius, *Dieting for an Emperor,* a translation of Books 1 and 4 of Oribasius' *Medical Compilations* with an introduction and commentary by Mark Grant

The Poughman's Lunch (Moretum), a poem ascribed to Virgil, trans. and edited by E. J. Kenney (Bristol, 1984)

3 THE QUEST FOR PERFECT BALANCE
Taste and Gastronomy in Imperial China

Anderson, E. N., *The Food of China* (New Haven and London, 1988)

Blanchon, Flora (ed.), *Asie III: Savourer, Goûter* (Paris, 1995), pp. 9–26

Buell, Paul D., and Eugene N. Anderson, *A Soup for the Qan: Chinese Dietary Medicine of the Mongol Era as Seen in Hu Szu-hui's Yin-shan Cheng-yao* (London and New York, 2000)

Chang, K. C. (ed.), *Food in Chinese Culture: Anthropological and Historical Perspectives* (New Haven and London, 1977)

Clunas, Craig, *Superfluous Things: Material Culture and Social Status in Early Modern China* (Cambridge, 1991)

Gao Lian, *Yin Zhuan Fu Shi Jian* (Discourse on Food and Drink), 1591; reprint edited by Tao Wentai (Beijing, 1985)

Gernet, Jacques, *Daily Life in China on the Eve of the Mongol Invasion 1250–1276* (Stanford and London, 1962; originally published Paris, 1959)

Ho Chui-mei, 'Food for an 18th-century Emperor: Qianlong and his entourage', *Life in the Imperial Court of Qing Dynasty China. Proceedings of the Denver Museum of Natural History,* Series 3, no. 15 (1 November 1998), pp. 75–83

Lai, T. C., *Chinese Food for Thought* (Hong Kong, 1978)

Li Dou, *Yangzhou Huafang Lu* (Record of the Painted Pleasure-Boats of Yangzhou) 1795 (reprint, Jiangsu Guangling Guji, 1984)

Newman, Jacqueline M., *Food Culture in China* (Westport, CT, and London, 2004)

Ryor, Kathleen M., 'Fleshly desires and bodily deprivations: the somatic dimensions of Xu Wei's flower paintings' in Wu Hung and Katherine R. Tsiang (eds), *Body and Face in Chinese Visual Culture* (Cambridge, Mass., 2005), pp. 121–45

So, Yan-kit, *Classic Food of China* (London, 1992)

Sterckx, Roel (ed.), *Of Tripod and Palate: Food Politics, and Religion in Traditional China* (Basingstoke and New York, 2005)

Waley, Arthur, *Yuan Mei, Eighteenth Century Chinese Poet* (London, 1956)

Wilkinson, Endymion, *Chinese History: A Manual* (Cambridge, Mass., 2000)

Xu Wei, *Xu Wei Ji* (Works of Xu Wei), 4 vols (Beijing, 1983)

Yuan Mei, *Suiyuan Shidan* (Beijing, 1984)

Zhang Dai, 'Tao'an Meng Yi', n.d., in *Zhongguo Wenxue Zhenben Congshu,* 23 (Taibei, 1936)

4 THE PLEASURES OF CONSUMPTION
The Birth of Medieval Islamic Cuisine

An Anonymous Andalusian Cookbook of the Thirteenth Century trans. Charles Perry at website http://www.daviddfriedman.com/Medieval/ Cookbooks/Andalusian

Al-Baghdadi, Ibn al-Khatib, *Wasf al-At'ima al-Mu'tada,* 'Description of the familiar foods', trans. Charles Perry in *Medieval Arab Cookery: Essays and Translations* (Totnes, 2001)

Arberry, A. J., 'A Baghdad cookery book', *Islamic Culture,* 13:1 (January 1939), pp. 21–47

—, 'A Baghdad cookery book', *Islamic Culture,* 13:2 (April 1939), pp. 189–214

Eigeland, Tor, 'The Cuisine of al-Andalus', *Aramco World,* 40 (September–October 1989), pp. 28–35

Gelder, G. J. H. van, *God's Banquet: Food in Classical Arabic Literature* (New York, 2000)

Marin, Manuela, 'Beyond taste: the compliments of color and smell in the Medieval arab culinary tradition', in Sami Zubaida and Richard Tapper (eds), *Culinary Cultures of the Middle East* (London, 1994)

Miranda, Ambrosio Huici, *Traduccion española de un manuscrito anónimo del siglo XIII sobre la cocina hispano-magribi* (Madrid, 1966)

Nasrallah, Nawal, *Delights from the Garden of Eden: A Cookbook and History of Iraqi Cuisine* (Bloomington, 2003)

Perry, Charles, 'Elements of Arab feasting' in *Medieval Arab Cookery,* op. cit.

—, 'Medieval Arab fish: fresh, dried, and dyed' in *Medieval Arab Cookery,* op. cit.

—, 'The *Sals* of the Infidels' in *Medieval Arab Cookery,* op. cit.

—, 'What to order in ninth century Baghdad' in *Medieval Arab Cookery,* op. cit.

Roden, Claudia, 'Middle Eastern cooking: the legacy', *Aramco World,* 39:2 (March–April 1988), pp. 2–3

Rodinson, Maxime, 'Studies in Arabic manuscripts related to cooking', trans. Barbara Inskip in *Medieval Arab Cookery,* op. cit.

—, 'Venice, the spice trade and eastern influences in European cooking', trans. Paul James in *Medieval Arab Cookery,* op. cit.

Rosenberger, Bernard, 'Arab cuisine and its contribution to European culture' in Flandrin and Montanari (eds), *Food: A Culinary History from Antiquity to the Present* (New York, 1999)

Waines, David, *In a Caliph's Kitchen* (London, 1989)

Wright, Clifford, *A Mediterranean Feast* (New York, 1999)

5 FEASTING AND FASTING
Food and Taste in Europe in the Middle Ages

Adamson, Melitta Weiss (ed.), *Regional Cuisines of Medieval Europe: A Book of Essays* (New York and London, 2002)

Aebischer, P., 'Un manuscrit valaisan de Viandier attribué a Taillevent', *Vallesia,* 8 (1953), pp. 73–100

Albala, Ken, *Eating Right in the Renaissance* (Berkeley and London, 2002)

Beaune, H., and J. d'Arbaumont (eds), *Mémoires d'Olivier de la Marche,* 4 vols (Paris, 1883–88)

Carlin, Martha, and Joel T. Rosenthal (eds), *Food and Eating in Medieval Europe* (London, 1998)

Cavaciocchi, S. (ed.), *Alimentazione e nutrizione secc. XIII–XVIII: atti della 'Ventottesima settimana di studi' 22–27 aprile 1996* (Prato, 1997)

Effros, Bonnie, *Creating Community with Food and Drink in Merovingian Gaul* (Basingstoke and New York, 2002)

Henisch, Bridget Ann, *Fast and Feast: Food in Medieval Society* (University Park, PA, and London, 1976)

Hieatt, C. B., and S. Butler (eds), *Curye on Inglysch: English Culinary Manuscripts of the Fourteenth Century (Including the Forme of Cury),* Early English Text Society, Supplementary Series, 8 (1985)

Lambert, C. (ed.), *Du Manuscrit à la table: essais sur la cuisine au Moyen Âge et répertoire des manuscrits médiévaux contenant des recettes culinaires* (Montreal, 1992)

Laurioux, Bruno, *Le Règne de Taillevent: livres et pratiques culinaires à la fin du Moyen Âge* (Paris, 1997)

—, *Manger au Moyen Âge: pratiques et discours alimentaires en Europe aux XIVe et XVe siècles* (Paris, 2002)

Menjot, D. (ed.), *Manger et boire au Moyen Âge,* 2 vols (Nice, 1984)

Mennell, Stephen, *All Manners of Food: Eating and Taste in England and France from the Middle Ages to the Present* (Oxford, 1985)

[Rey-Delqué, M. (ed.)], *Plaisirs et manières de table aux XIVe et XVe siècles* (Toulouse, 1992)

Scully, Terence, *The Art of Cookery in the Middle Ages* (Woodbridge, 1995)

—, 'Du fait de cuisine par Maistre Chiquart 1420', *Vallesia,* 40 (1985), pp. 101–231

Stouff, L., *Ravitaillement et alimentation en Provence aux XIVe et XVe siècles* (Paris, 1970)

Woolgar, C. M., D. Serjeantson, and T. Waldron (eds), *Food in Medieval England: Diet and Nutrition* (Oxford and New York, 2006)

6 NEW WORLDS, NEW TASTES
Food Fashions after the Renaissance

Albala, Ken, *Eating Right in the Renaissance* (Berkeley and London, 2002)

Bryson, Anna, *From Courtesy to Civility: Changing Codes of Conduct in Early Modern England* (Oxford, 1998)

Camporesi, Piero, *Bread of Dreams: Food and Fantasy in Early Modern Europe,* trans. David Gentilcore (Cambridge and Chicago, 1989; originally published 1980)

—, *Exotic Brew: The Art of Living in the Age of Enlightenment* (Cambridge, 1994; originally published 1990)

Coe, Sophie D., and Michael D. Coe, *The True History of Chocolate* (London, 1996)

Cowan, Brian, *The Social Life of Coffee: The Emergence of the British Coffeehouse* (New Haven and London, 2005)

Elias, Norbert, *The Civilizing Process, vol. 1, The History of Manners*, trans. Edmund Jephcott (Oxford and New York, 1978; originally published 1939)

Elliott, J. H., *The Old World and the New* (Cambridge, 1970)

Ferguson, Priscilla Parkhurst, *Accounting for Taste: The Triumph of French Cuisine* (Chicago, 2004)

Flandrin, Jean-Louis, 'La Diversité des goûts et des pratiques alimentaires en Europe du XVIe au XVIIIe siècle', *Revue d'Histoire Moderne et Contemporaine*, 30 (1983), pp. 66–83

Flandrin, Jean-Louis, and Massimo Montanari (eds), *Food: A Culinary History from Antiquity to the Present* (New York, 1999)

Girard, Alain, 'Le Triomphe de "La Cuisinière bourgeoise": livres culinaires, cuisine et société en France aux XVIIe et XVIIIe siècle', *Revue d'Histoire Moderne et Contemporaine*, 24 (1977), pp. 497–522

Guerzoni, Guido, 'The courts of Este in the first half of the XVIth century', *La Cour Comme Institution Economique* (Paris, 1998)

Heal, Felicity, *Hospitality in Early Modern England* (Oxford, 1990)

Isaac, Rhys, *The Transformation of Virginia: 1740–1790* (New York, 1988; originally published 1982)

Martino, Maestro, *The Art of Cooking: The First Modern Cookery Book*, edited with an introduction by Luigi Ballerini, trans. Jeremy Parzen (Berkeley and London, 2004)

Mennell, Stephen, *All Manners of Food: Eating and Taste in England and France from the Middle Ages to the Present*, 2nd edn (Urbana, Ill., 1995)

Mintz, Sidney W., *Sweetness and Power: The Place of Sugar in Modern History* (New York and London, 1985)

Montanari, Massimo, *The Culture of Food*, trans. Carl Ipsen (Oxford, 1994; originally published 1988)

Norton, Marcy, 'A New World of Goods: A History of Tobacco and Chocolate in the Spanish Empire, 1492–1700 (Ph.D. dissertation, University of California at Berkeley, 2000)

Peterson, T. Sarah, *Acquired Taste: The French Origins of Modern Cooking* (Ithaca, NY and London, 1994)

Platina, *On Right Pleasure and Good Health*, trans. and edited by Mary Milham (Tempe, AZ, 1998)

Smuts, R. Malcolm (ed.), *The Stuart Court and Europe* (Cambridge, 1996)

Stavely, Keith, and Kathleen Fitzgerald, *America's Founding Food: The Story of New England Cooking* (Chapel Hill, NC, 2004)

Wheaton, Barbara Ketcham, *Savoring the Past: The French Kitchen and Table from 1300 to 1789* (New York, 1996; originally published 1983)

7 THE BIRTH OF THE MODERN CONSUMER AGE
Food Innovations from 1800

Alimentarium Vevey, Musée de l'alimentation, une fondation Nestlé (ed.), *Objektgeschichten – Histoires d'Objects* (Vevey, 1995)

Andritzky, M. (ed.), *Oikos. Von der Feuerstelle zur Mikrowelle. Haushalt und Wohnen im Wandel, Katalogbuch zu einer Gemeinschaftsausstellung des Deutschen Werkbundes Baden-Württemberg des Design Center Stuttgart und des Museums für Gestaltung Zürich* (Gießen, 1992)

Andritzky, M., and T. Hauer (eds), *Das Geheimnis des Geschmacks. Aspekte der Ess- und Lebenskunst* (Frankfurt, 2005)

Barlösius, E., *Soziologie des Essens* (Munich, 1999)

Ellerbrock, K.-P., *Geschichte der deutschen Nahrungs- und Genußmittelindustrie, 1750–1914* (Stuttgart, 1993)

Fenton, A. (ed.), *Order and Disorder: The Health Implications of Eating and Drinking in the Nineteenth and Twentieth Centuries* (East Linton, Scotland, 2000)

Fenton, A., and Eszter Kisbán (eds), *Food in Change: Eating Habits from the Middle Ages to the Present Day* (Edinburgh, 1986)

Gollmer, R. (ed.), *Die vornehme Gastlichkeit der Neuzeit. Ein Handbuch der modernen Geselligkeit, Tafeldekoration und Kücheneinrichtung* (Leipzig, 1909)

Hartog, A. P. den (ed.), *Food Technology, Science and Marketing: European Diet in the Twentieth Century* (East Linton, Scotland, 1995)

Heckmann, H., *Die Freud des Essens. Ein kulturgeschichtliches Lesebuch vom Genuß der Speisen – aber auch vom Leid des Hungers* (Munich, 1979)

Heischkel-Artelt, E. (ed.), *Ernährung und Ernährungslehre des 19 Jahrhunderts* (Göttingen, 1979)

Hengartner, T., and C. M. Merki (eds), *Genußmittel. Ein kulturgeschichtliches Handbuch* (Frankfurt and New York, 1999)

Hietala, M., and T. Vahtikari (eds), *The Landscape of Food: The Food Relationship of Town and Country in Modern Times* (Helsinki, 2003)

Jacobs, Marc, and Peter Scholliers (eds), *Eating Out in Europe: Picnics, Gourmet Dining and Snacks since the Late Eighteenth Century* (Oxford, 2003)

Lesniczak, P., *Alte Landschaftsküchen im Sog der Modernisierung. Studien zu einer Ernährungsgeographie Deutschlands zwischen 1860 und 1930* (Stuttgart, 2003)

Oddy, Derek J., and Lydia Petránová (eds), *The Diffusion of Food Culture in Europe from the Late Eighteenth Century to the Present Day* (Prague, 2005)

Sandgruber, R., *Konsumverbrauch, Lebensstandard und Alltagskultur in Österreich im 18 und 19 Jahrhundert* (Munich, 1982)

Schärer, M., and A. Fenton (eds), *Food and Material Culture* (East Linton, Scotland, 1998)

Schlegel-Matthies, K., *'Im Haus und am Herd'. Der Wandel des Hausfrauenbildes und der Hausarbeit, 1880–1930* (Stuttgart, 1995)

Teuteberg, H. J., 'The General Relationship between Diet and Industrialization' in E. and R. Forster (eds), *European Diet from Pre-industrial to Modern Times* (New York and London, 1975), pp. 60–109

—, 'The Beginnings of the Modern Milk Age in Germany' in A. Fenton and T. Owen (eds), *Food in Perspective* (Edinburgh, 1981), pp. 283–311

—, 'From famine to nouvelle cuisine: change of diet as result of industrialization and urbanization' in W. Blockmans and P. Clark (eds), *The Roots of Western Civilization* (Danbury, CT, 1994), vol. 1, pp. 81–92

—, 'Old Festive Meals of German Country Folk: The Intensification of Urban Influences, c.1880–1930' in P. Lysaght (ed.), *Food and Celebration: From Fasting to Feasting* (Ljubljana, 2002), pp. 169–177

— (ed.), *European Food History: A Research Review* (Leicester and New York, 1992)

— (ed.), *Die Revolution am Esstisch. Neue Studien zur Nahrungskultur im 19/20 Jahrhundert* (Stuttgart, 2004)

Teuteberg, H. J., and G. Wiegelmann, *Unsere tägliche Kost. Geschichte und regionale Prägung* (Stuttgart, 1986)

—, *Der Wandel der Nahrungsgewohnheiten unter dem Einfluß der Industrialisierung* (Göttingen, 1972; 2nd edn, Münster, 2005)

Wiegelmann, G., *Alltags- und Festtagsspeisen. Wandel und gegenwärtiger Stellung* (Marburg, 1967)

Zischka, U., H. Ottomeyer and S. Bäumler (eds), *Die anständige Lust. Von Eßkultur und Tafelsitten* (Munich, 1993)

8 CHEFS, GOURMETS AND GOURMANDS
French Cuisine in the 19th and 20th Centuries

Aron, Jean-Paul, *The Art of Eating in France: Manners and Menus in the Nineteenth Century*, trans. Nina Rootes (London and New York, 1975; originally published 1973)

Beaugé, Bénédict, *Aventures de la cuisine française. Cinquante ans d'histoire du goût* (Paris, 1999)

Berchoux, Joseph de, *La Gastronomie ou l'homme des champs à table* (Paris, 1803; originally published 1800)

Brillat-Savarin, Jean Anthelme, *La Physiologie du goût* (Paris, 1826)

Carême, Marie-Antonin, *L'Art de la cuisine française au XIXe siècle* (Paris, 1833)

—, *French Cookery* (London, 1836)

Chatillon-Plessis, *La Vie à table à la fin du XIXe siècle. Théorie pratique et historique de gastronomie moderne* (Paris, 1894)

Courtine, Robert J., *Le Nouveau savoir-manger* (Paris, 1960)

—, *La gastronomie* (Paris, 1970)

Curnonsky, *Souvenirs littéraires et gastronomiques* (Paris, 1958)

Curnonsky and Pierre Andrieu, *Les Fines gueules de France: Gastronomes, gourmets, grands chefs, grands Cordons-bleus, grands relais* (Paris, 1935)

Curnonsky and Marcel Rouff, *La France gastronomique. Guide des merveilles culinaires et des bonnes auberges françaises* (Paris, 1921–28)

Dubois, Urbain, *La Nouvelle Cuisine bourgeoise* (Paris, 1888)

Escoffier, Auguste, *A Guide to Modern Cookery* (London, 1907; originally published as *Guide culinaire*, Paris, 1902–7)

Grimod de La Reynière, A.-B.-L., *Almanach des gourmands servant de guide dans les moyens de faire excellente chère*, 8 vols (Paris, 1803–12)

—, *Manuel des amphitryons* (Paris, 1808)

Guérard, Michel, *La Grande Cuisine minceur* (Paris, 1976)

Guillot, André, *La Grande Cuisine bourgeoise* (Paris, 1976)

Mesplède, Jean-François, *Trois étoiles au Michelin* (Paris, 1998)

Nignon, Edouard, *Eloges de la cuisine française* (Paris, 1992)

Pitte, Jean-Robert, *French Gastronomy: The History and Geography of a Passion*, trans. Jody Gladding (New York, 2002; originally published 1991)

9 DINING OUT
The Development of the Restaurant

Aron, Jean-Paul, *The Art of Eating in France: Manners and Menus in the Nineteenth Century*, trans. Nina Rootes (London and New York, 1975; originally published 1973)

Bercovici, Konrad, *Around the World in New York* (New York and London, 1924)

[Blagdon, F. W.], *Paris As It Was and As It Is* (London, 1803)

Bradford, Ned, and Pam Bradford, *Boston's Locke-Ober Café: An Illustrated Social History with Miscellaneous Recipes* (New York, 1978)

Brillat-Savarin, Jean Anthelme, *The Physiology of Taste: or, Meditations on Transcendental Gastronomy*, trans. M. F. K. Fisher (New York, 1949)

Courtine, Robert J., *La Vie parisienne* (Paris, 1984–)

Frischauer, Willi, *The Grand Hotels of Europe* (New York and London, 1965)

Deghy, Guy, and Keith Waterhouse, *Café Royal: Ninety Years of Bohemia* (London, 1955)

Grimod de La Reynière, A.-B.-L., *Almanach des gourmands, servant de guide dans les moyens de faire excellente chère*, 8 vols (Paris, 1803–1812)

Hogan, David Gerard, *Selling 'em by the Sack: White Castle and the Creation of American Food* (New York, 1997)

Hungerford, Edward, *The Story of Louis Sherry and the Business he Built* (New York, 1929)

Jacobs, Marc, and Peter Scholliers (eds), *Eating Out in Europe: Picnics, Gourmet Dining and Snacks since the Late Eighteenth Century* (Oxford, 2003)

[Jarves, James Jackson], *Parisian Sights and French Principles Seen through American Spectacles* (New York, 1852)

Kuh, Patric, *The Last Days of Haute Cuisine: The Coming of Age of American Restaurants* (New York, 2001)

Mennell, Stephen, *All Manners of Food: Eating and Taste in England and France from the Middle Ages to the Present* (Oxford and New York, 1985)

Newnham-Davis, Lieutenant Colonel Nathaniel, *The Gourmet's Guide to London* (London and New York, 1914)

Newnham-Davis, Lieutenant Colonel Nathaniel (ed.) and Algernon Bastard, *The Gourmet's Guide to Europe* (London, 1903)

Pitte, Jean-Robert, *French Gastronomy: The History and Geography of a Passion*, trans. Jody Gladding (New York, 2002; originally published 1991)

Ranhofer, Charles, *The Epicurean: a complete treatise of analytical and practical studies on the culinary art, including table and wine service, how to prepare and cook dishes... etc., and a selection of interesting bills of fare of Delmonico's from 1862 to 1894. Making a Franco-American culinary encyclopedia* (New York, 1894)

Revel, Jean-François, *Culture and Cuisine: A Journey through the History of Food*, trans. Helen R. Lane (Garden City, New York, 1982)

Ritz, Marie Louise, *César Ritz: Host to the World* (Philadelphia, New York and London, 1938)

Schriftgiesser, Karl, *Oscar of the Waldorf* (New York, 1943)

Seitz, Erwin (ed.), *Cotta's Culinarischer Almanach*, no. 12 (Stuttgart, 2004)

Spang, Rebecca L., *The Invention of the Restaurant: Paris and Modern Gastronomic Culture* (Cambridge, Mass., 2000)

Spencer, Colin, *British Food: An Extraordinary Thousand Years of History* (London, 2002)

Street, Julian, *Where Paris Dines: with information about restaurants of all kinds, costly and cheap, dignified and gay, known and little known; and how to enjoy them together with a discussion of French wines, and a table of vintages, by a distinguished amateur* (London and Garden City, New York, 1929)

Strong, Roy, *Feast: A History of Grand Eating* (London, 2002 and New York, 2003)

Symons, Michael, *A History of Cooks and Cooking* (Urbana, Ill., 2000 and Totnes, 2001)

Thomas, Lately, *Delmonico's: A Century of Splendor* (Boston, 1967)

Trager, James, *The Food Chronology: A Food Lover's Compendium of Events and Anecdotes, from Prehistory to the Present* (New York, 1995 and London, 1996)

Trubek, Amy B, *Haute Cuisine: How the French Invented the Culinary Profession* (Philadelphia, 2000)

Wheaton, Barbara Ketcham, *Savoring the Past: The French Kitchen and Table from 1300 to 1789* (Philadelphia, 1983)

10 NOVELTY AND TRADITION
The New Landscape for Gastronomy

Beck, Ulrich, *Risk Society: Towards a New Modernity*, trans. M. Ritter (London, 1992)

'Family food in 2002/2003', Report by the Department for Environment, Food & Rural Affairs, http://statistics.defra.gov.uk/esg/publications/efs/2003 (3 July 2005)

Food and Agriculture Organization (FAO) of the United Nations, Statistics Division, web site: http://www.fao.org/es/ess/

Fiddes, Nick, 'The omnivore's paradox', in David W. Marshall (ed.), *Food Choice and the Consumer* (London, 1995), pp. 131–51

Fischler, Claude, *L'Homnivore: le goût, la cuisine et le corps*, 3rd edn (Paris, 2001)

Frewer, Lynn, Einar Risvik and Hendrik Schifferstein (eds), *Food, People, and Society: A European Perspective of Consumers' Food Choices* (Berlin and London, 2001)

Goldstein, Darra, and Kathrin Merkle (eds), *Culinary Cultures of Europe: Identity, Diversity and Dialogue* (Strasbourg, 2005)

Grignon, Claude, and Christiane Grignon, 'Long-term trends in food consumption: a French portrait', *Food & Foodways*, 8:3 (1999), pp. 151–74

Grunert, Klaus, et al., 'Food-related lifestyle: a segmentation approach to European food

consumers' in L. Frewer, et al., *Food, People and Society*, op. cit., pp. 211–30

Helstosky, Carol, *Garlic and Oil: Politics and Food in Italy* (Oxford, 2004)

Jacobs, Marc, and Peter Scholliers (eds), *Eating Out in Europe: Picnics, Gourmet Dining and Snacks since the Late Eighteenth Century* (Oxford, 2003)

Laudan, Rachel, 'A plea for culinary modernism: why we should love new, fast, processed food', *Gastronomica*, 1:1 (2001), pp. 36–44

Levenstein, Harvey, *Paradox of Plenty: A Social History of Eating in Modern America* (New York and Oxford, 1993)

Maddison, Angus, *The World Economy: A Millennial Perspective* (Paris, 2001)

Macbeth, Helen (ed.), *Food Preferences and Taste: Continuity and Change* (Oxford and Providence, RI, 1997)

Marshall, David W. (ed.), *Food Choice and the Consumer* (London, 1995)

Mennell, Stephen, *All Manners of Food: Eating and Taste in England and France from the Middle Ages to the Present* (Oxford, 1985)

Mintz, Sidney W., *Tasting Food, Tasting Freedom: Excursions into Eating, Culture, and the Past* (Boston, 1996)

Murcott, Anne (ed.), *The Nation's Diet. The Social Science of Food Choice* (London and New York, 1998)

Pendergrast, Mark, *For God, Country, and Coca-Cola: The Definitive History of the Great American Soft Drink and the Company That Makes It* (New York, 2000)

Petrini, Carlo, *Slow Food: The Case for Taste*, trans. William McCuaig (New York, 2003)

Poulain, Jean-Pierre, *Sociologie de l'alimentation. Les mangeurs et l'espace social alimentaire* (Paris, 2003)

Rappoport, Leon, *How We Eat: Appetite, Culture, and the Psychology of Food* (Toronto, 2003)

Régnier, Faustine, 'Spicing up the imagination: culinary exoticism in France and Germany, 1930–1990', *Food & Foodways*, 11:4 (2003), pp. 189–214

Ritson, Christopher, and Richard Hutchins, 'The consumption revolution', in J. M. Slater (ed.), *Fifty Years of the National Food Survey, 1940–1990* (London, 1991), pp. 35–46

Sarasùa, Carmen, Peter Scholliers and Leen van Molle (eds), *Land, Shops and Kitchens: Technology and the Food Chain in Twentieth-Century Europe* (Turnhout, 2005)

Schot, Johan, et al. (eds), *Techniek in Nederland in de Twintigste Eeuw. III. Landbouw. Voeding* (Zutphen, 2000)

Sloan, Donald (ed.), *Culinary Taste: Consumer Behaviour in the International Restaurant Sector* (Oxford and Amsterdam, 2004)

Sombart, Werner, *Luxus und Kapitalismus* (Munich, 1922)

Urry, John, *The Tourist Gaze: Leisure and Travel in Contemporary Societies* (London, 1990)

Warde, Alan, *Consumption, Food and Taste: Culinary Antinomies and Commodity Culture* (London, 1997)

PICTURE CREDITS

Advertising Archives 249, 336, 344; akg-images: 68 Erich Lessing, 252, 255, 257, 258, 259, 322, 323 Ullstein Bilderdienst; Alamy Images/Worldwide Picture Library 300–301; Alan K. Outram 42, 46; American Museum of Natural History, New York 52; Ancient Art & Architecture Collection 141; Archaeological Museum, Florence/Art Archive 57; Archaeological Museum, Strasbourg/Art Archive 58; Archaeological Museum, Thessaloniki 77; Art Archive/ Dagli Orti 39; Ashmolean Museum, Oxford/Bridgeman 54; Asian Art Museum of San Francisco 101 below, 103, 114, 115; Bahlsen 242 below; Biblioteca Apostolica Vaticana, Rome 145; Biblioteca Estense, Modena 176; Biblioteca Medicea-Laurenziana, Florence 174; Bibliothèque des Arts Décoratifs, Paris 212, 213; Bibliothèque des Arts Décoratifs, Paris/Bridgeman 228, 267, 272, 317; Bibliothèque Municipale, Rouen 175; Bibliothèque Nationale de France, Paris: 4, 142, 170, 171, 231, 265 below, 266 Bridgeman; Boxgrove Project 40; BPK 232, 237, 241, 248; British Library, London 134, 138, 139, 151, 155, 167, 169, 190–191, 201; British Museum, London 59, 92–93, 104, 106, 109, 113, 148, 154; Cairo Museum 137; Camera Press: 146–147 Heeb/laif, 158–159 Gamma; Castello di Issogne, Val d'Aosta/Scala 168; Christie's Images 120–121, 124, 129; Corbis: 24–25 Clara Cortes IV, 29 Carlos Cazalis, 37 Michael Freeman, 245 E. O. Hoppé, 262–263 Louie Psihoyos, 291, 292, 296 Owen Franken, 298 Desgrieux/Photo Cuisine, 332 Envision, 343 John Madere, 346 Pitchal Frederic/Sygma; 350 Gideon Mendel; Devizes Museum/Art Archive/Eileen Tweedy 56; Ecole de la Boucherie, Paris/Bridgeman 268; Empics 347; Foto Marburg 9, 65; Freer Gallery of Art, Washington, DC/Art Archive 107; French Ministry of Culture and Communication, Regional Direction for Cultural Affairs – Rhône-Alpes, Regional Department of Archaeology, Lyons 44 below; Getty Images: 41 Richard Dobson, 44–45 top Joanna McCarthy, 130–131 Tim Hall, 286 Hulton Archive, 287 Eliot Elisofon, 312 Hulton Archive, 329 Bill Brandt, 338 AFP, 339 John Zoiner, 354 Stephen Chermin; Ronald Grant Archive 13 Cinevista, 84–85; Guardian Newspaper/Jonathan Watts 357; Johnny van Haeften Gallery, London/Bridgeman 204–205; Hirmer Fotoarchiv 72; Historiska Muséet Stockholm/Art Archive/Dagli Orti 36; Hunan Provincial Museum, Changsa 101 top; Hunterian Art Gallery, University of Glasgow, Mackintosh Collection, Glasgow, Photo Media Services, Glasgow University 326; Leeds Museums and Art Galleries, Temple Newsam House/Bridgeman 217; Liaoning Provincial Museum, Shenyan 118; Louvre, Paris 91, 216; Louvre, Paris/Bridgeman 75, 270–271; Julia MacKenzie 330; Mauritshuis, The Hague 211; Monastery of Monte Oliveto Maggiore 10; Musée d'Art Islamique, Cairo 136; Musée d'Art Thomas Henry, Cherbourg/Bridgeman 276; Musée des Beaux-Arts et d'Archeologie, Besançon/Bridgeman 126; Musée des Beaux-Arts, Rouen/Bridgeman 282–283; Musée des Beaux-Arts, Tourcoing 278; Musée des Beaux-Arts, Tours/Bridgeman 196–197; Musée Carnavalet, Paris 274; Musée Cernuschi, Paris/Art Archive/Dagli Orti 102; Musée Condé, Chantilly/Bridgeman 166; Musée Nationale de Château de Versailles 275; Musée d'Orsay, Paris 316; Museo Correr, Venice 208–209, 218; Museo Gregoriano Profano, Vatican/Scala 83; Museo Mandralisca, Cefalu 80; Museo de Mallorca, Palma 157; Museo Nazionale, Naples/Scala 62–63; Museo Nazional, Naples 87; Museo Ostiense, Ostia Antica/Scala 94; National Archaeological Museum, Naples 81, 95; National Gallery of Art, Washington, DC, Collection Mr and Mrs Paul Mellon 28; National Palace Museum, Taiwan/Art Archive 98–99; New York Historical Society/Bridgeman 319; New York Public Library, Buttolph Menu Collection, Rare Books Division, Astor, Lenox and Tilden Foundations 31; Palace Museum, Beijing 117, 123, 110–111 Werner Forman Archive; Palais des Papes, Avignon/Bridgeman 172; Plantin-Moretus Museum, Antwerp 214; Prado, Madrid: 2 Fotografia Digital Madrid, 210 Art Archive/Dagli Orti, 304 Arxiu Mas; Private Collection/Bridgeman 234, 247, 276 top, 277, 281, 306, 328; Roger-Viollet/Rex Features 273; Royal Geographical Society 152; Russian State Museum, Moscow/Scala 21; Edwin Smith 88; Smithsonian Institution, Washington, DC 53; Staatliche Antikensammlungen, Munich 74, 76; Staatliche Museen, Berlin 14, 69; Städel Museum, Frankfurt 221; Hans J. Teuteberg 235, 241, 246, 250, 251; Galleria dei Candelabri, Vatican/Zigrossi/Musei vaticani/IKONA 89; Vatican Museums and Galleries, Vatican State/Scala 198; Victoria & Albert Museum, London/Bridgeman 160, 162; Villa Albaini 86; Wellcome Trust Photo Library 201 top.

LIST OF CONTRIBUTORS

PAUL FREEDMAN is Chester D. Tripp Professor of History at Yale University. His field of particular interest is the medieval period and he has written on Spain (particularly Catalonia), the power of the Church, and the social condition of the peasantry. He is the author of *Images of the Medieval Peasant* and has a forthcoming book on the demand for spices in the Middle Ages.

ALAN K. OUTRAM is Senior Lecturer in Archaeology at the University of Exeter. He is an environmental archaeologist and palaeoeconomist who specializes in zooarchaeology, the study of human exploitation of animals in the past. Particular research interests include the importance of fat in prehistoric diets and the domestication of the horse. He is the author of many academic papers and is an editor of the journal *World Archaeology*.

VERONIKA GRIMM is Lecturer in Classics and Ancient History at Yale University. She is the author of *From Feasting to Fasting, the Evolution of a Sin* and her research interests include the social and intellectual history of the Roman Empire, religions of the Roman Empire, and food and diet in the Ancient World.

JOANNA WALEY-COHEN is Professor at New York University, where she has taught the history of China since 1992. Her research interests include Chinese imperial and military culture, Chinese social and cultural history, and the long history of China's interactions with others around the globe. Among her publications are *The Culture of War in China: Empire and the Military under the Qing Dynasty* and *The Sextants of Beijing: Global Currents in Chinese History*. She is currently preparing a history of cooking and consumption in early modern China.

H. D. MILLER is an Assistant Professor of History at Cornell College in Mount Vernon, Iowa. He is currently finishing a book on the history of the Mozarabs, the Arabized Christians of medieval Iberia, and preparing a new translation of Ibn Hazm's *Tawq al-Hamamah*.

C. M. WOOLGAR is Reader and Head of Special Collections at the University of Southampton Library. His research interests include day-to-day life in medieval England, encompassing the history of food. Among recent publications are *Food in Medieval England: Diet and Nutrition*, which he edited with Dale Serjeantson and Tony Waldron, and *The Senses in Late Medieval England*.

BRIAN COWAN holds the Canada Research Chair in Early Modern British History at McGill University in Montreal. He is the author of *The Social Life of Coffee: The Emergence of the British Coffeehouse*, which was awarded the Wallace K. Ferguson Prize from the Canadian Historical Association in 2006, and he is a co-investigator with the Canadian Social Sciences and Humanities Research Council's Major Collaborative Research Initiative on 'Making Publics: Media, Markets and Association in Early Modern Europe, 1500–1700'.

HANS J. TEUTEBERG is Professor Emeritus of Modern Social and Economic History at the University of Münster (Westphalia). From 1989 to 1996 he was the first president of the International Committee for Research into European Food History (ICRFH). He has written and lectured extensively on food history and has been a visiting professor in England, the USA, Japan, China and Austria. His many publications include *European Food History: A Research Review* and *Revolution am Esstisch. Neue Studien zur Nahrungskultur im 19/20 Jahrhundert*, of which he was editor.

ALAIN DROUARD is Director of Research at the National Centre for Scientific Research, Paris. He has specialized in the history and sociology of education and the social sciences, and his present field of research is the history of food in France and in Europe. His publications include *Histoire des cuisiniers en France (XIXe – XXe siècle)* and *Les Français et la table: Alimentation, cuisine et gastronomie du Moyen Age à nos jours*.

ELLIOTT SHORE is Chief Information Officer, Director of Libraries and Professor of History at Bryn Mawr College in Pennsylvania. He is a social historian with interests in the history of publishing, advertising and ethnicity. His recent books include two co-edited works, *Advertising and the European City: Historical Perspectives* and *The German-American Encounter: Conflict and Cooperation Between Two Cultures, 1800-2000*.

PETER SCHOLLIERS teaches social, cultural and economic history of the 19th and 20th centuries in the History Department of the Vrije Universiteit in Brussels. His research focuses on the standard of living in Europe (work, wages, cost of living, food, material culture) and industrial archaeology. He recently edited (with C. Sarasua and L. Van Molle) *Land, Shops and Kitchens: Technology and the Food Chain in 20th-century Europe*.

INDEX

Page numbers in *italic* refer to illustrations